SOUTHERN BIOGRAPHY SERIES

CRACKER MESSIAH

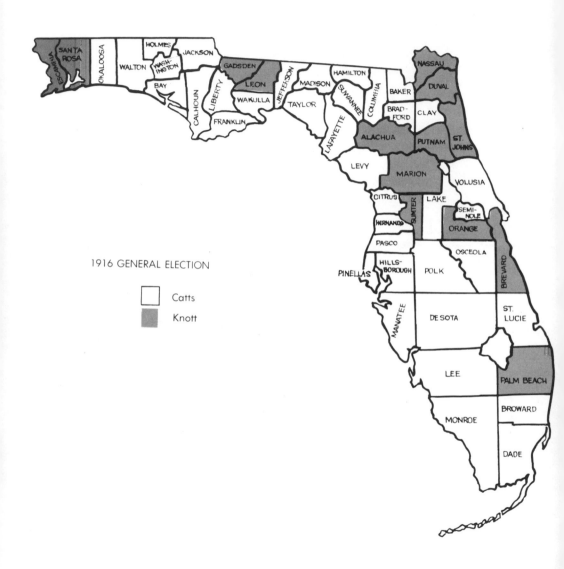

1916 GENERAL ELECTION

☐ Catts

▨ Knott

CRACKER MESSIAH

Governor Sidney J. Catts of Florida

WAYNE FLYNT

Louisiana State University Press / Baton Rouge

Designer: Dwight Agner
Type face: VIP Caledonia
Typesetter: The Composing Room of Michigan, Inc., Grand Rapids
Printer and binder: Kingsport Press, Inc., Kingsport, Tennessee

LIBRARY OF CONGRESS CATALOGING IN PUBLICATION DATA

Flynt, Wayne, 1940–
    Cracker messiah, Governor Sidney J. Catts of Florida

    (Southern biography series)
    Bibliography: p.
    Includes index.
    1. Catts, Sidney Johnston, 1863–1936. 2. Florida—Politics and
government—1865–1950. 3. Florida—Governors—Biography. I.
Title. II. Series.
F316.C27F59   975.9'06'9024 [B]   76–57664
ISBN 0–8071–0263–6

For David and Sean

Contents

Illustrations

Following page 144

Governor Sidney Catts in inaugural parade
Governor Catts reads inaugural address
Florida state Chautauqua headquarters
The Catts home in DeFuniak Springs
Governor Sidney Johnston Catts
Joe L. Earman
J. B. Hodges

Maps

Preface

THE SOUTH HAS PRODUCED an impressive array of politicians who may be defined as demagogues. Characterized by their emotional appeals to irrational issues, they have posed formidable interpretive problems. Once in office, they have sometimes become champions of progressive reform, articulating the frustrations and prejudices of the masses. Such a man was Sidney J. Catts. Few contemporaries had difficulty deciding how they felt about "Old Sid"; many loved him as a clerical messiah come to save the abused farmers and laborers of Florida; others despised him as a cynical hypocrite who used his ministerial office to seduce gullible Baptists, while repudiating in private the morality he proclaimed publicly.

Later generations have been more ambivalent in judging Catts. There was much that was noble about his vision of providing a voice for the common man. His programs, though frequently killed by a recalcitrant legislature, were well ahead of his times. Although the controversy surrounding his later career clouded Catts's earlier idealism and cast doubt upon his entire career, there is no reason to question his dedication to the cause of what he defined as the common man. Catts understood what some others have forgotten, that the masses could be bigoted as well as noble; that they might seek to enlarge their own opportunities at the expense of not only conservative business interests, but of Catholics and Negroes as well.

The task of evaluating Catts is made harder by the destruction of his official correspondence which was stored in Tallahassee. Aside from extensive files in the J. B. Hodges papers at the University of Florida, there is no major body of materials from the governor.

In the absence of such collections, I have acquired many debts. I especially appreciate the assistance of Governor Catts's three daughters. Mrs. Ruth Cawthon, Mrs. Elizabeth Paderick (now deceased), and Mrs. Alice May Stiegel helped in many ways, managing to discuss their father realistically, though lovingly. The late Jerry Carter, Florida's "Mr. Democrat," offered a balanced and critical appraisal of his onetime mentor. Jerry Carter, Jr., whose mimic of Sidney Catts is unsurpassed, provided additional aid. Two student secretaries, Carolyn Hooper and Suzanne Holden, provided clerical assistance worthy of significantly greater recognition and salary than either received.

Library staffs at the P. K. Yonge Library of Florida History, Florida State University, and Samford University made my research as simple as possible. I owe special thanks to Professor Arthur O. White of the University of Florida for his insights into Florida education, and to Eddie Akin for numerous errands and help. Marlene Rikard offered her considerable artistic talents to prepare the charts included in this volume, while Sam Mitchell of the Samford University English department shared his ideas on southern politics. This research was undertaken under grants numbers one and fifty-six provided by the Samford University Research Fund, whose chairman, David Vess, has provided friendship and advice worth more than the generous SURF grants. Finally, I wish to thank my wife, Dorothy, whose proofreading and literary criticisms have been invaluable, and David and Sean, who have shared their father with Sidney J. Catts for more years than any of us care to remember.

CRACKER
MESSIAH

ONE

Sitting Like Frogs
Waiting for the Rain

THE REVEREND SIDNEY JOHNSTON CATTS concluded his sermon on the sultry Alabama Sabbath but did not immediately dismiss the congregation. He had long boasted that his rural Baptist church at Fort Deposit was the strongest between Montgomery and Mobile. To bolster this allegation, he had pledged that his church would contribute more to missions than any other congregation in the state Baptist convention. The convention was to meet in annual session in 1905, and Catts had determined to collect several hundred dollars from his charge for a missions offering. Declaring at the close of his sermon that he would not take with him a report of short contributions, the parson proposed that subscriptions begin with gifts of fifteen dollars. His parishioners were mainly farmers who had experienced a succession of bad crop years, and only three or four responded to Catts's appeal. When he asked for ten dollar pledges, profound silence settled over the congregation, broken only by the noontime braying of a hungry mule waiting impatiently outside the little red brick church.

Catts wiped sweat from his neck and face with a handkerchief while fanning himself briskly with his large palmetto leaf fan. At length he boomed: "I don't intend to stand here long and see you sitting like frogs waiting for it to rain. If I cannot have the support of my congregation, I shall offer my resignation." And to the dismay of his astonished, but still silent congregation, resign he did. He pronounced the benediction, went directly home, wrote his resignation, and submitted it to the church. Months later, Catts returned to the parish to confess his uncontrollable temper and ask the forgiveness of those whom he had offended. The reunion and "love feast" that followed healed the wounds between parson and congregation.[1] Sidney Catts was a visceral man who lived by the emotion of the moment, and many a temper tantrum would be followed by many a remorseful apology; but not all the objects of his outbursts were destined to be as forgiving as the faithful Baptists at Fort Deposit, Alabama.

Whenever Catts was asked about his ancestry, he related himself to religious controversy by claiming that his paternal ancestry dated to Jacob Catts, a Dutch poet sometimes called the Shakespeare of Holland. Prominent in letters and public affairs, Jacob Catts had been selected minister plenipotentiary to the Court of St. James's to plead against Catholic persecutions of the Dutch Reform Calvinists of Holland. Although the claim is unsupported by reliable evidence, Sidney Catts boasted of the relationship as positive fact.[2] His claim of ancestry with a man of intellect who waged war against Catholicism is more revealing of Sidney Catts than of his genealogy.

In the eighteenth century Michael Catts and his two brothers had migrated from Holland to Baltimore. Michael Catts settled in Cecil County, Maryland, and in 1755 a child was born to the family and christened Michael. This second Michael Catts appeared in the 1790 federal census as a Quaker resident in North Susquehannah, Cecil County, the father of seven children. One of these children, Samuel Catts, moved to Alexandria, Virginia, and reared a family of eleven children, one of whom was Samuel Walker Catts, born on May 8, 1825. When a young man, he settled on a plot of land three miles west of the town of Pleasant Hill in Dallas County,

    1. Hayneville (Ala.) *Citizen-Examiner*, August 28, 1902; New York *Times*, May 29, 1921.
    2. Sidney Catts's claim of descent from Jacob Catts is made in a biographical sketch prepared by him while he served as governor of Florida and is found in B. J. W. Graham, *Baptist Biography*, II (Atlanta: Index Printing Co., 1920), 57–58. Catts's chief biographer mentions that the claim is based only on speculation, though the name *Jacob* occurred frequently among Sidney's ancestors; see John R. Deal, Jr., "Sidney Johnston Catts, Stormy Petrel of Florida Politics" (M.A. thesis, University of Florida, 1949), 3.

Alabama, on June 17, 1850. He was accompanied part way on his journey by his first cousin, William Bloxham, whose son, William D. Bloxham, became governor of Florida.[3]

Samuel Walker Catts managed a successful plantation and attained considerable wealth. He loved horses and kept a stable of fine Kentucky-bred animals. In 1851 he married Adeline Rebecca Smyly, daughter of a prominent Alabama family. Adeline's Scottish grandfather had been a linen-mill owner in Carie Tergus, Ulster, Ireland. He had left Ireland for the Edgefield district of South Carolina, settling there prior to the Revolutionary War. John Smyly, Adeline's father, had come to the Georgia-Alabama frontier in 1808 with his family and slaves, taking the ninety-ninth patent on land in the region. He prospered on a plantation that ultimately reached five thousand acres. Adeline enjoyed the benefits of planter affluence, attending Judson College, a Baptist woman's college in the Alabama black belt town of Marion. She was one of four young women in the college's first graduating class. While a student she converted from her father's Presbyterian affiliation to Baptist.[4]

Samuel Catts and his bride inhabited a fine two-storied, columned plantation home near Pleasant Hill, but also maintained a commodious residence in town built in colonial architectural style. This idyllic pastoral life was interrupted by the Civil War, when Samuel Catts organized the Pleasant Hill Cavalry Company and served as its captain.[5]

Samuel and Adeline Catts had three children; a son, Smiley, was born in 1851; Lilian was born three years later; and their second son, Sidney Johnston, was born on July 31, 1863, on the family plantation.[6] The baby was named in honor of General Albert Sid-

3. Deal, "Sidney Johnston Catts," 3–4.

4. Jacksonville *Florida Times-Union*, December 24, 1916; Graham, *Baptist Biography*, II, 57; Deal, "Sidney Johnston Catts," 4.

5. Interview, Mrs. Ruth Cawthon, DeFuniak Springs, Fla., May 8, 1972. Mrs. Cawthon has an original painting of the home, which was destroyed by fire many years later; Jacksonville *Florida Times-Union*, December 24, 1916.

6. Sidney J. Catts to W. T. Cash, August 12, 1929, in Catts files, Florida State Library, Tallahassee.

ney Johnston, who had died on the battlefield at Shiloh the year before.

Information concerning the boy's childhood is sketchy but significant. At age three, when he was playing, he asked his Negro nurse to throw a pair of scissors to him, a request with which she complied all too literally. The point of the scissors struck him and blinded his left eye. His disconsolate parents gave him a figurine to comfort him, a token he kept and treasured all his life. [7]

Sidney, whose childhood hero was John Randolph of Roanoke, embodied the Virginian's ferocious disposition. One story relates an incident involving nine-year-old Sidney and his cousin, Samuel W. Catts of Montgomery, also about nine. Sidney, who had inherited his father's love for horses, had a colt of which he was particularly fond. In playful scuffling, Sidney seized his cousin and placed him on the colt, who bolted, threw the boy off, then ran until he collapsed from exhaustion. Sidney, angry and fearing that his colt would die, refused to speak to his cousin for the rest of the day. When the colt recovered, the boy gave Samuel a dollar to forget the incident. [8]

Unlike many antebellum planters, the Catts family did not experience financial collapse during Reconstruction. It retained much of its prewar status and affluence. By 1870, when he was forty-five, Samuel Catts had broadened his economic interests to include a dry goods store in Pleasant Hill. His real estate holdings were valued at fifteen thousand dollars, and his personal property was placed at a comparable figure. This combined estate made him the wealthiest man in Pleasant Hill and one of the most affluent men in the rich black belt county of Dallas. [9]

Despite the death of Samuel Catts in October, 1874, the family's prosperity allowed Mrs. Catts to provide her youngest son with all the education he desired. After receiving most of his prelimi-

7. Jacksonville *Florida Times-Union*, December 24, 1916; interview with Mrs. Alice May Stiegel, May 12, 1972, Jacksonville.
8. Deal, "Sidney Johnston Catts," 6.
9. *1870 Census Population Schedules, Alabama, Dallas County*, on microfilm, Samford University Library, Birmingham.

nary work in the private schools of Dallas County, Sidney left home as a thirteen-year-old to study at Auburn, Alabama. Although he lived in the home of his tutor, a Professor Dunklin, he suffered from homesickness for Dallas County and his mother. Upon completion of his preliminary schooling, he enrolled at Alabama Polytechnical Institute (now Auburn University) in 1877, where he remained through the 1879–1880 school year.[10] There is no available explanation for his failure to graduate, but in 1880 he transferred to Howard College, a Baptist institution in Marion, Alabama. During the academic year 1880–1881 he was enrolled in English composition and rhetoric, mathematics, Latin, elocution, logic, and political economy. Again he failed to complete requirements for graduation, and received none of the certificates of distinction, or medals for elocution.[11] In 1881 he enrolled in the law class at Cumberland University in Lebanon, Tennessee, where he was awarded an LL.B. degree on June 1, 1882.[12] Although Catts did not excell as a student, or possess the discipline necessary to achieve an undergraduate degree, he was not the ignorant, back-country farm boy that his Florida political opponents later depicted. But he acquired a lifelong interest in the classics, history, and language, and close associates remembered him as a man who retained details, and whose speeches often drew analogies from Greek and Roman history.

Sidney returned to Dallas County to manage the family plantation for his widowed mother, who, while he pursued his education,

10. Graham, *Baptist Biography*, II, 54; *Alabama Baptist*, October 3, 1901; Albert F. Killian (Auburn University registrar) to author, August 7, 1970.

11. *Thirty-Eighth Annual Catalogue and Register of Howard College, 1880–1881* (Selma, Ala.: James S. Jacob Publishers, 1881).

12. *Catalogue, Cumberland University, Lebanon, Tennessee, 1881–1882* (N.p., n.p.), 6. Virtually every biographical reference to Catts gives a different description of his academic accomplishments. The most reliable biography, the one by John R. Deal, Jr., lists him as graduating from Marion Institute, a military college at Marion, Alabama, after departing Auburn ("Sidney Johnston Catts," 7). Christine O. Gillis wrote a biographical sketch of Catts in 1916 which listed him as attending Howard College three years, Auburn three years, and Cumberland Law School, receiving degrees from all three (Jacksonville *Florida Times-Union*, December 24, 1916). Catts's own biographical sketch correctly lists the sequence and mentions a degree only from Cumberland (Graham, *Baptist Biography*, II, 54). The confusion apparently developed when Howard College moved to Birmingham, causing

had operated the farm and dry goods business with only a Negro servant to help.[13] Sidney found the role of entrepreneur not entirely to his liking, so he practiced law on the side. In 1882, with his Dallas County ventures prospering, he decided to begin a law partnership with a friend in bustling, industrial Birmingham.

Catts might well have spent the remainder of his life practicing law but for a spiritual experience that deflected his life in a new direction. A Baptist congregation was located only a short distance from the family residence in Pleasant Hill, and the church had always been important in his life. The pastor and visiting ministers enjoyed an open invitation to the Catts's hospitality, and Mrs. Catts was known as a deeply religious woman as well as an entertaining conversationalist. The fact that her fatherless son had never affiliated with a church concerned her, and during a "protracted meeting" at the Baptist church in 1886, she prayed earnestly that he would "be saved." One evening after a visit to his mother's home and before his return to Birmingham, the young attorney attended the revival meeting and proclaimed his conversion. With characteristic brashness and without formal theological preparation, he immediately entered the ministry, becoming pastor of several part-time country churches in Dallas and Lowndes counties. His mother, who had been ambitious for her son's legal career, jokingly confessed that God had answered her prayers too well.[14]

The year 1886 was doubly eventful for him because he also met and married Alice May Campbell, the daughter of Marcus B. and Alice May Campbell, Scottish descendents of Lord Colin Campbell. A Methodist, young Alice May came to Pleasant Hill from her

---

irate local planters to form Marion Institute which claimed to be the real successor to old Howard College, assuming even its founding date and alumni. However, Marion Institute has no record concerning Sidney Catts (John M. Fultz, Marion Institute Office, to author, July 14, 1970).

13. *1880 Census Population Schedules, Alabama, Dallas County,* on microfilm at Samford University.

14. *Alabama Baptist,* November 25, 1897; interview with Mrs. Ruth Cawthon, May 8, 1972, DeFuniak Springs. Fla.

home in Montgomery to teach school, but married the Baptist minister instead. Their wedding ceremony was performed in an antebellum home at Collirene which had been owned for generations by the Lyon family. Catts's wedding became a celebrated joke as the "Animal Wedding of Collirene." In addition to the Catts and Lyons families, guests included Wolves, Baers, Foxes, and a Mr. Hare. Catts good-naturedly accepted the joking and later turned his family name into a political asset.[15]

The young preacher became a popular religious leader in the black belt of central Alabama, serving as pastor of the Baptist church at Lowndesboro in the late 1880s. The frame building seated four hundred, and in rural communities such a church was an important social institution and the revival meeting a central event. A fellow pastor, Joshua Hill Foster, preached a revival for Catts and left a vignette which described Catts's evangelistic fervor. Preaching had dominated the morning and afternoon, with a break for "eating on the ground" at noontime. The climax of the services came when a little girl asked Foster to pray for her grandfather, a wicked man whom no one liked. The old man, eighty-nine and blind, was a former state senator and lifelong troublemaker in the community. Catts and Foster visited him after the service, reminding him that God had blessed him with wealth and longevity. He replied that he had worked hard for everything he possessed and that they were wasting their time: "I'm going to hell and deserve to go there if there is a hell." The two ruffled divines, refusing to surrender the recalcitrant sinner, began to pray urgently for the old man, until, finally, he weakened and invited them back the next day. The following morning he went to church with them, was converted, and baptized by Catts.[16]

During the 1890s the Reverend Catts served a number of part-time churches near Pleasant Hill, none of which could afford a reg-

---

15. Graham, *Baptist Biography*, II, 57; Florence A. Middleton to editor, Montgomery *Advertiser*, July 13, 1958 (clipping in possession of Mrs. Elizabeth Paderick, Jacksonville).

16. Joshua Hill Foster, *Sixty-Four Years a Minister* (Wilmington, N. C.: First Baptist Church, 1948), 39–42.

ular pastor. He also worked in Baptist activities, presenting reports at associational meetings, attending the state convention, and contributing regular reports to the state Baptist journal. At the end of 1892 he left Pleasant Hill to accept a "call" from the Bethel Baptist Church at Fort Deposit in the southern part of Lowndes County. Because the small congregation provided inadequate support for a complete church program, Catts held services only on the second and fourth Sundays. He preached at Steep Creek on alternate Sabbaths.[17]

The parson enthusiastically set his fellow clerics an example by visiting country districts around Fort Deposit, establishing preaching stations as he went. In addition to his two half-time pastorates, he preached evening sermons at Kirksville on each second Sunday, at Calhoun every third Sunday and at Sharpsville on the second Sunday of the month. "Better wear out than rust out," he explained to concerned friends. His revivals and "protracted meetings" were frequent and usually successful. Between January 1 and September 1, 1893, he baptized ninety-two persons, a notable record even in the revivalistic years of the late nineteenth century.[18]

Among his new friends was W. B. Crumpton, the director of Baptist organizational activity in Alabama. As spokesman for state missionary efforts, Crumpton praised Catts's rural work as a model for other ministers. Catts was described by other Baptist officials as "a strong preacher" who was "rising in the ministry." A correspondent for the Hayneville *Citizen* who heard him preach at Fort Deposit agreed with this estimate, calling him "one of the best impromptu speakers I ever listened to."[19] His ample gifts as a pulpit orator were widely employed, not only in revivals throughout the black belt, but also as advocate of increased mission offerings for the denomination and as speaker for the local militia company.

Although Catts was well liked and successful at soul saving, he

17. *Alabama Baptist*, February 20, March 20, August 14, 1890.
18. *Ibid.*, May 18, September 21, 1893.
19. *Ibid.*, February 8, 1894, January 5, June 22, 1893.

found that the life of a small-town Baptist parson was not easy. As his family grew, his financial condition declined. The state mission board paid him fifty dollars to support his rural ministry, but his churches had increasing difficulty paying his salary. Agricultural depression struck the nation in the 1890s, and his mainly rural parishioners could not pay his salary. During one disastrous crop year, when the Fort Deposit church lacked $180 of his annual stipend, the young parson told the church that he could not accept the money, and that the congregation should consider the debt to him paid in full. The people responded by payment "in kind"; his 1893 Christmas gifts included twenty bushels of potatoes, "one fine porker, ready dressed," two young pigs, three turkeys, Christmas toys for the children, a buggy, embroidery, calico, canned jellies and fruits, and tableware.[20]

Even during these difficult years, he proved adept at raising money for causes in which he believed, a skill he later utilized in his political campaigns. He raised two hundred dollars for one of his mission churches in Lowndes County, and he constantly prodded his congregations to contribute to mission causes. His parishes provided subscriptions to the *Alabama Baptist* for widows and clothing for orphans.

Catts's social and political action first emerged over the issue of prohibition. He entered the struggle against "demon rum" early in his ministerial career when Lowndes County, which had voted dry for many years, faced a liquor referendum. Like most Baptists, he opposed legalization, though he privately enjoyed spirituous Christmas eggnog and did not consider such a harmless pleasure inconsistent with his public professions on the subject. His wife took a much firmer position, participating actively in the Women's Christian Temperance Union and frowning even on holiday spirits. A revival speaker at Catts's church during the heat of the county prohibition election also attacked "ballot box stuffing, 'Blind

20. *Ibid.*, May 9, 1901, January 18, February 22, 1894.

Tigerism,' waltzing, vulgar anecdotes and such things," much to the delight of the pastor.[21]

Southern Baptists became more deeply politicized in the decade of the 1890s than historians have noted, involving themselves in a number of political issues. Prohibition was their most frequent object, but once enmeshed in this social concern, Baptists often adopted other causes. *The Alabama Baptist,* which Catts read faithfully, commented frequently on prohibition, gambling, and prostitution. Catholics received almost weekly attention, with criticism ranging from alleged clerical immorality to papal corruption of American politics. Catts read nativistic editorials supporting the anti-Catholic American Protective Association and opposed a Catholic layman who ran for mayor of Mobile. Most moral problems somehow involved Catholicism: "There is one peculiar fact about Catholicism. Wherever it prevails you observe a low state of morals. Marital ties set lightly. Fornication and adultery are common. The Sabbath has been changed from a holy day to a holiday. Gambling is fashionable. Saloons are numerous and prosperous. . . . There is no question that rum and Romanism go together. Indeed, the very stronghold of rum in this country is Romanism."[22]

Anti-Catholicism was not the only legacy from Catts's Baptist heritage. The same paper that castigated Catholics sympathized with oppressed agrarians and praised the Farmers' Alliance. Baptist clerics in Alabama debated furiously the proper function of the minister in politics, and many activist preachers entered the Populist movement. By 1892 Baptist congregations across the state were torn by political factionalism. Disputes over economics made it impossible for some churches to function effectively, and the Reverend Sidney Catts determined to prevent such division within his parishes. He recorded a successful revival at the Steep Creek

---

21. *Ibid.,* August 2, 1894; interview, Mrs. Elizabeth Paderick and Mrs. Alice May Stiegel, May 12, 1972. As soon as the youngest Catts daughter, Alice May, was old enough, Mrs. Catts turned over the unpleasant duties of making alcoholic eggnog to her.

22. *Alabama Baptist,* January 11, February 15, 1894.

church in 1892 despite the advice of many "that we could have no meeting on account of politics." "If the Lord is not stronger than politics," he preached, "it is the fault of his servants." In the midst of the Populist campaign two years later, denominational leader W. B. Crumpton visited the Fort Deposit church on a mission tour. After two days of discussions with Catts, he wrote: "Though the male members differ in their political views, they have never allowed that to disturb their church relations. This speaks well for the Church and their wise pastor. So many churches and pastors by their imprudence have allowed this question of politics to well nigh ruin them."[23]

Despite his skillful administration, internal tensions and financial difficulties took their toll on Catts's enthusiasm. His optimistic reports to the *Alabama Baptist* and his apparent success disguised the inner unhappiness that characterized the rest of his life. He was never satisfied with any church or later with his political career in Florida. One evening as Catts sat reading a chapter entitled "The History of the Jews," he penned a prayer of frustration in the margin of the book: "Fort Deposit—1894. Sidney J. Catts. O hasten the day when I shall go to happier lands."[24]

Catts received an answer to his prayer three years later when the Baptist church in Tuskegee invited him to become its pastor. He left Fort Deposit without rancor and with the congregation begging him to reconsider. The people expressed their love for him in many ways, and Deacon V. H. Bell recalled Catts's ministry as "one of unselfishness and loyal devotion."[25] When he left the Bethel church for Tuskegee, it had grown to 350 members.

Tuskegee was not unlike Catts's earlier pastorates. Macon County was similar to Dallas and Lowndes in its black belt location, though it was farther east in central Alabama. The town was already becoming a center for black education, thanks to the Tuskegee In-

---

23. *Ibid.*, August 11, 1892, March 22, 1894.
24. Book in possession of Mrs. Alice May Stiegel, Jacksonville. Catts frequently wrote in the margins of books in his extensive library, most of which are still in the possession of Mrs. Ruth Cawthon, DeFuniak Springs.
25. *Alabama Baptist*, May 9, 1901.

stitute headed by Booker T. Washington. The church was far smaller than his Fort Deposit parish, numbering only 88 members in 1901.

Catts's ailing mother, who moved to Tuskegee to live with him, died in the fall of 1897. She left him the plantation at Pleasant Hill and considerable property which temporarily stabilized family finances. Each autumn Catts obtained permission from his church to return to the plantation to oversee the harvesting which was done by tenant farmers. The Catts children eagerly anticipated this time each year which gave them a chance to savor the opulence of the antebellum South for a few weeks.[26]

The church at Tuskegee was a difficult challenge. It had experienced an unfortunate sequence of pastors, the one preceding Catts having divorced his wife. The church had also been torn for some years by political differences partly stemming from the prohibition struggle in Macon County. His preaching won part of the congregation, and most parishioners supported his work in surrounding mission stations.[27] The Tuskegee *News* reported in 1899 that the church had paid all its back debts as well as the preacher's salary for the year, which apparently was a noteworthy event for the congregation. Catts and his people were "thoroughly united."[28]

The pastor spent much of his time reading and preparing sermons. Using the large library that he inherited from the Smyly family and from his mother, he continued a lifelong habit of reading several hours each day. His acquaintance with classical subjects and biblical and secular history was impressive, and he even acquired some knowledge of Greek and Hebrew. Much of the poetry he quoted was his own, and he attempted unsuccessfully to have some of it published. His sermons were well organized, and he usually prepared detailed outlines, occasionally with a complete manuscript, an atypical practice in the Baptist ministry of his day.

26. Interview, Mrs. Elizabeth Paderick and Mrs. Alice May Stiegel, May 12, 1972, Jacksonville.
27. Bessie Conner Brown, *A History of the First Baptist Church, Tuskegee, Alabama, 1839–1971* (Tuskegee: First Baptist Church, 1972), 22.
28. *Alabama Baptist*, December 21, 1899, quoting the Tuskegee *News*.

The sermons were enlivened by an extensive vocabulary, his travels to Washington and New York, as well as his broad reading interests. A sermon titled "Types of Religious Beliefs" relied heavily on a book by British philosopher Sir John Lubbock and discussed not only Christianity, but Atheism, Totemism, and Shamanism. Although he quoted much scripture, he favored historical allusions to theological discussion, perhaps reflecting his lack of formal theological training. References to Lycurgus, Solon, Demosthenes, and Cicero appear frequently, but Napoleon held a special fascination which continued into his political oratory.

In a commencement sermon delivered at nearby Notasulga in May, 1900, Catts maintained that each part of nature and society revealed a perfecting process moving from lower to higher forms, which was leading to the perfection of the human species. He refused to call this process evolutionary, preferring instead the term *difference in type*. Discussions of light defraction and x-ray demonstrated a passing knowledge of science. His sermons did not emphasize the Old Testament, or the negative, judgmental aspects of Christianity. Most of his theology was based on New Testament concepts, with strong emphasis upon the Protestant ethic of individual responsibility, hard work, and personal morality.[29]

Self-reliance assumed a paramount place in Catts's personal and ministerial thought. In a sermon to his congregation in 1900, he discussed the elements of permanence which allow civilizations to endure. The central stabilizing force was the moral order, which he interpreted as self-reliance "or grit to carve out your own destiny." He illustrated the point by citing the response of a workman offered charity by Cornelius Vanderbilt: "We do not want charity. We want work." The world owed a man a living, the preacher concluded, only in that it owed him a chance to work. Personal frugality and morality were inextricably connected, and Catts frequently

---

29. Catts's sermon notebook, original in possession of Mrs. Elizabeth Paderick, Jacksonville; microfilm copy in Samford University Library, Birmingham. These sermons were written for the church at Tuskegee, but most were preached at his subsequent charges at Fort Deposit and DeFuniak Springs.

cited a dictum that he tried to practice: "Save fifty cents of every dollar you make."[30]

The parson also manifested interest in the young people of his parish. A sermon titled "The Glory of Young Men Is Their Strength" developed the theme that the church depended on its young, and moral strength resided in heredity and a "temperate and pure life." He warned against drinking, gambling, dancing, and idleness, to the chagrin of some parishioners. The sure ruin of a child, he warned in another sermon, originated when parents gave him too much money, upheld him when he was wrong, allowed him to have bad companions, or to "loaf down town in the day time." He cultivated the young people of his church, inviting them for dinner on special occasions.[31]

His extensive reading led him to an interest in public affairs, unusual for a Baptist clergyman of that day. Like the prominent social gospel advocate Josiah Strong, he saw American imperialism as a method to further God's kingdom on earth. God's plan for winning the "heathen" consisted of "vassal nations" absorbing "the conqueror's religion," a historical pattern verified by numerous examples: Rome and Britain, America and the Indians, Cortez and Mexico, Pizarro and Peru, the South and slaves.

Social morality also attracted his attention. When discussing the morals of the young, Catts noted that sins of the flesh might rob a man of physical strength, but the more serious problem was intellectual integrity. One did not have to leave Alabama to find examples of dedication to learning, he noted, referring to mental health reformer Dr. Peter Brice, who was "the friend of the poor insane." His later attention to reform in the treatment of prisoners, the mentally ill, and juvenile offenders, was no cynical political expediency; it began early in his ministerial career as a result of his careful study of and humanitarian commitment to such change.

Sidney Catts, like most evangelical ministers, was ambivalent

---

30. *Ibid.*; interview, Jerry Carter, Jr., May 8, 1972, Tallahassee.
31. Catts's sermon notebook; interview, Mrs. W. O. Willham (wife of former pastor of Tuskegee Baptist church), May 8, 1972, DeFuniak Springs.

on social questions. As eager as he was to achieve prohibition and
other social reforms, he could not admit that the kingdom of God
consisted of earthly activism. His eschatology was grounded not in
the temporal but in the spiritual—in the end of time. The Christian was a "Prisoner of Hope" who "does not care to change earthly
lands." [32]

Although he lived and worked in the midst of Negro education,
surrounded by young blacks who were seeking new directions for
their people, Catts did not deviate from his white supremacy up-
bringing. His sermons did not deal specifically with race for he considered the inferiority of blacks to be a demonstrated reality, not a
debatable subject. He warned his listeners that "it is a bad plan to
let small children come too much under the influence of negroes
for they will ground these African superstitions into their hearts so
that manhood and womanhood will not shake them off." He discussed evolution in a commencement sermon, expressing the belief that each genus of organism "clings to its . . . class with a tenac-
ity amounting to knowledge"; among humans this was expressed in
the progression of the five racial branches—Negroes, Malays, Indian, Mongolian, Caucasian—from lowest cannibalism to "the perfection of the human species." [33]

As with his anti-Catholicism, Catts succeeded in keeping his
racism abstract, and his personal relations with blacks were as con-
genial as his personal relations with individual Catholics. On one
occasion Mrs. Catts was sitting on the front porch when a neatly
attired Negro man passed in front of the house. She asked him if he
would like a job doing some yard work; the man politely declined,
but assured her that he would send someone to work for her. The
family was embarrassed to discover that the polite stranger was
Booker T. Washington, the president of Tuskegee Institute. [34]

Washington apparently took no offense at the incident, for sev-

32. Catts's sermon notebook.
33. *Ibid.*
34. Interview, Mrs. Elizabeth Paderick and Mrs. Alice May Stiegel, May 12, 1972,
Jacksonville.

eral times he asked the young minister to speak at the institute. One of the lectures, "Persecutions and Martydoms [sic] of the Church," demonstrated that Catts's anti-Catholicism was not politically inspired as some of his opponents later claimed. Religious periodicals in Alabama were devoting much of their space to the "Catholic menace," and Catts revealed this same bias in his 1900 lecture. He announced to the black audience that he had been "struck with awful force by the cruelties of the Roman Catholic Church towards others when in her power." Seen through Catts's prejudice, western history was God's prophetic judgment on Catholicism. The defeat of the Spanish Armada by the Protestant British, Napoleon's loss to the Russians (apparently the Orthodox Church avoided the iniquity of its Roman counterpart), and secularistic Italian political unification were all divinely inspired historical shafts directed at Catholicism. Furthermore, in America "every movement of Jehovah seems to be directed against the temporal power of the Pope, and for enlightenment and good government." Andrew Jackson might have beaten the Spanish in Florida by himself, but according to the Reverend Catts, the Tennesseean was only an agent of a Catholic-hating God.[35] His lecture demonstrated a remarkable and detailed knowledge of historical facts, together with a subjective frame of reference.

Although his lecture in February indicated a harmonious relationship with Tuskegee Institute, the situation was altered dramatically some months later. Catts established himself as an unofficial censor of radicalism on the Tuskegee campus, and it proved to be a cause célèbre. Two pastors from Trinity Church in Boston spoke on the campus, allegedly insulting "southern manhood" and advocating integrated schools where ignorant children, both white and black, could receive an education. The lectures strained Catts's patience, and in a temperamental outburst he recounted the excesses of Reconstruction and warned of violence to anyone who attempted the imposition of a neo-Reconstruction policy on the South. It was time "to call a halt," and "if any such effort is ever made in reality

35. *Alabama Baptist*, February 1, 1900.

here is one man who will change his commentaries into works on military tactics—his pen and plow into a sword and . . . go down to Dallas and Lowndes and organize the boys for war."[36] This flamboyant rhetoric characterized both his clerical and political careers. Apparently Washington forgave this attack, for in 1901 Catts was once again invited to lecture. Confining his remarks to more traditional themes, he discussed the origins of the Bible, what the new century demanded of ministers, the minister as a citizen, and Christian courtesy.[37]

Not everyone, white or black, appreciated the ministry of the Reverend Catts. His troubles ranged from personality conflicts, to impulsive and tactless administrative decisions, to resentment over some of his religious concepts involving personal morality. One wealthy, invalid parishioner had a phone installed in the pulpit so she could listen to Catts's sermons at home. The parson could not remain still when preaching, and his movement around the pulpit frustrated her expensive attempts to hear him. Many Sunday sermons were followed by Monday telephone calls reprimanding him for his pulpit mobility.[38]

Since the parsonage was inadequate for his expanding family, Catts bought a house on the outskirts of Tuskegee and left the manse empty, without the permission of his congregation. He also demonstrated little interest in the Sunday school program, which survived only because of a group of loyal women. The ladies also resented his lack of attendance at associational meetings. The Tuskegee Baptist Association met each year in October during the time when the church granted Catts permission to tend affairs on his Pleasant Hill plantation. Associational members were offended that the largest church in the county was unrepresented, and even considered changing the name of the group because the pastor of the Tuskegee church did not participate. Membership at Catts's parish dropped to its lowest level in many years, and the official

36. Sidney Catts to editor, *ibid.*, May 2, 1901.
37. The speech outline is in Catts's sermon notebook.
38. Interview, Mrs. W. O. Willham, May 8, 1972, DeFuniak Springs.

church historian dismisses him with several unflattering sentences:
he was "very impulsive" which "at times placed him in some unpleasant situations"; during his last years in Tuskegee he became
"very anxious to make money and resigned in 1901 to give his attention to business and politics."[39]

The disenchantment was mutual. In a pattern characteristic of
his career, Catts believed the trouble stemmed from his controversial philosophical and moral positions, and had nothing to do with
personality. The trouble began on June 23, 1900, when he
preached a sermon entitled "Be Sure Your Sin Will Find You Out."
The sermon was an atypically "fire and damnation" effort, which,
according to Catts's marginal note, "raised very hell in Tuskegee."
He began by warning his congregation that there were "some sins
and sinners of this community we want to talk about today." Beginning with the dance hall that had been established at a local army
camp, he enumerated the community's iniquities: gambling, ir-
reverence in God's house, nonenforcement of Sabbath and curfew
laws by town officials, and the sale of liquor to minors.

The town's leaders attacked Catts's remarks, as did some of his
members. One young woman reacted to his strictures against dancing by calling him "an old idiot" who "has no sense." The local
Methodist minister, Tuskegee's mayor, and five others refuted his
charges. Years later, memories of the affray still festered in Catts's
mind, and he appended an almost gleeful marginal note to his sermon notebook. The young woman who had accosted him had two
years later "given birth to an illegitimate child and in disgrace was
following a Congressman around as his mistress." There were others also that he "had his eye upon as to God's justice on account of
their treatment of me about this sermon." Two of them had died
since the controversy, an unmistakable sign of God's judgment. In
a plea for complete vindication, Catts concluded: "O God! thou
ruler of heaven and earth do what is right, vengence [sic] is thine."
Unhappy with the divine timetable, he wrote later: "Father thou

39. Brown, *History of the First Baptist Church, Tuskegee,* 22–23.

hast said vengence [sic] is mine—will you repay? How? and when? I will keep watch."

His unhappiness deepened in the following months. A sermon concerning Israel's loss of glory because of her faithlessness contained the notation: "certainly true of Tuskegee when I was there." At the top of a sermon delivered on September 22, 1900, he pleaded: "How long! O Lord! will I write sermons from this place."[40]

He soon received an answer to his prayer. Within months he terminated his ministry of five years. Several additional factors influenced his decision, one of them the economic distress mentioned by the church chronicle. A Dunn and Bradstreet rating had listed his wealth at fifty thousand dollars when he went to Tuskegee, but five poor crop years on the family plantation had produced a severe crisis.[41] Financial difficulties of some degree plagued him for the rest of his life. Also, his former pastorate, Bethel Baptist at Fort Deposit, sought his leadership again in 1901. The membership had declined by fifty following Catts's departure, and on August 29, 1901, he returned. Before departing Tuskegee he hurled a final indignity at the local citizenry. His new home there was next door to a particularly influential deacon who had led the anti-Catts faction of the church. When Catts received his "call" from Fort Deposit, he sold his parsonage to a Negro.[42]

Catts's return to Fort Deposit launched the church into a program of rapid expansion. During his first year of leadership, seventy-eight new members were added, pushing total membership beyond three hundred. The new pastor's innovations included an open-air meeting on Friday evenings and a young men's prayer meeting for Fort Deposit's businessmen. His interests continued to be multifaceted, as he dabbled in community life, denominational affairs, and politics, in addition to his ministerial duties.

40. Catts's sermon notebook.
41. Jacksonville *Florida Times-Union*, December 24, 1916.
42. *Alabama Baptist*, May 16, 1901; Brown, *History of the First Baptist Church, Tuskegee*, 22.

Preaching offered Catts an avenue to extend his popularity throughout the central Alabama area, and he missed few opportunities to take advantage of the revival circuit.[43]

Baptist politics offered another outlet for his varied interests. Catts's involvement was exceptional in an era when few Baptist ministers were educated or pastored full-time churches affluent enough to allow them to participate in denominational life. He was in charge of devotions at the Alabama Baptist state convention in November, 1901. With the improvement of his personal finances he pledged fifty dollars each year for four years to an endowment drive for Howard College, a state Baptist school. He had become angry at the institution for moving from Marion to Birmingham, and also because it was not managed in a businesslike manner. But when a new president took the reins of the college, Catts felt that "order and system" had been restored. He urged practical oriented reform of the college curriculum, a philosophy he would later propose in Florida, insisting that the faculty include a teacher who would give one lesson per day on Bible study, pastoral duties, and sermon delivery.[44]

When not restructuring schools or protecting the morals of students, the Reverend Catts showered his attention on the provincial citizens of Fort Deposit. Responding to popular requests in 1903, he related experiences from his trip to New York City to a large and appreciative audience.[45] The next year, his diverse interests finally carried him into politics.

On March 20, 1904, Fifth District congressman Charles W. Thompson died suddenly. Only twenty days remained before the state Democratic primary, but six candidates announced for the post. The favorite was J. Thomas Heflin, a bombastic orator and storyteller from LaFayette who had served four terms in the state legislature, as a member of the 1901 constitutional convention, and

43. Hayneville Citizen-Examiner, August 28, 1902; Alabama Baptist, May 16, 1901, August 27, 1902, December 23, 1903.
44. Catts to editor, Alabama Baptist, August 17, 1904.
45. Ibid., October 3, 1901, April 15, 1903.

who was currently serving as secretary of state. District newspapers endorsed him, and he also won commitments from most of
the "courthouse gang" of county clerks, state examiners, sheriffs,
and mayors who controlled Alabama politics. Heflin's aides confi-
dently predicted that their candidate would win more than 9,000 of
the estimated nine-county total vote of 14,000.[46]

The Reverend Catts announced his candidacy on March 31, but
he had already begun a strenuous campaign to translate his
ministerial reputation into votes. He drew 250 persons to his first
political rally at Tallassee, then toured the northern half of the district, speaking three and four times a day. Catts's campaign was in
stark contrast to that of the witty, jocular Heflin. Catts tried no
anecdotes, and his speeches were described as "solid," "business
like," "earnest," and "patriotic"; he kept all remarks on "a high
plain" and did not mention or ridicule his opponents. For issues,
he concentrated on rural mail delivery, good roads, and a federally
financed school of technology to provide practical education in the
fifth district, perhaps an indirect result of his contact with Tuskegee Institute. He opposed immigration, saying that "America
was for Americans, and for the children of Americans." He made
few promises, pledged to carry out the ones he made, and assured
his listeners that he would not be a "social flame" or "drink intoxic-
ants, or . . . gamble."[47]

His emphasis upon sobriety, honesty, and a Christian spirit did
not excite enthusiasm among the people of his district, and he
made several grievous political blunders. He gave one politician
$250 to canvass a county for him, only to discover that the man had
bet the entire amount that Heflin would defeat him.[48] Even with a
faultless campaign, his task would have been formidable, for the

46. Hayneville *Citizen-Examiner*, March 13, 1904; Montgomery *Advertiser*, April 10,
1904.

47. Montgomery *Advertiser*, April 7 and 9, 1904.

48. The man who took Catts's money without delivering any votes was not forgotten
and took a tongue lashing from the newly elected governor when Catts spoke in Birmingham
in 1916. Catts, who discovered that the man subsequently had moved to the industrial city,
pledged that "if I ever see him I will whip him, so help me God." See Birmingham *Age-
Herald*, December 14, 1916; New York *Times*, May 29, 1921.

witty Heflin moved easily among rural voters, drawing frequently from his collection of drolleries and stories to entertain them.

Despite Heflin's obvious advantages, Catts won several of the black belt counties and ran second in the six-man field. Heflin doubled Catts's vote, but the preacher-turned-politician learned some valuable lessons. If one intended to beat a well-established Democratic organization, he had to find issues that would inflame the populace. Polite, issue-oriented politics that omitted personal references to one's opponent could not be translated into votes. He learned his lessons well.

Catts never recovered from the political mania that infected him in 1904. He returned to his ministerial duties with restlessness he could not shake off. Perhaps this fact explained the increasing tension which developed in his Fort Deposit church.

A parishioner had written in 1902 that Catts was "a wise and aggressive leader in the church and community," and the church had grown and prospered under his direction.[49] During the year following his political initiation, however, his relationship with the church deteriorated. Finally, his general dissatisfaction with ministerial life, ill health, and his volatile temper combined to produce the tempestuous outburst that ended his pastorate at Fort Deposit.

The next few years were transitional in the life of the Catts family. Sidney took his growing family back to the plantation at Pleasant Hill, where he farmed, tended to his mercantile business, and preached part-time. He believed that "the greatest riches in this world is [sic] a large family of children," and of his eight off-spring, he declared, "We have a fine mess of them." He remained active in the state's Baptist work, pastoring small part-time churches at Sandy Ridge and Mt. Willing and frequently preaching revivals. He appeared on the program of the Alabama Preachers' Conference, appropriately speaking on "The Preacher and Poli-

49. C. H. Priester to editor, *Alabama Baptist*, July 9, 1902.

tics," and he also wrote the report for the Selma Baptist Association in April, 1905.[50]

Catts's health had not been good during the last years of his Fort Deposit pastorate, and the invigorating physical activity and close family relations at Pleasant Hill proved therapeutic. He enjoyed riding and maintained a stable of fine saddle horses, a carriage for himself, and a surrey for his wife. He was completely devoted to his wife Alice May, a gentle, shy woman who cared little for politics and had learned to cope with her husband's quick temper. She disputed his decisions only once in the memory of the children, a confrontation she regretted. She adapted to his gregariousness which was best demonstrated by his penchant for inviting unexpected guests to Sunday dinner, and she maintained the plantation's reputation for hospitality.

The children remembered their father as a man of considerable temper who recovered his good humor almost as quickly as he lost it. The family was close and devoted. Catts expected his children to work but provided for their recreation. Each boy received a horse, and Catts constructed tennis courts next to the house. Nearby villages furnished social life for the young people, and black tenants did most of the yard work and house chores.

Religion remained the central feature of family life. Every night the family gathered for Bible-reading and prayer. The Baptist congregation was located nearby the plantation home, and the family attended every service at the church. The children remembered Catts's religion as simple and devout; he told them that they should not try to understand theology, that the only way to comprehend Christianity was to keep it simple.[51]

During the years following his resignation as pastor at Fort Deposit, his economic condition deteriorated. The boll weevil ap-

50. Catts to editor, *ibid.*, March 18, 1903; *Alabama Baptist State Convention, Report for 1904*, p. 46, in Archives of Alabama Baptist Historical Collection, Samford University, Birmingham.
51. Interview, Mrs. Ruth Cawthon, May 8, 1972, DeFuniak Springs; interview Mrs. Elizabeth Paderick and Mrs. Alice May Stiegel, May 12, 1972, Jacksonville.

peared in his cotton fields, and bad crop years were complicated by
trouble with his tenant farmers. Catts acquired a reputation locally
for treating his tenants unfairly, a fact that may explain the mysterious destruction of two of the plantation's sawmills.[52] Faced with
mounting financial burdens, he decided to become a professional
orator and journeyed to Chautauqua headquarters in New York to
join the popular lecture organization.

Catts's career might have taken a new direction but for the intervention of a Mr. Vinson, a banker from Georgianna, Alabama.
Vinson had become a close friend of Catts when the preacher had
conducted revivals in the Georgianna Baptist church. The banker
had moved to DeFuniak Springs, Florida, during Catts's self imposed retirement, and when he found that his friend was able to
speak again and was in financial difficulties, he persuaded the
church at DeFuniak Springs to call Catts as pastor.[53] The church
was small and supported by the Baptist Mission Board, but Catts
was in no position to be selective, and when the pulpit committee
extended a call in June, 1911, Catts hurried back from New York.
He went to Florida immediately, his family remaining behind in
Alabama until September to dispose of the plantation. His three-
year pastorate at DeFuniak Springs only accentuated his frustration, torn as he was between a ministerial career, which seemed to
be his only source of financial stability, and his increasing political
ambitions.

52. A former chief justice of the Florida Supreme Court worked for a Pensacola lawyer
after finishing law school, and in 1922 when Catts filed a bankruptcy petition with the west
Florida law firm, the young attorney was dispatched to Alabama to make a routine investigation. The lawyer was told by several older residents that when settlement time came on the
plantation and sharecroppers asked for their money, they had been known to disappear
"suddenly, mysteriously and permanently." Confidential source to author. Such charges
followed Catts throughout his career, however, and cannot be confirmed.

53. Interview, Mrs. Elizabeth Paderick and Mrs. Alice May Stiegel, May 12, 1972,
Jacksonville.

TWO

Peddling God, Insurance, and Sidney J.

DEFUNIAK SPRINGS was a thriving county seat in 1911, containing the state Chautauqua headquarters and dominating Walton County, Florida. It was located in the middle of the Florida panhandle, a tier of counties stretching from the capital of Tallahassee in Leon County westward along the Gulf of Mexico to Pensacola. It had been one of the earliest and most heavily populated regions of the state, with an economic base of cotton and timber. The panhandle's economy, heavy concentration of blacks, and political attitudes were similar to patterns in adjacent south Alabama, and the ties between the two areas were, in many respects, closer than those which bound west Florida to the southern part of the peninsula.

The population of the panhandle retained much of the political power it had enjoyed from antebellum days. In 1910 one-fourth of Florida's 750,000 inhabitants resided in the area, so its power in the state legislature was not so disproportionate as it would soon become with the rise in population of central and south Florida.

Just as the panhandle shared south Alabama's racial composition and economic base, it also reflected its evangelical religious bias. Black membership in National Baptist churches led all denominations with some 16,000 members, followed by white Southern Baptists, who counted nearly 14,000 members; the Methodist Episcopal Church South with slightly over 12,000; and the African Methodist Episcopal church with some 10,000. Three panhandle counties listed a combined total of 149 Catholics in the national religious census of 1916, although this figure is obviously too low. Pensacola in Escambia County, for instance, had a sizable Catholic community but did not report any members of that church.[1]

Walton County contained some 16,000 inhabitants when Catts moved there in 1911. Its religious community was equally divided between white and black Baptists, each with about 1,300 members—some 900 white Methodists and slightly more than 500 black Methodists. The First Baptist Church was the most significant parish of the county, though it had a tradition as a difficult and stormy church.[2] The church paid Catts less than one hundred dollars a month, and he was never happy as pastor. After three years of directing its ministries, a combination of factors led to his resignation in 1914; the church's refusal to raise his salary; the now familiar clash of personalities between strong-minded parson and unhappy congregation; Catts's renewed interest in politics.[3] The preacher's own explanation of the affair was typically abrupt: "My church told me to do something that I would not do. They insisted and I told them where to go. Then I went into the insurance business." He also conceded that his new job with the Fraternal Life Insurance Company as a salesman was simply a way to make a living "while I ran for the governorship."[4]

His new employment as a traveling insurance salesman took him into the tiny hamlets and rural areas of the panhandle and put him into contact with the "little people." He listened to their grievances and frustrations, and he would soon become the most articulate spokesman in Florida for their causes. Just as being a traveling salesman would one day be the prelude to the careers of Louisiana's Huey Long and Alabama's Jim Folsom, Catts's 1914 decision to sell insurance was invaluable to his dream of once again offering for public office.

1. Census, *Religious Bodies, 1916*, Pt. 1, "Summary and General Tables" (Washington: Government Printing Office, 1919), 248–49.
2. Interview, Mrs. W. O. Willham, May 8, 1972, DeFuniak Springs.
3. Interview, Mrs. Elizabeth Paderick and Mrs. Alice May Stiegel, May 12, 1972, Jacksonville; *Florida Baptist Witness*, June 29, 1916.
4. Birmingham *Age-Herald*, December 14, 1916.

Although Catts's schedule kept him away from his children more than before, the family remained close. He insisted that each child obtain a job, a decision prompted both by his rigorous Calvinist work ethic and by economic necessity. Sidney, Jr., entered Palmer College, a prep school in DeFuniak Springs, and graduated in 1915. He worked on a survey crew in Birmingham to raise money to enter his father's alma mater, Cumberland Law School. Walter took a job delivering ice while completing his studies at the local high school, and Elizabeth taught music in a nearby village.

Catts allowed the children considerable latitude in reaching their own decisions. When young Walter entered an essay in a high school contest, he included a fundamentalist religious comment on immortality. One man on the panel of judges, a Unitarian-Universalist, took exception to the reference and insisted that the young man substitute another phrase in order to receive first place. Walter asked his family to help him decide what to do, but his father insisted that it was not a family decision; only Walter could make the judgment. The boy retained the original wording and finally received the prize when the controversial judge resigned.

Walter suffered from a kidney ailment, the result of a childhood case of measles, and after finishing high school, traveled to Birmingham to join his brother Sidney and be nearer his doctors. Shortly after arriving in the city, he suffered a serious kidney malfunction, and Mrs. Catts rushed to his side. She reached her husband in Jacksonville, where he was seeking political support in preparation for his gubernatorial race, telling him their son was not expected to live. Catts had to borrow the cash from friends to purchase a railroad ticket and finally arrived in Birmingham only hours before his son died.[5] Mrs. Catts grieved long for her son, but politics left her husband little time for mourning.

Catts's audacious scheme to become governor of Florida really began secretly in 1914, after he had resided in the state for only three years. One of his earliest confidants was Jerry W. Carter, an itinerant sewing machine salesman from west Florida. Carter was a

5. Unidentified newspaper clipping in possession of Mrs. Elizabeth Paderick; interview, Mrs. Elizabeth Paderick and Mrs. Alice May Stiegel, May 12, 1972, Jacksonville.

genuine Florida "cracker" with an intuitive understanding of the
aspirations of the poor farmers of the Florida panhandle. Part of his
territory stretched to Marianna and DeFuniak Springs, and while
in the latter town, he first heard Catts speak to a group of Masons at
the Chautauqua headquarters. He encouraged the pastor's political
interests, though he urged him to try for a congressional seat rather
than for the governorship. Catts had decided already on the
statehouse, however, and asked Carter to help in his campaign.
The friendship endured through many stormy conflicts, and Carter
was virtually the only man to retain Catts's trust throughout his
political career. Carter's lifetime loyalty to Catts merited such
faith.

Not all members of the Carter family shared Jerry's enthusiasm. Catts frequently borrowed money from Carter that he did
not always bother to repay. Mrs. Carter was never very fond of
Catts, resenting both the time and money her husband spent working for him. The first memory that their son, Jerry Carter, Jr., had
of Catts was as a boy of five or six. The Carters pinned young Jerry's
name on his shirt and put him aboard the train bound from
Marianna to Pensacola. Catts, a passenger on the same train, saw
the boy's nametag, and inquired if the youngster knew who he was.
Young Carter innocently replied, "Yes sir, you are Rev. Catts who
borrowed fifty dollars from my father you never paid back."[6]

Enlisting Carter was characteristic of Catts's egotism. His desire to dominate and his inability to work cooperatively with others
caused him to eschew the traditional political power structures in
Florida. His impatient ambition left him no time to cultivate entrenched power bases he probably could not have won anyway. He
chose the improbable route of involving the apathetic masses.
"Win the little people" was the theme of Catts's early campaign.
Listen to the "crackers," flatter them, attend their churches and
fraternal meetings, stir them up, make them mad, frighten them,
win their respect, talk politics—mixed with insurance and

6. Interview Jerry W. Carter, Tallahassee, May 15, 1964, July 29, 1970; interview
Jerry Carter, Jr., May 8, 1972, Tallahassee.

religion—but always talk politics. The choice of Jerry Carter as one of his earliest compatriots was a careful one; it proved to be the heart and soul of the Catts magic. Carter was cracker Florida in microcosm: good natured, uneducated, but intuitively and practically bright and witty, genuinely sympathetic to the problems of panhandle farmers and laborers.

Actually, the political course open to Catts never afforded other options. If opponents judged him harshly for his irrational emotionalism, they should divide their blame with the Democratic hierarchy.

Florida had no political machine in the strict sense of a highly disciplined cadre organized behind a single figure such as a Harry Byrd or a Huey Long. Powerful interests representing insurance, utility, and railroad companies financed candidates who were receptive to their needs, but such arrangements were amorphous and hardly constituted a machine. The state's elongated geography and economic dichotomy made it nearly impossible for one individual to control the entire peninsula. Rather, the state Democratic party was characterized by factionalism, dispersion of power, and personal followings. Nevertheless, the party leadership did constitute a loosely organized club whose members informally set demanding rules for participation. Philosophical deviation within certain parameters could be tolerated, but the proper route to preferment within the party had been carefully drawn and all were expected to follow.[7]

In earlier decades, philosophical conservatism had been a requirement for high public office in the Sunshine State. Governors in the 1880s and 1890s—William D. Bloxham, Edward A. Perry, Francis P. Fleming, and Henry L. Mitchell—might occasionally flirt with reform, but they were wedded to the interests of timber companies, railroads, bankers, and the New South dream of rapid

7. Interviews, Judge James R. Knott and Professor Jerrell Shofner, May 4, 1974, Tallahassee. This description runs counter to the later one by V. O. Key, Jr., *Southern Politics* (New York: Vintage Books, 1949), 82–105. However, the state had undergone considerable urbanization in the southern portion by the time of Key's analysis. The "courthouse gangs" did possess less power in Florida than in other southern states.

economic development even if such progress required the exploitation of the state's citizenry and resources. When progressivism appeared, as in the persons of Senator Wilkinson Call or Governor
Sherman Jennings, it usually flowered in a man whose family connections or long political service in lesser offices made excusable
his deviation from orthodoxy.

Only one man who reached the governorship before Catts
lacked both orthodox views and a prominent political connection.
Governor Napoleon Bonaparte Broward, who distinguished himself as a reform leader between 1904 and 1908, rose from the
obscurity of Duval County (Jacksonville) sheriff to the statehouse.
Broward, unlike Catts, focused on the political and economic issues
without side excursions into demagoguery.

In many ways Broward's task had been simpler. His opponents
had fallen under the domination of conservative railroad influence,
providing Broward a perfect target in a progressive, antitrust era.
Also, Broward had won the state's attention during the 1890s, and
though he had never held a major state office, he did have a powerful base of support in Jacksonville, the most populous city in the
state. His reform faction dominated Duval County politics, and his
progressive allies furnished enthusiasm and political savvy for his
campaign.[8]

Catts, by contrast, had to run against four men who were all
stamped by the Broward era, as were most Florida politicians after
1908. Issues were muddled and largely refurbished from earlier
campaigns, but in main they reflected progressivism. Catts not
only was no hero; he had resided in the state only five years. De-
Funiak Springs was hardly a significant power center, and even
there Catts had few political ties. Whatever professional politicians
joined his ranks would come only after he had surprised the experts
by winning the Democratic primary.

---

8. For a brief but adequate survey of the political climate of Florida, see Chaps. 16–21
of Charlton W. Tebeau's *A History of Florida* (Coral Gables: University of Miami Press,
1971). The standard study of Napoleon B. Broward, which includes a perceptive political
view of the reform movement, is Samuel Proctor's *Napoleon Bonaparte Broward: Florida's
Fighting Democrat* (Gainesville: University of Florida Press, 1950).

Although the Broward era had left the Democratic hierarchy considerably more progressive, it had made it only slightly more inclusive. Success still came by way of a carefully prescribed formula: a prominent family affiliation provided a distinct advantage; that failing, one could convert years of loyal service to the party and a successful law practice into a legislative seat or cabinet post. Using this as a platform for public attention, an aspiring politico could parlay his influence into statewide political alliances in preparation for a race for the statehouse or the United States Senate.

All of Catts's opponents in 1916 had traversed the prescribed route to success: William V. Knott of Tallahassee, the state capital, had been state treasurer and was currently state comptroller; Ion L. Farris was a progressive Jacksonville attorney who had twice served as speaker of the house and who was then in the state senate; Frederick M. Hudson, a Miami lawyer, was a special counsel for the Florida Railroad Commission, and in 1908 had been president of the senate; Frank A. Wood was a St. Petersburg banker who had already served an apprenticeship in the lower house. It was a respectable, traditional slate, if somewhat bland and unexciting, and it met the demands of Democratic party tradition.

With the traditional road to power closed to him, Catts sought an alternate path among the plain people of the panhandle. Through them he discovered the formula that would lead to the wildest campaign in Florida's history.

Religion as a political issue in Florida must be understood in a broader setting. The ambivalent character of the American Progressive Era is nowhere better demonstrated than in religion. Although some churches, especially southern denominations, clung stubbornly to fundamentalism, most adopted a more liberal theology. All of them, even the southern sects, showed greater interest in social and political problems. This "liberal" interest in the social arena oftentimes flowed from their increased political involvement on behalf of prohibition. A long history of nativism and anti-Catholicism sometimes was strengthened by the increasing social involvements of Protestant churches. Many evangelicals believed that their battle against alcohol, which was one of their major social reforms, was hindered by Catholics, whose European tradition treasured the fruit of the vine as one of God's choicest pleasures. Heightened immigration from southern and eastern Europe in the last three decades of the nineteenth century accentuated the conflict. Many Protestant nativists combined support of progressive reforms for labor and even sympathy for socialism with a fanatical hatred of Catholics.[9] For reasons both traditional and political, America experienced a powerful upsurge in anti-Catholicism in the early twentieth century.

An editorial in the *Independent* in 1912 took notice of the national phenomenon. A new organization called the Guardians of Liberty, organized in 1911, claimed a membership in the hundreds of thousands. Headquartered in New York City, it boasted a prominent list of high ranking military figures, clergymen, businessmen, and even some Jewish rabbis. The Reverend Augustus E. Barnett of New York City was the "Chief Recorder," General Nelson A. Miles, former United States chief of staff, was the "Chief Attorney," Charles D. Harris the "Chief Guardian," Rear Admiral O.W. Baird "Chief Vigilant," and Major-General D. E. Sickles "Chief Custodian." The semisecret organization was often compared to the Masons. Its "Declaration of Principles" affirmed supreme loyalty to the Constitution as opposed to any "temporal allegiance," favored complete separation of church and state, opposed the expenditure of any public funds on parochial schools, and pledged to protect the public schools against "foreign menacing influence." The Catholic press interpreted the new organization as directed against Catholicism and charged it with reviving "Know-Nothing" nativism, a view which the editor of the *Independent* shared. Its real goal, thought the editor, was to defeat Catholic politicians; as such it was "proscriptive and unAmerican," a "menace to our political peace."[10]

9. John Higham, *Strangers in the Land: Patterns of American Nativism, 1860–1925* (New York: Atheneum Press, 1963), 180–82.

10. Editorial in the *Independent*, LXXIII (July 11, 1912), 103–104; for a fuller discussion, see Higham, *Strangers in the Land*, 182–84.

The South was a receptive audience for the new movement. Religious fundamentalism thrived there, and the nativist cause became less urban and more rural dominated in the years after 1900. Centered in Alabama, Georgia, and Florida, the anti-Catholic mania infected every southern state; one national writer, Charles P. Sweeney, observed that "bigotry is as much a product of a considerable section of the South as is cotton!"[11] Sweeney also concluded that bigotry in the South was intensified by fraternalism; he specified the Guardians of Liberty and also the Masons, American Mechanics, Knights of Pythias, Woodmen of the World, Odd Fellows, Junior Order American Mechanics, True Americans, Sons and Daughters of Washington, and the nascent Ku Klux Klan.[12] Not incidentally, Catts in one of his earlier biographies listed himself as member of the Masons, Woodmen of the World, Junior Order of American Mechanics, Knights of Pythias, Guardians of Liberty, and the Baptist Church.[13]

The national mood and fraternalism were not the only causes of the spread of religious intolerance in Florida. Protestant religious denominations traditionally had viewed Catholics with suspicion, and the national growth of intolerance only intensified the theological conflicts. Although all evangelical sects in Florida damned Catholic theology, the state's Baptists raised the strongest outcry.[14] The explanation for this fear is more historical and traditional than contemporary, for Catholics obviously posed no threat to Florida. Southern Baptists numbered more adherents in 1916 than any other white Protestant denomination in the state, with 57,732 members organized into 686 churches. The Methodist Episcopal

11. Charles P. Sweeney, "Bigotry Turns to Murder," *Nation*, CXIII (August 31, 1921), 232–33. Since the state previously had demonstrated little religious intolerance, the spread of it is particularly interesting. Catholics had been elected to high office and held a disproportionate number of elective and appointive offices. The state's senior senator, Duncan U. Fletcher, was a Unitarian.

12. Charles P. Sweeney, "Bigotry in the South," *Nation*, CXI (November 24, 1920), 586.

13. Graham, *Baptist Biography*, II, 57.

14. For an example of theological conflict, see the article "Catholics and the Bible," *Florida Baptist Witness*, November 2, 1916. Also, see Edward Earl Joiner, *A History of Florida Baptists* (Jacksonville; Convention Press, 1972), 91.

Church South trailed just behind with 51,505 communicants in 590 parishes. Roman Catholics listed a membership of 24,650, making it the fifth largest church behind Negro and white Baptists and Methodists, with 7.5 percent of the total church population of the state in 1916. Even its financial situation limited its effectiveness, for it lagged in sixth place in value of property.[15]

Although Florida had made a determined effort to attract immigrants in the years following the Civil War, many residents had withdrawn their welcome by 1900. Religious prejudice was one important factor in this rising nativism.[16] One of the most powerful sources of anti-Catholicism in the state actually emanated from across the Georgia state boundary. Thomas E. Watson, former Populist leader and still a respected spokesman for many southern agrarians, had begun a series of articles in 1909 on "The Roman Catholic Hierarchy" in his *Jeffersonian* newspaper. The paper numbered many subscribers in Florida, and secret anti-Catholic societies began to spread. In 1910 the Patriotic Sons of America, urged its members not to vote for Lewis W. Zim, a St. Augustine Catholic who was campaigning for a congressional seat against Frank Clark.[17] Zim's defeat encouraged the politicizing of the secret groups.

Four years later in 1914, United States Senator Nathan P. Bryan recommended the appointment of Peter Dignan, a highly respected member of the Jacksonville city council and a Catholic, as Jacksonville postmaster. Such a routine appointment would have been innocent enough before 1914, but in that year an aggressive young Scotsman arrived in the city from Pennsylvania. Billy Parker was a religious enthusiast and Catholic baiter. Almost immediately he began attacking Catholics in speeches on the city's street cor-

15. Census, *Religious Bodies, 1916*, pp. 160–62.

16. George E. Pozzetta, "Foreigners into Florida: A Study of Immigration Promotion, 1865–1910," *Florida Historical Quarterly*, LIII (October, 1974), 164–80.

17. W. T. Cash, *History of the Democratic Party in Florida* (Live Oak: Democratic Historical Foundation, 1936), 123–24. This chapter by Cash, "Catts and Catholicism," is still the most perceptive contemporary account of Catts, written by a shrewd political opponent the year of the former governor's death.

ners. He organized a chapter of the Guardians of Liberty, and the *Menace,* a weekly anti-Catholic magazine published in Missouri, soon circulated throughout Florida. Protestant speakers wandered across the state fanning religious prejudice. The appointment of Dignan served as convenient excuse for vituperative attacks on Catholics and on Bryan. He was advised by friends to drop the appointment, but Bryan held to his pledge. Although a Methodist, he bitterly resented the introduction of religion into politics. Anti-Catholic groups began to hold meetings in the city to draft someone to oppose Bryan. Governor Park Trammell had already announced his candidacy for Congressman from the first district, but the Protestant activists promised such strong support that he finally agreed to oppose Bryan.[18]

It was within this context of a state already boiling with religious ferment that an itinerant insurance salesman hungry for the statehouse began searching for issues. In subsequent months the state press would accuse Catts of introducing the religious argument to Florida politics. Historians and political observers remembered him as the man who "hanged the Pope to every oak tree in West Florida during the years between 1910 and 1925," or the nativist who along with Tom Watson set the stage for the emergence of the Ku Klux Klan in Florida.[19]

Far from denying these charges, Catts reveled in them, boasted of his role, and substantially enlarged it over reality. The best account by Catts of the origins of his gubernatorial campaign came shortly after his election. He visited his son and daughter-in-law in Birmingham, just before his inauguration. The Alabama city con-

---

18. The best summary of these behind-the-scenes developments can be found in a manuscript written by William V. Knott, "The Guardians of Liberty: The Origin and Purpose of the 'Guardians of Liberty' and the Influence of the Organization on the 1916 Florida Elections," September, 1957. Original in possession of Judge James R. Knott, West Palm Beach, Florida. For published, edited copy see Wayne Flynt (ed.), "William V. Knott and the Gubernatorial Campaign of 1916," *Florida Historical Quarterly,* LI (April, 1973), 423–30.

19. Fuller Warren, *How to Win in Politics* (Tallahassee: Peninsular Publishing Co., 1949), 175; and David Chalmers, "The Ku Klux Klan in the Sunshine State: The 1920's," *Florida Historical Quarterly,* XLII (January, 1964), 209.

tained a large Catholic minority and seethed with religious conflict stirred primarily by the secret nativists True Americans. Dr. O. T. Dozier, a leading anti-Catholic spokesman, learned of Catts's visit and asked him to address a Birmingham audience on the subject, "How I Did It, or How I Smashed the Machine in Florida." On December 13, 1916, Catts addressed a hastily assembled but huge audience at Cable Hall. The governor-elect was introduced by Dr. A. J. Dickinson, pastor of Brimingham's First Baptist Church, a collection was taken for renting the hall, and a meeting of the Ku Klux Klan was announced to follow immediately after the adjournment of the address.

Catts's speech began with a disclaimer of any political ambition. Although he had seen the "pernicious influence" of Jesuit domination in Florida, he had never really thought of running for governor. Then two events had propelled him into the race: the assassination of an anti-Catholic lecturer named Black in Texas, and the inspiration of Tom Watson, "the greatest leader of our cause, Americanism." Thunderous applause followed. He related his version of the tragic reality of Florida politics: less than one-fifth of the population was Catholic, yet they held two-thirds of all offices. Through "unseen and invisible methods," they controlled the government and press: "The Catholics were about to take Florida, and I told the people about it wherever I went. I was trampling on their toes and raising the devil to such an extent that many of the Catholics wanted to kill 'Old Catts.'" None of the gubernatorial hopefuls would speak out on the real issues of Catholic control of government, press, and public education.

According to contemporary newspaper accounts, Catts's voice "quivered with emotion" as he recounted in dramatic manner his decision to enter the race: "For weeks before I announced, I could not sleep at night. I felt a call that I was trying to resist. I firmly believe, and was finally convinced that I was called of God to make that race. And after I got into the fight I was more and more convinced of the truth of my vision."[20]

---

20. Birmingham *Age-Herald*, December 14, 1916.

Even allowing for the fact that Catts, as usual, was swept along by his own evangelical rhetoric, this is a misstatement of the facts. His occasional flights into religious mysticism make such a statement thoroughly believable; however, this one seemed more designed for public consumption than it was a revelation of his motivation for entering the contest. Such explanations received an enthusiastic reception in rural Florida, and they better reflect Catts's increasing political sagacity than his naïve theology. The true origin of his gubernatorial ambition contradicts his December explanation in Birmingham.

Two years before the 1916 gubernatorial race, Catts had resigned his pastorate at DeFuniak Springs, and the insurance job he took in 1914 was a temporary position that allowed him to meet the "little people" and discover the issues which perplexed them.[21] After toiling away his days peddling insurance, he spent his nights lecturing in tiny schoolhouses and churches scattered throughout north and west Florida. It was from this discovery of the fears of rural Floridians that his "movement" sprang. In a later interview he acknowledged that his campaign was fathered by the Guardians of Liberty, the True Americans, and similar nativist groups.[22] W. T. Cash writes that Catts, an intuitively accurate observer of the cracker mentality, saw the anti-Catholic sentiment already sweeping Florida, and on his trips to teach Sunday school classes or sell insurance in fish camps, he came to understand "a great many people whom political leaders of Florida had previously ignored." Cash emphasizes the pragmatic politics that dominated the demagoguery of Catts, noting that the fishermen who were attracted to Catts by his demand for an overhaul of state game policy were mostly Catholics; however, Catts never mentioned Catholicism while listening to their grievances in a hundred fishing villages be-

21. Evidence of his decision to run by no later than 1914 is abundant. His home town paper boasted that he had secretly lined up support for two years before the 1916 race began (see Jacksonville *Florida Times-Union*, July 17, 1916, quoting Lakeland *Telegram*); Jerry Carter, one of his earliest enthusiasts verifies this (interview, Jerry Carter, July 29, 1970, Tallahassee), as does Catts himself in an autobiographical sketch (Graham, *Baptist Biography*, II, 56).

22. Interview in Birmingham *Age-Herald*, December 14, 1916.

tween 1914 and 1916.[23] His Baptist heritage bequeathed him a fear
of Catholicism, and he opposed Catholics who sought public office;
but this did not sour his personal relations with individual members of the faith, and he did not emphasize this anti-Catholicism in
communities where such sentiments might harm him politically.

Jerry Carter, who also emphasized this strain of shrewd pragmatism in Catts, denied that Catts ever felt personal animosity
towards Catholics. When the minister-turned-politician visited
Pensacola on one of his first campaign trips, he cultivated every
potential supporter, including Catholics, Protestants, businessmen, and laborers. Carter contended that it was not until Catts
visited Jacksonville, a center of anti-Catholicism, that the Catholic
issue emerged, forced on him by people like Billy Parker (who
endorsed Catts publicly only in the spring of 1916). Once the issue
was raised, there was only one side to join in an increasingly
nativist Florida. After Catts's election, he secretly instructed Carter to obtain the names of the most influential Catholics in the
various communities; he desired to make peace with them, win
their trust, and perhaps even appoint several to public office.[24]

An interesting postscript, which might further clarify the nature of Catts's anti-Catholicism, occurred in 1920 in an article published in the Jacksonville *Metropolis*. The paper, in opposing
Catts's candidacy for the United States Senate that year, accused
him of Machiavellian expediency. According to the editor of the
paper, Catts had stopped by, after winning the governor's race in
1916, to thank him for his fairness in the just completed campaign.
The editor asked Catts why he had attacked Catholics so bitterly.
The governor-elect replied that Napoleon Broward had been elected governor of Florida with the battle cry of Everglades drainage:
"When I decided to enter the Governor's race, I had to have a

23. Cash, *History of the Democratic Party in Florida*, 124, 128. His opponent, William
V. Knott, also emphasizes the influence of "cracker" nativism on Catts as he traveled the
state: "Apparently he sensed the political possibilities that might come from the prejudice
and division that was being preached." Knott, "The Guardians of Liberty," 6.

24. Interview, Jerry Carter, July 29, 1970, Tallahassee. A brief survey of nativism in
Florida emphasizes the pragmatism behind Catts's use of the issue while focusing on pre-
1916 anti-Catholicism; see David Page, "Bishop Michael J. Curley and Anti-Catholic
Nativism in Florida," *Florida Historical Quarterly*, XLV (October, 1966), 101–17.

battle cry which would stir up the people, and after careful thought I decided to choose 'the Catholic question.' I worked it to a finish—and I won."[25]

Jerry Carter has summarized the political realities of Florida politics in the years 1914 to 1916 as well as any twentieth-century observer. To understand Catts, he said, one must remember that a very close and narrow clique completely controlled state politics when Catts arrived on the scene. To win, he had to smash completely the influential Democratic leadership in Tallahassee because power and offices were obtainable only through them.[26] To accomplish this, Catts had to discover what issues frightened and perplexed the crackers, which disputes he could fashion into programs that would distinguish him from the other candidates; he must jar the "little people" from their apathy into an angry political movement; and he found the issues.

25. St. Petersburg *Times*, June 6, 1920, quoting Jacksonville *Metropolis*.

26. Interview, Jerry Carter, July 29, 1970, Tallahassee. Knott admits that the reason no one considered Catts a contender was that he was the only candidate without Florida political connections; Knott, "The Guardians of Liberty," 5.

THREE

Protestant Rednecks and Catholic Fishermen

THE ELECTION YEAR OF 1916 opened without a hint that it would be one of the most unusual political years in Florida history. The urban daily press, insulated from discontent in the rural areas and small hamlets, spent its major attention on the U.S. Senate race between incumbent N. P. Bryan and his challenger, Governor Park Trammell, who was trying to become one of the few men in Florida history to move from the governor's mansion in Tallahassee to the Senate in Washington. The leading gubernatorial candidates were cut from essentially the same cloth and inspired little enthusiasm among the press or the voters. Few paid any attention to the obscure west Florida insurance salesman who was stumping in rural schools, churches, and fish camps. William V. Knott of Tallahassee was generally acknowledged to be the leading candidate. His long residence in the state capital, his loyalty to the Democratic party, and his effective record as an officeholder, provided many assets. Knott's political career was a classic example of traditional access into Florida's Democratic hierarchy. He had served as deputy clerk of the circuit courts in Sumter and Putnam counties for four years; from this base he had run for state treasurer, an office he held for nine years; for the next five years, he served as state comptroller.

When interviewed later concerning the 1916 campaign, Knott reminisced that he had run to combat the rising tide of religious bigotry in Florida. However, he did not mention Catts in his an-

nouncement, and at that time religion did not threaten to be an
important issue in the campaign. Actually Knott had long aimed for
the statehouse.[1]

Through the years political friends had urged him to run for
governor. Their assurances convinced him that he could win hand-
ily, and his candidacy depended on political friendships rather than
on selection by a narrow leadership clique within the Democratic
party. In past campaigns his friends had contained his opposition,
eliminating serious candidates, but they had no influence with Sidney Catts. Though a man of great integrity, affable, and an experienced officeholder, Knott was untested on the stump against strong
competition.[2]

After marshaling strength for some months, Knott announced
his platform on February 11, 1916. While not a very exciting or
controversial statement, it was solidly progressive within the
ideological framework of the Broward era. It called for economy in
government, equalization of tax rates, good roads, establishment of
a free school system, Everglades drainage, encouragement of agriculture, and increased pensions for Confederate veterans. His
only unpredictable plank endorsed the relaxation of restrictive libel
laws in order to provide greater freedom of speech and press. His
emphasis on public service and efficiency fitted nicely into what
one historian of the recent South calls "business progressivism."[3]

Knott had assiduously courted political leaders across Florida
and had already committed many to his candidacy. William
Bloxham Crawford of Kissimmee, scion of one of the most powerful
political families in the state, was an early Knott enthusiast and

1. Deal discounts Knott's statement, emphasizing the candidate's political ambition:
"Sidney Johnston Catts, Stormy Petrel of Florida Politics," 17. The candidate's son, though
only a boy of six, remembers hearing much discussion of the campaign in later years. He
writes: "I think it is safe to say that my father did not enter the governor's race primarily to
counter the rise of anti-Catholic sentiment in Florida represented by Catts' platform
speeches." James R. Knott to author, August 6, 1970.

2. Interview, Judge James R. Knott, May 4, 1974, Tallahassee.

3. See text of platform in Jacksonville *Florida Times-Union*, February 12, 1916. For a
fuller treatment of "business progressivism" in southern politics, see George B. Tindall,
The Emergence of the New South, 1913–1945, Vol. X of *A History of the South* (Baton
Rouge: Louisiana State University Press, 1967), 224.

used his considerable influence on Knott's behalf.[4] His father had been a long-time Florida secretary of state, and Crawford himself was a power within the state Democratic executive committee. Considered a progressive, he had led the struggle for a presidential primary in 1912 which had helped Woodrow Wilson's presidential candidacy in Florida. Another early backer was J. B. Hodges, prominent Lake City lawyer and political figure, who would later switch to Catts and play a key role in Knott's defeat.[5] Newspapers, both conservative urban dailies and progressive rural weeklies, considered Knott the front runner, and many endorsed him. So convinced of the primary victory was Knott that he did not join the other candidates for a May tour of west Florida, explaining that his official duties required his attention in Tallahassee.[6]

Knott considered his chief rival for the nomination to be Frederick M. Hudson, Miami lawyer, former president of the state senate, and special council for the Florida Railroad Commission. Like Knott, Hudson favored better schools, higher assessment of railroad property, and a franchise tax. Hudson tried to link comptroller Knott's financial policies to an unusually large number of bank closings in Florida and proposed creation of a state commission to supervise banks.

Frank A. Wood, a retired St. Petersburg banker and former state legislator, was given only an outside chance of winning, but he embarrassed Knott by his attack on the state comptroller's handling of banking matters. Since most statewide interest had centered on a series of joint debates between senatorial hopefuls N. P. Bryan and Park Trammell, Wood challenged Knott to a similar confrontation. The debates, beginning March 20, placed Knott increasingly on the defensive over bank failures. At Lynn Haven,

4. J. B. Hodges to W. B. Crawford, May 4, 1916, in Box 12, J. B. Hodges Papers, P. K. Yonge Library of Florida History, University of Florida, Gainesville.

5. W. V. Knott to J. B. Hodges, May 14, 1916, in Box 12, Hodges Papers. Hodges not only guaranteed his loyalty to Knott as late as May, 1916, but helped organize the county for him; he did detect, however, a disenchantment with Knott from the earliest stages of the race, and a steady drift within the county to Catts.

6. For examples of newspaper support, see Jacksonville *Florida Times-Union*, January 26, 1916, quoting DeLand *Record*, Jasper *News*, May 19, 1916. Interestingly, neither paper mentions Catts at all until just before the June primary.

where the local bank had just collapsed, Knott was introduced and endorsed by former major J. M. Hughey, who explained that he had investigated charges that Knott's policies had caused the crisis, and had found them invalid. Despite this assurance, Knott felt obligated to spend most of his speech on a detailed explanation of complicated banking practices and the international financial situation.

Many observers considered the most progressive gubernatorial candidate to be Ion L. Farris of Jacksonville, popular attorney and orator of wide renown, who twice had been speaker of the House and was currently a state senator. In his platform, announced on March 19, 1916, Farris proposed renewal of the Broward plan of Everglades drainage, improved education and industrial schools for boys and girls, salaries for county officials to replace the fee system, abolition of the convict lease system, better roads, and a revision of state libel laws. He charged that there had been more bank failures during the administration of Comptroller Knott than under the direction of his predecessors. Detecting the Catts threat earlier than other candidates, Farris faced the religious issue squarely. While hesitatingly assuring voters that he was a Methodist, he ridiculed Catts's anti-Catholicism and argued that religious affiliation should not be a political issue. He equivocated on the liquor issue, opposing statewide prohibition, but announced that he personally had voted dry in local option elections.[7]

During the early sparring for position, Catts ranged across Florida, though concentrating his activities in the northern and western portions of the state. In 1910 the twenty-seven counties of the panhandle and north Florida contained slightly less than half of Florida's population, 358,426 of 752,619.[8] Lack of financing dictated much of his political strategy. He claimed to have had only

---

7. Jacksonville *Florida Times-Union*, March 19, April 27, 1916.

8. North and west Florida are used only in a general sense to refer to the areas north of Gainesville (north of and including Alachua, Putnam, and St. Johns counties), with Jacksonville the major metropolis, and the panhandle. Contemporary purists insisted that "west Florida" referred only to that area west of the Apalachicola River. The territory between the Suwannee and Apalachicola rivers, including Suwannee County, was technically "middle Florida." See *Florida Democrat and Weekly Record*, May 23, 1924.

two hundred dollars when he began campaigning actively for the nomination, and he spent that almost immediately on newspaper publicity. He estimated that the entire campaign cost only seventeen thousand dollars, most of it collected by passing the hat at his rallies, while he charged that Knott spent one hundred thousand dollars. Political ally Jerry Carter knew of no large donations to Catts, although DeFuniak Springs millionare J. J. McCasskill may have made modest contributions just before the general election in the fall when Catts appeared a sure winner. Carter verifies Catts's claim that most money was collected by passing the hat during rallies. Between collections, Catts frequently had no funds at all, and when the primary campaign ended with the candidate at Tampa, he watched the vote count there because he had no money for a railroad fare home.[9]

Lack of funds caused Catts to concentrate his efforts on rural audiences in country schools and churches. Explaining his strategy simply, he told an interviewer: "I stuck to the country and made speeches at night. The other candidates stuck to the cities. I covered the state from end to end. When I ran entirely out of money, I would take up a collection to get enough to go the next county." After a day of selling insurance in a hamlet, he would scurry across the hinterland soliciting votes. On one such journey, he walked more than ten miles in a midsummer sun to address a precinct meeting of only seventeen voters.[10]

Despite his desperate lack of money, Catts was not without assets. He was a striking man physically, dressed in white suit with turned back collar and vest; he also had acquired an uncanny capac-

9. Birmingham *Age-Herald*, December 12, 1916; New York *Times*, May 29, 1921. Independent sources tend to validate this claim since he had to borrow money to buy inaugural clothes for himself and his family. Later, he received contributions from J. J. McCasskill. Interview, Mrs. Elizabeth Paderick, May 12, 1972, Jacksonville. Estimates of his campaign expenditures were found in the Jacksonville *Florida Times-Union*, October 30, 1919, quoting the Branford *Progress*. See also Birmingham *Age-Herald*, December 14, 1916, New York *Times*, May 29, 1921. These estimates are consistent with his known expenditures and contributions. Catts's meager campaign expenditures also were confirmed in an interview with Jerry Carter, July 29, 1970, Tallahassee.

10. Birmingham *Age-Herald*, December 14, 1916; New York *Times*, May 29, 1921.

ity to remember names. W. V. Knott, a prominent Baptist layman himself, recalled that he had first seen Catts at a Baptist convention in 1914. Catts was an impressive figure, six feet tall, weighing about two hundred pounds, with a shock of unruly and thinning red hair. Although they were introduced only briefly at the Baptist conference, Catts startled Knott by recalling his name when they met more than a year later.[11]

Catts's ministerial duties had accustomed him to public appearances, and he was by far the most entertaining speaker in the gubernatorial field. Former governor Fuller Warren emphasizes Catts's humor and almost legendary powers on the stump. Knott's son explained Catts's transformation from obscure insurance man to governor through "the force of his cracker rhetoric [which] became felt among the largely rural population to the extent that he became almost a minor folk hero to 'the great unwashed,' with their (until then) unarticulated prejudices and fears regarding Catholics and other unassimilated or non-conforming groups."[12]

Catts usually began his speeches with some humorous reference to his name which invariably provoked laughter. After his election, he quipped, instead of calling him "Old Catts" or "Blatherskite Catts," his opponents could address him simply as Governor Catts. Next, he attacked the Catholic conspiracy in earthy but compelling language. A master storyteller, he captivated his audiences for an hour or longer, spinning them into alternating moods of attentive silence, uproarious laughter, or clamorous applause. Rural audiences were moved by his account of how he had decided to enter the gubernatorial contest. While riding between insurance appointments, something had bothered him; so he stopped, propped himself against a charred stump, and prayed until suddenly God's will came to him: "Run for governor." The speech usually ended with Catts pointing to the sky, asking his

11. Deal, "Sidney Johnston Catts," 16. Mrs. Catts had vests especially made for her husband, a half dozen at a time. He insisted on the white vests, which did not come with his suits, because he needed them for his pocket watch and chain. Interview, Mrs. Elizabeth Paderick and Mrs. Alice May Stiegel, May 12, 1972, Jacksonville.

12. Warren, How to Win in Politics, 175–76; Knott to author, August 6, 1970.

audiences if they could not see Jesus Christ sitting on a cloud, while angels strummed harps, observing the decisions of Floridians as they decided the political fate of their state.[13] A reporter covering his speech in Birmingham, Alabama, in December, 1916, provides the fairest evaluation of his oratorical style:

> Mr. Catts has a peculiar power as an orator and speaker. He has a massive frame and powerful physique. His voice, while practically broken down from the 3,000 addresses he made during his campaign, has exceptional oratorical possibilities. A wonderful sense of humor, and the ability to tell stories in a style that would do credit to the most experienced raconteur, he has no trouble holding the attention of his audience. His entire style of speaking, his general appearance, and his methods of campaigning mark him as a unique but extremely forceful character. He could say things that in other speakers would sound coarse and possibly offensive, and escape the slightest censure from his hearers.[14]

The platform adopted by Catts was similar to his opponents'. In a speech at Gainesville on March 3, he called for economy in government, increased taxes on corporations and land syndicates, larger pensions for Confederate soldiers, and more equitable railroad shipping rates. He favored improved education but, continuing a theme from his 1914 Alabama platform, warned that the state was training the minds of children rather than their hands; he therefore proposed establishing three dozen normal schools for manual training of white youth. In a stand similar to that of former Mississippi governor James K. Vardaman, he opposed both vocational and classical education for Negroes. Given his earlier favorable impressions of Tuskegee Institute, this argument appears to be a purely expedient racial appeal for white votes. With some variations all the candidates favored these "reforms"; what distinguished Catts's candidacy was his emphasis on statewide prohibition, the Catholic menace, and his bitter opposition to the conservation policies of Shell Fish commissioner T. R. Hodges.

The burden of selling his policies to the voters of Florida fell

13. Interview, Jerry W. Carter, Jr., May 8, 1972, Tallahassee.
14. Birmingham *Age-Herald*, December 14, 1916.

almost exclusively on Catts. He had neither the money nor the political loyalties to form an organization even remotely comparable to Knott's. J. V. Burke managed the campaign, with Jerry Carter in Pensacola, Van C. Swearingen in Jacksonville, and other novices providing assistance; but the general strategy was determined by Catts.[15]

By springtime, 1916, Catts's efforts were winning him many friends in north and west Florida. The Lake City *Index* surveyed the gubernatorial candidates in May, eliminating them one by one. Knott was too closely identified with the railroads and the successful attempt to move the University of Florida from Lake City to Gainesville; Wood was a rich banker who would favor banks over "the common people" and was rumored to be a "wet"; Farris had no chance and was a wet in addition. The editor added a note of concern over Catholic political power and concluded that Catts had more "original, inherent, characteristic ability" than any other candidate. He was "almost an exact duplicate of Ben Tillman twenty years ago, when the latter fought for the common people of South Carolina." Catts might make mistakes, but it would be "a blunder of the head and not of the heart—an honest error and not a political trick."[16]

J. B. Hodges, an ambitious attorney in Lake City, favored Knott but admitted privately that the sentiment in Lake City seemed to be opposed to all incumbent officeholders. He told a Knott aide that Catts had developed "a strength that surprised me, and people seem to be following him." To another friend who favored Catts he confided: "Your friend, Catts, was here last night. He is some Catt. He is strong[er] than I thought he was."[17]

Despite the diversity of his platform, Catts quickly perceived the contagious effect of his anti-Catholicism and promoted this into the preeminent issue. His attack on the other four candidates

15. Interview, Jerry Carter, May 15, 1964, Tallahassee.

16. St. Petersburg *Times*, May 26, 1916, quoting Lake City *Index*.

17. J. B. Hodges to W. B. Crawford, May 4, 1916, Hodges to James B. Alexander, May 4, 1916 in Box 12, Hodges Papers.

centered on their refusal to join his crusade against "the continuance of Roman domination" of America. He had gone to see them all, but they only had ridiculed "Old Catts": "They knew nothing about our American platform and they cared less."[18] Thus, Catts had to carry the banner of Americanism alone.

In 1916 Florida contained just enough Roman Catholics to frighten many Protestant voters but insufficient numbers to furnish political protection for themselves at the polls. The state's 24,650 Roman Catholics were concentrated in eleven counties (Duval and St. Johns in north Florida; Dade and Monroe in south Florida; Brevard, Hillsborough, Orange, Pasco, Pinellas, Polk, and Volusia in central Florida) which contained 21,477 of the reported census total. Outside these counties, anti-Catholicism became an emotional political issue, thriving on rural ignorance and evangelical intolerance.

The level of intensity and even the nature of Catts "demagogy" varied with the audience. To more sophisticated urban gatherings covered by the press, he opposed Catholic influence in government, parochial schools, and private closed institutions such as convents and monasteries. He insisted on a law providing state inspection of all "closed institutions." Even Woodrow Wilson's personal secretary, who was a Catholic, came under fire. Catts also managed to connect religious and racial prejudices. During the campaign, Governor Park Trammell used state powers to arrest three Catholic parochial schoolteachers for instructing Negroes in their classrooms. Sister Mary Thomasine of the Sisters of St. Joseph went on trial in St. Augustine for violating a state law that prohibited whites from teaching black students. The allegation that a white Roman Catholic taught black students created a tremendous public reaction and forcefully illustrated the subversive influence of parochial education; many Floridians concluded with Catts that the extension of Catholic control would inevitably bring racial changes. The Catholic diocese paper attacked Trammell's handling

18. Birmingham *Age-Herald*, December 14, 1916.

of the affair, provoking many Protestants to write the governor supporting his determination to control the "Catholic menace." M. F. Green from Taylor County typified the response of many Floridians, writing Trammell: "I think most of us in Florida (in Taylor County, at least) has [sic] enough of Bryanism, Negroism, and Catholicism, they can all go to H—for my part."[19]

There are no complete or reliable accounts of Catts's speeches in rural areas, and the religious charges made there were certainly embellished by his opponents. However, given the popularity of Tom Watson's obscene accounts of life in monasteries and convents and the wide use of such materials Southwide, there may be some validity in the reports that Catts delighted rural audiences with accounts of sensual priests and nubile nuns. Almost certainly he told rural audiences that Catholics were planning an armed revolt to take over America and were at that moment storing arms and munitions in the cellar of a cathedral in Tampa.[20] A single cliche, admitted by Catts and oft repeated in 1916, summarized his stand: "Nothing in Florida above the nation's flag; the red school house against the parochial school; all closed institutions in Florida to be opened by process of law and America for Americans first, last, and forever."[21]

It was this nativistic religious issue that provided an effective counterweight to the well-established Democratic organization backing Knott. Most contemporary observers and later historians

19. David Page, "Bishop Michael J. Curley and Anti-Catholic Nativism in Florida," *Florida Historical Quarterly*, XLV (October, 1966), 110–11; M. F. Green to Park Trammell, May 12, 1912, in Reel 1, Park Trammell Papers, microfilm, P. K. Yonge Library of Florida History, University of Florida, Gainesville. A similar view was expressed by many other correspondents; *i.e.*, see William Collins to Park Trammell, May 15, 1916, in Reel 1, Trammell Papers. For Catts's stand on these issues, see Jacksonville *Florida Times-Union*, January 13, March 4, May 6, 12, 16, 1916.

20. Opponents such as Ion Farris claimed that Catts pledged to search Knights of Columbus halls looking for munitions caches, and Fuller Warren records the same general speech. See Jacksonville *Florida Times-Union*, April 27, 1916; Warren, *How to Win in Politics*, 176; William V. Knott, "The Guardians of Liberty: The Origin and Purpose of the 'Guardians of Liberty' and the influence of the Organization on the 1916 Florida Elections," September, 1957, p. 6, in possession of Judge James R. Knott, West Palm Beach.

21. B. J. W. Graham, *Baptist Biography*, II, 55.

have ignored the powerful Guardians of Liberty whose members
rallied energetically behind their fraternal brother Sidney Catts.
The exact membership of the Guardians in Florida is unknown;
Catts declared it to have numbered 40,000 members, while the
Panama City *Pilot,* bitterly hostile to him, lowered the estimate to
"approximately" 35,000. Either estimate represents significant
strength, and the tightly knit and enthusiastic clubs performed
yeomanlike service in both the primary and general elections. Following his victory, Catts acknowledged that the unqualified support of the Guardians of Liberty together with the prohibitionist
vote had been the key to his triumph.[22]

The fire of religious hatred fanned by Catts grew into a wild
conflagration by spring, and the regular Democratic forces belatedly tried to contain it. T. J. Appleyard—state printer, publisher of the Tallahassee *Florida Record,* and sympathetic to
Knott—distributed copies of the constitution and bylaws of the
Guardians of Liberty. He also charted a strategy designed to arrest
the cracker revolt in north Florida. Appleyard had discovered that
E. J. Long, editor of the *American Citizen,* a publication of the
Guardians, was a Negro. Long had proposed to send 100,000
copies of his journal to Florida during the campaign, and
Appleyard believed the revelation of his race would more than balance this journalistic blitz. He urged Knott loyalists to utilize the
Negro issue and promised to supply a photograph of Long
momentarily.[23] Herbert Felkel, who edited the *Florida Record* for
Appleyard, wrote Bradford Byrd of the Atlanta *Journal* commis-
sioning a cartoon showing white and black men taking the Guardian of Liberty oath together and quoting from the pledge. Felkel
told the Atlanta newspaperman that Appleyard also wanted the At-

22. Birmingham *Age-Herald,* December 14, 1916; Panama City *Pilot,* July 3, 1916. For
Catts's view, see the Birmingham *Age-Herald,* December 14, 1916. William V. Knott
agreed that the Guardians played a decisive role. Knott, "The Guardians of Liberty," 6. For
a broader discussion of the organization and the spread of nativism in the South, see
Higham, *Strangers in the Land,* 180–86, 291–92.

23. J. B. Hodges to T. J. Appleyard, April 7, 1916, Appleyard to Hodges, April 7, 1916,
in Box 13, Hodges Papers.

lanta *Journal* to release the story on the same day it was released by the *Florida Record*, thus strengthening credibility. The two Florida journalists expressed confidence that the story would defeat both Trammell and Catts. However, Appleyard badly misjudged Byrd, who sent the correspondence to his friend Park Trammell and replied to Felkel's letter with a curt reprimand. He had been an admirer of Felkel, but was deeply disappointed at such underhanded politics. He did not know Catts, nor did he care about him; but he chided: "Why pick on Catts, he's harmless. He's not the man your candidate will have to beat."[24] Appleyard and Felkel, undismayed by the uncooperative Georgia paper, released the story and charged that the Guardians accepted Negro members and treated them on the basis of equality with whites. The *American Citizen*, they argued, was published in Philadelphia and hated the South and the Democratic party. The Guardians were advocating nothing less than "political miscegenation."[25]

Other newspapers debated the legitimacy of using religion as a political issue. The Panama City *Pilot* contemptuously wrote of a new denomination in Florida, the "Cattsites"; while this was the sixteenth branch of the Baptist Church in the United States, it was the "only Baptist denomination that permits its pulpits to be made political rostrums." Other papers agreed that Catts's only issue was religion and that this was not a proper topic of political debate. As the DeLand *News* editorialized: "Politics itself is nasty enough without being polluted by so-called religion, which is nothing but prejudice or the desire to milk the suffering public of some pieces of silver."[26]

This feeble counterattack failed to blunt the issue, and religious turmoil intensified. Observers predicted that anti-Catholicism would aid Catts in the governor's race, and Park Trammel in the

24. Bradford Byrd to Park Trammell, March 15, 1916, Byrd to Herbert Felkel, March 14, 1916, on Reel 1, Trammell Papers.
25. Jacksonville *Florida Times-Union*, March 24, April 1, 1916, quoting Panama City *Pilot* and Ocala *Star*.
26. Panama City *Pilot*, July 3, 1916; Jacksonville *Florida Times-Union*, January 1, 1916, quoting DeLand *News*.

senatorial campaign.[27] The *American Citizen* allegedly had begun a
subscription fund to help Governor Trammell defeat incumbent
Senator N. P. Bryan; as a consequence, Bryan blasted the Guardians of Liberty, perhaps thus contributing to his defeat. Catts attributed Trammell's primary victory to the Guardian's activity on
his behalf.[28] Unquestionably Catts's interjection of religion into the
campaign aided Trammell. The governor unhesitatingly climbed
aboard the Guardian of Liberty bandwagon and profited from its
support. S. G. Bartow, editor of another Guardian newspaper, the
Menace, which was published in Missouri, corresponded with
Trammell, and the local chapters instructed members to vote for
both Catts and the governor. Many voters assumed that Trammell
was a member of the organization. One Fort Myers correspondent
inquired about a spurious telegram allegedly sent by Catts which
complained of his treatment by the governor: "The two of you are
backed by the same parties. We want no split. . . . We are up
against a hard bunch that will stop at nothing to get you two out of
the way."[29] The Gainesville *Sun* sadly observed that "never in the
history of Florida has politics been worse mixed than at the present
time. Personal friends hold aloof from discussing political candidates . . . because religious prejudice has entered into the fitness
of men for office, and feeling is so tense that they realize it is useless to discuss the merits of candidates."[30]

Subtle evidence of the strange new element in state politics
began to appear in statements of local candidates. An aspirant in
Jacksonville announced in his publicity that he was not a member

27. Jacksonville *Florida Times-Union,* April 1, 1916, quoting Ocala *Star; ibid.,* February 24, 1916.

28. *Ibid.,* February 24, 1916; Birmingham *Age-Herald,* December 14, 1916.

29. For anti-Catholic support for Catts/Trammell, see "Correspondence concerning
Roman Catholic Issue in 1916 Election," on Reel 1, Trammell Papers. See especially S. G.
Bartow to Park Trammell, May 15, 1916; R. C. Boulvare to Trammell, May 23, 1916, on
Reel 1; and L. C. Stewart to Trammell, May 29, 1916, on Reel 3. Many politicians also
supported both men. See J. S. Blitch to Trammell, April 18, 1916, on Reel 3, Trammell
Papers.

30. Jacksonville *Florida Times-Union,* April 12, 1916.

of the Guardians of Liberty or the Catholic church. Ion Farris deplored Catts's intolerance, but reasserted that he was a member of the Methodist church.[31]

One attempt to check the rise of religious bigotry had the ironic effect of strengthening it, providing Catts with a straw man of monumental proportions. Amidst the spectacular increase of anti-Catholicism, the state Democratic executive committee met in Jacksonville on January 6, 1916. R. B. Sturkie of Pasco County, chairman of the resolutions committee, introduced a resolution that triggered public wrath. The proposal began innocently enough, pledging the voters in Democratic primaries to support the victor in the general election. The fourth section, however, required the voter not to be influenced in his voting "by any religious test or on account of religious belief, denomination or sect with which the candidate is affiliated." The fifth section proved even more incendiary, requiring the Democratic voter to pledge "that he is not a member of any secret organization which attempts in any way to influence political action or results."[32] In the executive committee only one dissenting vote was cast against the proposal.

The resolution had been drafted by Jacksonville city attorney John M. Barrs, a prominent progressive, and a long-time ally of Napoleon Broward and Senator Nathan P. Bryan. Barrs, though not a member of the state committee, was promoting the candidacy of Ion Farris for governor and the reelection of Bryan. Barrs conceived the idea of excluding members of secret political clubs from the Democratic party without thinking specifically of Catts, despite the popular belief, manipulated masterfully by Catts, that the resolutions were aimed solely at him. At the time that the resolutions were adopted, Catts was not considered even a remote threat, and the real object was Billy Parker and the burgeoning ranks of the Guardians of Liberty in Jacksonville, where Barrs had observed

31. *Ibid.*, May 24, April 27, 1916.
32. *Ibid.*, January 7, 1916.

their potential threat.[33] Sturkie explained that he introduced Barrs's resolution at the request of Catholic voters who numbered 65 percent of the total registration in his home county. Whatever Sturkie's motive, it was not concern for the Catholic "bloc" in Pasco County. Although the county did contain the sixth largest recorded Roman Catholic population of the counties in Florida, there were only 447 communicants compared to 819 Southern Baptists and 592 white Methodists. Politics appears to have had more influence on Sturkie than the religious preferences of his constituents.

Catts attended the controversial committee meeting on January 6 as an observer. Following the meeting, he confided to his campaign manager, who was an active member of the Guardians of Liberty, that he might just as well withdraw from the race. Burke persuaded him to stay in the campaign, arguing that his presence would help make the resolution unpopular. Burke established a political paper to lead the attack, and Catts subsequently directed much of his oratory against the state Democratic committee.[34]

J. S. Smith of Green Cove Springs was one of the few members of the executive committee who recognized the danger posed by the resolution. He wrote an open letter calling the resolutions undemocratic and "not in accord with the wishes of the Democratic voters of the state."[35] Each passing week demonstrated the understatement of his protest.

The Bartow *Courier-Informant* spoke for many Floridians when it called the resolutions an attempt to "Romanize Florida inaugurated by the state Democratic committee."[36] Former governor A. W. Gilchrist and incumbent Park Trammell lost no time in opposing the Sturkie resolves as undemocratic and in effect setting religious qualifications for voting. Catts, not to be outdone, charged

33. James R. Knott to author, August 6, 1970; Cash, *History of the Democratic Party in Florida*, 127–28. The account of the Sturkie resolutions by Cash is the most reliable reference and contains information he could have acquired only from participants.

34. Knott, "Guardians of Liberty," 2.

35. J. S. Smith to editor, Jacksonville *Florida Times-Union*, January 8, 1916.

36. Quoted in Cash, *History of the Democratic Party in Florida*, 127.

that the members of the committee were "under the influence of liquor" when they passed the resolution.[37]

Public outrage swept across the state. A mass meeting in Tampa, hometown of executive committee chairman George P. Rainey, demanded that the state committee rescind the resolution. Two days later a similar gathering met in Leesburg. A mass meeting at Montbrook, led by state senator J. S. Blitch, who supported both Catts and Trammell, drafted a statement opposing sections four and five. On January 29 the Hillsborough County Democratic Committee voted twenty-six to fourteen to condemn the resolution.[38] During February the resolutions were condemned by mass meetings at River Junction in Gadsden County, Bushnell in Sumter County, Palmetto (Manatee County), Lake Helen (Volusia County), and Palatka (Putnam County). The Macclenny *Standard* and Leesburg *Commercial* joined a growing list of newspapers that denounced the state committee; and the Brevard County Democratic Committee by unanimous vote refused to abide by sections four and five "on the grounds that said resolution is unconstitutional, undemocratic and would jeopardize the freedom of a true Democrat and a true American."[39] Similar resolutions were adopted in many other counties across the state.

The Florida State Federation of labor met in the midst of the controversy on February 2 to debate a resolution demanding another meeting of the state executive committee and damning the Sturkie resolution as "an encroachment of the rights of Democrats" which sought to deny them "their liberty of freedom and thought." In the heated exchange that followed, party loyalist T. J. Appleyard of Tallahassee and Catholic state senator Lewis W. Zim of St. Augustine led opposition to the motion. J. H. Mackey, a Jacksonville labor spokesman, introduced the resolution and was assisted in the

---

37. Jacksonville *Florida Times-Union*, January 13, 16, February 12, 1916. Trammell's opposition to the Sturkie resolution greatly aided him among members of the Guardians of Liberty. See Fred Taylor to Park Trammell, May 28, 1916, on Reel 1, Trammell Papers.

38. Jacksonville *Florida Times-Union*, January 27, 29, 30, 1916.

39. *Ibid.*, February 3, 6, 1916.

debate by C. T. Barry, also of Jacksonville. On a voice vote, over-
whelming sentiment favored the condemnatory labor resolution.[40]

The party hierarchy rallied behind the Sturkie resolution which
accomplished nothing except to deflect the torrent of abuse from
the executive committee to themselves. W. V. Knott endorsed the
controversial sections, as did Senator Bryan, though Bryan denied
persistent charges that he was responsible for authoring the document. The Duval County Democratic Committee, home of both J.
M. Barrs and Bryan with whom the resolution originated, overwhelmingly endorsed the Sturkie resolve and denounced what it
called "this reincarnated Know Nothing organization" (the Guardians of Liberty).[41] The state press rallied to the Sturkie resolution
and a preponderance of newspapers endorsed the controversial
sections. The Jacksonville *Florida Times-Union* estimated that the
Florida press endorsed the proposal by a margin of two or three to
one.[42] Interestingly, however, some papers that initially favored
the resolution later switched positions, and the Plant City *Courier*
observed that the strength of the Guardians of Liberty and the
confusion over religion had combined "to cause some wonderful
sail-trimming in Florida political seas."[43]

By late January, reaction to the Sturkie resolution had become
so tumultuous that chairman Raney consented to call another meeting of the executive committee if a majority of the fifty-one members requested it. Despite a statement by Park Trammell claiming
that at least twenty-six members desired to reconsider, Raney refused to summon the members, saying that of the thirty-seven responses he had, sixteen favored and twenty-one opposed another

40. *Ibid.*, February 3, 4, 1916.
41. *Ibid.*, January 16, 28, February 24, 1916.
42. *Ibid.*, January 24, 1916. Perusal of state press opinion validates this estimate. Papers defending the Sturkie resolution included the Jacksonville *Florida Times-Union*, St.
Petersburg *Independent*, Panama City *Pilot*, Miami *Herald*, Lake City *Citizen-Reporter*,
Tallahassee *Record*, Lakeland *Telegram*, Okaloosa *Leader*, Punta Gorda *Herald*, Gainesville
Sun, Orlando *Reporter-Star*, Tampa *Times*, and St. Petersburg *Times*.
43. Jacksonville *Florida Times-Union*, February 19, 1916, and quoting Plant City
Courier, February 15, 1916.

meeting.[44] Pressure continued to mount, and on February 14 Raney called the committee back into session.

When the executive committee met in Jacksonville on February 24 to discuss sections four and five, such a large crowd gathered to observe events that the members had to move from the Seminole Hotel to the Morocco Temple. The debate lasted two hours, after which controversial sections four and five were repealed by a vote of twenty-six to fourteen. Counties whose representatives voted to maintain the sections contained 473,000 people, while those voting for repeal numbered only 339,000; generally, delegates from the northern counties where the Guardians of Liberty were strongest voted for repeal, whereas members from urban counties and centers of party strength such as Hillsborough (Tampa), Duval (Jacksonville), Alachua (Gainesville), Escambia (Pensacola), and Leon (Tallahassee) voted to retain them. The Jacksonville *Florida Times-Union* attributed repeal to the activity of the Guardians and predicted: "We may now look for the nastiest, most abusive campaign that Florida has ever known, and it will probably be attended with loss of life."[45] The entire affair aided Catts immeasurably, since it appeared to confirm his estimate of a Catholic conspiracy; and by the time repeal came, the resolution seemed to have been aimed directly at his candidacy. Astute political observer W. T. Cash believed that without the momentum given Catts by the Sturkie resolution, he could not have been elected governor; W. V. Knott wrote years later that this issue propelled Catts from relative obscurity into the role of a major contender.[46]

One additional issue differentiated Catts from the other candidates and influenced the primary election returns. The state legislature had passed conservation laws in 1913 to protect fish and oys-

44. *Ibid.*, February 1, 2, and 6, 1916. The February 1 and 16 issues contain a list of executive committee members who wanted another meeting.

45. *Ibid.*, February 25, 1916. This issue also gives a tally of how each delegate voted.

46. Cash, *History of the Democratic Party in Florida*, 127; Knott, "Guardians of Liberty," 3.

ters, and T. R. Hodges, the state Shell Fish commissioner, had enforced the laws with a passion. Viewing himself as "practically a sheriff for the entire state of Florida," he policed the fish and oyster laws over a coastline of three thousand miles. Strict enforcement of seasonal restrictions and legal methods of fishing had resulted, Hodges claimed, in more demand for oysters, cheaper market prices, and better quality.[47]

Fishermen along the Florida coast had three main objections to the conservation policy. They felt that any restrictions on their trade were unnecessary. Also, to finance the Shell Fish commissioner and his department, the state had levied a fee on fishing boats; fees were also charged on retail and wholesale fish dealers. By 1916 their anger had focused on a boat named the *Roamer*, which had been purchased by the state legislature for fifteen thousand dollars to patrol the Gulf Coast. Animosity intensified to such an extent that an armed clash broke out in which one of Hodges' deputies was killed by a fisherman. A sympathetic jury returned a verdict of innocent in the case, and threats against Hodges' life became so frequent that he installed two 1-pound cannons on the vessel.[48]

From his earliest visits to the west coast fish camps, Catts had detected the deep hostility toward Hodges, and he made this a key point of his campaign. He maintained that had he been governor, he would have vetoed the legislature's appropriation for the *Roamer*. If elected, he pledged to fire Hodges, sell the *Roamer*, and allow fishermen to pursue their occupation without interference from Tallahassee.[49]

The *Roamer* issue would not have been such an advantage to Catts but for a fortuitous chain of circumstances early in the campaign. W. V. Knott, after a speech on the coast, was unable to get a train to his next stop. Exhausted, he accepted an invitation from his

47. T. R. Hodges to editor, Jacksonville *Florida Times-Union*, April 6, 1916.
48. *Ibid.*
49. Jacksonville *Florida Times-Union*, March 4, 1916.

friend T. R. Hodges to spend the night on the *Roamer* and take the boat to Tampa for a speech the next day.[50] Catts manipulated the incident into an obvious alliance between Knott and Hodges and won the commercial fisherman vote, despite the fact that many of them were Catholics.

As the June 6 primary approached, the only certainty was that confusion would prevail on election day. This was guaranteed by the Bryan primary law of 1913 which had placed the canvassing of state returns under the authority of the Florida State Canvassing Board and had imposed a ceiling of four thousand dollars on campaign expenditures. It also had eliminated runoff primaries by substituting second-choice votes. The size of the state had contributed to the large number of candidates who usually ran for each office. Oftentimes the large field of candidates had precluded anyone from obtaining a majority and had forced an expensive runoff. Under the Bryan law each voter cast a first and second choice in all races. If his candidates finished first and second, only the first-choice vote counted; if his first-choice was eliminated but his second choice finished among the top two candidates, the second-choice ballot was counted. Conceivably a voter might vote for two candidates who both finished third place or worse, in which case neither vote influenced the outcome. The winner would be the candidate who received the greatest total of first- and second-choice votes combined. The 1916 election would be the first statewide race employing the new system, and county officials had not been adequately instructed in its use. Moreover, many people did not vote a second choice for fear it would affect their first. Some Democratic county executive committees sent letters to all voters emphasizing the importance of voting for a second-choice candidate; but many confused voters decided not to exercise their option when election day arrived. In addition, the Guardians of Liberty considered the

50. Deal, "Sidney Johnston Catts," 44. Knott admitted the hostility of state fishermen to Hodges, whom he considered "a good man, a good official, but he liked to make a show"; see Knott, "Guardians of Liberty," 6.

second-choice votes to be part of a conspiracy against them and advised members to vote only first choice, denying their opponents all second-choice ballots.[51]

A nonpartisan Jacksonville-based newsgathering organization conducted a poll on election eve with disconcerting results. Although Knott had slightly over 50 percent of the first-choice votes in the gubernatorial race, Catts was in second place with 34 percent, and was reported to be gaining rapidly in most counties. The reports noted particularly Catts's strength in rural sections of all counties.[52]

Early election returns were confused but revealed a very close race. Unusual delays in reporting returns occurred due to differing interpretations over the method of counting second-place votes. Some initial returns listed first- and second-choice votes separately, while others combined them into one figure for each candidate; the returns from Orange County (Orlando) were delayed because the election officials incorrectly tabulated second-choice votes. On June 8, returns were still trickling in with no victor; Knott issued a statement expressing his confidence that the complete count of second-choice votes would give him the victory despite his trailing Catts significantly in first-choice ballots. However, local officials were so confused that on June 12, six days after the election, no returns whatever had come in from Washington County, no second choice votes from Hillsborough, and only partial returns from Okaloosa and Wakulla counties. In addition, county officials who had reported their tabulations were constantly changing the official canvass. Newspapers grumbled about the obvious inadequacies of the Bryan primary law. On June 22, sixteen days following the election, newspapers announced that Catts, with a lead of 176 votes, based on official returns from fifty of fifty-two counties, had won. Information flowing into Knott headquarters indicated many errors, mostly against their candidate, so they decided to contest the election based on the charge that there was

51. L. C. Stewart to Park Trammell, May 29, 1916, on Reel 3, Trammell Papers.
52. Jacksonville *Florida Times-Union*, June 4, 1916.

confusion in counting second-choice votes, and that these ballots were not counted at all in over one hundred precincts.[53] Final official returns confirmed Catts's triumph, with 30,092 first- and 3,891 second-choice votes for him, to 24,765 and 8,674 for Knott. The compiled totals, 33,983 to 33,439 gave Catts a margin of 544 votes.

Catts's strength was scattered throughout the state, though his strongest backing came from the panhandle and central Florida. The four counties with the largest numbers of Roman Catholics (Duval, Hillsborough, Monroe, and St. Johns) all voted for Knott; but in three other counties that contained substantial Catholic minorities (Dade, Pasco, and Polk), Catts won. The final irony for R. B. Sturkie must have been Pasco, where his alleged 65 percent Catholic constituency voted for Sidney Catts.

Catts's jubilation was short-lived because his opponents vowed to take the election to the courts, and he feared that they would control the judicial system. Even before the first hearings, the governor-elect began to protest the tactics of his opponents. His cry soon became a shrill crescendo heard across the Sunshine State.

53. For view of the chaos, follow election returns *ibid.*, June 7–June 22, 1916. Also, see Knott, "Guardians of Liberty," 3, 6. See map, page 62 herein.

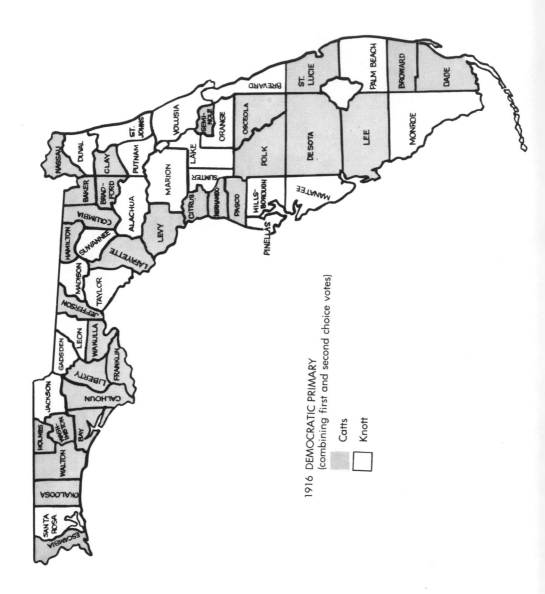

1916 DEMOCRATIC PRIMARY
(combining first and second choice votes)

Catts

Knott

FOUR

The Crackers'
Three Friends

SIDNEY CATTS'S FEARS were soon realized, and the scheme to
deny him the nomination evolved into legal wrangling and court
proceedings. Regular Democrats searched frantically for ways to
withhold the nomination from him, and this maneuvering replaced
the issues of Catholicism, the Sturkie resolution, and T. R. Hodges
as the chief concern of voters in the November 7, 1916, general
election. The Democratic party would successfully deny Catts its
nomination, but in so doing it created a new target for his barbs:
the corrupt Democratic "machine" and its lackey, the Florida Supreme Court.

The cacophony emanating from the Democratic camp could not
have been more to his advantage had Catts directed it himself.
When election returns were all completed and Catts declared the
party nominee, most Floridians accepted this no matter how dis-
agreeable it might be.

Newspaper reaction to the delayed count varied, but most papers editorialized that when the State Canvassing Board declared
Catts the victor, that decided the issue. Although a number of
these papers were to reverse their positions by November, they
had already done immeasurable harm to the Knott cause. The Sanford *Herald* had backed F. M. Hudson in the primary but announced support for Catts on June 23, simply because he had been
nominated by the majority; the St. Petersburg *Times* regretted his
victory based on a religious issue, but proclaimed him the victor in

its June 9 issue; the Panama City *Pilot* conceded Catts the election, while warning that the development of the state had "been set back at least ten years."[1] The Ocala *Star* believed that religion had been too significant an issue, but added that there were many people who were tired of the way Florida had been governed, that Catts might do much good and deserved a chance to serve: "We will not join any combination of liquor dealers and railroad interest [*sic*] to count him [out]." The Lake City *Citizen-Reporter* and Tavares *Herald* believed so much confusion had prevailed that the best course would be to put both Catts and Knott on the general election ballot as Democratic nominees and let the people decide between them.[2]

Neither the state party structure nor W. V. Knott was willing to concede so graciously. From the first, many pro-Knott newspapers pressured him to contest the primary results. They rejected proposals for a dual candidacy in November, convinced that their candidate would win a court-ordered recount. the Ocala *Banner* epitomized this viewpoint in a July editorial: "We hope that Mr. Knott will not let the Democratic editors with populistic tendencies keep him from having a retabulation of the count."[3]

The legal maneuvering which began in June and lasted for four months assembled stacks of data and testimony, but to this day no one can be certain who won the Democratic primary. The judicial conclusion did not convince the voters of Florida, and it does not sway the historian. Knott's appeal to the courts hinged on five contentions: second-choice votes were not counted at all in many precincts; in others they were counted incorrectly; exhausted election inspectors in several places allowed nonofficials who were friends

1. Jacksonville *Florida Times-Union*, June 23, 1916, quoting the Sanford *Herald;* St. Petersburg *Times*, June 9, 1916; Jacksonville *Florida Times-Union*, June 19, 1916, quoting Panama City *Pilot*. For a brief summary of this election, see Dorothy Lord, "Sidney J. Catts and the Gubernatorial Election of 1916," *Apalachee* (1967), VI, 45–64.
2. Jacksonville *Florida Times-Union*, June 20, July 12, 18, 1916, quoting Ocala *Star*, Lake City *Citizen-Reporter*, and Tavares *Herald*.
3. *Ibid.*, July 4, 1916, quoting Ocala *Banner*. Many other papers agreed, including the Lakeland *Telegram* and Sumter County *Times;* even more interesting, by mid-July the Panama City *Pilot* and Ocala *Star* argued that Knott should contest.

of Catts to assist in tabulating votes; some precincts carried by Catts had more votes than there were eligible voters; and non-Democrats had been allowed to vote.[4] Catts countered by instituting mandamus proceedings to force a count of one Alachua precinct that had given him a seventy-four-vote majority which had been disallowed because of irregularities.

The sequence of legal moves is especially significant because Knott refused to campaign actively while the courts were adjudicating the case. He did seek an injunction to prevent the state canvassing board from certifying returns in the June primary while court proceedings were underway. The circuit court denied this petition on June 26, allowing the canvassing board to declare Catts the Democratic nominee, an official action that lent credence to Catts's later charge of fraud.

Knott's initial court action asked for a recount of precinct votes in twenty-seven counties. The worst irregularities, said Knott, had occurred in Polk, Holmes, and Calhoun counties. According to Knott's evidence, voters in one Calhoun County precinct with fifty-nine qualified registrants had cast 140 ballots. Although the courts took the issue under advisement, the secretary of state and attorney general delivered official certificates of nomination to Catts on July 2.

In early July the courts began ordering recounts, the first coming in Suwannee, Madison, Hamilton, and Duval counties. Such recounts almost invariably added second-choice votes for Knott because of unintentional errors. The vote recount in five Jacksonville precincts gave Knott a gain of eleven votes. By August 23 the recount showed Knott leading by 134 ballots. Other kinds of irregularities were also investigated, including a charge by L. V. McKay, deputy sheriff of Hillsborough County, that seven hun-

4. For original legal documents submitted to the supreme court by Knott and Catts, together with corroborating documents, briefs, evidence, and the original and amended county by county returns, see State of Florida, *Democratic Primary, June 6, 1916, Office of the Secretary of State*, I, n. p., in office of secretary of state, Tallahassee. This volume contains all the court appeals, sworn testimony, etc., relating to state of Florida Ex Rel. *Sidney J. Catts vs. H. Clay Crawford, Thomas F. West, and J. C. Luning.*

dred Tampa Socialists had changed their registration to Democratic in order to vote for Catts.[5]

On September 5 the Florida Supreme Court issued a writ against the State Canvassing Board, requiring it to tally the amended returns from counties were Knott had obtained a recount. By this time, the court-ordered recount had added 481 votes to give Knott a 221 vote lead. The canvassing board refused to certify the recanvassed tally, explaining that affidavits were on file alleging widespread fraud.

The reluctance of the canvassing board raised spirits in the Catts's camp. Hal W. Adams, a Catts aide, predicted that the board would now pursue the charges of fraud and discover convincing proof of wrongdoing in Hamilton and Madison counties. Adams urged Catts's allies to locate voters in the disputed precincts who would testify before the supreme court. The canvassing board opposed the court-ordered retabulation because of this documented evidence of ballot box tampering furnished by local Catts backers.[6] The court ruled, however, that the three cabinet officials who constituted the canvassing board—Secretary of State H. Clay Crawford, Attorney General Thomas F. West, and State Treasurer J. C. Luning—assumed the burden of proof to demonstrate that fraud had actually taken place in the recount of disputed boxes, and, failing this, they had to certify the revised figures.[7] Catts also followed the route of judicial protest but with an unsatisfactory outcome. On July 17 the supreme court denied Catts's attorney a writ to prevent a recount in Duval County; on August 8 the same court overruled a Catts's challenge of the Bryan primary law and the legality of recounts; on October 10 it denied a petition by Catts's

5. Jacksonville *Florida Times-Union*, July 6, 23, 1916. For a summary of the recount from a pro-Knott perspective, see *ibid.*, August 23, 1916; Deal, "Sidney Johnston Catts, Stormy Petrel of Florida Politics," 104.

6. Hal W. Adams to J. B. Hodges, September 14, 1916, in Box 13, J. B. Hodges Papers.

7. The supreme court had listened to testimony charging fraud in the recount. It was alleged that in some counties several persons had keys to the room where the ballot boxes were kept. See *Democratic Primary, June 6, 1916, Office of the Secretary of State*, I.

attorney, W. W. Flournoy, to count 69 votes for Catts in a disputed precinct in Alachua County.[8]

Finally, the canvassing board reconvened on the morning of September 21, 1916, as ordered by the supreme court, recanvassed the returns, and declared Knott the Democratic nominee by a plurality of 21 votes. Two weeks later on October 7 the state's highest court rejected Catts's petition to count the disputed 69 votes from Gainesville. This decision, four months and a day after the primary, gave Knott the legal nomination.

Catts's general election campaign centered on the alleged fraudulence of the recount. Undoubtedly there were unintentional irregularities in counting second-choice votes just as Knott contended. The widespread opposition to Catts by Democratic officials and the peculiarities of the recount, however, raise serious questions about the correctness of the final decision to name W. V. Knott the party nominee. Unknown to candidate Knott, whose integrity was seldom questioned even by Catts, strange events occurred in some precincts. In a Greenville voting place (Madison County, in north Florida), Catts originally had received 74 first-choice and 21 second-choice votes, to 5 first and 5 second-choice ballots for Knott. In the recount the courts required the clerk to adjust the tally so that Catts received a total of 57 (compared to 95) and Knott 30 (compared to 10). Incensed Catts backers obtained affidavits from every man who had voted in the precinct, establishing the accuracy of the original count.[9] The countywide tally from Madison shows wild inconsistencies. The initial vote in the county had been 336 for Catts to 610 for Knott (combining first- and second-choice votes). The recount reduced Catts's total by 116 votes (107 first-choice, 9 second), while adding 57 ballots for Knott (21 first, 26 second), for a huge net gain of 173 votes for Knott in a county that cast only 946 for both men.[10]

8. Jacksonville *Florida Times-Union*, July 18, August 9, 10, 1916; State of Florida, *Cases Adjudicated in the Supreme Court of Florida*, LXXII, 1916, pp. 255–57.

9. Jacksonville *Florida Times-Union*, July 30, 1916.

10. For conflicting election returns, see "Exhibit C" introduced as evidence by Catts, *Democratic Primary, June 6, 1916, Office of the Secretary of State*, I.

Two other counties showed inexplicable variations between initial returns and the recount. Amended returns in Suwannee County, which Knott also had carried, reduced Catts's vote by 22 (15 first, 7 second-choice), while Knott's total increased by 76 (26 first, 50 second-choice), for a net gain of 98. The recount in Hamilton County did not substantially alter Catts's totals or first-choice votes for Knott, but did add 53 second-choice votes for Knott. One Hamilton County citizen testified that he had seen county officials in the courthouse tampering with ballots; following his testimony, perjury charges were filed against him.[11] The adjustments in Suwannee and Hamilton counties were more believable than those in Madison, because they came primarily in the confusing second-choice ballots. In Madison the change of 138 first-choice ballots about which no confusion existed strains credibility.

Other irregularities also affected the outcome of the election. One entire box which had gone overwhelmingly for Catts in Baker County mysteriously disappeared; Knott accused Catts of stealing the box to prevent exposure of fraud, and Catts called the affair a "frameup." W. W. Flournoy, Catts's attorney, sought a court order requiring the canvassing board to add 69 votes from precinct three in Alachua County. The supreme court disallowed the motion because the state board had canvassed the precinct improperly. Court inconsistency became obvious when the judges allowed the count of precincts carried by Knott in which similar irregularities had occurred.[12]

Catts fared no better with the state Democratic executive committee. At its August 24 meeting, Hal W. Adams of Lafayette County, a Catts supporter on the committee, proposed a resolution endorsing his candidate as the nominee; but a hostile majority immediately adjourned without taking any action. On October 7, the same day that the supreme court rejected Catts's last petition, the

11. *Ibid.;* Jacksonville *Florida Times-Union,* September 11, 1916.
12. Jacksonville *Florida Times-Union,* August 19, September 2, 1916; *Cases Adjudicated in the Supreme Court of Florida,* LXXII, 1916, p. 225; Deal, "Sidney Johnston Catts," contains an excellent discussion in Chapter 4, especially 90–92. Deal especially challenges the justice of not allowing the Catts vote in precinct three in Alachua County, p. 105.

committee reconvened at the Seminole Hotel in Jacksonville. Hal Adams gained the floor and proposed that the names of both Knott and Catts be listed on the November ballot. The delegates rejected this course by a vote of 31 to 10. The Catts forces, abandoning this strategy, proposed next that the body refuse to endorse a candidate for governor, an obviously unacceptable alternative that was promptly rejected by the Knott contingent. Chairman Raney took the floor and explained that he had called the special session because the Democratic party faced a danger unprecedented in three decades. He had voted for Hudson first choice and Knott as second, he continued, but now pled for endorsement of Knott as the only hope for holding the party in its traditional pattern. This substitute resolution was endorsed by the committee 28 to 13 even before the court had declared Knott the winner. The final recount declared him the victor with a total of 33,439 votes to 33,169 for Catts.[13]

The obvious tactical question for Catts to resolve was how to get on the November general election ticket. From the inception of litigation, Catts had concluded that the party hierarchy and courts would deny him the nomination; therefore, he and his advisers had considered several alternative strategies. J. B. Hodges, an opportunistic but fervent convert to "Cattsism," warned Hal Adams that Knott would win the legal manuevering. He proposed summoning a state convention which would nominate Catts and certify him as the nominee; he could then run under Section 212 of the Florida Codes which allowed any certified caucus or convention nominee of a party or faction to appear on the general election ballot.[14]

The complexity of the Hodges proposal created technical problems, and the plan was discarded in favor of two alternate suggestions by campaign manager J. V. Burke. The more difficult route was to gain ballot position by the petition method. Burke obtained petitions from the secretary of state's office to be circulated in each county. Under the complicated state formula, a specified number

---

13. Jacksonville *Florida Times-Union*, August 25, October 8, 13, 1916.
14. J. B. Hodges to Hal W. Adams, September 1, 1916, in Box 197, Hodges Papers.

of signatures had to be obtained from counties in each region of the state. Burke also contacted the leaders of the tiny Prohibition party to persuade them to reconvene and nominate Catts. The party had met in Jacksonville following the June Democratic primary and had endorsed Trammell and Catts. Its progressive platform had endorsed the major national and state reforms of the era, while opposing officeholders who owed allegiance "to any foreign sovereign, prince, potentate, or ecclesiastic."[15] Burke believed that for the nomination to be legally acceptable the party would have to reconvene and formally name Catts. If each of these routes proved impossible, Burke agreed to Hodges' "Progressive Democrat" convention as a last resort.[16]

Even though petitions were widely circulated in the late summer and fall, Burke preferred the Prohibition party route which had the advantage to tying Catts more closely to the popular cause of prohibition.[17] On the night of August 4 and again the next day, John C. Coffin, chairman of Florida's Prohibition party, came to Burke's office to confer. Coffin declined to make an immediate commitment on reconvening the Prohibition convention and retired to his Johnstown home to reach a final decision. Coffin's decision was affirmative, and the Prohibition party formally nominated Catts together with all other Democratic nominees except two.[18] On October 9, two days after the Democratic party formally denied him the nomination, Catts informed the secretary of state that he would consent to have his name certified as the Prohibition party nominee. After four months of confusion, Catts was at last assured a place on the general election ballot.

Although the neophyte politician had run an amateur campaign in the spring, his effort took on a professional quality during the

15. Jacksonville *Florida Times-Union*, June 21, 1916.
16. J. V. Burke to J. B. Hodges, September 4, 1916, in Box 197, Hodges Papers.
17. For petition activity, see J. B. Hodges to Hal W. Adams, September 21, 1916, Hodges to J. V. Burke, October 12, 1912, in Box 12, Hodges Papers; Jacksonville *Florida Times-Union*, October 1, 1916.
18. J. V. Burke to J. B. Hodges, August 5, 1916, in Box 197, Hal W. Adams to Hodges, September 14, 1916, in Box 13, Hodges Papers.

summer. Some of the state's shrewdest politicians had caught the drift of Florida political tides and recognized that Catts had tapped emotions seldom articulated before.

Leading the Catts organization was J. V. Burke, who ran the campaign from headquarters in the Baldwin Building in Jacksonville. He mapped strategy with legal adviser W. W. Flournoy and performed efficiently in dispatching speakers and producing publicity; but he also became the focus of friction in the Catts camp. Some criticized him privately because he sought the advice of Billy Parker, whose rabid anti-Catholicism and Republican party affiliation appalled more moderate followers of Catts.[19] He was also a heavy-handed manager according to south Florida lieutenants, who claimed that Burke milked the Tampa area dry of funds and in the process created many enemies by his financial pressure. Even in Jacksonville, some Catts aides concluded that Burke's influence was negative.[20]

The resentful south Florida organization was led by Dr. W. H. Cox of Brooksville, who managed the south Florida Catts Democratic committee, C. T. Frecker, secreatry, R. T. Joughlin, treasurer, and organizer Goode M. Guerry. Guerry was one of Florida's most popular newspapermen, but gave up his occupation in Lake County after a bitter dispute with Burke over campaign strategy and joined Catts's Tampa office as organizer of Catts clubs. Guerry allegedly maintained close contacts with Florida racetrack and sporting interests.[21] Catts could also boast an unprecedented array of colorful stump speakers to agitate the backwoods. Jerry Carter directed his matchless wit at many a receptive cracker audience. State senator J. S. Blitch of Williston had been converted to the cause early and spent the summer and fall speaking almost every day. Van C. Swearingen, former mayor of Jacksonville, cov-

19. St. Petersburg *Daily Times*, October 17, 1916. Attorneys who helped determine legal strategy included a Mr. Butler, Van C. Swearingen, E. B. Donnell, and three men identified only as Maxwell, Campbell, and Alexander. See J. V. Burke to J. B. Hodges, September 4, 1916, in Box 197, Hodges Papers.

20. C. T. Frecker to J. B. Hodges, November 9, 1916, in Box 197, Hodges Papers.

21. *Ibid.*; also, see Deal, "Sidney Johnston Catts," 77.

ered northeast Florida. Bryan Mack, newspaperman from Pensacola, spoke for Catts as frequently as he wrote editorials endorsing
him. Edgar W. Waybright, an aspiring Jacksonville legislator with
liberal credentials and labor backing, also aided the campaign.

The most important convert following the Democratic primary
was J. B. Hodges, a prominent Lake City attorney, who had served
as mayor, as president of the city council, and as a representative
in the lower house. Hodges had backed Knott enthusiastically
through the June primary, and he also served as a railroad lobbyist
which made his switch to Catts, who favored tighter regulation of
railroads, even more opportunistic. He cited a number of factors
that contributed to his altered loyalties: Knott had allowed his
friends to steal votes in Madison, Suwannee, and Alachua counties,
and he had attempted in court to reverse the decision of the Democratic primary which made him in essence a party bolter.[22]

Before the June primary Hodges had ridiculed Catts's "anti-
Catholic wagon," had supported the Sturkie resolution, and had
dismissed Catts as an inconsequential candidate; but in July he
volunteered his services to Burke and was soon engaged in writing
friends on behalf of Catts and addressing rallies for him.[23] He used
his influence on the Democratic executive committee against
chairman Raney, devoted his full time to the campaign beginning
in late October, and even gave up liquor, becoming a teetotaler. In
the last days of the race, he spoke three times in Jacksonville, in
Gainesville, St. Petersburg, and on election eve addressed four
thousand persons in Tampa.[24]

Hodges' conversion was complete as one can judge by his oratory which rang with opposition to "the sale of whiskey and the

22. J. B. Hodges to J. E. Hall, June 13, 1916, Hodges to Guyton Parks, November 11,
1916, in Box 20, Hodges to M. F. Brown, October 18, 1916, in Box 12, Hodges Papers.

23. J. B. Hodges to J. E. Hall, June 13, 1916, in Box 20, ibid. For examples of his
electioneering on behalf of Catts, see Hodges to Nat R. Walker, August 30, 1916, in Box
197, M. F. Brown to Hodges, October 16, 1916, in Box 13, ibid.

24. For his role in the campaign, see J. B. Hodges to Joe Earman, August 5, 1924, in
Box 53, Hodges to J. V. Burke, October 9, 1916, and copy of telegram from Hodges to Catts
Democratic Committee, October 30, 1916, in Box 12, Hodges to Guyton Parks, November
11, 1916, in Box 20, ibid.

participation of Catholics in primary election[s]." T. J. Appleyard, an old friend of Hodges who endorsed Knott, expressed surprise at a resolution drafted by Hodges attacking the Federated Catholic Societies. Having always considered Hodges a "Progressive Democrat," he could not understand this evidence of religious prejudice. Hodges' reply revealed his capitulation to the drift of Florida politics. He accused Appleyard and Knott of defending Catholicism, and charged that Catholic sympathizers contributed to the Knott campaign for "the purpose of seizing control of the state government of Florida."[25] It also seems likely that Hodges, always a shrewd student of state politics, had become convinced that Catts was going to win.

Many attorneys, local Democratic officials, and state employees endorsed Catts, though some still preferred to do so privately. R. J. Patterson of the Florida Office of the Tax Commission typified many lower echelon Democrats. He had voted for Hudson and Farris in the primary and was convinced that the Knott forces had stolen the election from Catts. In his view Catts was the party nominee, "while Knott is the nominee of the 4 R's (RUM, ROMANISM, RAILROADS, AND REDLIGHTS)."[26] In Jasper, Florida, where Catts alleged that Knott forces had stolen votes, the chairman of the Hamilton County Democratic Executive Committee, W. T. Ruse, resigned from the committee and announced that he would vote for Catts in November. The Duval County Democratic Executive Committee, elected in the June primary, opposed the court-ordered recount of votes in Jacksonville by a vote of twelve to four; they called Knott's contesting of the election "un-Democratic and . . . a menace to the interests of the party and . . . an attempt to defeat the expressed will of the majority of the Democratic voters of the state." The committee met in mid-October and again condemned Knott. So bitter did the feud become that committeemen were summoned to a third meeting on November 1. The pro- and

25. J. B. Hodges to B. B. Johnson, August 26, 1916, in Box 20, Hodges to Colonel T. J. Appleyard, September 11, 1916, in Box 197, *ibid.*
26. R. J. Paterson to J. B. Hodges, October 9, 1916, in Box 197, *ibid.*

anti-Knott factions locked into such a stormy debate that seventeen stalked out of the meeting; the remaining nineteen committeemen drummed their duly elected colleagues out of the party and elected a slate of replacements.[27]

On July 24 the Clay County committee met at Green Cove Springs, unanimously declared Catts to be the "true and lawful nominee of the Democratic party," and called on county Democrats to stand by Catts on November 7. They deplored Knott's legal maneuvers, then adjourned to a public rally where they organized a Catts club.[28]

These clubs became an important element in the Catts strategy. Orators who spanned the state left a club in every community where they spoke. Unlike so many Florida Democratic campaigns which had been organized from the top down by party functionaries, the Catts clubs enrolled the masses and sprang from cracker enthusiasm for the charismatic, antiestablishment preacher. The clubs constituted the basic element for systematic Catts organizations that appeared in every county by late August. Goode M. Guerry, who led the statewide club effort, reported that by August 25, Catts headquarters had received the names of 25,561 qualified voters who were officially enrolled in one of the Catts clubs.[29]

Of course, the active presence of the Guardians of Liberty provided another structured base of support. Organized into "courts" and numbering approximately 40,000 members, they constituted a formidable army of enthusiasts for distributing propaganda, nailing up posters, and intimidating local politicians.[30]

Support for Catts was developing so rapidly that Dr. W. H. Cox and J. B. Hodges decided on a bold move to further embarrass Knott. Following the state Democratic executive committee endorsement of Knott, Cox proposed that "the greatest piece of thunder that we could stage" would be a meeting of the sizable

27. Jacksonville *Florida Times-Union*, October 24, July 16, November 2, 1916.
28. *Ibid.*, July 28, 1916.
29. Goode M. Guerry to J. B. Hodges, August 25, 1916, in Box 197, Hodges Papers.
30. For an example of their activity, see Ed M. Wolff (Master Guardian of Liberty, Court No. 39, Lakeland, Florida) to J. B. Hodges, October 9, 1916, in Box 197, *ibid.*

Catts minority on the committee just before the November election. The group could condemn the committee endorsement of Knott and provide legitimacy for Catts's claim to be the rightful nominee. Hodges immediately assumed leadership of the rump meeting scheduled for Jacksonville.[31]

The feverish level of activity demanded sizable expenditures of money, and this became Catts's chief concern. Without personal resources, he had to rely on contributions. His lack of ties in Florida gave him no financial base to appeal to and his iconoclastic candidacy did not attract supporters from the business and industrial communities. Small contributions at his rallies had financed his preprimary race but could not support the staff and level of activity required after June. Goode M. Guerry, an aggressive fund raiser, privately estimated that the minimum cost for organizing the counties and maintaining state headquarters would be six thousand dollars. Since most of Catts's backers were people of moderate economic resources, financial problems plagued his efforts.[32]

Enough key backers became convinced that Catts could win that some funds did begin to trickle into his treasury. His friends finally raised a total of $8,000, sufficient to finance his organizational activities, run the Jacksonville *Free Press*, and purchase a new Ford automobile to expedite his campaigning. Some of these funds even paid grocery bills for the Catts family.[33]

Catts also initiated private fund-raising efforts, not all of which

31. W. H. Cox to J. B. Hodges, October 23, 1916, in Box 197, Hodges to Cox, October 25, 1916, in Box 12, *ibid.*

32. Goode M. Guerry to J. B. Hodges, August 25, 1916, in Box 197, *ibid.* Deal claims that Guerry was "hired" by Catts (77), but personal friends claimed that the Catts campaign funds did not even cover his expenses. See C. T. Frecker to Hodges, November 9, 1916, in Box 197, *ibid.*

33. Birmingham *Age-Herald*, December 14, 1916. Jerry Carter recalled no large donations before the June primary, though he conceded that there may have been some in the fall when it appeared very likely that Catts would win the general election; interview, Jerry Carter, July 29, 1970, Tallahassee, Florida. J. J. McCasskill of DeFuniak Springs was the most likely major contributor. Interview, Mrs. Elizabeth Paderick and Alice May Stiegel, May 12, 1972, Jacksonville. Catts later claimed that some of his associates siphoned funds into their own pockets, a charge they bitterly denied; see Joe Earman to J. B. Hodges, May 27, 1924, in Box 53, Hodges Papers.

were consistent with his ministerial background. One key financial backer was Joe L. Earman, popular West Palm Beach newspaper editor. Earman had represented the National Wholesale Liquor Dealers Association in earlier years, but fell under the spell of Catts's charm in 1916 and loaned him $700 during the next year. Part of the money was a $100 loan from Barnett National Bank in Jacksonville, made for Catts on October 16, 1916.

Earman also was involved in the most bizarre fund-raising incident of the race. Catts wrote Carter R. Bibb of Okeechobee, Florida, stating that if Bibb would send him $400 to use for election expenses, he would appoint Bibb Florida fish and game warden following victory in November. After the election Catts feared that a hostile legislature might discover the importunate letter and impeach him, so Earman and other political friends were dispatched to "purchase" the letter from Bibb in return for the original $400 "contribution." Earman not only successfully completed this transaction, but during the next four years loaned Catts an estimated $15,000.[34]

That portion of his funds spent on a Model T Ford made his campaign as remarkable technologically as it was politically. Previous campaigns had been circumscribed by the limitations of rail; many hamlets, farming communities, and fishing villages had never been visited by a candidate for governor. Catts, the first candidate to use the automobile in a statewide Florida political campaign, would oftentimes motor into town without previous advertisement, and start talking wherever he could find a crowd. He also introduced the loudspeaker; it was installed on his car, and he would cruise up and down the primitive streets extolling curious citizens to vote for Sidney J. Catts on November 7. J. V. Burke elaborated the Model T strategy by arranging tours of the state by Catts backers who also owned automobiles. The cars allowed them

34. Joe L. Earman to J. B. Hodges, August 1, 1922, in Box 197, *ibid.* This letter, an eleven-page indictment of the governor that implicates him in many corrupt episodes, came after a bloody break with Earman in 1920. Although his charge appears valid, apparently few men knew of the episode. Jerry Carter years later denied that Catts ever took a payoff for a state job or pardon. Interview with Jerry Carter, July 29, 1970, Tallahassee.

to cover the smaller communities where Burke and Catts believed the election would be won or lost. In a state which had fewer than three thousand registered automobiles, curiosity attracted many voters to Catts's allies. In his use of the automobile and speaker system, Catts anticipated by more than a decade Huey Long's remarkable campaigns in Louisiana, where the Kingfish utilized sound trucks to blitz rural areas and small towns during the 1930s.[35]

Whether addressing a few curious farmers on an obscure street corner or a massive rally in one of Florida's cities, Catts struck one major theme: the Democratic machine, supported by partisan courts, had stolen the nomination from the people's choice. Crowds turned out in unprecedented numbers to hear his colorful, earthy charges. Hostile newspapers called his rallies "the largest political gathering ever held in Gainesville," or "one of the largest political crowds in the City's history"; at Morriston in Levy County no hall could hold the throng, so Catts spoke from a wagon in the open air. Even the posters advertising his rallies emphasized these themes. They were nailed to pine trees across Florida, and a typical one announcing a rally in Washington County invited: "Everybody come and hear the truth regarding the Counts, Recounts, Discounts, and Outcounts following the Primary election of June 6th." Another poster promised that Catts was "the most eloquent speaker in the South" and would keep the crowd "spellbound for hours."[36]

He frequently began his address by asking all who had voted for Knott in the primary but planned to switch to him in November to raise their hands; hands invariably waved across the auditorium. Then he detailed how the Knott forces had stolen the primary from him, concluding: "If they [the courts] mandamus me to give that

35. For Catts's campaign innovations, see Warren, *How to Win in Politics*, 176; Deal, "Sidney Johnston Catts," 40; J. V. Burke to J. B. Hodges, October 2, 1916, in Box 197, Hodges Papers. There were only 2,820 autos registered in Florida in 1915–16; see State of *Florida, Report, Secretary of State, 1915–1916*, Pt. 3, "Automobiles," 4–125. For Huey Long's similar uses of sound trucks, see T. Harry Williams, *Huey Long* (New York: Alfred A. Knopf, 1969), 466–67, 587.

36. Jacksonville *Florida Times-Union*, September 2, 21, 22, 1916; posters in possession of Mrs. Elizabeth Paderick, Jacksonville.

certificate [of nomination], I am not going to make any resistance. . . . I will go to jail, and stay there until you people set me free November 7, by snowing Knott under by 30,000 majority." When elected, his first act would be to "kick the Bryan primary law into smitherines," after which he would advocate legislation to recall "them infernal judges," the "five little tin gods" on the supreme court.[37]

In some of his speeches Catts embellished the basic story. According to one account, Knott had visited Hayes Lewis of Jacksonville, had broken into tears, then admitted that he had telegrammed his south Florida managers that no more votes were needed there for him to win the recount. Knott termed the charge a vicious lie, and Catts dropped the tale, blandly commenting that he had heard Lewis recount the event, but wanted to be fair to Knott.[38]

An even sharper refinement linked Catholic conspriacy to Democratic fraud in a grotesque explanation of the events in June. Catts charged that Knott had given Cardinal Cromwell Gibbons $180,000 to elect him governor. Knott personally did not want to steal the votes, but his "Catholic lawyers" forced him to "pay his financial debts to the machine or take their stolen votes." The chief conspirator had been Charlie Jones, "that old Catholic lawyer sitting back smoking twenty-five cent cigars bought with money stolen from Cardinal Gibbons." Building to a climax, Catts described how Knott had "called one lawyer to hold his nose and another to hold his chin whilst that Catholic lawyer creased [greased?] his throat and swallowed his dose."[39]

Catts also linked Knott and Cardinal Gibbons to the Jacksonville political machine that traditionally had controlled Democratic affairs, especially to J. M. Barrs and Pleasant Holt. In Catts's colorful phrase, Knott "got with the dirtiest set of men in the state

37. Jacksonville *Florida Times-Union*, September 11, November 2, 1916.
38. *Ibid.*, August 7, 18, 1916.
39. Miami *Herald*, October 18, 1916. The *Herald* gives details of Catts's speeches found nowhere else. Catts denied making many of the more flamboyant statements attributed to him, so the *Herald*, in an attempt to discredit him, sent stenographers to his rallies to get verbatim accounts.

of Florida, and he is as dead politically as a dead pig in the sunshine."[40]

Jerry Carter and Bryan Mack provided an additional dimension to "the issue." Concluding that they could aid Catts more from a jail cell than from the stump, they tried to provoke the court into a confrontation. Carter borrowed the official certificate declaring Catts the Democratic nominee, had a photographer make a copy, then circulated it throughout Florida captioned, "The Legal Nominee of the Democratic Party." He also reproduced copies of the court-ordered recanvassed returns which were labeled, "The Nominee of the Court of Supreme Contempt." Mack contributed a scathing editorial, and both were soon embroiled with the now livid members of the state supreme court. On September 23 Pensacola's sheriff arrested Percy Hayes, editor and manager of the Pensacola *News*, and Mack, special writer for the paper. The supreme court held them in contempt for their editorial which had charged that the justices were hostile to Catts and prejudiced against his case. Carter quoted a phrase that traveled the southern states tickling many rural audiences and catching the spirit of his rural constituency: "The Florida crackers have only three friends: God Almighty, Sears Roebuck, and Sidney J. Catts!"[41]

Catts used the jailing of Mack to take another swipe at the court. He recounted for his audiences the dramatic and hilarious scene when Mack stood before the bench to defend himself: "'Your honor, I was raised by a mother who taught me to tell the truth and I have told it. . . . Gentlemen, I said you were a partisan court and told the truth,' and they seemed to accept that as a good plea, and fined him only thirteen dollars and seventy-five cents. I don't know what that seventy-five cents was for, but I suppose it was for pocket change for the court and for them to buy chewing gum with."[42]

40. *Ibid*. Catts's phrases are better than his analysis of political machines, for Barrs and Holt were usually on separate sides of the Duval County conservative-progressive split.
41. Interview, Jerry Carter, May 15, 1964, Tallahassee; Jacksonville *Florida Times-Union*, September 24, 1916.
42. Miami *Herald*, October 18, 1916.

Such "poetic license" sometimes gave way to emotional flights into unreality. Preceding a rally in Jacksonville, he became incensed when he observed several high school girls loitering on the streets. Minutes later in his speech he attacked the declining public morality as evidenced by girls standing on corners showing "how low they could cut their dresses at the top and how high they could cut them at the bottom." In a Miami speech he inveighed against the Catholic menace and promised his rooters: "Catts is going to open those convents for inspection; Catts is going to make them pay taxes; Catts is going to make those priests turn their collars right and marry good American girls."[43]

Catts's genuine conviction that a sinister conspiracy was trying to deny him his victory only complicated his inability to handle his own emotions. Jerry Carter's prime concern during the fall was controlling his candidate's ferocious temper. If Catts heard some provocative rumor just before a speech, he would favor his audience with a profane outburst that alienated many people who did not think such language appropriate for a Baptist preacher. In Pensacola he offended many local citizens by referring to a prominent official as a "damn liar" because of unsupported rumors which reached Catts just before he spoke.[44]

Catts's oratory manifested an almost psychotic anti-Catholicism. In his predictions of counties he would carry in November, he excluded St. Johns (St. Augustine) which was "controlled by Catholics." He warned that local Catholic officials had entered a conspiracy to arrest him and that in Apalachicola a cabal of Catholics intended to assassinate him. To protect himself, he carried two revolvers which he displayed prominently on the podium to quiet unruly crowds and awe his followers: "At some places I would speak with both hands on big pistols which were loaded in every chamber." Such derring-do coupled with provocative oratory sometimes provoked his audience to a frenzy. A policeman who at-

43. Jacksonville *Florida Times-Union*, August 24, 1916; interview, Jerry Carter, Jr., May 8, 1972, Tallahassee.
44. Miami *Herald*, October 25, 1916.

tempted to arrest Catts at a Lakeland rally was almost choked to death by angry supporters before Catts could persuade his zealots to release the unfortunate lawman.[45] There seemed to be an obvious conspiracy against him, and he was so completely incapable of understanding its origins that he probably believed such preposterous charges in the closing days of the campaign. Catts's fantasies did not completely obscure his more rational issues, though substantive proposals clearly receded into the background of the campaign. He reiterated his promises to lower taxes, procure election reforms, create industrial schools at Jacksonville and Tampa for boys and girls, and achieve other reforms, but such discussions were not what his audiences came to hear.

Because of or perhaps despite his theatrical platform antics, Catts's campaign was obviously wrecking the Democratic party in Florida. Goode Guerry courted his newspaper friends, and his wooing won results in late summer when a number of papers that had backed Hudson and Farris in the Democratic primary switched to Catts. Before the November general election, Catts had won the support of the Tampa *Tribune*, Jacksonville *Metropolis*, Miami *Metropolis*, Pensacola *News*, Palm Beach *Post*, Palatka *Herald*, Mulberry *Herald*, Lakeland *Star*, Tallahassee *Democrat*, Fort Lauderdale *Sentinel*, Daytona *Journal*, and many smaller weeklies.[46] Catts's headquarters in Jacksonville also published an official campaign paper called the *Free Press*.

An excellent study of the Florida press during the 1916 campaign emphasizes the fluctuation which occurred between the Democratic primary and the general election. Utilizing a daily analysis of editorial references, the author concludes that before the June ballot, the press generally had dismissed Catts as a back

45. Jacksonville *Florida Times-Union*, August 24, 1916; Birmingham *Age-Herald*, December 14, 1916.

46. Goode M. Guerry to J. B. Hodges, August 25, 1916, in Box 197, Hodges Papers; Tampa *Tribune*, October 24, 1916. Smaller papers supporting Catts included the Zolfo *Truth*, Bradford *Times*, DeFuniak *Breeze*, Avon Park *Press*, Arcadia *News*, Raiford *Tribune*, Wauchula *Advocate*, Brooksville *Argus*, Lake City *Index*, Bronson *Times-Democrat*, Palmetto *News*, Sebring *White Way*, Arcadia *Enterprise*, Lake Wales *Highlander*, and Williston *Progress*.

country buffoon from the panhandle; but after the supreme court denied him the nomination, many papers defended him as the real party nominee. These newspapers made Catts a symbol of reform against the corrupt, status-quo Democratic organization. By mid-August fourteen papers had either endorsed Catts or favored him, while thirty-five endorsed or favored Knott.[47]

The most revealing explanation for this journalistic switch to Catts can be found in the pages of the influential Tampa *Tribune*. Before the June Democratic primary, the paper had made little mention of Catts or the governor's race. It had supported Knott, but with minimum comment. After the primary the editor dismissed Knott's charges of fraud and irregularities and accepted the decision of the canvassing board as binding. When Secretary of State H. Clay Crawford telephoned the Jacksonville *Metropolis* that Catts had a decisive lead, the *Tribune* had declared him the victor. In an election summary, the editor called it the most remarkable campaign in Florida history. When Catts had announced, he had been a stranger to the state; without funds, his candidacy had been dismissed as a joke. The liquor interests had opposed him, as had almost all officeholders, the state press, and the Catholic church. The editor offered no analysis of what happened or what "strange and new features it may inject into our politics and government"; but he was convinced of one point: "Certain it is that it has happened—and certain it is that the election was an honest and a fair one and that the will of the voters of the party was expressed—and still more certain it is that the Democratic Party of Florida is in duty bound to carry out the verdict of its primary and elect S. J. Catts Governor, as its duly accredited and selected nominee."[48]

47. Too little attention has been paid to the rural press of 1916, as demonstrated by Jean Carver Chance in her thorough study. Florida's 1916 rural population was 513,478 compared to 406,720 in urban areas. The state had 26 daily and 5 semiweekly newspapers, most in cities and larger towns; but it also had 155 weeklies, 3 semimonthly, and 11 monthly newspapers. See Jean Carver Chance, "Sidney J. Catts and the Press: A Study of the Editorial Coverage of the 1916 Governor's Race by Selected Florida Newspapers" (M.A. thesis, University of Florida, 1969).

48. Tampa *Tribune*, June 16, 18, 1916.

The paper advised Knott to accept the primary verdict graciously and to eschew friends who advised him to appeal to the courts. When Knott decided to contest, the *Tribune* affirmed its faith in his integrity and conceded that he must have a "well-grounded belief" that the returns were incorrect; "but this does not prevent our conclusion that nothing could be fraught with more danger to the party, disturbance of the peace of the State or injury to Mr. Knott's own standing as a citizen and a Democrat than a contest of the gubernatorial primary." In conclusion to one of the most balanced and judicial evaluations to come from the Florida press, the editor added that it was well known that a combination of powerful men regarded Catts's nomination as contrary to their interests, "and their welfare, be it known, is not always synonymous with the welfare of the people or of the State." This clique had been "conferring, devising, and planning for days, with a view to arriving at some means by which the said nomination may be circumvented." Although Knott had no connection with this sinister group, he would be identified with it in the public mind. The *Tribune* believed that Knott was being poorly advised and would ultimately abandon his appeal.[49]

By early October, with mounting evidence indicating that the courts would declare Knott the official nominee, the *Tribune* began a cautious retreat from its tacit support of Catts. It chastized him for circulating petitions to get on the ballot; such tactics compromised his position with rank and file Democrats, wrote the editor. Also, he was bound by oath to support the party nominee, and he still might win his appeal to the supreme court. By mid-October, the paper had decided to back Knott. The editor offered agonized apology in response to charges of bad faith and inconsistency, explaining that he had led the fight for recognition of Catts as the rightful nominee. When the matter had been fought out in the courts and a decision reached favoring Knott, a verdict acceptable to the Democratic executive committee and the canvassing board, only two choices remained: the editor could accept the deci-

49. *Ibid.*, June 17, 23, 28, 1916.

sion and support the nominee, or refuse that decision and withdraw from the Democratic party. The *Tribune* reserved "the right
to continue to entertain our own views as to the truth, justice and
virtue of the action taken," but "esteemed its Democratic fealty
above its individual conviction" and urged a solid Democratic vote
in November. The editor observed, however, that no matter who
won the election, "party integrity" had been besmirched, and it
would require years "to affect a complete reconciliation of the es-
tranged elements." He blamed George P. Raney and the Democratic executive committee for the party's disruption. The Sturkie
resolution and the committee's subsequent endorsement of Knott
even before the supreme court had reached its decision had compromised the integrity of the party. In his final statement before
election day, the editor urged his readers to vote for Knott or
Catts, but counseled the loser to accept his loss gracefully, and
encouraged all Democrats to unite following the ballot.[50]

Knott's attempt to regain momentum floundered because of his
ineffective strategy and inability to deal with the emotional issues
raised by his opponent. Bound by his concept of political honor,
Knott refused to campaign until after the courts had reached a decision. Since the supreme court did not make a final disposition of
the case until early October, this left only a month to counter the
energetic, and by now well-organized Catts forces. Knott later admitted that this delay dealt a fatal blow to his chances.[51]

During the lengthy interval between the primary and the court
decision, the Democratic press attacked Catts. The great majority
of the state's daily newspapers backed Knott. Many of them continued a by now familiar charge that Catts was a demagogue who
appealed only to prejudice. The Panama City *Pilot* and Miami
Herald were the most obvious representatives of such journalism.
The Panama City paper employed its own illogic on Catts by alleg-

    50. *Ibid.*, October 5, 13, 14, November 5, 1916.
    51. William V. Knott, "The Guardians of Liberty," 7. Knott's son believes that relaxing
active campaign efforts—"in conformity with what he considered proper"—was a mistake
which left him too little time and "this alone was a large factor in his defeat." James R. Knott
to author, August 6, 1970.

ing that his chief support in the town came from the liquor interests and the Guardians of Liberty, a most unlikely alliance. According to the editor, the city counted over a hundred members of the Guardians, all of whom paid twenty-five cents apiece to support the Catts cause in Bay County. Since the state organizer for the society resided in Panama City and published the state journal there, the Guardians did constitute a powerful local force in politics. The editor of the *Pilot* blasted the whole Catts movement with little attempt to understand the complex causes that spawned it: "Cattsism and Prejudice are synonymous terms. But to illiberality should be added hellish hate, which is the foundation principle of Cattsism. It reeks of ignorance, weakness of judgment and the reason of fools, but above all else stands out in opposition to the doctrine of love taught by our Saviour."[52]

The Miami *Herald* matched Catts's emotional excesses with a fanaticism of its own. It had completely ignored him before the June primary, but in October and November virtually every issue of the paper carried two or three editorials attacking him. It did not so much question his personal character as it pronounced him a public menace who based his campaign on the "wholly fictitious issue" that the state was endangered by the Catholic church. In its goal to discredit his cause, the paper used some of Catts's tactics. It pictured him as the tool of a secret and destructive force. Since he had no money or political experience, "it is apparent that . . . Catts is merely the tool of some stronger, abler, subtler mind." It was evident to the editor "that Catts and all his deluded followers are merely the puppets of some stronger force, some sinister conspiracy against the liberties of the people." In a masterpiece of circumlocution, the editor explained the nature of the conspiracy as "an invisible government, something as yet hardly defined, that is guiding and controlling this singular movement, a power that is ably playing on the passions, the prejudices of ignorant men to accomplish some purpose not yet fully disclosed."[53]

52. Panama City *Pilot*, August 10, October 26, August 8, 1916.
53. Miami *Herald*, June 10, November 2, 1916.

The paper urged the Democratic executive committee to launch a vigorous campaign lest many disgusted Democrats bolt the party entirely and vote Republican. When the committee began to purge those Democrats who refused to back Knott, the paper rejoiced. In answer to rumors that petitions were circulating in the panhandle calling for secession from the state and merger with Alabama in the event of a Catts defeat in November, the editor opined that losing the panhandle was not too great a price to pay for ridding Florida of the Catts movement. In rebuttal to the *Herald's* contention that only ignorant people supported Catts, signs sprang up on trees in Dade County which read: "To the Miami *Herald:* We may be ignorant, but we will not steal."[54]

Other papers publicized research into Catts's Alabama background which was designed to discredit him. One account misrepresented Catts's 1904 race against Tom Heflin by contending that although Catts had been a well-to-do farmer, he had posed as a poor man. The ruse had failed, and he had lost every county in the district, a charge that was also untrue.[55] A more damaging revelation involved Catts's hot temper which had resulted in his shooting a Negro in Alabama. Relatives of Catts described the event quite differently from the Florida press. According to his grandson, Catts was talking to a friend on the front porch of a small country store in Dallas County. A Negro who had been drinking walked by, cursing loudly and insulting the two men. There were women in the store, so Catts had told the offender to be quiet and move on. He had turned around to continue his conversation, when his companion shouted a warning. Catts whirled around in time to see the black man rushing at him with a knife. Snatching a shotgun that was leaning against the wall, Catts had killed the man with a single blast. Catts defended his actions in almost every speech during the fall saying that he had killed "a nigger, because he was trying to kill

54. *Ibid.,* October 9, 10, 27, 24, 1916.
55. Jacksonville *Florida Times-Union,* November 7, 1916.

me"; he boasted that he had been freed on the testimony of several Negro witnesses.[56]

Another charge, also linked to his Alabama background, questioned whether he had resided in Florida sufficiently long to qualify to run for governor. The state constitution required that the governor be a resident of the state five years preceding the date of his election. Many papers interpreted the constitutional requirement to pertain to the Democratic primary; they considered him ineligible because they claimed he had not moved to Florida until July, 1911, when he had become pastor of the church at DeFuniak Springs. Catts, his memory temporarily failing him, claimed to have come to the town "on or about" January 10, 1911. The Tampa *Tribune* brushed the entire issue aside, pointing out that the primary was not the election, and that to qualify he only need have lived in Florida five years prior to November 7, 1916.[57]

Opponents also charged that Catts was telling rural audiences that if he were not declared governor in November, he would march to Tallahassee with ten thousand citizens armed with rifles and take the capitol by force. Catts issued a weak denial, adding that while he would not take the governor's seat by force, the people might storm Tallahassee and seat the person they chose if the November election were stolen as the primary had been.[58]

The most unlikely indictment emanating from the Knott camp alleged an agreement between Catts and R. B. Sturkie, author of the infamous resolution. Catts had revealed a series of telegrams between Sturkie and Knott indicating voting irregularities in Dade City. Knott called the telegrams a "frame," and said that Sturkie, while pretending to be helping him, was actually backing Catts. Sturkie embarrassed Knott by denying that he favored Catts and

56. Deal, "Sidney Johnston Catts," 103. See also Jacksonville *Florida Times-Union*, August 24, 1916. The number of Negro witnesses varies. In this account Catts said there were nineteen; in a speech recorded in the Miami *Herald* (October 18, 1916) there are nine.
57. Jacksonville *Florida Times-Union*, February 12, 1916; Tampa *Tribune*, June 18, 1916. Actually, Catts had arrived in DeFuniak Springs in June, 1911. See Chapter 1, 28.
58. Jacksonville *Florida Times-Union*, August 7, 18, 1916.

adding that despite Knott's unkind allegation, he was still loyal to his old friend.[59]

Throughout the fall, loyalist Democrats rallied to the banner of party regularity. With few genuine issues to rationalize their actions, they depicted the Catts camp as a hybrid assortment of malcontents. The Gainesville *Sun* charged that Billy Parker, who had toured Florida in the spring lecturing against Catholics and organizing for the Guardians of Liberty, was canvassing the state in the fall on behalf of the Republican candidate for governor, George W. Allen.[60] S. C. Martin, a Knott aide, charged that Dr. Cox, Catts's manager in south Florida, had been a Populist in the 1890s, then a Socialist until 1912 when he had joined the Bull Moose movement of Theodore Roosevelt. A state senator backing Knott charged that Catts's campaign manager in Holmes County, a Mr. Weeks, had once been a candidate for governor on the Populist ticket. At a Catts rally in St. Petersburg chaired by the Reverend J. W. VanDeventer, the parson closed the meeting by saying that though not a Democrat he supported Catts; in fact, he intended to vote for Republican Charles Evans Hughes for president. Catts allegedly told voters to cast their ballots for Republican Allen if they would not vote for him; but he did deny persistent charges that he would not support the Democratic presidential ticket, pledging to vote for Woodrow Wilson and to appoint to office all nominees of the Democratic party in Florida.[61]

After the supreme court finally loosened the legal knot that had bound the loyalists to inactivity, they labored valiantly to restrain straying Democrats. On October 19 F. D. Brennan, a state labor leader, endorsed Knott because of his advocacy of the eight-hour day and other labor reforms. The Democratic executive committee

59. *Ibid.*, August 15, 16, 17, 21, 1916.
60. *Ibid.*, October 23, 1916. This is a credible charge. The Pennsylvanian was a Republican and may have had hurt feelings when he asked to speak on behalf of Catts, an offer that was vetoed by Jerry Carter who felt he would do more harm than good. Interview, Jerry Carter, March 1, 1962, Tallahassee.
61. Jacksonville *Florida Times-Union*, November 6, October 23, 1916; St. Petersburg *Times*, October 25, November 3, 1916; Miami *Herald*, October 19, 1916. Also, see S. J. Catts to editor, Jacksonville *Florida Times-Union*, July 27, 1916.

circulated a sworn statement by Democrats in Fellsmere, Florida, saying that Catts had urged them to vote for the Republican gubernatorial candidate if they would not vote for him.[62] The committee also issued publicity sheets, one of which was entitled "Truth About Recount." It discussed examples of errors that had deprived Knott of the election. Another committee letter urged all Democrats to vote the party ticket, and enclosed the names of Democratic electors together with the names of other candidates. The same mailing inclosed a sheet refuting Catts's charges against Knott while reminding voters that Catts's staff included two railroad lawyers, A. J. Henry and J. B. Hodges. The propaganda also noted that Knott had been a member of the Baptist church for thirty-five years, was a deacon and trustee, and referred those who were interested in further information to the Reverend Dean Addcock, pastor of the Baptist church in Tallahassee.[63]

Knott belatedly tried to appease Florida's fishermen by issuing a statement concerning their problems. He promised to recommend legislation to improve conditions and suggested that they select representatives to visit Tallahassee to help the legislature frame new bills.[64]

He also marshaled most prominent Democrats in the state to help him in the final two weeks of the race. Endorsements rolled in from Florida's United States Senators Duncan U. Fletcher and Nathan P. Bryan; Governor Park Trammell urged a vote for all party nominees; Ion Farris backed his old opponent, as did former governors Sherman Jennings and Albert W. Gilchrist. The list of state dignitaries who addressed Knott rallies read like a bluebook of Florida politics: state chemist R. E. Rose, United States Congressmen Frank Clark and W. J. Sears, state treasurer J. C. Luning, and Jacksonville political boss Pleasant Holt. Most of the

62. F. D. Brennan to editor, Jacksonville *Florida Times-Union*, October 19, 1916. Also see November 4, 1916.

63. "Truth About Recount," copy in Box 197, Hodges Papers; "Some Facts to Count and to Recount" and form letter, George P. Rainey to "My Dear Sir," October 31, 1916, both in Box 197, Hodges Papers.

64. Jacksonville *Florida Times-Union*, October 31, 1916.

state's bankers and county officials also were found in the Knott camp.[65]

This strategy did not always work. On November 3 at a Knott rally in Tampa, many distinguished luminaries were displayed; but the speakers were subjected to such frequent and abusive interruption that they could not continue their arguments. The audience shouted and catcalled; the last part of the rally was "practically a joint debate between the speaker and members of the audience."[66] Catts had no qualms about joining the issue with anyone, regardless of position, and assailed Democratic officials who attacked him. When the popular Congressman Frank Clark assumed a major role in the loyalist drive, the Catts camp contacted him privately, warning him to keep his "hands off of the Knott-Catts controversy." Catts took a more direct approach, urging his audiences to vote for the Prohibition party candidate against Clark in the November election. He also advised them to vote for Republican John K. Cheney who was a candidate for the now discredited Florida Supreme Court.[67]

Catts had saved one more dramatic move for election eve. On November 4 he dispatched a telegram to the United States attorney's office requesting federal poll watchers for the general election. This accentuated the entire issue of fairness and sent many loyalist newspapers into a near apoplectic frenzy. The election returns left no doubt as to the "people's choice"; Catts had 39,546 votes to 30,343 for Knott, 10,333 for George W. Allen, and 2,470 for Socialist C. C. Allen. Catts led Knott in thirty-eight counties, while losing only fourteen. By isolating the twenty counties in which Catts received his largest percentages and comparing the results to the seven counties in which Knott received his highest margin, a geographical pattern emerges. Half of Catts's twenty counties were in north Florida and the panhandle, while five of

65. Lewis O'Bryan to J. B. Hodges, November 9, 1916, in Box 13, Hodges Papers.
66. Jacksonville *Florida Times-Union*, November 4, 1916.
67. John R. Rogers to J. B. Hodges, October 10, 1916, in Box 13, Hodges Papers; St. Petersburg *Times*, October 28, 1916.

Knott's strongest centers were in the same region. Catts showed more balanced strength, with three of his strongest counties on the southeast coast, two in central Florida and three on the west coast. Outside north Florida, only two central Florida counties went strongly for Knott. In the rural panhandle, Catts carried nine counties to only two for Knott (one of which was urban Escambia containing the city of Pensacola). Knott's strength in north Florida was largely urban. Of the five north and panhandle counties in which he received a high percentage of votes, three contained urban voting areas (Duval/Jacksonville, Leon/Tallahassee, and St. Johns/St. Augustine). [68] Although Catts would run three times statewide in the future, he would never again attract such broadly based strength.

The New York *Times* called the 1916 race "one of the most spectacular gubernatorial campaigns ever waged in the United States." Catts won, said the *Times*, without money, and with the aid of a Bible and two revolvers. The victor's analysis differed very little from this viewpoint: "The Guardians of Liberty had triumphed over the Knights of Columbus... and the doctrines of the 'little red school-house' were in the ascendency as opposed to the parochial schools." He added that he had also "smashed the powerful democratic machine in Florida and defeated its candidate, not only once, but twice."[69]

Certainly religion played a critical role. Catts's rallies were often moderated by preachers, and the core of his Wednesday night crowds often had just adjourned from a prayer meeting.[70] The state Baptist paper's analysis of the election revealed much about the pro-Catts Protestant mind. Catts's platform, wrote the editor, had been so "radical" that politicians had regarded him as a

68. For the official tabulation by county, see *Report of the Secretary of State, 1915–1916*, insert. See map, frontispiece, herein. Even though they carried approximately the same areas, Catts added ten counties to his primary total. Knott added only two, Nassau and Escambia.

69. New York *Times*, May 29, 1921; Birmingham *Age-Herald*, December 14, 1916.

70. For instance, see St. Petersburg *Times*, October 25, 1916; Miami *Herald*, October 19, 1916.

joke. The Democratic executive committee had assisted him immeasurably by trying to exclude his name from the ticket, a move
"no doubt inspired by fear or favoritism toward the Catholics." He
had pledged that he would not appoint a bachelor to office if he
could find a worthy married man and that he would not appoint a
man who drank liquor, or was a Catholic or a non-Democrat. The
masses had elected him: "Somehow the common people feel that
Catts is one of them, and that he is interested in them. Many
people voted for him because they fear the political influence of the
Catholic church. Its political career has been a very unhappy one
for dissenters, and there is no reason to think that its spirit has
changed." The editor called for Baptists to unite behind him
whether they had preferred him or not. They ought not to com-
plain, "and let us hope that he will never give us cause to feel
ashamed."[71] That sentence would one day prove significant.

The impact of the 1916 race reverberated beyond Florida.
Thomas E. Kilby copied some of its features, notably the convent
inspection proposal, for his 1918 gubernatorial bid in Alabama.
Catts almost overnight became a major spokesman for anti-
Catholicism in the South, even inspiring books on the subject.
When he brought his rhetoric to Birmingham in December, 1916,
he provoked a Catholic priest, Father James E. Coyle, to respond
in several letters to local newspapers. The priest, complaining of
the extensive reporting of Catts's speech, wrote that it was full of
"stuff that has heretofore found place and space only in the
malodorous gutter press of Georgia and Missouri, but not till today
in the pages of any Alabama newspaper of standing."[72]

Far from inspiring more controversy, Catts was conciliatory in
his victory statement. He sought to allay the fears of those Flori-

71. *Florida Baptist Witness*, June 29, 1916.
72. Birmingham *Age-Herald*, December 15, 1916. See also Sweeney, "Bigotry in the
South," 585–86. Catts's visit to Birmingham in December, 1916, and his account of the 1916
campaign, inspired local poet O. T. Dozier to write a book attacking Catholicism that borders on obscenity. See the Birmingham *Age-Herald*, December 16, 1916; O. T. Dozier,
Response of Doctor O. T. Dozier to Priest James E. Coyle (privately published, n. p., 1917).
Father James E. Coyle, who tried to answer Catts's charges, was later shot to death in 1921
by a Methodist minister crazed with hatred of Catholics.

dians who had come to view him as a half-crazed fanatic: "I am a broadminded man, and not a fanatic, as has been so often charged in this heated campaign, and will work to upbuild, and not tear down." He promised to work loyally with the Democratic party: "I am very sorry that the state Democratic executive committee did not consider me a good Democrat, but if I am permitted I will show it that I am just as loyal a Democrat as ever lived. In fact, I have always insisted that this was a family row. I have frowned upon, and would not tolerate, a negro vote coming in to settle a Democratic fuss." Retreating from the feverish emotionalism of the stump, he pled for unity, assuring citizens that he would never try to enforce his religious views on anyone else, nor would his administration impose "blue laws": "You have honored me by your vote, and whether you be Catholic or Protestant, gambler or saint, rich or poor, you will receive fair and considerate treatment at my hands."[73]

Mayor J. E. T. Bowden of Jacksonville praised this statement, but for many bitter Florida Democrats who still controlled the party machinery and the legislature, reconciliation would not come so easily. The Miami *Herald* did not concur with Catts's call for harmony; refusing to even call him a Democrat, the paper ominously announced that it would participate in no "honeymoon" with the governor-elect: "In electing a man of the character of Mr. Catts, the *Herald* believes the people of Florida have made a grievous mistake, that the state has been dishonored and humiliated, and that the people will eventually regret the action taken on Tuesday."[74]

---

73. Quoted in Jacksonville *Florida Times-Union*, November 9, 1916.

74. Miami *Herald*, November 9, 1916. This negative reaction was not universal, and many editors urged Floridians to unite behind the new governor or at least adopt a policy of "watchful waiting." See Jacksonville *Florida Times-Union*, November 11, 1916.

FIVE

Taking Care
of Friends

FLORIDIANS DID NOT HAVE to wait long to catch a glimpse of the political style that would characterize the Catts administration. He summoned two hundred close supporters to a November banquet at his DeFuniak Springs home where plans for his inauguration were put in final shape. J. S. Lewis, chairman for arrangements, announced plans for an inaugural parade of two hundred cars to replace the traditional horse-drawn buggies.

Preparations for the event at the Catts household were frantic. The seemingly endless campaign had drained the family's meager financial resources, and even the purchase of clothes for the Tallahassee festivities posed problems. Genial West Palm Beach publisher Joe Earman rescued the family with a note payable to Mrs. Catts to buy an inaugural wardrobe for herself and the children. Earman also sent a check for forty-eight dollars to Levy's, a Jacksonville clothier, to pay for a suit for Catts.[1]

Five thousand people crowded the streets of Tallahassee on January 2 to watch the ceremonies. The parade forming at the outskirts of town had a place for members of the supreme court, but the justices, still sulking from the verbal abuse heaped on them by

---

1. Joe L. Earman to J. B. Hodges, August 1, 1922, Box 197, Hodges Papers. Catts's daughters affirm that the family had very little money when they moved to Tallahassee; interviews, Mrs. Ruth Cawthon, May 8, 1972, DeFuniak Springs, Florida, and Mrs. Elizabeth Paderick and Mrs. Alice May Stiegel, May 12, 1972, Jacksonville, Florida.

Catts, refused to participate. Attorney W. W. Flournoy, who had handled Catts's court appeals during the disputed primary, learned of their recalcitrance, visited them, and after much argument persuaded them to join the caravan.[2] A color guard of Confederate veterans on horseback led the procession of fifty gaily decorated automobiles, followed by many more that were unadorned. Catts's auto sported crepe paper spokes, three American flags, and a boastful sign attached to the side: "THIS IS THE FORD THAT-GOT-ME THERE."[3] In keeping with Catts's innovative campaign, the inauguration was the first ever filmed in Florida with a motion picture camera.

A newly constructed platform in front of the capitol had been draped with bunting and was surrounded by a huge throng of spectators. Chief Justice Jefferson B. Browne administered the oath which was followed by the traditional address. Old timers could not remember any governor quoting so much scripture or drawing so many historical allusions. Catts declared that his victory had been like the triumph of Cromwell over the English aristocracy or the French Revolution over the Catholic nobility, or the American colonies over Great Britain. It had been a victory for the people of Florida over "the onslaughts of the county and state political rings, the vast corporations, and the railroads, the fierce opposition of the . . . press, and organization of the negro voters . . . the judiciary of the state . . . and the power of the Roman Catholic hierarchy." Against this malevolent combination, "the common people of Florida, the everyday masses of the cracker people, have triumphed, and the day of your apotheosis has arrived, and you can say, as said the ancient Hebrew devotee, 'Lift up your gates, and be ye lifted up, ye everlasting doors, and let the Lord of Glory in.'"

He explained his program in folksy but earnest phrases: the supremacy of the public "little red schoolhouse" over sectarian

2. Jacksonville *Florida Times-Union*, January 3, 1917.
3. In the traditional legends that thrive on the Catts mythology, the sign supposedly read "This is the car that got me here"; *i.e.*, see Fuller Warren, *How to Win in Politics* (Tallahassee: Peninsular Publishing Co., 1949), 176.

schools; freedom of speech, conscience, and press; complete separation of church and state; the appointment of no man to public
office "who owes his allegiance to a foreign national potentate, or
foreign ecclesiastical power"; suppression of the whiskey traffic;
Everglades drainage; elimination of governmental waste; strengthening the board of equalization in order to more equitably tax
private estates, corporations, and railroads; revision of the confusing Bryan primary law; election reforms including initiative,
referendum, and recall; state police inspection of all "closed institutions"; taxation of all church property except parsonages and
church buildings; creation of industrial schools for boys and girls
where they could learn practical trades instead of "dead languages";
and effective regulation of freight rates. In a Jacksonianlike reference to officeholding, Catts suggested that officials who held office
too long became inefficient and extravagant: "Our ideas will be to
effect changes in these matters by rotation in office and putting in
new men as we can do so practically."[4]

His proposals for reform, no less than his inaugural parade of
automobiles, announced the dawning of a new day for the Sunshine
State. Magnifying the contrast with previous administrations, Catts
refused to attend the inaugural ball and excluded "punch" from the
formal banquet. Both actions were acclaimed by Protestants as
examples of the high moral tone of the new administration, though
they were inconsistent with his occasional imbibing of alcoholic
eggnog. The Baptist *Georgia Christian Index* commented favorably
on Catts's remarkable victory and his precedent-shattering inaugural: "It is a great thing for the Governor of a state to take a firm
stand for righteousness. We congratulate both Governor Catts
and the state of Florida."[5]

The governor wasted little time implementing his plan to rotate
office. Since this became the most controversial element of his administration, some explanation is required. The 1884 state constitution, written by conservative Redeemers, had created a weak

4. For text of Catts's inaugural address, see Jacksonville *Florida Times-Union*, January
3, 1917.
5. *Alabama Baptist*, January 17, 1917, quoting *Georgia Christian Index*.

executive branch. The office of lieutenant governor had been abolished entirely, and the governor had been forbidden to run for a second consecutive term. To further limit the governor's power, the six-man cabinet had been made elective, a unique constitutional provision. Often cabinet members serving on ex-officio administrative boards had more power than the governor. The main reservoir of power remaining to the governor in 1916 was found in the eighteen hundred jobs on state boards, commissions, and within counties. Although he could not completely control such positions, the governor could appoint some directly and influence many others. Even in normal times Florida had exhibited a spoils system by which governors had rewarded the faithful; and the times were abnormal in 1917. The recent governor's race had created wide fissures within the Democratic party; the faction in power had opposed Catts, and he had to find jobs for many friends, few of whom held public office. Should he entertain further political ambitions—and by the end of 1917 he already was looking toward the Senate—he would need to create his own party faction. What better source of nourishment for his loyalists could there be than the cornucopia of the public trough?

Four elements explain his policy toward officeholding: like President Andrew Jackson, he believed philosophically in rotation of office; he desired to punish entrenched Democrats who had opposed him and reward his legion of neophytes; he needed a disciplined cadre of followers for future battles which could be welded together only with the solder of patronage; and he was determined to eliminate corruption from all levels of government. The fundamental choice he made was neither exceptional nor wicked, though it did reach extremes. In a satirical editorial, the Arcadia *Enterprise* replied to his critics: "Governor Catts has been accused of the heinous crime of appointing his friends and supporters to office. Every impulse of gratitude and common justice would dictate that he deal out the choice plums of public patronage to his most cantankerous enemies."[6]

6. Jacksonville *Florida Times-Union*, July 1, 1919, quoting the Arcadia *Enterprise*.

Although the governor reserved to himself the ultimate decision over appointments, he depended for advice on recent convert J. B. Hodges. The Lake City attorney was deluged by job applications in January, 1917, and endorsed someone for every position available. Catts usually respected his opinion. His nominees obtained access to the governor, and Catts frequently consulted him on patronage, particularly posts involving Columbia County in which Lake City was located.[7]

Despite his prodigious efforts for the governor in the last weeks of the election, Hodges sought no appointment for himself, preferring to continue his lucrative law practice and involvement in local politics. Catts offered him the office of attorney general when it came open in the fall of 1917, but Hodges would have been forced to run statewide for election in the approaching primary and so declined. He did accept an appointment to the State Board of Control which governed all colleges and state institutions, and continued his valuable service on the Democratic executive committee.[8]

Hodges' efforts did not go unrewarded. He became the most influential lawyer handling appeals before the State Pardons Board. Since the governor was a dominating voice on the board, Hodges' services were sought for more reasons than his ample legal skills. Although many of these cases came to Hodges unsolicited, the governor's influence obtained others for him.[9]

One of Catts's first acts violated his postelection pledge to appoint all duly elected Democratic nominees. A number of elective

7. For examples of job applications, see J. B. Hodges to Judge Otis R. Parker, January 15, 1917, L. S. Moody to Hodges, February 8, 1917, Hodges to Moody, February 10, 1917, in Box 13, Hodges Papers. For Hodges' influence, see Sidney Catts to Hodges, January 19, 1917, in Box 13, Catts to Hodges, September 14, 1917, Catts to Hodges, January 4, 1918, in Box 25, Hodges Papers.

8. J. B. Hodges to Judge Otis R. Parker, January 15, 1917, in Box 13, telegram from A. B. Small to Joe Earman, August 27, 1917, Hodges to L. E. Roberson, September 3, 1917, in Box 25; Hodges Papers. Hodges served as president of the city council in his home town.

9. Box 13 of the Hodges Papers contains a phenomenal number of requests for legal help based on his official connections. For Catts's influence in soliciting legal business for Hodges, see J. B. Hodges to A. E. McLeary, January 5, 1918, in Box 25, J. L. Kirby to Hodges, April 9, 1917, in Box 13, Sidney J. Catts to Hodges, September 30, 1918, in Box 28, Hodges to L. E. Roberson, September 3, 1917, in Box 25, Hodges Papers.

offices required the additional consent of the governor. Rumors
began to circulate in December, 1916, that he would refuse appointments of General J. Clifford R. Foster as state adjutant general, and Justice R. F. Taylor to the state supreme court, despite
their renomination without opposition in the Democratic primary.
On January 11 the Jacksonville *Florida Times-Union* reported that
Foster, who had held the office since 1901, definitely would not be
reappointed. The move was viewed as an attempt by Catts to purge
the Knott "regulars" from state government, but a more obvious
reason was his desire to reward a long-time friend and supporter, J.
B. Christian. A native of Camden in Wilcox County, Alabama, and
former classmate of Catts at Auburn, Christian was currently a
highly respected jeweler in Tallahassee, where he had resided for
five years. He termed himself "a black belt Jeffersonian Democrat," and had been one of Catts's earliest supporters in 1914.
Christian was not without military experience, having been active
in the Alabama militia before moving to Florida. Catts explained
his appointment of Christian in terms consistent with his inaugural
statement. Twelve years in office was long enough for General Foster to hold the position.[10]

Foster had close ties with many prominent politicians, and a
torrent of criticism was directed at Catts's appointee. The incumbent adjutant general refused to surrender his office, denying that
the governor had authority to appoint him. Christian was forced to
obtain an order from Catts removing Foster before he could assume his duties. The ousted official considered contesting his removal before the 1917 state senate, but ultimately decided against
this maneuver. When asked to comment on the Florida fracas, Dr.
Leonard Wood, senior major general of the regular army, referred
to Foster in less than exuberant terms as a leader of the "National
Guard Lobby."[11]

Governor Catts, not content to let the issue die, poured fuel on

10. Jacksonville *Florida Times-Union*, December 28, 1916, January 11 and 12, 1917;
Deal, "Sidney Johnston Catts," 112.
11. Jacksonville *Florida Times-Union*, January 12 and 23, February 1, 1917.

the conflagration by announcing the transfer of National Guard headquarters from St. Augustine to Tallahassee. The move was attributed to Catts's dislike of St. Augustine, which he considered a center of Catholicism and which had voted against him in 1916. The governor admitted that the relocation caused him to be "knocked good and hard" but resignedly added that he was accustomed to such abuse.[12]

William W. Flournoy, like Christian, had been one of Catts's early converts. As mayor of DeFuniak Springs and a respected attorney, he had served faithfully throughout the gubernatorial race. The strain of handling various legal appeals as Catts's personal attorney had left him exhausted; by late January, 1917, he was critically ill, having suffered a nervous collapse and contracted typhoid fever. The governor had rushed to his side, and when his old friend recovered in the summer of 1917, he offered him the position as attorney for the Internal Improvement Board, a lucrative post paying thirty-five hundred dollars a year. Criticism of the governor had become routine by this time, and Flournoy, with a wisdom not shared by the governor, realized the potential embarrassment of the situation. He had resumed his role as Catts's personal legal counsel, and with a $3 million bond issue for Everglades drainage requiring extensive legal work for the Internal Improvement Board, Flournoy recognized the obvious conflict of interest. He rejected the job, explaining that he "would accept no position surrounded by conditions that would tend to afford grounds for any criticism of the governor."[13]

Catts sought an even juicier plum for his attorney in the summer of 1917, the office of state attorney general. He proposed a bill to the state legislature creating a sixth place on the Florida Supreme Court, then leaked word to the press that he planned to appoint Attorney General Thomas F. West should the bill become law. He could then appoint Flournoy attorney general. The bill failed, however, submerged in legislative suspicion that the governor might be trying to pack the supreme court.

12. *Ibid.*, January 12, 1917.
13. *Ibid.*, January 28 and June 9, 1917.

In spite of his frustrated plans to reward Flournoy, the governor provided his friend with whatever assistance he could. Flournoy was a frequent guest at the governor's mansion in Tallahassee and continued to handle much of Catts's legal business. Like Hodges, he profited from his influence with the state's chief executive. He was a moderately wealthy man who owned extensive bay shore land in the panhandle, and in 1918 he obtained Catts's assistance with Treasury Department officials for the establishment of a new national bank in Pensacola.[14]

Rewarding campaign manager J. V. Burke was a simpler matter. He was appointed as the governor's secretary, a position paying three thousand dollars per year. After resigning on September 6, 1917, because of eye trouble, he was appointed to the office of state tax commissioner at a salary equal to his former post. An additional explanation for Burke's resignation was reportedly friction with former Jacksonville mayor Van Swearingen, who along with Burke had been a key supporter in Catts's 1916 victory; however, the administration denied that internal dissension figured in the change.[15]

Swearingen had joined the administration in late August. The resignation of a supreme court justice finally allowed Catts to appoint Attorney General West to the bench, thus opening a major cabinet post. Three men were rumored to be under consideration by the governor: state senator Glenn Terrell of Leon County, one of Catts's few friends in the upper house, J. B. Hodges, and Milton Pledger. The governor huddled with a number of key advisers on August 28, and two days later appointed Swearingen attorney general.[16] Actually, the post had been offered to J. B. Hodges who had declined and urged the appointment of Swearingen; Hodges offered his congratulations and pledged his support in the forthcom-

14. *Ibid.*, March 31, 1918. According to Jerry Carter, Flournoy was more independent than the public record indicates, favoring Catts when it suited him and opposing him when it did not. Interview, Jerry Carter, July 29, 1970, Tallahassee.

15. *Ibid.*, September 7, 1917.

16. Those present at the August 28 strategy conference included Major A. B. Small of Lake City, a Hodges ally; Sheriff Hayes Lewis of Duval County; Joe L. Earman; J. S. Blitch; South Florida manager Dr. W. H. Cox; and F. L. Tatum, D. B. Murphree and W. W. Jennings, all from DeFuniak Springs. *Ibid.*, August 30, 1917.

ing primary. For once the governor's appointment evoked general approval from the state press, which praised both West and Swearingen.[17]

No one had labored longer or harder for the governor than Jerry W. Carter. One of the original cadre of backers in 1914, he had even named his fifth son Sidney, in honor of the chief executive. Catts pondered an adequate reward for his friend, finally deciding on the job of state hotel commissioner. The post was already occupied by A. L. Messer, a technicality that the governor removed by suspending the incumbent. Messer proved uncooperative, refusing to surrender his job until ordered to do so by the courts. Catts sought legal advice from Flournoy, Hodges, and other attorney friends, admitting that "our friend Jerry Carter is going to be up against a good and hard fight." Hodges replied that the governor could remove Messer under the constitutional provision giving him power to suspend "all officers that shall have been appointed or elected, and that are not liable to impeachment."[18]

Catts successfully removed Messer and appointed Carter to succeed him, but a hostile state senate failed to uphold the suspension and reinstated Messer, whose term expired on June 8, 1918; the following day Catts finally succeeded in installing Carter as hotel commissioner. Reminiscing about the episode years later, Carter recalled: "Yes, I was a fire-eater. The truth of the matter is that no Governor ever could have appointed me anything more than convict inspector except Catts, and he appointed me Hotel Commissioner. The newspapers said I spelled 'hotel' with two 't's,' and to be perfectly frank with you I don't doubt at all that it was true."[19]

Another loyal veteran from the gubernatorial campaign, J. S.

17. J. B. Hodges to L. E. Roberson, September 3, 1917, Hodges to Van C. Swearingen, September 4, 1917, in Box 25, Hodges Papers. For examples of press reaction see quotes from the Ocala *Star* and Winter Haven *Chief,* in Jacksonville *Florida Times-Union,* September 10 and 20, 1917.

18. Sidney J. Catts to J. B. Hodges, June 21, 1917, Hodges to Catts, June 22, 1917, in Box 25, Hodges Papers.

19. St. Petersburg *Times,* October 14, 1962.

Blitch of Levy County, occupied three successive positions within the new administration. Blitch had long been active in the progressive wing of the Democratic party, and according to press reports, Catts had promised him appointment as a state tax commissioner.[20] As good as his word, the new governor named Blitch to the tax commission in April, 1917. He had held the job only five months when the governor's secretary, J. V. Burke, resigned and Blitch exchanged jobs with him on September 6. He held that office for more than a year at which time he became superintendent of the state prison farm. There he made his most notable contributions to the reform of penology in both Florida and the nation.

One of the most sensitive spheres of patronage was the State Board of Control, which administered the University of Florida, Florida State College for Women, the Florida School for the Deaf and Blind, and Florida A. and M. College. During the bitterly contested campaign, Catts had vowed to purge the board and bring state institutions under tighter control. Rumors circulated that Catts planned many personnel changes, including the appointment of new presidents at the Florida State College for Women and the University of Florida.[21] As a consequence, the state's college administrators lived in constant dread during the early months of 1917. University of Florida president A. A. Murphree expressed chagrin at published rumors that the governor also intended to remove Pensacola's P. K. Yonge, chairman of the board, and J. G. Kellum of Tallahassee, the board's secretary.

Yonge had served on the board for twelve years and was acknowledged to be one of the state's most capable experts on state institutions. He feared that Catts would carry out his promise to interject politics into educational policy, and at first decided not to accept reappointment even should it be offered. Kellum, however, persuaded Yonge to compromise by allowing a Catts man to be-

20. To understand the connection of Blitch to Florida progressive politics, see J. S. Blitch to Thomas E. Watson, May 29, 1908, in Thomas E. Watson Papers, University of North Carolina. See also Jacksonville *Florida Times-Union*, February 10, 1917, quoting Levy *Times-Democrat*.

21. Cash, *History of the Democratic Party in Florida*, 131.

come chairman. Joe Earman wanted the chairmanship, Kellum confided, but was inexperienced and would botch the position so badly that he would not be able to hold the office more than four months. He predicted that Yonge would dominate board policy regardless of who held the chairmanship. Dr. Edward Conradi, president of Florida State College for Women, advised the same strategy.[22] Yonge acquiesced, agreeing to accept reappointment should Catts offer it. In a gesture inconsistent with his desire to avoid involving the board in partisan politics, Yonge proposed that the incumbent members elect a new chairman before the Catts members took their places, but Frank E. Jennings, a retiring board member, dissuaded him by emphasizing that this act would itself constitute a purely political action.[23]

Meanwhile, Catts already had made his decision regarding board personnel. A friend of Yonge surreptitiously copied a letter from Catts to a supporter who was urging the governor to continue Yonge on the board. The chief executive explained that he had decided to appoint Professor H. Clay Armstrong in place of Yonge. To do otherwise would leave a preponderance of carry-overs from the Knott era, "and I am determined to have three Catts men and two Knott men on the Board." As news spread that Yonge would not be reappointed, hostility to the governor intensified. The Tampa *Times* called Yonge one of the ablest men ever to serve on the board. Former United States senator Nathan P. Bryan sent his regrets concerning Yonge's dismissal, and predicted that Catts's purge of the board would start a revolt that would make people come to their senses.[24] University of Florida president A. A. Murphree was disconsolate. If Yonge were not retained, he confided to J. G. Kellum, he would "be greatly tempted to accept the first

22. P. K. Yonge to J. G. Kellum, June 12, 1917, Kellum to Yonge, May 8, 1917, in Box 4, P. K. Yonge Papers, P. K. Yonge Library of Florida History, University of Florida, Gainesville.

23. Frank E. Jennings to P. K. Yonge, June 11, 1917, in Box 4, Yonge Papers.

24. F. F. Bingham to P. K. Yonge, June 22, 1917, N. P. Bryan to Yonge, June 29, 1917, *ibid*; Tampa *Times*, June 16, 1917.

decent position which may offer itself."[25] During this period of despair, Kellum informed Murphree that he too was "doomed to be replaced by some two-by-four" political friend of the governor who was to be rewarded with the position of board secretary and business manager of the colleges. In his mood of utter frustration, Murphree exclaimed: "Ye Gods! Save the state from this horrible political autocracy!"[26]

By midsummer, 1917, Murphree felt reassured, having received information that Catts's appointees were "capable, reasonable and fair minded." Although he deplored the removal of several board members for purely political reasons, he had been assured that Catts had "no designs on Conraddi [sic] and myself."[27]

The source of this optimism was Joe L. Earman. The West Palm Beach publisher, Catts's choice as board chairman, wrote Yonge that "governor Catts instructed the other two new members and myself when he handed us our commissions to eliminate politics from these two boards." He assured Yonge that these instructions would be followed, and even sought advice from Yonge on board policy.[28] There is no evidence to refute this incident, and Catts generally avoided meddling in specific board matters.

The governor notified J. B. Hodges on June 15 that he would soon appoint him, Earman, and H. Clay Armstrong, an outstanding Pensacola educator, to four-year terms on the board of control, replacing P. K. Yonge and two other incumbents. At the July 23 meeting of the board at Jacksonville, Earman was elected chairman with his own vote and the support of Hodges and Armstrong against the opposition of holdover members E. L. Wartmann and

25. A. A. Murphree to J. G. Kellum, June 9, 1917, Murphree to Kellum, June 15, 1917, in Box 4, A. A. Murphree Papers, University of Florida, Gainesville.

26. A. A. Murphree to P. K. Yonge, July 3, 1917, in Box 5, Yonge Papers.

27. A. A. Murphree to J. G. Kellum, June 28, 1917, Murphree to John A. Thackston, July 9, 1917, in Box 4, Murphree Papers.

28. Joe L. Earman to P. K. Yonge, August 23, 1917, in Box 5, Yonge Papers. The "two boards" that Earman refers to include the State Plant Board whose membership was the same as the Board of Control.

T. B. King. He was only the third chairman in the board's history, having been preceded by N. P. Bryan, who had served one four-year term, and P. K. Yonge, who had served two terms. The Catts majority left no doubt as to the governor's power by electing his old Pensacola crony, Bryan Mack, secretary of the board at an annual salary of three thousand dollars. Wartmann and King pledged that they would cooperate despite Catts's July coup.[29]

Catts's friendship with Earman demonstrates the governor's cynicism about moral issues. Though he professed to be a prohibitionist, the governor worked closely with Earman, who had spent twenty-five years with the Robert W. Simms Company, a Jacksonville wine importing concern. In 1908 Earman had represented the National Wholesale Liquor Dealers Association by lobbying for the wets in an Osceola County liquor referendum. By the time he had retired from the Simms company in October, 1916, he had risen to vice-president and was one of its largest stockholders. In September, 1913, he had entered a partnership with Donald Herbert Conkling to organize the Palm Beach *Post,* which they operated as a semiweekly until January 1, 1916, when they transformed it into a morning daily. It subsequently became one of the state's most influential papers. Despite his past business affiliation, he claimed that he never drank alcohol and numbered many friends among state prohibitionists. He had always been politically active, idealistically championing reapportionment and other reforms, and he had contributed financially to Catts's victory.[30]

E. B. Donnell, circuit court judge in West Palm Beach and a Catts legal adviser during the recent campaign, wrote President Murphree that he knew both Hodges and Earman, and that the state institutions were in safe hands. He admitted that Earman had once sold whiskey but claimed that there were worse crimes. Through the years he had handled Earman's legal work, and he

29. Sidney J. Catts to J. B. Hodges, June 15, 1917, in Box 25, Hodges Papers. Also, see E. L. Wartmann to editor, Jacksonville *Florida Times-Union,* July 25, 1917.
30. Jacksonville *Florida Times-Union,* April 17, 1917; Joe Earman to J. B. Hodges, June 25, 1924, in Box 53, Hodges Papers.

thought that the new chairman would be fair to Murphree and the University of Florida: "Earman has an exalted opinion of you and of the good work you have done and are doing. . . . You will find that he is more than willing to confer with you and to recognize your worth as a leader in your work. You can talk to him as freely as any man you have ever worked with. . . . If I mistake not the men on the Board of Control, you are going to find that policy [the president running the university without interference from the board] lived up to during this administration." [31]

Murphree was obviously relieved by Donnell's evaluation. He replied that he had not believed the "unfair attacks" on Earman by some of the antiadministration newspapers. Some of the charges in these publications were "so perfectly absurd and ridiculous as to fill one with disgust if not nausea." [32] Considering Murphree's earlier private statements, one detects more relief than sincerity in this response.

Hodges and Earman provided continuity and quality leadership for the board, but there was considerable fluidity in the other position. Armstrong served only a few days before resigning and was followed in turn by Henry J. Brett of DeFuniak Springs, J. T. Diamond, a Santa Rosa County educator, and Catts's legal advisor, W. W. Flournoy.

Friends of the governor also were put in control of the State Board of Health. Dr. W. H. Cox, who had headed Catts's south Florida headquarters during the campaign, became the state health officer. Charles T. Frecker of Tampa, who had been secretary of Catts's south Florida office, was appointed president of the Board of Health. They remained in office until a bitter confrontation with the governor in 1919 resulted in the dismissal of both and the appointment of Earman to the presidency of the board.

Less prestigious and remunerative jobs went to secondary figures whose loyalty was untested or who had joined the Catts juggernaut late in the 1916 race. One of Catts's managers had writ-

31. E. B. Donnell to A. A. Murphree, July 30, 1917, in Box 4, Murphree Papers.
32. A. A. Murphree to E. B. Donnell, August 3, 1917, ibid.

ten county officials during the campaign requesting that they state their choice for governor, and this list served as a patronage guide. Voting patterns in the 1916 legislature provided a more reliable estimate of service and furnished the basis for many additional appointments.

The lot of his appointees was not always easy, as one of his nominees for rural school inspector discovered. The Constitution provided that the governor should appoint inspectors "upon the nomination of the state Superintendent of Public Instruction." Superintendent William N. Sheats never got along well with Catts. A Methodist by religious preference, his resentment against Baptists was almost as obvious as the governor's antipathy toward Catholics. During the campaign he privately referred to Catts as "a renegade from Alabama," and believed that Catts's election inspectors not only had stolen votes for Catts, but also had tried to defeat Sheats. Relations did not improve after the governor took office, and Sheats wrote his wife in September, 1917, that because he could not "do everything in a jiffy, Gov. Catts is already insinuating that I am not keeping up with my business."[33]

Complicating the personality clash between the governor and his cabinet official was Catts's conviction that the office of rural school inspector constituted a legitimate patronage opportunity. As early as February, 1917, he recommended to Sheats a certain individual for inspector, writing that "no man did better work and service for us than he did in the late campaign." Sheats made little effort to be cooperative, and in the fall of 1919, recommended the appointment of William T. Cash of Perry, Florida, a prominent state legislator, and Madison County superintendent of education George W. Tedder, along with the reappointment of R. L. Turner of Inverness. Catts reappointed Turner but refused to name a second inspector, instructing Sheats to nominate two additional per-

---

33. William N. Sheats to Bishop W. A. Candler, January 6 and November 11, 1916, H. H. McCreary to Sheats, June 19, 1916, on Reel 2, Folder 35, Sheats to Mrs. W. N. Sheats, September 13, 1917, on Reel 2, Folder 40, all in William N. Sheats Papers, on microfilm at P. K. Yonge Library of Florida History, University of Florida, Gainesvillle.

sons. Actually, Catts had announced in Jacksonville on July 6,
1919, that he would appoint Cash. This statement had been well
received, but Cash had refused, complaining that the governor had
imposed a condition that he could not accept. The Taylor County
Herald, which had applauded the initial announcement, expressed
surprise that Catts would try to offer a "deal" to a man of Cash's
integrity: "'You scratch my back and I'll scratch yours,' is the Cat-
tocratic creed to the exclusion of public welfare, of merit, of justice,
of honesty and integrity."[34]

Sheats responded to Catts's rejection by recommending Tedder
a second time, but substituting the name of Miss Maud Schwal-
meyer of Florida State College for Women in place of Cash. Again
Catts rejected the slate, causing Sheats to offer as additional options, Miss Francis Davis and Miss Hortense Broward. These
pleased the governor no better than the other nominees, provoking
him to seek an advisory opinion from Attorney General Van C.
Swearingen as to whether the governor had the right to make an
independent appointment. Receiving an affirmative reply, he
chose William M. Holloway, a Baptist layman and long-time opponent of Sheats who had lost the race for state superintendent in
1913 by only eight thousand votes. Sheats, who considered Holloway a personal enemy, refused to pay his salary and appealed to the
supreme court on the grounds that Catts's independent appointment violated the constitution. Catts responded by warning
Sheats, who had entered an Atlanta hospital, that he had been absent from his post too long, and denouncing him for refusing to sign
Holloway's requisitions; the governor demanded an immediate explanation from the superintendent. Sheats's reply was a public and
vindictive philippic aimed at Holloway: "Mr. Holloway, having
done me a great wrong, has been the bitterest and most unscrupu-
lous enemy I have ever had. This fact was... known to any man
familiar with Florida political history for the past 16 years. Aside
from past political differences between Mr. Holloway and myself,

34. Sidney J. Catts to J. D. Godges, February 6, 1917, on Reel 2, Folder 38, Sheats
Papers; Jacksonville *Florida Times-Union,* August 5, 1919, quoting Taylor County *Herald.*

my long acquaintance with Mr. Holloway compels me to consider
him wholly incompetent for the discharge of the duties of rural
school inspector."[35] On December 11, the Supreme Court ruled
unanimously that Catts had no power to appoint a rural school inspector, leaving Holloway without a job.

The enduring enmity between Catts and the state Democratic
organization expressed itself even in local appointments. In 1920
Catts ignored the recommendation of the Brevard County Democratic Executive Committee in appointing M. S. Jones, Jr., to fill
the office of sheriff. The committee, located in a county that had
gone two to one for Knott in 1916, protested that the governor had
pledged originally to appoint their nominee, who had also been
endorsed by the county commissioners. When Catts reneged on
his promise, the committee condemned his appointment, calling
the action "undemocratic and un-American, in that it tramples the
principles of democracy in the dust, and is a travesty on justice."[36]

Not all applicants for jobs obtained the governor's dubious
blessing. One example was T. R. Hodges, controversial Shell Fish
commissioner whom Catts had vowed to dismiss. Swallowing his
pride, the commissioner had written patronage boss J. B. Hodges
in December, 1916, entreating Hodges to use his influence with
the governor to save his job. He also lobbied in the state legislature, persuading a representative to introduce a bill, subsequently
killed, to remove this position from the governor's appointment
and place it in the hands of the commissioner of agriculture. All his
efforts failed, and Catts fulfilled his campaign promise by replacing
T. R. Hodges with J. A. Williams of Gainesville, who was said to be
the father of the original shellfish conservation law and one of the
most knowledgeable men about the state's fishing industry.[37]

---

35. Sidney J. Catts to W. N. Sheats, October 27, 1919, on Reel 2, Folder 43, Sheats
Papers. For text of correspondence between Catts and Sheats, see Jacksonville *Florida
Times-Union*, November 16, 1919. For text of Catts's request for an advisory ruling and
Swearingen's opinion, see State of Florida, *Biennial Report of the Attorney General of the
State of Florida, from January 1, 1919 to December 31, 1920* (Tallahassee: T. J. Appleyard,
1921), 97–99.

36. Jacksonville *Florida Times-Union*, March 19, 1920.

37. T. R. Hodges to J. B. Hodges, December 4, 1916, in Box 13, Hodges Papers;
Jacksonville *Florida Times-Union*, June 5, 1917.

Even the governor's friends were not immune from disappointment, especially when they became enmeshed in the patronage struggle between Catts's north and south Florida factions. The southern contingent complained that the Jacksonville clique that had run the state headquarters during the campaign dominated patronage. Charles Frecker, secretary to the south Florida forces, was especially perturbed, writing J. B. Hodges an insistent letter endorsing Catts Club organizer Goode M. Guerry for the post of gubernatorial secretary. The appointment of Guerry, he wrote, was essential to balance the volume of patronage directed to the Jacksonville leadership. Once again the north Florida clique received the prize with the appointment going to former state campaign manager J. V. Burke.[38]

An analysis of the officeholding rolls between 1916 and 1920 reveals a dramatic change in personnel. Such "house cleaning" regularly occurs in two-party states where Democratic and Republican parties are closely balanced, a process that has required the need for civil service protection. In the Democratically dominated southern states, factional purges within state government have occurred, but few have had the sweep generated by the Catts administration.

Comparing lists of state officials in 1915–1916 at the close of the Trammell administration to 1919–1920 in the last years of the Catts term demonstrates the fluidity. Catts had replaced all four supervisors of state convicts (some twice), the Shell Fish commissioner, all five members of the State Board of Examiners for Nurses, a majority of the board of control, all three members of the State Board of Dental Examiners, all five representatives on the State Board of Medical Examiners, three of the five members on the State Road Department, plus appointing twenty-two members of new boards created during his administration. Numerous changes also had occurred on less significant state commissions. Furthermore, a selective sampling of state boards during the last two years of the Trammell administration indicates that only five mem-

38. Telegram from Buck Lanier to J. B. Hodges, November 10, 1916, Ct. T. Frecker to Hodges, November 9, 1916, in Box 197, Hodges Papers.

bers resigned and none were suspended; in the comparable period of Catts's term, sixteen members resigned and six were suspended.[39]

Even such extensive utilization of state jobs did not provide enough patronage, and the governor supplemented his rewards with local offices, usually vacated by executive dismissals of county officials. No office was of too little consequence, and the governor appointed his allies to such county positions as probation officer, justice of the peace, constable, county commissioner, superintendent of public instruction, and even to membership on community school boards. Though such jobs were provincial in nature, Catts did not allow any local adviser to dictate appointments; he sought their advice but usually reserved the ultimate decision on all patronage to himself.

The press attacked many of his appointments but directed its most devastating criticism at his relatives, who filled a growing list of positions. Sidney J. Catts, Jr., one of the governor's four surviving sons, had planned to enter Cumberland Law School, but the newly elected chief executive persuaded the boy to enroll at the state university. The boy enrolled in the school's ROTC program, but resigned to enter the army when war was declared and was sent to Fort McPherson, Georgia, in May, 1917, for training. At Fort McPherson he had obtained the rank of captain and had been recommended by the adjutant general and post officers as one of the best soldiers in the camp. Following his training, however, he won reassignment to Florida, where his father appointed him captain of Company B, Florida National Guard, located in Tallahassee. Some members of the unit wired the commanding officer of the military district that they would not serve under the younger Catts, to which he replied that they could not elect officers since the unit had been federalized for service overseas.[40]

39. For mobility of officeholders, compare lists in *Report of the Secretary of State, 1915–1916, Part I*, 11–26, to *Report of the Secretary of State, 1919–1920, Part I*, 13–26.
40. Jacksonville *Florida Times-Union*, July 24 and 25, 1917. Also, see unidentified newspaper clipping in papers of Mrs. Elizabeth Paderick.

Young Sidney's strong recommendation from Fort McPherson lends credence to newspaper reports that most of the dissatisfaction resulted from encouragement by Catts's enemies and was confined to only a minority of the troops. Lieutenant H. Clay Crawford, Jr., son of a powerful establishment-oriented Democratic family, led the protest and was removed from his rank by Governor Catts on charges of insubordination. The insurgents then contacted Congressman Frank Clark, no friend of Catts, who advised them to elect officers of their own choosing and promised to help them out of trouble should any result. On August 2 forty-six members of the company met secretly outside Quincy, Florida, to elect officers. Clay Crawford, Jr., nominated Catts, who did not receive a single vote; J. Douglas Hopkins of Tallahassee was elected captain, while Crawford was chosen second lieutenant. Even though a few of the troops present held written proxies, the meeting was not representative of the preferences of the 111-member company. The chief executive asked J. B. Hodges to represent his son should the affair demand legal action.[41]

Congressman Frank Clark, who was considered a likely gubernatorial candidate in 1920, kept the issue alive. He persuaded one officer to recommend that the War Department establish a committee to examine Captain Catts mentally, physically, and morally. He also challenged the governor to a public debate on the proposed topic that the state's chief executive should be impeached. This assault on himself and his son aroused the governor's seldom dormant temper. According to the governor, his son had been treated wretchedly by the army. The boy had been hounded out of service by Cardinal Gibbons and others. He had offered to make the boy state adjutant general but Sidney had refused. Then he had offered Sidney the post of private secretary, but the young man had replied that he wanted only to serve his country.

The charges by Clark were part of a concerted effort to embarrass the governor and his family. Governor Catts crowned his of-

---

41. Jacksonville *Florida Times-Union*, July 25, August 3, 4, 1917; J. B. Hodges to L. E. Roberson, September 3, 1917, in Box 25, Hodges Papers.

fensive with an open letter to Clark published in most Florida
newspapers in which he quoted correspondence from the commanding general of the army denying that there had been an investigation into the conduct of Captain Catts. Furthermore, the governor wrote, Clark was using the entire episode to advance his own
gubernatorial aspirations and obtain funds from his "corporation
and law-breaking friends," who hated Catts. The governor concluded the letter vituperatively by referring to an earlier race when
Clark, armed with a hickory stick, allegedly had met Governor
William S. Jennings with the intention of thrashing him; instead,
Jennings had wrestled the stick away from him and had administered a sound beating. Catts, alluding to the affair, warned: "if you
ever interfere with me or any of my children anymore, or meddle
with my business again . . . I will give you . . . a debate a la Jennings
via the hickory stick plan."[42] Tempers cooled but Catts never forgave Clark and helped arrange stout opposition against him in the
1918 elections.

The governor did not ignore his other children either, obtaining an officer's rank in the National Guard for son Rozier and the
position of inspector of naval stores, secretary to the governor (after
the resignation of Blitch), and finally Duval County tax collector for
K. R. Paderick, his son-in-law. When Paderick resigned as his secretary, Catts offered the post to John G. Kellum, business manager of the Florida State College for Women and formerly secretary to the Board of Control. After Kellum rejected the offer, he
appointed his daughter, Ruth Catts, to the job. Hotel commissioner Jerry Carter selected Catts's oldest son, Edward Douglas,
for a post on the hotel commission.[43]

The appointments of Paderick and Ruth Catts would not have
provoked such a furor but for Sidney, Jr.'s, assumption of a high
state office. Following the controversy over his position in the local
guard unit, this outfit had been federalized as part of the 31st Division and sent to France, where it arrived two months before the

42. Jacksonville *Florida Times-Union*, August 26, 1917, September 3, 1918.
43. *Ibid.*, September 11 and 18, 1918; interview, Mrs. Ruth Cawthon, May 8, 1972,
DeFuniak Springs.

armistice. When the war ended, Catts interceded to have his son sent home and appointed to active duty at Gainesville so he could complete his law course. When Secretary of War Newton D. Baker denied the transfer, the governor changed tactics. Forgetting his promise not to meddle in university affairs, he asked the Board of Control and President A. A. Murphree of the University of Florida to agree to let young Catts come to the campus as an officer of the National Guard. James McCants, a Catts protégé who had replaced Christian as adjutant general, agreed to the appointment of an instructor who would drill local boys on campus.[44] Wishing to speed his son's return, the governor wrote General John J. Pershing and federal officials, pressuring them to reassign his son from the occupation force in Germany to Gainesville. In dealing with the university, Sidney, Jr., proved to be a shrewd negotiator, realizing the leverage of his father's office. He demanded a higher salary than the $110 per month provided by the adjutant general's office and suggested that the sum be supplemented by the university or the Board of Control. Murphree privately resisted this demand, arguing that no additional funds were available.[45]

Sidney, Jr.'s, ambition proved too expensive for the Board of Control, so the governor provided another option. On September 2, 1919, only days after the salary dispute had ended, Adjutant General McCants was persuaded to resign, and Sidney was appointed to his place. The Florida press enjoyed the affair immensely, noting that McCants, who had been an original Catts supporter, had found the governor too dictatorial and meddlesome.[46] A more likely explanation of the resignation is Catts's desire to provide an office for his son.

44. Newton D. Baker to Sidney Catts, May 28, 1919, Catts to Joe L. Earman, June 5, 1919, Earman to Catts, June 13, 1919, all in Box 12, Murphree Papers; Catts to Earman, June 5, 1919, in Box 33, Hodges Papers.

45. J. B. Hodges to A. A. Murphree, August 22, 1919, Murphree to Hodges, August 27, 1919, Hodges to Murphree, August 29, 1919, all in Box 12, Murphree Papers.

46. Jacksonville Florida Times-Union, September 8, 1919, quoting Plant City Courier. When Sidney, Jr., finally did enter the university's law school, President Murphree shrewdly took great pains to expedite his law program, a course of action that won the governor's praise. A. A. Murphree to Sidney Catts, Jr., February 21, 1920; Catts to Murphree, June 7, 1919, in Box 12, Murphree Papers.

Whatever the reason for the change, the press blistered the chief executive. The Miami *Herald* noted that Sidney was the fourth adjutant general to serve since the 1916 election, an unprecedented number, and linked the appointment to those of Ruth Catts and Paderick to illustrate the extent of nepotism within the administration.[47]

The governor resorted to another of his acrid public letters to answer the press charges. Without really refuting the allegation of nepotism, he noted that family appointments were a common practice among all of Florida's cabinet officers, except for two whose children were still in school. He observed that Secretary of State Crawford had employed his son on the public payroll until the boy had joined the army; then in 1919 he had appointed his daughter to his office staff. The son of State Treasurer Luning held a position in his father's office, as did the daughter and son of Superintendent of Public Instruction Sheats. Comptroller Amos employed both his father and his wife. Catts concluded that the governor dispensed some eighteen hundred jobs, and undue criticism had been attached to the four which had gone to his children. Less formally, he explained the matter to cracker audiences by asking: "Did you ever see an old cat that wouldn't take care of its kittens?"[48]

Young Sidney attempted to justify his father's confidence by reorganizing the Florida National Guard to bring unit strength up to quotas. An adequately staffed guard was necessary, said young Catts, "to combat the great spirit of Bolshevism and unrest" in America. At the time that he assumed direction of the guard, there were no units recognized as adequate by the War Department.[49]

Even greater than the criticism of his appointments or nepotism was the opposition to his removal of public officials. Hav-

47. Jacksonville *Florida Times-Union*, September 12, 1919, quoting The Miami *Herald*. Also see *ibid.*, September 6, 1919, quoting Ocala *Star*, Tampa *Times*, Lakeland *Telegram*, and Clearwater *Sun*.

48. Sidney J. Catts to editor, *ibid.*, September 26, 1919; interview, Mrs. Ruth Cawthon, May 8, 1972, DeFuniak Springs.

49. For text of his reorganization plan and condition of the Florida guard, see Jacksonville *Florida Times-Union*, September 20, 21, 1919.

ing been forewarned in his inaugural address, few incumbents were surprised when he began "rotating" officials; but the extent of his removals created a public scandal in Florida. During his administration approximately one hundred county and state officials were removed. Such dismissals included the entire Volusia County board of commissioners and the sheriffs of Duval, Pinellas, Escambia, Monroe, Sumter, Citrus, and Clay counties. Many of these removals resulted from vigorous examinations of county finances conducted by State Auditor J. Will Yon. From the first days of his administration, he had announced his intention to eliminate corruption from the statehouse level down to the lowest county officials. He instructed the state auditors to inspect all public financial transactions, but particularly those involving local tax collectors.[50] Catts pushed the investigations and when shortages appeared, promptly removed the erring official. The Nassau County tax collector was removed when a state audit revealed an $8,000 shortage; S. I. Revell, clerk of the Liberty County circuit court, was suspended after Yon's audit disclosed a $2,600 deficit; Yon's audit of Jefferson County tax collector J. B. Horne located a $3,057 shortage. In addition, Horne was charged with habitual drunkenness and improper "overtures and approaches" to his secretary, Miss Willie Mae Davis. Other dismissals resulted from equally obvious malfeasance of office; when Sheriff J. H. King of Clay County was removed on June 28, 1917, he had been absent from the county and state for a month and no one knew his whereabouts.[51]

Catts's rigid if inconsistent standards of morality also figured prominently in his suspensions. Nowhere did his ministerial background affect him more directly or hypocritically than in his judgment of the conduct to be expected of public servants. The most obvious examples involved drinking and prostitution. Although Catts drank privately, he maintained his public posture as a prohi-

---

50. New York *Times*, April 16, 1921; interview, Mrs. Elizabeth Paderick and Mrs. Alice May Stiegel, May 12, 1972, Jacksonville.

51. Jacksonville *Florida Times-Union*, April 24, 1919, August 5, 1920, May 6, 1919, June 29, 1917.

bitionist and informed political advisor J. B. Hodges that he was
determined to remove Hamilton County judge B. B. Johnson who
was rumored to drink heavily. Hodges cautioned against precipi-
tate action because of Johnson's support by Hamilton County's
senator as well as by the legislative delegations of adjoining districts. The Lake City attorney concluded that the action would be
futile because the senate would merely reinstate the judge. Besides, such action might solidify opposition to Catts's appointees:
"[Johnson's] friends in Jasper are not our friends; we know their
methods; we know that their speciality is the bringing to bear [of]
influences in a secret and insiduous manner, and in the case of the
removal of Johnson they will at once actively begin to lay their
plans to defeat his removal, and, at the same time, lay plans to
defeat other appointments that necessarily must be made."[52]

Catts did not heed this advice, bringing the very consequences
about which Hodges had warned. Johnson appealed his dismissal
to the state senate. Catts summoned Hodges to the capital in a vain
attempt to keep the upper house from reappointing the judge, and
vowed to remove Johnson again should he regain his office.[53]

Excessive drinking also figured in the suspension of many other
officials. He removed Sheriff G. R. Carter of Citrus County because of drunkenness, and even some of his own appointees became suspect. Hodges had won appointment for a Lake City friend
and state legislator, W. J. Roebuck, as state convict inspector.
Catts, obviously perturbed, wrote Hodges in 1917 that he had
heard rumors that Roebuck drank; despite Roebuck's loyalty in the
1917 legislature, Catts intended to dismiss him if the offending
conduct continued. Hodges' vigorous defense preserved Roebuck's
job until 1919 when he voluntarily resigned.[54]

A bitter struggle developed in Escambia County when the governor threatened to remove Judge C. Moreno Jones of the
Pensacola court of record. The controversy arose because the

52. J. B. Hodges to Sidney J. Catts, February 24, 1917, in Box 13, Hodges Papers.
53. Sidney J. Catts to J. B. Hodges, April 3, 1917, *ibid.*
54. J. B. Hodges to Sidney J. Catts, June 16, 1917, in Box 25, *ibid.*

county sheriff had raided a service club run by J. C. Hillard. Hillard, complaining that he had a liquor license and conducted his business in accord with law, obtained an injunction against the sheriff from Judge Jones. The sheriff appealed to Catts who wrote another of his renowned public letters, warning that Jones's judicial opinions carried no more weight than a "negro guinea" and that the judge had better "get right" on the liquor question or he would be viewing that issue as a private citizen instead of as a judge. Members of the Pensacola Bar Association expressed their outrage in a resolution condemning the governor for trying to "intimidate" the judiciary of Florida. Catts, visiting the port city to attend the wedding of political henchman Bryan Mack, was unimpressed by the bar association and its resolution, calling them "the same old crowd that attempted between last June and November to rob me of the nomination for governor"; furthermore, the members were "falsifiers" and "upholders of blind tigers."[55] Once again J. B. Hodges tried to restrain Catts, advising the governor in mid-November that the removal of Jones would be a serious mistake. It would give the chief executive's opponents in the panhandle a weapon against him. Catts, somewhat mollified, replied that the "crowd over there at Pensacola are [sic] sorter scared and I think they are as anxious to drop it as anybody can be. We will sit still and watch what we see."[56]

Such confrontations with drinking and its advocates continued throughout his administration, though they diminished after legal prohibition came to Florida. Catts obviously utilized prohibition to fulfill pledges he had made to his rural, evangelical constituency; the zeal with which he fought the "liquor traffic" is quite remarkable in a man who was not personally committed to abstinence.

Prostitution also attracted the governor's attention, although on this issue his concern appears to have been genuine. The construction of military facilities brought demands from the Departments

55. Jacksonville *Florida Times-Union*, November 2, 4, 1917.
56. J. B. Hodges to S. J. Catts, November 14, 1917, Catts to Hodges, November 15, 1917, in Box 25, Hodges Papers.

of the Army and Navy to eliminate the redlight districts that flourished in many Florida cities. Part of Catts's assault on Pensacola's government resulted from its toleration of prostitution in the city, and the governor acted on a request of Secretary of the Navy Josephus Daniels to clean up the town. The chief executive, once again exercising his penchant for private snooping, wrote J. B. Hodges of Lake City that a local woman had complained to him that Columbia County sheriff J. W. Perry allowed houses of prostitution in Lake City; according to Catts there were twenty-three houses of "ill fame" in the small town, creating a condition worse than anything "this side of the western dives." He asked Hodges to tell the sheriff "that if he doesn't clean up, things will get busy in regard to his holding office." Some temporary reforms occurred before the small town returned to its former condition as the prostitution capital of northern Florida, a reputation it maintained into the 1960s.[57]

On July 7, 1917, Catts summoned Monroe County sheriff Jaycocks and county attorney Roberts, both of Key West, to explain why they had not closed down the town's "disorderly houses." The War Department had complained to the governor that American soldiers in uniform frequented these "disreputable resorts." Catts delivered an ultimatum, giving the officials two weeks to clean up their community. Jaycocks admitted the charges, but complained that he had received no support from the prosecuting attorney or county judge. He had made ten arrests, but the county attorney often had refused to prosecute, and when tried, the judge dismissed prostitutes with a nominal fine of one dollar.[58] This explanation did not convince Catts, and on September 14, the sheriff joined the lengthening ranks of unemployed former Florida officeholders.

No single governmental unit bore the brunt of Catts's dismis-

57. Jacksonville *Florida Times-Union*, August 7, November 17, 1917, Sidney J. Catts to J. B. Hodges, April 14, 1917, copy of letter from Catts to J. W. Perry, April 14, 1917, in Box 13, Hodges Papers.
58. Jacksonville *Florida Times-Union*, July 8, 1917.

sals so heavily as Duval County. During the January, 1917, municipal elections, many local Jacksonville politicians had requested the governor to investigate alleged corruption in the city. Ion L. Farris, leader of the reform group seeking an audit, complied with Catts's request to obtain a petition bearing the names of 20 percent of the city's voters. Catts dispatched the state auditor for a preliminary examination, and the official submitted his report to the governor on February 18. Catts studied the findings until mid-March, then removed Duval County solicitor L. D. Howell from office for drunkenness and "disorderly conduct." Completion of a more thorough audit triggered a sensational scandal. Duval County tax collector J. W. Rast had been ailing for some time and took leave for major surgery. In the early fall of 1918, Catts suspended him, appointing the governor's son-in-law, K. R. Paderick, to the vacated post. On September 25, Rast was arrested on charges of embezzling $140,000 of public funds. Rast denied the charges and ran for reelection in November, 1918, hoping that a voter referendum would exonerate him. Attorney General Van Swearingen ruled that due to a technicality, his name could not be placed on the ticket, but Rast obtained a court order granting him a ballot place and then launched a campaign aimed mainly at Catts's nepotism. Rast won reelection by a landslide, reflecting voter disgust at what appeared to be a purely political dismissal to make way for yet another of the governor's relatives. Paderick ran a poor third in a three-man race.[59]

Despite Rast's vindication by the voters, Catts refused to issue a commission. On January 23, 1919, he filed ten suits against Rast totaling $275,000. The governor's persistence finally triumphed in February, 1919, when a Jacksonville jury found Rast guilty of embezzling $138,000 of state and county funds and sentenced him to ten years in the penitentiary.

Duval County Sheriff W. H. Dowling also felt the brunt of Catts's wrath. In February, 1917, Catts privately requested J. B.

---

59. *Ibid.*, January 30, March 9, 10, 1917, September 11, 26, October 26, November 6, 1918.

Hodges to investigate liquor law violations in Duval County. In another example of moralistic politics wedded to pragmatic patronage, Catts suspended Sheriff Dowling in June, for "malfeasance, misfeasance, and neglect of duty"; he replaced Dowling with Henry Hayes Lewis, former collector of internal revenue and a Catts aide. The Ocala *Star* condemned Lewis as a "Cattocrat," and charged that the governor would remove any elected official in order to create a job for one of his henchmen.[60]

The charge seemed valid when considered in the context of a fierce power struggle in Duval County between Catts and party regulars led by Pleasant A. Holt and Senator Duncan Fletcher. J. B. Hodges had discovered shortly after the 1916 election that Fletcher intended to displace Lewis from his job as collector of revenue in the Jacksonville office of the Internal Revenue Service. Hodges wrote the senator referring to Lewis as a loyal Democrat and close personal friend, and also arranged a strategy conference with Governor Catts. Fletcher agreed to confer with Hodges upon returning to Florida but remained firm in his decision to punish Lewis for disloyalty. In the spring of 1917 he accomplished the purge, appointing his secretary to replace Lewis. Hodges, frustrated in the attempt to preserve his friend's job, wrote Catts a furious letter calling Fletcher a "so-called Democrat" whose action was "characteristic of the independentism [sic] bred by the State Committee last year, and reared and fostered by the Florida State Senate this year—that no man shall hold an office who is thoroughly democratic, and who . . . is able to recognize its voice when it proclaims to the adherents of the party the name of its nominee for Governor."[61] The governor decided to appoint Lewis to a new job in restitution for this loss of employment.

---

60. J. B. Hodges to Sidney J. Catts, February 10, 1917, in Box 13, Hodges Papers; Jacksonville *Florida Times-Union*, June 15, 1917, and June 21, 1917, quoting Ocala *Star*. As in so many of Catts's dismissals, time vindicated his decision on the Dowling matter. Governor C. A. Hardee removed Dowling as sheriff in 1922 because of his alleged association with Duval County bootleggers; Joe Earman to Hodges, June 9, 1922, in Box 44, Hodges Papers.

61. J. B. Hodges to Duncan U. Fletcher, February 12, 1917, Hodges to Hayes H. Lewis, February 17, 1917, Fletcher to Hodges, February 15, 1917, Hodges to Sidney J. Catts, May 22, 1917, all in Box 13, Hodges Papers.

Catts visited Jacksonville on June 30, explaining his appointment in typically blunt fashion to one thousand citizens who crowded the county armory. He had pledged to clean up the port city and had removed Dowling because the sheriff would not enforce state liquor laws. The governor denied a rumor that Hayes Lewis had paid him two thousand dollars for the office and promised to "plant his fist where it would do the most good" if anyone made that charge to his face. As for local complaints that he had taken funds from liquor interests during the recent campaign, he admitted that some "liquor money" had been received and used by his paper, the *Free Press;* but, he declared, he had not cared where the money came from so long as it was going for a good cause. As for his appointment of Lewis, he candidly admitted that it was in payment of a political debt. Lewis, then collector of revenue, formerly had supported Knott and had lost his job when he switched to Catts. He revealed in the speech that Lewis had been the first man to tell him of the election frauds in Madison, Hamilton, and Suwannee counties. After the rally ended, the sympathetic audience gave Catts a roaring vote of confidence, and even the usually critical *Florida Times-Union* defended his actions.[62]

The following day, the governor spoke to the Florida Press Association meeting in the city. Elaborating on his earlier remarks, Catts said that Dowling had admitted that he could not enforce the liquor laws in Duval County. Catts exploded with wrath, warning that "if Hayes Lewis don't carry out the law and clean up this city so help me God I'll remove him as quick as I would a guinea nigger."[63] That same day Dowling was elected by the city council to the county board of commissioners in an obvious slap at the governor.

In September, 1917, the chief executive summoned the Duval County commissioners to Tallahassee to answer charges against them, and just before leaving office in 1920, he finally removed Luther L. Meggs, chairman of the Duval board. The *Florida*

62. Jacksonville *Florida Times-Union*, July 1, 14, 1917.
63. *Ibid.*, July 1, 1917.

Times-Union editorialized that the governor had been trying to get
Meggs for a long time and that the paper was only thankful it had
taken so long. It praised Meggs as an unusually competent man in a
job frequently corrupted in other counties.[64]

Neither Catts's friends nor his enemies fully understood the
governor's frequent dismissals. He removed officials for valid reasons, often because they violated one of his moral legalisms; but
the jobs thus vacated proved a fortuitous way of rewarding political
friends. Catts candidly admitted his determination to make places
for his friends, a course in which he saw no sin. On one occasion he
dismissed four state inspectors, explaining frankly that they were
not in harmony with the administration.[65] His Jacksonville explanation of the Lewis appointment bears the same mark of credibility. Therefore, there is no reason to disbelieve his explanation that
he had removed men because of their drunkenness, inefficiency, or
malfeasance. Furthermore, he often reappointed officials when
hearings before the governor convinced him that the charges were
invalid. Following such hearings, he reinstated the Volusia County
Board of Commissioners, the state's attorney for the fifteenth judicial circuit, a member of the state road department, and even
Duval County sheriff Dowling who was reappointed when a hearing before Catts could not substantiate the specific claims of
wrongdoing. The governor frequently issued public statements ef-
fusively regretting suspensions in cases where charges were not
sustained. As in his ministerial career in Alabama, his impulsive
temper led to hasty action which in turn created public embarrassment.

Those officials who did not fare so well often appealed to the
state senate for vindication. The senate, center of legislative opposition to Catts, usually obliged them. The legislature overrode
many of his suspensions, threatened him with impeachment, and
considered a constitutional amendment restricting gubernatorial
removals. The 1919 legislature reimbursed a dozen suspended offi-

64. *Ibid.*, August 11, 1920.
65. *Ibid.*, June 31, 1917.

cials a sum amounting to over eighteen thousand dollars. Among officials reinstated were Duval County commissioner L. L. Meggs, Polk County sheriff John Logan, and Escambia County sheriff J. C. Van Pelt. [66]

Punitive legislative action bothered the governor very little, for he had rationalized such actions with his devil's theory of state politics. In a pamphlet entitled "Open Letter to the Public," Catts replied to those legislators who sought his impeachment on the grounds of his dismissal of state officials and partisan appointments. He promised to continue expelling incompetents even if the senate did reappoint them. The truth was that "all of these knocks that Catts is getting come from the Catholics, the Tampa *Times*, *Dixie*, Ocala *Star*, Orlando *Reporter-Star*, and such papers, the politicians who desire to fool the people and a bunch of corporation lawyers who have had control of Florida for the past thirty years, and who do not desire to resign their positions of bossism." The attempt at impeachment was the inevitable result of his standing up to "every politician, the Catholic Heirarchy, the big corporation interests, and every other agency of power."[67]

The administration of Sidney J. Catts was traumatic for public officials who for reasons of incompetence, moral turpitude, or, more rarely, political disagreement, came under the governor's meticulous scrutiny. There is no reason to question the judgment of W. T. Cash, historian of Florida's Democratic party and himself a legislator during the Catts years, who wrote that county officials lived in more dread under Catts than in any other four-year period in the state's history. This conclusion alone does injustice to the governor and his administration, however, for the quality of public officials was often inferior, and the governor exercised restraint at least to the degree that he granted hearings and frequently reinstated suspended officials when charges against them could not be sustained. Cash conceded that "a number [of officials] were re-

---

66. *Ibid.*, September 1, 1919; unidentified clipping in Ruby Diamond Papers, Florida State University, Tallahassee.
67. "Open Letter to the Public," undated pamphlet in Box 13, Hodges Papers.

moved justly and there were grounds for complaint in nearly every case."[68] One opposition newspaper recorded Sheriff Hayes Lewis' zealous prosecution of the law in Duval County, and then editorialized: "Whatever else he may have done, Governor Catts has certainly stirred up Tampa, Jacksonville, Key West, Pensacola, and Miami, and the officers in these cities are enforcing the law as never before. To be sure, the war department got behind him, but Gov. Catts summoned the county officials to Tallahassee, held a little conference with them, chopped off a few heads—and the law is now being enforced vigorously. The Governor deserves some credit for his decisive instructions to the officials."[69]

Judged by their performance, many of Catts's appointees distinguished themselves. Joe Earman won almost universal praise for his handling of the Board of Control. The Leesburg *Commercial* had originally opposed Earman's appointment, as it had most of the Catts administration; but when he resigned to become head of the Board of Health, the paper concluded that "no man in public office in Florida in recent years has made a more consistently good record," a judgment shared by much of the state press.[70] W. T. Cash recorded the somber predictions made by leading Democrats of a purge of the state's educational institutions, then analyzed the performance of Catts's appointees, concluding that they had actually strengthened the institutions: "Fortunately he selected excellent men who were able to work a satisfactory compromise. The governor was allowed to put in one of his friends as secretary of the Board [Bryan Mark]... but was kept by diplomacy and otherwise from making more drastic changes."[71]

Although not all his appointees to the Board of Control had the educational credentials necessary to guarantee intelligent decisions, they did possess a dedication to higher education that

68. Cash, *History of the Democratic Party in Florida*, 131–32.
69. Jacksonville *Florida Times-Union*, August 4, 1917, quoting DeLand *News*.
70. *Ibid.*, July 16, 1919, quoting Leesburg *Commercial*, and August 1, 1919, quoting St. Lucie *Tribune* and DeFuniak Springs *Breeze*.
71. Cash, *History of the Democratic Party in Florida*, 131.

allowed Florida to experience exceptional development in its college system. Decisions made by the board were as carefully considered as before the new personnel took control; Earman and Hodges, though the least qualified of his appointees based upon prior training, championed innovative extension programs and avoided the wartime hysteria that threatened academic freedom on many American campuses.

Even Catts's relatives occasionally attracted praise. When Adjutant General Sidney Catts, Jr., left office in 1920, the Ocala *Star*, long a bitter foe of the administration, reversed its harping criticism: "While the Star did not approve of Lieutenant Catts' appointment . . . it must in fairness say that he has done good work, and it is our opinion that his work has weighed more heavily with him than the salary or prestige of the office."[72]

Succeeding governors indirectly confirmed the competence of many of his appointees. J. B. Hodges, a flexible and resilient politician who changed alliances with every new political breeze that swept Florida, would serve in many important posts, including chairman of the state Democratic executive committee. Most immediately, he continued his activities on the Board of Control under Governor Cary A. Hardee.

The appointment of Jerry W. Carter as hotel commissioner proved to be a splendid mating of man and job. Carter's background as a sewing machine salesman had carried him across the state, and the itinerant drummer knew the inadequacies of Florida's commercial hotels as few men of the period.[73] He enacted so many improvements that two succeeding governors reappointed him, a record of longevity unequaled in Florida history. W. T. Cash praised Carter and also J. S. Blitch, who served capably in several offices before becoming superintendent of the state prison

---

72. Jacksonville *Florida Times-Union*, April 28, 1920, quoting the Ocala *Star*.
73. The Jerry W. Carter papers are deposited at the Florida State University Library, Tallahassee, and are rich in materials relating to Carter's activities as hotel commissioner and as railroad and public utilities commissioner. Correspondence and materials before the 1920s are regrettably slim, however.

farm where he distinguished himself as "one of the outstanding prison superintendents in the United States."[74]

The near hysterical charges of nepotism, political purges, and incompetent appointments followed Catts throughout his political career, completely obscuring the legitimate accomplishments of his administration. The Democratic establishment that finally grasped power from him in 1920, abetted by the 1917 and 1919 legislatures, propounded a myth of insane demagoguery coupled with a vindictive craze for revenge that caused the governor to retaliate against the entire body of public officials who had united against him in 1916. Reality presents quite a different story.

The governor, faced with hostile officials, removed enough of them to make way for his own lieutenants and close relatives. In addition, he determined to dismiss officials who drank heavily as he had promised in his campaign and to end prostitution because it offended his own moral sensibilities and because of urgent prodding by the War Department. When removing erring officials, he suspended many who had opposed him, inevitably raising charges of political prejudice. He just as regularly restored his enemies when hearings did not sustain charges against them. In cases where the inept official was a Catts protégé, the governor expressed no less determination to eliminate him. Furthermore, many of his untried associates—notably Earman, Hodges, Blitch, and Carter—proved to be unusually competent men who, long shut out of Florida's rigid political system, contributed meaningfully to the state after being brought into government.

---

74. Cash, *History of the Democratic Party in Florida,* 132.

SIX

Stirring up
Dry Bones

FLORIDA'S CHIEF EXECUTIVE could seek to exercise power in two ways: he could make policy through appointments to various state boards, and he could propose a program to the legislature. In a one-party state such as Florida, policy was determined by the candidate, not the party. He formulated positions during the campaign, then after his election, claimed a mandate from the people to enact his platform. The key to success was the first legislative session after election in which the governor usually wielded the most power he would possess. If his program failed in that session, he could urge voters to elect a new legislature more sympathetic to his wishes, but such appeals rarely succeeded. To a large extent the governor was bound by the ideological predispositions, prejudices, and prior alliances of the legislature.[1]

Even before the first session of the legislature convened in April, 1917, Catts was implementing his campaign promises. Having already disposed of the Shell Fish commissioner, T. R. Hodges, he also removed the guns from the Fish and Game Commission steamer, the *Roamer*. In April, 1917, the federal government expropriated all vessels registered in the customhouse to use as patrol craft during World War I. The *Roamer*, with guns remounted,

1. For a brief, interesting treatment of power relationships in Florida government, see Alice S. Chambers, "The Governor as Chief Administrator" (M.A. thesis, Florida State University, 1953).

saw service once again on the Florida coast; but during the Catts administration it protected Floridians from the "German Menace" rather than harassing state fishermen.

The remainder of his 1916 pledges were incorporated in his first address to the Florida legislature, delivered on April 3, 1917. Catts's message was one of the most progressive up to that time in Florida history, largely restating the goals already outlined in his inaugural speech. He called for sweeping changes in state government predicated on the premise that many laws were antiquated, overly technical, and incomprehensible. His major proposals included: passage of a statewide constitutional amendment to prohibit the sale of alcoholic beverages; use of several hundred convicts for road construction which would allow the state to qualify for federal matching highway funds; economy in government so as to require no additional taxes; a graduated inheritance tax; creation of industrial schools for vocational education; replacing the Bryan Primary Law with runoff elections; the addition of one state auditor to help investigate county financial records; the adoption of initiative, referendum, recall, and a statewide vote which could override judicial decisions; taxation of all church property except church buildings and parsonages; opening all closed ecclesiastical institutions to state inspection; sale of drained Everglades land and transfer of drainage operations to private companies; increasing the number of justices on the supreme court from five to six; creation of a bank guarantee and reserve fund whereby the state would insure deposits against bank failures; and a vague statement calling for reform of labor conditions.[2]

Two of his suggestions deserve further consideration because of their uniqueness and the controversy they provoked. His concept of tax reform necessitated enlarging the powers of the state tax commission. Noting that legislative loopholes allowed many large corporations and estates to escape taxation, he asked that the commission be empowered to investigate untaxed property so that it

2. See State of Florida, *Journal of the House of Representatives*, 1917 (Tallahassee: T. J. Appleyard, 1917), 14–31.

could assume "its just proportion of the burdens of government."[3]

The second proposal was creation of a state prison post to be known as the Friend of the Convicts. Calling the job "a new provision in the history of the world," Catts defined it. An individual would live in the prison in order to hear the convicts' problems. He would "learn their heart-throbs of sorrow and disconsolateness and form a fiduciary relation with these men to such a degree that [he] will take their part as an advocate even as the Son of Man came to earth and took the part of a lost and ruined world with our Heavenly Father."[4] No matter whether the legislature enacted his plan, Catts hoped that the ensuing debate would popularize the concept in other states and lead to its widespread adoption. Many political opponents alleged that the proposal was politically inspired and that the large quantity of pardons granted to convicts during his term were purchased with bribes; but this ignores the genuine sympathy that Catts always had expressed toward men "down on their luck." From his ministerial past he had acquired the belief that when a man erred, he should have a chance to redeem himself, that it was oftentimes the circumstance that provoked criminality. He maintained a naïve faith that if most prisoners had a second chance, they would become productive citizens.[5]

Reaction to his message was favorable, perhaps reflecting the relief of many Floridians over the contrast between the strident emotionalism of his gubernatorial campaign and the moderate reasonableness of his message. In a backhanded compliment, the Gainesville *Sun* disagreed with his advocacy of referendum, recall, and some other reforms, but said that the message had fewer objectionable features than any of the previous three administrations. The paper commended several of the proposals and concluded that Catts was "better posted concerning conditions in Florida than

3. *Ibid.*, 17.
4. *Ibid.*, 33.
5. Interviews, Jerry W. Carter, July 29, 1970, Tallahassee, Mrs. Elizabeth Paderick and Mrs. Alice May Stiegel, May 12, 1972, Jacksonville, Mrs. Ruth Cawthon, May 8, 1972, DeFuniak Springs.

many supposed him to be." The Ocala *Banner* applauded the governor's "mild and conservative production" which was couched in "simple phrases." The conservative *Florida Times-Union* criticized portions of the proposed tax reform, initiative and recall, and the creation of industrial schools; but the editor endorsed the idea of Friends of the Convicts, calling it an innovative concept originated by Catts but destined to spread to other states. President A. A. Murphree of the University of Florida, obviously much relieved by the absence of hostility toward the state's colleges, sent an effusive congratulatory note. He called the message "statesmanlike," said it had a "clear grasp of our peculiar problems of government," and predicted that the document "will stand out conspicuously as a State paper in the history of the various administrations of Florida."[6]

From Catts's allies came predictable votes of confidence. Joe Earman pledged the support of the Palm Beach *Post* on behalf of the governor's program. Tom Watson's Catholic-baiting paper, the *Jeffersonian*, published those parts of the governor's message that dealt with taxation of church property, convent inspection and election reforms. It editorially praised "our friend and champion, Sidney J. Catts," who was "stirring up the dry bones in Florida."[7]

Recognizing the difficulties he would face in the legislature, Catts sought to forge alliances in several directions. The same day that he addressed the legislature, he staged a banquet for members of the cabinet, legislators, and the capital press corps, who were generally hostile to him. In an atypical gesture of humility, he asked his guests to cooperate with his administration.

In negotiations more in keeping with his temperament, Catts sought to fashion a lobby on behalf of his proposals. A number of political friends contributed to a fund for the establishment of a

6. Jacksonville *Florida Times-Union*, April 7, 10, 1917, quoting Gainesville *Sun* and Ocala *Banner; ibid.*, April 4, 1917; A. A. Murphree to Sidney J. Catts, April 6, 1917, in Box 4, A. A. Murphree Papers.

7. Joe L. Earman to J. B. Hodges, April 25, 1917, in Box 13, J. B. Hodges Papers; the *Jeffersonian,* April 12, 1917, copy in Florida VF, "Governors—Catts, Sidney J.," Florida State Library, Tallahassee.

Prohibition-Democratic headquarters in Tallahassee which would furnish lawyers and stenographers free of charge to aid the drafting of legislation. The chairman of the Duval County Democratic Executive Committee served as treasurer of the fund that financed operations during the entire 1917 legislative session. [8]

Catts also courted organized labor whose lobby exerted some influence. He had always sympathized with the workingman, a sentiment that stemmed from his belief that laborers were not provided adequate opportunities to better their conditions because of a lack of education. Jerry Carter verified the governor's genuine regard for laborers, but added that his interest in the late teens and twenties was also "damn good politics." Catts appointed John C. Privett, former lobbyist for the state Federation of Labor, to the position of State Labor Commissioner, and Privett frequently joined the governor at his public rallies and speeches. The Florida State Federation of Labor, representing twenty-four thousand members, met in Tallahassee during the second week of April and endorsed a legislative package similar to that of Catts. L. R. Campbell of Tampa remained in the capital as a lobbyist for the federation, urging passage of fifteen key measures, most of them included in Catts's address. [9]

The governor would need all such help because the upper house of the state legislature looked askance at most reform legislation. As early as December, 1916, Catts had predicted trouble with the senate. [10] This estimate was not so much a clairvoyant prediction as an accurate backward reading of the 1916 campaign. Numerous legislators, particularly senators, had actively campaigned for Knott, raising doubts as to their willingness to cooperate with the new governor. Nor was the rancorous campaign with its personal abuse likely to be forgotten when the doors to the senate and house chambers swung open in April.

8. Jacksonville *Florida Times-Union*, March 29, 1917.

9. Interviews, Jerry W. Carter, July 29, 1970, Tallahassee, Mrs. Ruth Cawthon, May 8, 1972, DeFuniak Springs. See also Jacksonville *Florida Times-Union*, April 4, 5, 12, 1917.

10. Birmingham *Age-Herald*, December 14, 1916.

The Jacksonville *Florida Times-Union* had written each state legislator in 1916, requesting that he summarize his views on matters to come before the legislature. During the succeeding five months, the paper printed each response. Perusal of these statements reveals that many legislators, particularly in the house, favored the same basic reforms proposed by the governor. Only the issue of what to do about the Bryan primary law seemed to divide them beyond hope of some kind of compromise. Many expressed interest in the guarantee of bank deposits, tax and election reforms, prohibition, improved education, reapportionment, and better roads.[11] Although conservatives dominated the senate, their public statements on substantive issues provided some room for compromise had not corporation pressure and personal animosity figured so prominently in the legislative process.

To gain leverage, Catts attempted to weld an administrative coalition among the legislators. His aides distributed a form letter to each member asking if he intended to support the governor's proposals.[12] From the responses, Catts detected his problems and strengths among the lawmakers. His most loyal lieutenant in the thirty-two-member senate was James E. Alexander of DeLand, representing the twenty-eighth district. Alexander was a native of Covington, Tennessee, and a former classmate of Catts at Cumberland Law School. He had previously served two terms in the legislature (1892 and 1908), where he had actively opposed child labor while favoring better schools and roads. He was a personal friend of the governor and seldom strayed from the administration camp.

J. B. Hodges exerted considerable influence on the Columbia County delegation which included Senator M. L. Plymton of Lake City who vowed to support the governor's general plan of legislation and dismissals. The county's two representatives, W. J. Roebuck and A. G. Withee, split their loyalties. Roebuck was an original Catts veteran from the beginning of the 1916 race; Withee

11. For legislative reports, see Jacksonville *Florida Times-Union*, December 3–12, 17, 21–23, 27–28, 1916, January 6, 10, February 6, 9–11, 13, March 22–23, 27, April 1, 1917.
12. Samuel F. Flood to J. B. Hodges, March 7, 1917, in Box 13, Hodges Papers.

was doubtful but was a client of J. B. Hodges, who felt that with Roebuck's assistance he might persuade Withee to side with the administration.[13]

Two representatives who performed important service for Catts were Arthur Gomez of Key West (Monroe County) and McQueen Chaires of Oldtown (Lafayette County). Gomez, who had been a barber before taking a law degree, became closely identified with the administration, often traveling over the state with the governor. Chaires sought spoils from J. B. Hodges and was responsive to the patronage available from the administration.[14]

The first day of the legislature was spent in organizing committees and selecting senate and house leadership. The little town of Live Oak in Suwannee County furnished both the president of the senate, John B. Johnson, and the speaker of the house, Cary A. Hardee. Friction between legislators and the chief executive developed immediately. On the second day of the session, Representative Roebuck warned Hodges that the "anti-administration forces are working both day and night."[15] The campaign wounds of 1916 had not healed.

More than anything else, the governor needed to cultivate the friendship and confidence of wavering legislators who knew of his emotionalism but were still willing to work with him for common objectives. The legislative process barely had begun, however, when Catts made another of his thoughtless extemporaneous speeches. Newspapers reported that while speaking at Tallahassee's Leon High School he had said that if any member of the legislature became drunk during the session, the governor would lock him in jail for sixty days. On April 5, with the session only three days old, a resolution was introduced in the senate censoring the chief executive for reflecting on the legislature and for actions "unbecoming the dignity of the high office of the governor." James

13. J. B. Hodges to Samuel F. Flood, March 15, 1917, W. J. Roebuck to Hodges, April 4, 1917, *ibid.*
14. J. B. Hodges to McQueen Chairs, January 11, 1917, *ibid.*
15. W. J. Roebuck to J. B. Hodges, April 4, 1917, *ibid.*

Alexander, Catts's floor leader, warned that if the bill came out of committee, he would amend the penalty proposed by Catts to provide 120 days in jail; he recalled that the Sturkie resolution had made Catts governor, and prophesied that this resolution would make him president. Cooler heads prevailed on both sides, and a legislative committee conferred with Catts, who explained that he had been misquoted. He had commented that whiskey had been used freely to defeat a prohibition bill in 1915, and had added that if any lawmaker became inebriated when the prohibition issue came up in 1917, he would have the errant legislator jailed.[16] This unconvincing explanation did not augur well for amicability between executive and legislature.

Fulfilling a postelection pledge, Catts recommended confirmation of all Democratic primary nominees. This action helped ease the tension and met approval in the press, though the governor was to make several exceptions later.

With preliminaries completed, lawmakers set the machinery of government going, and a steady stream of legislation began appearing in mid-April. One of the early acts dealt with prohibition, a topic on which Catts had taken a strong public stand. This issue had received much attention in Florida, and a majority of counties were already dry by local option. On April 4, William Jennings Bryan lent his prestige to the cause, addressing a large Tallahassee audience. Representative N. C. Bryan of Osceola County introduced a bill prohibiting the manufacture, sale, or use of alcoholic beverages by a constitutional amendment to be ratified in a statewide referendum in November, 1918; if passed it would become effective on January 1, 1919. The bill sailed through the house on April 10 by a vote of 64 to 6, ironically with several Catts supporters in opposition (Chaires and Gomez). It passed the senate on the same day by a 29 to 3 vote, with Jacksonville Senator Ion Farris, who normally voted with the administration on reform measures, also opposed.[17]

16. Jacksonville *Florida Times-Union*, April 6, 14, 1917.

17. See State of Florida, *General Acts and Resolutions Adopted by the Legislature of Florida*, 16th Reg. Sess., April 3–June 1, 1917, Vol. I (Tallahassee: T. J. Appleyard, 1917), 324.

Catts signed the bill on April 18, the first completed piece of legislation signed into law during his administration.

Two other perennial issues converged to provide a second major victory for the administration. During two decades of criticism, many southern states had abolished or at least substantially modified the system whereby state convicts were leased to work for private businessmen. Abuses and brutality had become flagrant, and public sentiment against the system had intensified in Florida. In 1911 Governor Albert W. Gilchrist had vetoed a bill that would have phased out the system gradually. Governor Park Trammell had opposed convict leasing, and a bill backed by him had passed the house only to fail in the conservative senate. The legislature did provide for a prison farm, but private leasing also continued.[18]

In the 1916 gubernatorial campaign, none of the candidates had advocated an end to leasing. Catts's residence in DeFuniak Springs had exposed him to the abuses visited on convicts leased to the turpentine camps, and he was determined to improve conditions; the influence of Jerry Carter reinforced this conviction. Carter's business frequently had taken him into the turpentine camps of the Florida panhandle where he had seen Negro convicts chained to their beds inside long barracks. The chains were barely long enough for them to reach the window, which served as the prisoners' toilet. One such barrack filled with convicts had caught fire, and the convicts, still chained to their beds, were helpless as fire engulfed them. A combination of Catts's concern and Carter's pleading brought a pledge from the governor to seek abolition of the system.[19]

Catts decided to utilize Florida's good roads movement as a vehicle for ending convict leasing. A state so dependent on tourism needed highways for the increasing volume of automobile traffic. The agitation for better roads became almost as intense in Florida as the pressure for prohibition, and providing a framework for im-

18. See N. Gordon Carper, "The Convict Lease System in Florida, 1866–1923" (Ph.D. dissertation, Florida State University, 1964).

19. Interviews, Jerry W. Carter, May 15, 1964, July 29, 1970, Tallahassee, Mrs. Ruth Cawthon, May 8, 1972, DeFuniak Springs.

plementing the program constituted one of the major accomplishments of Catts's administration.

Ed Scott, chairman of the Florida State Road Department,
submitted a lengthy report in January, 1917, aimed at extensive
improvement of highways. The report called for the use of prison
laborers and the appropriation of $280,000 over a two-year period
to maintain the convict labor force; such an appropriation would
allow the state to acquire matching federal funds. Financing could
come from a state license fee and bond issue. Local booster clubs
and good road associations vigorously endorsed the proposal, while
members of the State Road Department lobbied with the governor
on March 6. They recommended a system of state highways to be
built and maintained by the road department; these would be
supplemented by county or lateral roads left under the control of
county commissioners as in the past.[20]

The Florida State Good Roads Association held its twentieth
annual convention in Tallahassee in April, 1917, during the legislative session. It issued a statewide publication entitled *Good Roads
in Florida,* and constituted an effective political lobby. Catts accepted an invitation to address the group and pledged his support.
Ed Scott explained to the convention that Florida could not receive
its proportion of federal funds unless the legislature acted on the
governor's proposal to use state convicts to provide Florida's share
of matching funds.[21]

Representative Telfair Stockton introduced a package of state
highway bills in April, and on May 2 the senate passed the package
providing matching state highway funds, uniform auto laws, and
authorizing the State Road Department to construct roads and
bridges. It also provided for the appointment of members to the
road department and employment of a state road commissioner.
When the upper house rejected the use of convicts in road construction, state road officials adopted technical changes to make the

20. For full report see Jacksonville *Florida Times-Union,* February 1, 1917. For Road
Department recommendations, see *ibid.,* March 7, 1917.
    21. *Ibid.,* April 12, 1917.

bill more acceptable. The senate approved this modified version, and on May 28, the compromise was approved by the house. The Convict Lease Act provided that state prison doctors would examine all prisoners and grade them according to physical condition and the work they could safely perform. No prisoner could be worked more than sixty hours a week or eleven hours in any one day. Three hundred convicts were assigned to the State Road Department; but any Negro male convict not employed on the roads or prison farm still could be leased privately for two years.[22]

Implementation of the act required investigation of various types of convict road camps in other states. W. A. McRae, commissioner of agriculture, and Attorney General Van Swearingen were instructed to conduct this research and were impressed by what they called "model camps" at Atlanta, Charlottesville, and Trenton, New Jersey. One feature of these camps was the trustee system which eliminated chains on the convicts. By July, 1918, the road department had established five road camps using convicts, and their work was of high quality.[23]

Although use of convicts on road projects modified the leasing system, it by no means eliminated it. The state continued to work many convicts on the state prison farm at Raiford and offered 650 prisoners for lease at a minimum charge of three hundred dollars each. Abuses occurred both on the prison farm and with leased convicts, causing the governor to propose more radical changes to the following legislature.

The governor also had begun a practice of regular visitation to all state institutions, including the prison farm, which he continued throughout his administration. Catts's chief spokesman in the senate, James E. Alexander, introduced a concurrent resolution in May to send a committee of three representatives and two senators to inspect the prison farm. Alexander, reflecting Catts's own findings, revealed a pattern of inhumane treatment of prisoners in-

22. *Ibid.*, May 4, 29, 30, 1917; Carper, "The Convict Lease System in Florida, 1866–1923," p. 300.
23. Jacksonville *Florida Times-Union*, September 19, 1917, and July 17, 1918.

fected with tuberculosis who were forced to sleep with uninfected
cell mates. The prison physician, however, defended medical care
for prisoners, and Alexander's fellow senators ridiculed his proposal, calling it the result of a "junketing trip"; they offered ludicrous
amendments and called on the senator to pay expenses of the
committee if he were so interested in the health of prisoners.[24]
Catts would have to obtain basic reform by changing the personnel
administering the prison system, not by pricking the conscience of
the 1917 senate.

The issue which had dominated the campaign figured insig-
nificantly in the legislature. Perhaps the governor had attacked
Catholics for the cynical purpose of obtaining office; or he may have
observed that restrictive legislation would alienate many citizens.
Superintendent of Education William N. Sheats, a bitter foe, wrote
a distressed friend not to be unnecessarily alarmed at Catts's election: "I believe the Catholic fright will end in nothing. He and his
followers will learn that public sentiment will not endorse the agitation of religious questions."[25] Whether for this or other reasons,
Catts's only effort to impose restrictions on Florida's Catholics was
a convent inspection law. Representative W. G. Seals of Bradford
County introduced House Bill 304 by which the governor would
appoint a commission to inspect all privately owned institutions,
sectarian schools, seminaries, and convents. The bill sparked a divisive debate, and Bishop Michael J. Curley of St. Augustine
penned an open letter to house speaker Cary A. Hardee protesting
the bill. Opposition legislators termed the Seals bill an attack on
religious freedom and a bigoted piece of legislation, but it passed by
a vote of 56 to 11. The senate, despite the membership of only one
Catholic legislator, proved more reluctant, but a weakened inspection bill finally passed on May 30 by a vote of 18 to 12. The governor triumphantly signed the bill into law, and the act inspired similar action in other southern states. The punitive legislation was not

24. *Ibid.*, May 4, 1917.
25. William N. Sheats to Mrs. Katherine Baron, December 5, 1916, on Reel 2, Folder
36, William N. Sheats Papers.

enforced, however, and Catts made no serious attempt either to persecute Catholics or to pass more repressive measures.[26]

The legislature handed the governor another victory by confirming his decision to rid Florida of the *Roamer*. Although the federal government had temporarily expropriated the vessel, the state retained legal title. Representative A. G. Withee of Columbia County, a Hodges protégé, introduced a bill in the house to sell, loan, or lease the steamer. The house passed the measure with only one dissenting vote, and the senate quickly ratified this action. Catts signed the bill on May 12.[27]

Election reform also figured prominently in the legislative session amid widespread disgust over operation of the Bryan primary law. After two days of debate, a bill to "reform" electioneering practices passed the house on May 14 by a surprisingly lopsided vote of 55 to 7. The bill provided for a runoff primary in event that no candidate received a majority in the first vote. Section three of the bill, obviously aimed at Catts, required of all primary candidates a loyalty oath to neither vote for the nominees of any other party nor to accept the nomination of another political group. The senate adopted an amended version, and during a debate that lasted nearly the entire last night of the session, a conference committee approved a compromise acceptable to both houses. The Terrell primary bill, adopted on the last legislative day, was primarily the work of Senator Glenn Terrell of Tallahassee. It provided for a loyalty oath, a runoff primary, indirect election of the state Democratic executive committee, and ballots to be marked on a table in view of election managers. Even newspapers that opposed the administration blistered the Terrell Act as an "ill-

---

26. Bishop Michael J. Curley to Cary A. Hardee, April 21, 1917, published in Jacksonville *Florida Times-Union*, April 26, 1917. See David Page, "Bishop Michael J. Curley and Anti-Catholic Nativism in Florida," *Florida Historical Quarterly*, XLV (October, 1966), 115–16. For the legislative record of anti-Catholicism in Florida, see Robert B. Rackleff, "Anti-Catholicism and the Florida Legislature, 1901–1919," *Florida Historical Quarterly*, L (April, 1972), especially 362–64.

27. *Journal of the House of Representatives, 1917*, pp. 849, 1190–91, 1242, 1321, 1330; see also Florida, *General Acts and Resolutions Adopted by the Legislature of Florida*, 16th Reg. Sess., April 3–June 1, 1917, p. 276.

considered," last minute remedy that destroyed the secret ballot. One editor conceded that he had thought the Bryan primary law was "as rotten a measure" as could be devised; "but the Terrell Act showed "a progressiveness in rottenness that is simply amazing."[28]

Governor Catts agreed, calling even the ineffective Bryan law superior to the new measure. Complaining that inadequate consideration had been given the eleventh hour legislation, he vetoed the act on June 9. His veto won statewide approval, eliciting praise from most of the state press. The Milton *Gazette* editorialized that it was only "through the wisdom and courage of Gov. Catts that... [the Terrell Act] was prevented from being foisted upon the people." Even the vituperative Gainesville *Sun* admitted that Catts had done one deed which "we heartily approve."[29] The moment was a high hour for the otherwise harassed governor.

Several additional election bills were introduced, including Senator Ion Farris' constitutional amendment to provide for recall and referendum, but they were unsuccessful. A provision for woman suffrage revealed an inexplicable ambivalence in the governor. The bill, drafted by former Governor William S. Jennings and introduced in mid-April, extended the franchise to women, and Mrs. William Jennings Bryan addressed the Florida legislature on behalf of equal suffrage. The senate voted 19 to 9 against the woman suffrage amendment, but a number of senators were absent; upon reconsideration, the upper house submitted the amendment to a statewide referendum by a vote of 23 to 7. Catts's leader in the senate, James E. Alexander, voted for the act. When the amendment went to the house, it failed by five votes to receive the requisite three-fifths majority; 40 members favored it (including Gomez and Chaires), while 27 opposed. Despite the governor's frequent speeches endorsing woman suffrage, he made little effort to push the equal rights amendment through the legislature.

28. Jacksonville *Florida Times-Union*, May 15, June 2, 1917. For press reaction, see *ibid.*, June 11, 1917, quoting Lakeland *Telegram* and Bradenton *Herald*.
29. *Ibid.*, June 19, 1917, quoting Orlando *Reporter-Star*, Milton *Gazette*, and Gainesville *Sun*.

Of the fourteen bills which he vetoed in 1917, five of them were municipal suffrage bills which extended the vote to women in local elections. Catts claimed that the constitution restricted the ballot to men, and the legislature did not possess authority to permit a municipality to unilaterally enfranchise women. Only a constitutional amendment could legally accomplish that objective. He hopelessly confused the issue, however, by approving some local municipal suffrage bills while vetoing others.[30] Perhaps his attitude toward the issue was still evolving, for after 1917 Catts unequivocally supported woman suffrage.

Labor problems also assumed a high priority in the administration. Florida was more heavily industrialized than other southern states, with a consequent increase in workers engaged in manufacturing. Unionization also played a significant role in politics. Lobbyists for the American Federation of Labor found the governor receptive to their proposals, but confronted a reluctant legislature. L. R. Campbell of Tampa and John Privett enjoyed some success lobbying in the house but ran into strong opposition from the senate. The labor lobbyists centered their efforts on the passage of fifteen measures, including a statewide compulsory school attendance law, a maximum eight-hour day act, an anti-injunction bill, a provision for workmen's compensation, a law prohibiting child labor, a measure for semimonthly pay, a law creating a bureau of labor, a boiler inspection law to prevent explosions, and several other provisions.

Initial progress on these bills excited optimism among union leadership. A house committee reported favorably on Representative Arthur Gomez' bill establishing a maximum eight-hour day for laborers on state contracts and for all county and city employees. Representative James M. Johnson of Escambia County also won favorable treatment for his proposal requiring semimonthly pay-

30. *Ibid.*, April 17, 24, 26, 1917. The best study of woman suffrage in Florida is Kenneth R. Johnson, "The Woman Suffrage Movement in Florida" (Ph.D. dissertation, Florida State University, 1966). Johnson attributes Catts's inconsistency to personal political conflict with the legislature, which seems a likely possibility. See 178–80, 229, 243.

days by all businesses in Florida with a payroll of ten thousand dollars or more per month. The bill, reportedly aimed at the Louisville and Nashville Railroad, would have exempted small businesses. The committee also approved a measure introduced by Representative H. S. McKenzie of Putnam County guaranteeing a minimum weekly wage of five dollars for women employed six days a week. A bill requiring full crews on trains passed, but opponents rallied to strike out the enacting clause by a thirty-seven to thirty vote; Gomez and Chaires voted with labor against the majority, while Roebuck, another Catts loyalist, voted with the majority. Despite this defeat, lobbyist Campbell was elated over the progress of labor legislation in the house.

Organized labor did not fare so well in the upper chamber. Three men championed the interests of workers: Catts's senate leader, James E. Alexander, progressive Ion L. Farris, and Doyle E. Carlton. Farris, representing the labor stronghold of Jacksonville, had to leave school at sixteen to assist his father in the boilermaker trade, and carried from that experience a deep sympathy for workers. Carlton was a graduate of the University of Chicago and Columbia University law school serving in his first elective office from Tampa, the most active unionist city in Florida. Senator Glenn Terrell sometimes voted with the labor forces and himself wrote bills creating a state labor inspector and limiting the age and hours of child laborers.

Senator Farris introduced eight-hour-day and anti-injunction bills, while Carlton backed semimonthly pay, creation of a state bureau of labor, and a boiler inspection bill. Senator Alexander drafted Senate Bill Twenty-three that created a three-member industrial board appointed by the governor to judge injury claims lodged by laborers. The bill established sweeping compensation provisions and placed the burden of proof on employers. The fate of Carlton's semimonthly pay bill was typical of the entire labor slate. Opponents of the bill amended it to apply to any business employing one worker instead of the original twenty-five, convinced that this would kill it. Senator Farris charged that railroads, against whom the measure was directed, made interest on their

Sidney Johnston Catts rides on the back seat of his famous Ford for the inaugural parade at Tallahassee, 1917. His son Rozier is driving, and beside him is Catts's campaign manager, J. V. Burke.

Governor Catts reads his inaugural address, calling for major reforms in Florida government.

Florida state Chautauqua headquarters on the lakeshore in Catts's hometown of DeFuniak Springs was the site of many of his speeches.

The Catts home in DeFuniak Springs which the family occupied after they retired from the Governor's Mansion at Tallahassee in 1920.

Governor Sidney Johnston Catts.

Joe L. Earman, West Palm Beach
publisher who gave financial aid to
the Catts family, finally came to de-
test "Old Catts."

J. B. Hodges, a Lake City attorney, was a long-time crony of Catts.

money by paying their workers only once a month. Senate president John B. Johnson, who had represented railroads in his legal practice, led the forces seeking to amend the bill and won an eighteen to twelve victory. Senators Alexander, Carlton, and Farris all opposed the amendment, but organized labor left Tallahassee in 1917 with little to show for its vigorous lobbying.

The education lobby was more successful. In the first days of the session, Representative A. H. Williams of Leon County introduced bills requiring statewide school attendance and providing free textbooks. The latter proposal levied a one-half-mill tax to finance the bill. Following the most animated debate of the session, the house passed the free textbook measure by a vote of thirty-seven to thirty-two, with Gomez, Roebuck, and Withee siding with the majority. Doyle Carlton sponsored the legislation in the senate where, despite much support from the press, the bill was indefinitely postponed.

Representative W. T. Cash of Taylor County, a highly respected legislator who served as chairman of the house committee on education, tried to salvage the purpose of the Williams proposal by creating a state school book commission which would adopt a uniform series of school texts in order to reduce book prices. The bill passed the house on May 11 and the senate on May 28. The Uniform Text Book Act, which was finally signed into law, created a commission composed of two teachers from each of four levels—college, high school, elementary, and primary—plus two county superintendents. Cash also supported a bill creating a state board of examiners which would test schoolteachers and prescribe requirements for certification. The bill slipped through both houses of the legislature and was signed by Governor Catts on June 9. A final education bill which funded Florida's school system was passed in May.

Turning its attention to other matters, the house rejected by one vote a bill creating a second mental hospital to be located in southern Florida, while the senate passed Senator Carlton's bill allowing counties to establish tuberculosis hospitals. The legislature demonstrated more concern for diseased crops and animals than for infirm people, passing a nearly half-million-dollar appropriation to eradicate citrus canker and cattle ticks. The legislators also established a state marketing bureau to help farmers market their crops, and a state livestock sanitary board to suppress hog cholera and cattle ticks. The legislature adopted a state game law, but Governor Catts, in a veto which reflected the underlying conflicts between executive and legislative branches, rejected the proposal because the game warden was chosen by the Board of Commissioners of State Institutions rather than by appointment of the governor or by popular vote.[31]

Despite his occasional victory in minor skirmishes, the governor watched helplessly while the senate emasculated his program. His Friend of the Convicts concept made no progress, while attempted reforms in apportionment of the legislature, Everglades drainage, taxation, and banking practices encountered stiff resistance.

Drainage of Everglades swampland had been a major state priority since the administration of Governor Napoleon Broward. Catts had affirmed his determination to continue the project during the campaign but reversed himself in his legislative message when he proposed the sale of both drained land and remaining swampland to private companies. This reversal was consistent with recommendations of the Internal Improvement Board, administrator of the project, which had recommended that undrained lands be sold. South Florida counties touching the Everglades protested against the change and dispatched a delegation to visit the governor. The committee—consisting of Senator W. L. Hughlett of Cocoa and Representatives W. H. Marshall of Broward, John W. Watson of Dade, and J. M. Swain of St. Lucie counties—argued that undrained lands would sell for only five or six dollars an acre whereas after drainage the same land would bring fifty to one hundred dollars per acre. They offered an alternative to Catts's

31. For a brief comment on the legislative history of these measures, see Jacksonville *Florida Times-Union*, May 3, April 16, May 5, April 21, May 29, June 1, 1917.

scheme—an independent drainage commission. Catts was unconvinced, and the committee promised to oppose his move in the legislature even though Catts, in a fit of temper, countered by threatening to veto any drainage commission bill. More significant than the delegation's visit was the adherence of Joe Earman to the cause of continued drainage. Earman published his newspaper in Palm Beach County, one of the largest Everglades counties. He declared that the Everglades should forever remain in the hands of the trustees of the Internal Improvement Fund, composed of the governor and his cabinet. His newspaper urged a continuation of current drainage policy.[32]

Legislative proposals to alter Everglades policy were soon engulfed in furious opposition. When Senator W. M. Igou of Eustis introduced a bill authorizing the IIF trustees to sell swamplands, the senate committee on Public Lands and Drainage refused to recommend the bill, which was tabled.[33] A new lobby, the Everglades Drainage League, sponsored a bill to abolish the IIF, but the bill was substantially modified. The final legislation which finally was enacted created a new drainage district but altered the previous system very little. The state also provided fire protection for the volatile drained lands and created experiment stations. Catts apparently lost his enthusiasm for changing the system under the impact of Earman's opposition and played little role in the legislative wrangling.

Catts's unwavering endorsement of reapportionment contrasted with his equivocation on drainage policy. The inequity of legislative apportionment was obvious to even the most apolitical citizen. According to the 1915 state census, Florida had increased its population by 172 percent since the only reapportionment in Florida history had occurred in 1887; a 50 percent increase had occurred in the preceding decade alone. The result was a state with

32. *Ibid.*, April 11, 17, 1917.
33. State of Florida, *Journal of the State Senate of Florida, 1917* (Tallahassee: T. J. Appleyard, 1917), 809, 1551.

an estimated 1915 population of over 900,000 and one of the most
malapportioned legislatures in America.[34] In the November, 1916,
general election, Floridians had rejected a reapportionment
amendment which would have given even less representation to
the larger counties. The south Florida press harped on the issue,
promoting it to the status of a major crusade in the burgeoning
southern half of the peninsula.

Whether because of unfamiliarity with state government or lack
of interest, the new governor omitted any reference to reapportionment in his inaugural or legislative messages. This surprised no
one since the governor came from the overrepresented panhandle
which stood to lose power in any major reorganization. In mid-May
the governor shocked the legislature with a carefully researched
special message demanding equitable apportionment. He noted
that the state constitution provided for reapportionment every ten
years, an obligation unheeded for three decades. Catts pointed to
the glaring misrepresentation which had resulted: seven counties
(Nassau, Jefferson, Columbia, Bradford, Hamilton, Madison and
Putnam) contained a total population of 117,177 out of Florida's
nearly one million persons, but elected eight senators (25 percent
of the total), and fifteen representatives (20 percent of the house).
Duval, Hillsborough and Pinellas counties, rapidly growing urban
areas, contained 197,330 persons, yet elected only two senators
and five representatives. Dade, Broward, Palm Beach, St. Lucie,
and Brevard counties on the lower east coast elected only one
senator to represent a population of 54,827. In an obvious conclusion, Catts instructed: "The fundamental principles of democratic
government are based on equal representation, right and justice to
all classes of citizens. Your duty in this matter is plain."[35]

34. Richard E. Bain, "Legislative Representation in Florida: Historic and Contemporary" (M.A. thesis, Florida State University, 1960), 143–47. Also, see Douglas S. Gatlin and
Bruce B. Mason, *Reapportionment: Its History in Florida*, Civic Information Series No. 24
(Gainesville: Public Administration Clearing Service of the University of Florida, 1956),
8–9.
35. *Journal of the House of Representatives, 1917*, pp. 1679–80.

The special message was a remarkable document to come from the Catts administration. Not only did he represent a panhandle county which profited from the abuse he sought to correct, but in November, 1916, he had won five of the seven counties which he exposed as the most overrepresented. There are three possible explanations of his position. First, he genuinely believed that malapportionment was unconstitutional; secondly, while he had carried most of overrepresented northern Florida in 1916, he also had carried five of the eight counties which he pinpointed as the most underrepresented; thirdly, political alliances may have played some role, though he had powerful aides in both regions (Earman from Palm Beach on the south Atlantic coast, Hodges from Columbia County in north central Florida).

Whatever his motivation, the reaction of a malapportioned legislature was predictable. A motion in the house to consider a reapportionment bill lost on a tie vote thirty-one to thirty-one on May 12, though the lower house passed an innocuous resolution favoring the principle of reapportionment by a thirty-seven to twenty-six vote. The senate killed Senator Farris' reapportionment bill, then voted down a harmless resolution endorsing such reform in principle. A second message from the governor chiding the legislature for its failure to act arrived on the next to last day of the session and had no effect except to create a "strawman" for the uncooperative legislators. The senate passed a resolution which blamed the governor's tardy message for the failure to reapportion.

The legislature underestimated the intelligence of Floridians who howled with indignation at the resolution. The Daytona-Halifax *Journal* editorialized: "The joke of the legislature was the resolution . . . blaming the governor for its failure to pass a reapportionment bill. . . . At any rate they didn't blame it on the war." The Jacksonville *Florida Times-Union* reminded its readers that the constitution was perfectly clear on the subject, and the legislature needed no message from the governor to advise of its duties: "Naturally Governor Catts did not remind the legislature of this duty until late in the session. Naturally he thought the members would do what they swore they would do. . . . Every member was bound by oath to pass this measure."[36] A careful student of legislative representation in Florida concludes that Catts acted vigorously on reapportionment; however, the legislature's only response was to establish two new house seats by creating Flagler and Okeechobee counties.[37]

Catts's proposal for a law to guarantee deposits in state banks also died in the hands of the fickle legislators. Bank failures during 1916 had been frequent enough to contribute to the defeat of W. V. Knott, and Catts had proposed stringent controls of banking practices. C. F. Barber of Baker County introduced a bank depositor guarantee bill in the house, while Senator H. L. Oliver of Apalachicola proposed a similar measure in the upper house. The governor's aides suggested several shrewd moves designed to win passage for the proposal. J. B. Hodges wrote Catts's legislative leader W. J. Roebuck, suggesting that the administration forces investigate the comptroller's office with regard to the cause of recent bank failures, including one in Hodges' hometown of Lake City. Hodges believed that such an investigation would help pass the bank depositor guarantee bill pending in the house. In a similar proposal to Catts, Hodges reminded the governor that Florida's bankers had opposed him in 1916 and proposed an investigation if "it will show something to our advantage. . . . This is purely politics, and if you were running a campaign I would know how to proceed, but you are now running a great state government, and I do not care to prepare and secure the introduction of any resolution that might not be proper." Catts replied that he could not reach a decision on the matter, and would rely on the advice of Hodges and other friends.[38]

The threat of investigation had some effect, and the senate committee on banking reported favorably Senator Oliver's bill.

36. Jacksonville *Florida Times-Union*, June 11, 1917, quoting Daytona-Halifax *Journal*; *ibid.*, June 3, 1917.
37. Bain, "Legislative Representation in Florida," 147.
38. J. B. Hodges to W. J. Roebuck, April 10, 1917, Hodges to Sidney J. Catts, April 13, 1917, Catts to Hodges, April 21, 1917, all in Box 13, Hodges Papers.

Meanwhile, the house passed a bill regulating banks which provided that no financial institution in Florida could lend funds to any officer of the bank or lend an amount exceeding 15 percent of the aggregate capital and surplus to any bank official or company director. It also restricted a bank's investment in stock of another corporation. When the senate refused to act, Catts included a statement in his special message on reapportionment reminding the legislature of the disastrous bank failures of the previous two years. He considered the establishment of a fund to guarantee bank deposits "of very great importance," and advocated an assessment on banks to fund the proposal.[39] The senate ignored the governor's request, and the session ended without affirmative action.

Another central issue before the 1917 legislature was the governor's policy on removals and appointments of public officials. Although the press reaction in the spring of 1917 was negative, it could not affect the changes wrought by the governor. The legislature on the other hand held the prerogative of consenting to these changes or reinstating suspended officials. Since many of the changes affected friends of individual legislators, the angry solons wasted no time expressing their displeasure. The state senate rejected Catts's appointments of James E. Alexander and Milton Pledger to be respectively circuit judge and state attorney in the seventh district. Since Alexander was serving as a state senator and leader of the administration forces in the upper house, the rejection was interpreted as a rebuff of the governor.[40]

This was only the opening volley of a spring-long campaign. Representative Marion T. Jennings of Jacksonville introduced a bill restricting county or state officials from appointing relatives to public office, a move obviously aimed at Catts. In the senate W. M. Igou introduced a bill which allowed circuit courts to review gubernatorial suspensions; the bill passed 21 to 9 with Senators Alexander and Ion Farris among the opposition. Senator Farris of-

39. See *Journal of the State Senate of Florida, 1917*, Jacksonville *Florida Times-Union*, May 8, 1917. See also *Journal of the House of Representatives, 1917*, pp. 1679–80.
40. See Jacksonville *Florida Times-Union*, May 2, 1917.

fered a different approach, one more democratic and sympathetic to the governor. He proposed a constitutional amendment providing that when the governor suspended an official, instead of the senate deciding whether or not to uphold the suspension, the issue would be decided by the citizens directly involved in a special referendum. Farris' bill, however, conflicted with a measure already passed by the senate prohibiting salary payment to a state employee until after senate confirmation.[41]

The governor's opponents in the senate escalated their assault with introduction of the Fogarty bill. Senator J. N. Fogarty of Key West introduced a measure providing that all nominations by the governor had to be confirmed by the senate. Following "the sharpest and most spicy debate of the present session," the bill passed by a vote of twenty-one to ten. Fogarty's major argument in behalf of his bill was that Catts might be planning to withhold many of his appointments until after the legislative session adjourned. Senate President John B. Johnson led the proponents of the bill, while Senators Alexander, Ion Farris, Glenn Terrell, and Doyle Carlton directed the opposition. In a deliberate insult, the senators ignored the formality of referring to "the present executive," mentioning Catts by name in the rough debate. The Fogarty bill was referred to the committee on Judiciary A in the house where it faced tough opposition from a pro-Catts faction led by Representative Gomez of Key West. The committee killed the measure with an unfavorable report submitted by a six to two vote.[42]

All attempts to formally strip the governor of his appointive powers having failed in the house, the senate began a piecemeal attack. It confirmed some of his appointments such as J. S. Blitch and R. J. Patterson to the State Tax Commission, and even upheld many of his suspensions where flagrant abuse was obvious. But in other cases it ignored the governor's actions, restoring officials to office because of insufficient evidence of wrongdoing.[43]

41. *Ibid.*, May 12, 1917.
42. *Ibid.*, May 13, 1917.
43. For examples of the senate restoring officials who had been suspended by Catts, see *ibid.*, May 25, 26, 1917; *Journal of the State Senate of Florida, 1917*, p. 2052.

Catts's rebuttal was two-pronged. During the session, he increasingly alluded to drunken legislators who were trying to destroy him. The speech at Leon High School early in the session set the tone, but other public statements maintained the momentum. J. B. Hodges used the administrative organ, the *Free Press*, to publish drinking biographies of legislators. When Catts hired detectives during the legislative session, some representatives believed they were employed to snoop on the alcoholic consumption in the statehouse, and the house passed a resolution demanding that the governor explain their function. J. S. Smith, member of the state Democratic executive committee and a friend of Hodges and Representative Roebuck, misunderstood the political nature of the offensive and rushed a note to Hodges pleading that his name not appear in the *Free Press* drinking exposé.[44] The second phase of Catts's counterattack came after the session closed. He sought to purge the legislature at the polls.

While overruling many of his suspensions, the legislature paradoxically strengthened the governmental machinery that led to removals. Catts relied on state auditors for most of the investigations of financial irregularities, and his April request for an additional state auditor would increase his capacity to monitor local financial transactions. Whether because the legislature failed to perceive the political ramifications of the request or merely shared the governor's concern for honest government, it acceded to his proposal for an additional state auditor.[45]

The final controversy of the 1917 legislature swirled around the issue of tax reform. From the inception of his administration, Catts had championed a complete overhaul of the tax structure. His most apparent objective, elaborated in his April message to the legislature, was to strengthen the power of the State Tax Commission to equalize tax assessments. On May 22 Catts sent a special message "up the hill" asking for a state inheritance tax bill and for a law

44. Jacksonville *Florida Times-Union*, May 29, 1917; and J. S. Smith to J. B. Hodges, June 29, 1917, in Box 25, Hodges Papers.
45. *General Acts and Resolutions Adopted by the Legislature of Florida*, 16th Reg. Sess., April 3–June 1, 1917, Vol. I, 186.

requiring large corporations chartered by the state to make moderate annual payments based on their capital stock. The governor considered it unjust that corporations paid only a small initial fee to secure a charter and viewed the "reform" as a method of relieving tax burdens on the individual. Both requested bills failed; one suffered a quick burial in committee and the other a lingering demise on the senate floor.[46]

The key to Catts's proposal for the uniform assessment of taxes rested with the success of his request to enlarge the scope and powers of the State Tax Commission. Corporations and railroads, fearful of tax equalization, had fought tenaciously against the commission, trying to abolish it in the 1915 legislature and again in 1917. They constituted a formidable lobby in which Catts's dream of a strengthened commission floundered. The governor's plan died in the house, and the corporation forces, now in command, won a 42 to 25 vote to abolish the commission altogether. Opposition to the measure came mainly from administration forces led by Representative Gomez who charged that the impetus for abolition originated with railroads and corporations. A poll of the senate on April 25 revealed a similar abolitionist sentiment in the upper house, so J. V. Burke, Catts's secretary, warned that the governor would veto any bill that eliminated the commission.[47]

Heedless of the governor's warning, the senate quickly passed the house bill on April 26, despite opposition led by Ion Farris. Part of the legislative solidarity may have stemmed from the appointment to the board of Blitch and Patterson. Both men proved competent, however, and had provoked little opposition when they were confirmed by the same senate. John Neel, chairman of the tax commission, had opposed Catts in the 1916 election, so abolition could not have been a purely partisan issue. Successful lobbying by the railroads is a much more persuasive explanation for the legislature's actions.

John Neel commented on the "strong opposition and prejudice"

46. *Journal of the State Senate of Florida, 1917*, pp. 240, 1675–77, 2307.
47. Jacksonville *Florida Times-Union*, April 26, 1917.

against equal assessment, though without detailing the source of this opposition. Ironically, one of the anticommission lobbyists was a close ally of Governor Catts. J. B. Hodges of Lake City had been linked with the conservative wing of the Democratic party until his sudden conversion to "Cattsism" after the 1916 June primary. He had supported Senator Duncan U. Fletcher against a more liberal challenger in 1914, complaining that the word "progressivism" was thrown around too loosely. His correspondence reveals cooperation with Jacksonville's conservative ringmaker and arch enemy of Catts, Pleasant A. Holt.[48] His reward had come when Fletcher selected him as unofficial patronage boss for Columbia County.

Hodges' service as a railroad attorney had become an issue in the 1916 gubernatorial race when Catts had charged Knott with employing a "railroad lawyer" on his staff. In rebuttal the state Democratic executive committee had noted that Catts's staff included two railroad attorneys, Hodges and A. J. Henry, who served as attorneys for the Georgia, Southern & Florida railroad.[49]

Shortly after the 1916 Democratic primary, J. E. Hall, general counsel for the GS & FRR and Hodges' company intermediary, had requested his estimate of Catts. Hodges, already flirting with the idea of switching allegiance, admitted that the strength of the west Florida candidate had surprised him. The only information he could furnish on Catts's business philosophy was the candidate's advocacy of higher corporation taxes. Hodges concluded: "This is not the howl of the demogogue [sic]. It is a careful statement, and the people swallowed it. It may be that we will be able to show him that under the present system of taxation we are paying our share, or more. At any rate, if he tells the people we are paying enough and should be let alone, they will do so. It may be that he is beaten. I hope he is."[50]

48. *Ibid.*, March 24, 1918; J. B. Hodges to Hiram H. Hodges, May 12, 1914, Hodges to Duncan U. Fletcher, May 29, 1914, P. A. Holt to Hodges, January 27, 1914, Hodges to Holt, January 29, 1914, all in Box 16, Hodges Papers.
49. Form Letter from George P. Rainey, October 31, 1916, in Box 197, Hodges Papers.
50. J. B. Hodges to J. E. Hall, June 13, 1916, in Box 20, *ibid.*

Even assuming that Hodges wrote with his railroad audience in mind, this letter reveals the internal contradictions of the remarkable Catts coalition. When the opportunistic Hodges joined the Catts bandwagon, he brought his railroad friends along as baggage.

Although Hodges was uncertain of the governor's view on corporate taxation, he never feared the legislature's attitude. He wrote his friend Hall shortly after the 1916 primary that he had analyzed the roll of the 1917 legislature and that it was more favorable to railroads than usual. Nothing happened in the spring of 1917 to alter this opinion. Hodges reported in April that senate and house committees were in "very good shape" insofar as the railroads were concerned. Although there had been "some adverse legislation proposed in both houses," he wrote Hall that Catts had no disposition "to urge any legislation that would be adverse to us, except the enlargement of the powers of the Tax Commission." The governor probably would "be very favorable to us on the organized labor bills."[51]

Events soon challenged this estimate to the chagrin of Hodges' railroad clients. W. J. Roebuck wrote Hodges on April 13 that his railroad friends were "somewhat up in the air" because they had experienced "bad days in Court yesterday afternoon and last night." A franchise tax had been reported favorably by Roebuck's committee, while both house and senate committees reported bills increasing the powers of the Railroad Commission. Hodges replied that to say his friends were "'up in the air' hardly expressed it. They seemed to be lost." They were pressuring Hodges, but he complained that they had waited too late and that he was unable to help them. He doubted that the franchise tax would pass, but thought the Railroad Commission bill would become law. Once again Hodges proved to be a prophet. The legislature approved a measure giving the Railroad Commission authority to fix labor rates on toll bridges and causeway work. The house did kill a bill to equalize taxes on railroad property in Florida, causing the proad-

51. *Ibid.;* J. B. Hodges to J. E. Hall, April 7, 1917, in Box 13, *ibid.*

ministration Pensacola *News* to charge that the legislators were merely paying for the free railroad passes given to them.[52] Whether because of passes or pressure, the railroads certainly won more battles in the statehouse than they lost.

Railroad conquest of the legislature proved much simpler than persuading the governor. Catts issued an emphatic veto of House Bill 208 abolishing the tax commission, and elaborated in a stinging message to the legislature. Equality and uniformity of taxation might be an unrealizable dream, but that did not absolve government from the duty to attempt this objective. In order to obtain uniformity in taxation, power must be vested in some state agency with supervisory authority that could cooperate with local officers in a fair and uniform administration of tax statutes: "In my opinion the Tax Commission should not be abolished, but additional and necessary powers should be given it so that it may accomplish the purpose for which it was created." Apparently the message had some effect, for when the house took up the matter again, Catts's veto was sustained, with thirty-eight votes upholding the governor, to only thirty-one who voted to override. Gomez, Chaires, Cash, and Roebuck led those sustaining the veto.[53]

Catts's victory in the house proved illusory. In what was surely one of the weirdest conclusions to a legislative session in Florida history, the senate passed an appropriations bill to finance state agencies minus funds to operate the State Tax Commission. The house received the bill on the next to last legislative day, and countered with an appropriations bill including a thirty-thousand-dollar item for the controversial commission. The senate concurred with all house amendments except this one, and the resulting deadlock was referred to a conference committee. The committee reached a compromise of sorts by conceding that the expenses and salaries of

52. W. J. Roebuck to J. B. Hodges, April 13, 1917, Hodges to Roebuck, April 14, 1917, in Box 13, *ibid.;* Jacksonville *Florida Times-Union,* April 24, 1917, quoting the Pensacola *News.*

53. *Journal of the House of Representatives, 1917,* pp. 1029–31. For the roll-call vote, see 1031–32.

the tax commissioners were provided by statute anyway; so the house acceded to the senate version on the last legislative day. The final act also reduced the salary of Don C. McMullen, Catts's appointee as special counsel for the Railroad Commission, cut the expense account of another official, and restricted the governor's contingency fund.

Catts was outraged and furnished the legislators a spectacular climax to the session. After sending the appropriations bill to the governor, the legislators proceeded with the formality of instructing a committee to notify Catts that the session had ended. They discovered that the chief executive also had prepared a statement for them, and the committee returned with his "startling message." "Mr. Speaker: Your committee have [sic] performed the duty delegated to them.... We are directed by the governor to say to the house of representatives that inasmuch as it had cut out the tax commission [salaries], reduced D. C. McMullen's salary and cut the expense appropriation of Mr. Sheats, he will veto the appropriation bill." The legislators listened in disbelief; the stunned silence ended when the speaker, regaining composure, adjourned the session. Knots of legislators gathered to discuss the remarkable event and speculate about how Florida would finance state government for the following two years. After some reflection, the governor relented, vetoing only those sections of the appropriations bill affecting the salaries of McMullen and Sheats and his contingency fund. Attorney General West declared this selective veto null and void in July.[54]

Since all the governor's attempts to provide a more equitable tax system had been rejected, the individual taxpayer bore the burden of financing new legislation. In an obvious bit of hypocrisy, the legislature and loyalist press blamed Catts for raising taxes. The governor retaliated by blaming the legislature and startled his adversaries by announcing on June 30 that the tax levy would be only nine mills, two mills below the ceiling authorized by the 1917 legis-

54. Jacksonville *Florida Times-Union*, June 2, 5, July 14, 1917.

lature. Rigid governmental economies practiced by the administration allowed the reduction, the governor explained. The DeLand *News*, a frequent critic of the chief executive, saw through the legislative sophistry, stating that "Catts should not be blamed for the high state tax this year—the highest since reconstruction days. The legislature is responsible for the added tax burdens."[55]

During the session the state's lawmakers sent a pompous memorial to Congress requesting it to impose a graduated income tax and regulate war profits to provide more equitable financing of the war. Unfortunately, the Florida legislature's concern for fair taxation seemed to increase in proportion to its distance from the Sunshine State.

It is obvious that Catts faced insurmountable difficulties in the legislature. The absence of any personal political record and the public ignorance of his economic attitudes had allowed a wide range of conflicting interests to back him in 1916. He had drawn support from such disparate sources as populistic farmers and urban Socialists on one hand, to establishment advocates such as J. B. Hodges on the other. Winning an election amid such disparity proved much easier then welding together a reform coalition in the legislature. He had also offended the Democratic clique which controlled the legislative apparatus, especially the senate. Finally, his relatively liberal proposals would probably not have passed the conservative legislature no matter what his working relationship with it; given the additional factors of a year of personal animosity, Catts's ignorance concerning the machinery of government, and a bitterly hostile state senate, it is remarkable that he accomplished anything.

The center of opposition to Catts throughout his four-year term was the state senate, but the minority of that body which supported the governor reveals much about the nature of his administration. Four men—James E. Alexander of DeLand, Glenn Terrell of Tallahassee, W. A. MacWilliams of St. Augustine, and M. L.

55. *Ibid.*, June 21, 1917, quoting Lakeland *Telegram*, July 11 and May 3, 1917, quoting DeLand *News*.

Plympton of Lake City—were friends of the governor and could usually be counted on to loyally support his proposals. More significantly, two men who were not personally loyal to him and had not supported his candidacy almost always voted for his platform. Ion L. Farris of Jacksonville and Doyle E. Carlton of Tampa stood further to the liberal side of Florida politics, yet compiled a voting record equal to Senator Alexander's for supporting the Catts program of reapportionment, bank guarantee, and tax, labor, and educational reform. Farris even opposed stripping Catts of his often abused appointive powers, arguing that the people had known that the governor would have such authority when they elected him. In the house, W. T. Cash of Perry, another outstanding progressive who had opposed Catts, compiled a similar record of supporting the program if not the man. Unfortunately for Catts, the legislature contained too few men who voted for his measures either out of personal loyalty or philosophical preference; but given his surprising strength in the house, a less inflexibly conservative senate might well have made the 1917 legislature one of the most progressive in Florida history. To blame the failure of his reform program on his abrasive personality and ignorance of the machinery of government is to ignore the entrenched conservatism that dominated the Florida state senate. The ability of so many "liberals" to work with Catts, and the governor's own moderation concerning such issues as anti-Catholicism, suggest that pragmatism and reform played a more significant role in the administration than contemporaries realized.

Catts's response to the defeat of much of his program was a typically visceral one. Before the lawmakers adjourned, he warned them that he intended to stump Florida for two years to replace them with a more cooperative legislature. Catts was as good as his word; the offending legislators barely had departed Tallahassee when he announced his vendetta in a June 30 speech to the Florida Press Association meeting in Jacksonville. He denounced the senate for reversing gubernatorial suspension of a county judge who had been so drunk that he had been arrested by his own policemen. Surprisingly, the emotional speech drew frequent applause and a rising ovation at the end, confirming Catts's estimate of public support in his feud with the legislative branch.[56]

J. B. Hodges provided a sinister explanation for the governor's defeats. Appealing to Catts's phobia for Catholics, he explained that "the attitude of the Senate toward you is nothing more than the plan of Catholics." The senators had supported Knott; had cared nothing for the Democratic party, which they had tried to destroy; and only Catts had prevented their "devilish efforts." The senate's attempt to block his appointments was nothing "but a subterfuge, suggested and directed by Catholicism."[57]

Just as the governor sought the defeat of disloyal legislators, he offered lucrative rewards to his faithful. Columbia County's W. J. Roebuck received appointment as a state convict inspector in mid-June, 1917, though rumors of his drinking habit subsequently reached Catts and cost Roebuck his job. The governor rewarded Arthur Gomez on July 21 by removing the incumbent county solicitor for Monroe County and giving the job to his loyal legislator. David Sholtz, who had run against the "courthouse ring" in Volusia County and had supported most of the administration's program in the house, was appointed state food commissioner.[58] This policy rewarded his supporters and created a sorely needed reservoir of strength for Catts; but it also denied him their services in future confrontations, emphasizing the necessity of convincing Floridians to support his proposals and elect legislators who would enact them.

56. *Ibid.*, May 31, July 1, 1917.

57. J. B. Hodges to Sidney J. Catts, April 24, 1917, in Box 13, Hodges Papers.

58. Jacksonville *Florida Times-Union*, September 28, 1917. Also, see Merlin G. Cox, "David Sholtz: New Deal Governor of Florida" *Florida Historical Quarterly*, XLIII (October, 1964), 144.

SEVEN

Waging War and Peace in Florida

POLITICS NEVER FADED from the center of Sidney Catts's attention, but the adjournment of the 1917 legislature did allow him more time for personal interests. While touring the state in July, 1917, he purchased a forty-acre farm in newly established Flagler County where he planned to construct a winter home. A year later, more affluent than when he had taken office, he invested one thousand dollars in the Southern Pyrite Ore Company at Villa Rica, Georgia. The president of Lanier University in Atlanta, C. L. Fowler, interested Catts in the project, and the governor intended to add an additionalfive thousand dollars. Before completing the transaction, he requested a consulting engineer to investigate the project. Warned to be wary, the chief executive demanded the return of his initial investment and threatened to institute legal proceedings.[1]

No activities, whether political or personal, ever distracted the governor from his speaking schedule. From childhood he had been a talker, and his careers—legal, ministerial, sales, and public— utilized this verbosity. He seldom spent a week in Tallahassee without journeying somewhere to speak: to the Lake City Chautauqua, the Jacksonville George Washington birthday celebration, a DeLand barbecue, a Marianna farmers' meeting, or to

1. R. R. Sibley to Sidney J. Catts, August 19, 1918, Catts to Louis Fowler, August 22, 1918, in Box 13, J. B. Hodges Papers.

the Miami Rotary Club. Most Sundays found him in his ministerial role supplying the pulpit of a Baptist or Methodist church. Demand for his oratory outdistanced available time, but he still managed to range outside Florida to address a city-wide rally in Birmingham, to give the commencement sermon at Lanier University in Atlanta, and to preach at Central Baptist Church in Mobile.[2]

For recreation the governor arose near daylight, as had long been his custom, to work in his garden or to read. Catts was no simpleton, despite opinions of his political detractors to the contrary. His speeches reflected wide reading in history particularly. He appealed to rural audiences through a blend of emotion and poor grammar, only to confound urban antagonists with boasts that he had "possibly read all of the literature" that was "currently available in the libraries of the State and all private libraries" at his disposal. He modestly confided in an anonymously authored autobiography that he read "on a dead stretch of eight and ten hours, lying at length upon a couch with one arm thrown over his head and the other holding a book as he absorbs its contents."[3]

During his first months in the capital, such esoteric activity had to compensate for a limited social calendar. Tallahassee was a bastion of the regular Democrats, and the atmosphere was hostile to the new governor and his associates. Catts's daughters often experienced embarrassing confrontations with strangers who derided their father without realizing that the girls were related to him. Young Jerry Carter, Jr., even got into trouble with his schoolteachers because of the emotional 1916 campaign and his father's association with Catts.[4]

Catts's loquacious hospitality soon won friends, however, even among some residents who were initially hostile. The Jerry Carters lived near the governor's mansion, and the chief executive also

2. For examples of his speaking schedule, see Joe Earman to J. B. Hodges, November 24, 1917, in Box 25, Sidney J. Catts to C. Louis Fowler, August 22, 1918, in Box 13, Hodges Papers; *Alabama Baptist,* June 26, 1919.

3. B. J. W. Graham, *Baptist Biography,* II, 57.

4. Interview, Mrs. Elizabeth Paderick, Mrs. Alice May Stiegel, May 12, 1972, Jacksonville, Jerry Carter, Jr., May 8, 1972, Tallahassee.

maintained close relations with the Van Swearingens. New friends included J. G. Kellum, business manager of the woman's college who at first had feared Catts's appointees to the Board of Control; Judge Brown, a prominent Tallahassee jurist; and Judge James Bryan Whitfield, a Supreme Court justice who became a close advisor to the governor. The chief executive enjoyed hunting with Judge Brown, and the two men often journeyed to the outskirts of town, driven by Catts's youngest daughter, Alice May, to shoot quail. The governor's daughters even cultivated a friendship with W. V. Knott's children.

Alice May was only fourteen when the family arrived in Tallahassee, and because her brothers taught her to drive, she became the governor's occasional chauffeur. She would hide near the steps of the mansion and peep at her mother and father as they went out for dinner, Mrs. Catts usually elegantly attired in a black net dress with black necklace. Mrs. Catts labored to fit into the capital's social life, instructing her daughters in the social amenities of drinking coffee and singing to provide entertainment for their friends at the mansion. Unfortunately, none of the girls sang well, so Catts provided guitar lessons for Alice, and she attracted a boyfriend who sang for formal entertainments.

The family remained close despite Catts's busy life. The boys no longer lived with the governor, and Elizabeth, "Bess" to her father, resided in Jacksonville. When the governor visited the port city on official business, he stayed with her unless he had appointments which might disrupt her home. Alice May, named for her mother, was Catts's favorite and the only child still at home. On Sunday afternoons he would take his teenage "flapper" for walks in the woods behind the governor's mansion, discussing trees and Indian lore. On one occasion they saw a snake and the frightened girl ran; Catts stopped her, explaining that the snake would crawl away. The governor was sensitive to the feelings of his children, sensing that his youngest daughter, denied the attention of older sisters and a busy mother, needed companionship.[5]

5. Interview, Mrs. Elizabeth Paderick, Mrs. Alice May Stiegel, May 12, 1972, Jacksonville.

The governor's earlier interest in young people extended beyond his own children. He particularly took a liking to young Jerry Carter, Jr., who remembers the governor as quite different from his flamboyant public image. The governor was reserved, thoughtful, and considerate. On one occasion evangelist Billy Sunday came to the capital for a revival. The Catts family attended the meeting and invited young Carter to sit with them. As had been his ministerial custom, when the services ended he impetuously invited his young guest and the evangelist to visit the governor's mansion. Sunday, attired in a checkered suit and yellow button-up shoes, was a loud and sometimes vulgar speaker, and upon entering the official residence, slapped Mrs. Catts on the back, requesting: "Say Sister Catts, Do you have any food around? I'm starved." It was a difficult moment for the shy, genteel woman and for her angry husband. Although the Carter boy retained his admiration for the governor, he was somewhat disillusioned later as a teenager when he saw Catts with a group of political henchmen, all of them drinking despite the fact that the governor had so strongly advocated prohibition. Carter, retrospectively employing the perspective of a professional psychologist, attributes such inconsistent behavior to Catts's political disillusionment. After entering office as a genuine idealist, four years of frustrating combat with entrenched special interests soured him on reform. The passing of time made him cynical and self-serving.[6] There is some indication, however, that his drinking predated his disillusionment and is symbolic of a deeper contradiction in Catts.

When not engaged in prodigious reading or occupied with family affairs, the governor still found time for an occasional controversy, and the most compelling one in 1917 was the Camp Wheeler affair. On a trip to Washington, Catts had stopped at the Georgia army camp to visit Captain Sidney J. Catts, Jr., who was stationed there. His son related tales of wretched conditions, then introduced him to the commandant of the base who escorted the governor on a tour of the best parts of the facility. Catts, placated

6. Interview, Jerry Carter, Jr., May 8, 1972, Tallahassee.

by the tour, returned to his hotel where he met a woman who was
in tears; she explained that her son was sick and officials would not
let her visit him. She also reported epidemics of measles and
pneumonia at the base, lack of winter uniforms, and overcrowded
housing. The governor returned for a more thorough inspection
and found one thousand troops sick, many of them lying on floors
for lack of hospital beds. Catts immediately dispatched telegrams
to President Wilson, Chief of Staff General Peyton C. March, and
Secretary of War Newton D. Baker, threatening to recall all
Florida troops unless the government took prompt action. To
dramatize his urgency, the governor sent telegrams every hour
until Wilson replied to the fourth one. The president announced
that Major General W. C. Gorgas, surgeon general of the army,
was being sent to inspect the facility. The governor also filed a
vigorous complaint through the Washington office of Senator Duncan U. Fletcher. The senator was home in Florida resting, so his
secretary brought the matter to the attention of Secretary of War
Baker.[7]

As deaths from pneumonia mounted, numerous officials visited
the base, including Senator Hoke Smith of Georgia on November
21 and Surgeon General Gorgas on November 23. Repudiating
alarmist rumors, Gorgas declared the camp to be in fairly good
condition, despite many cases of pneumonia which had developed
from an epidemic of measles. He explained that many troops at the
camp came from the rural South where they had never been exposed to the childhood disease. Few comparable outbreaks had
occurred in northern camps because the draftees came from cities
where they had contracted measles in childhood and built up an
immunity to it. He admitted that some men might have suffered
from inadequate clothing, overcrowding, and unsanitary conditions, but claimed that these problems had been alleviated. Secretary of War Baker reported fifteen hundred cases of measles at
the overcrowded camp hospital but insisted that a new wing under

7. John R. Deal, Jr., "Sidney Johnston Catts, Stormy Petrel of Florida Politics," 152–
53; Jacksonville *Florida Times-Union,* November 17, 1917.

construction would eliminate this problem. Senator Fletcher visited the camp in early December on his way back to Washington, and President Wilson became progressively more concerned. The Senate Military Affairs Committee conducted hearings on the matter in late January, 1918, and Gorgas testified that the War Department had ignored his warnings about overcrowding and inadequate hospital facilities.[8]

Catts, unconvinced by assurance of federal action, visited Camp Wheeler to inspect for himself on December 9. Displeased with what he discovered and aware of the political potential of the situation, he announced that he would leave immediately for Washington to confront authorities with the necessity for drastic action. During his 1920 senatorial campaign against Fletcher he would contrast the incumbent senator's alleged inattentiveness to the plight of Florida troops to his own prompt action which brought relief.

His energy finally resulted in substantial changes, though not all of them were to his liking. The commanding officer of the camp was demoted two ranks, but not before he "busted" young Sidney to private and transferred him to Camp Sill. Despite the consequences to his son, the governor received national attention and praise even from the Florida press, and many soldiers from the Sunshine State who were stationed there never forgot his prompt attention to their troubles.[9]

The chief executive did not need to look for conflicts outside of Florida, for within the state the issue of uniform tax assessment generated enough strife to satiate even his voracious appetite for controversy. Before the legislature had adjourned in June, 1917, it had successfully blocked salary appropriations for the state tax commissioners. A circuit court injunction prevented administration efforts to bypass the legislative roadblock, and there the mat-

8. Ray Stannard Baker, *Woodrow Wilson, Life and Letters: War Leader, 1917–1918* (New York: Charles Scribner's Sons, 1939), 418, 444, 498; Jacksonville *Florida Times-Union*, November 24, 25, 1917.

9. Interview, Mrs. Ruth Cawthon, May 8, 1972, DeFuniak Springs.

ter remained until December, 1917. The state appealed the injunction to the state supreme court, with Attorney General Swearingen arguing the administration's case. The judges unanimously reversed the lower court injunction, arguing that since the law establishing tax commissioners had not been repealed, the state must pay its officials. After six months of economizing, the state tax commissioners drew back salaries, their first pay since legislative adjournment.

Using the favorable court decision as impetus, Catts once again endorsed uniform assessment in an address to the State Tax Association on December 20. Both large and small counties, he believed, ought to assess property at the same proportional rate of 50 percent of real value. The governor's speech amazed the assembled tax authorities, who commented favorably about how well versed the governor was on tax matters.[10]

The campaign against fair assessment conducted by state legislators and corporations finally took its casualties despite Catts's firm support. To remove tax commissioners from the patronage grasp of the governor, the Democratic executive committee placed the office in the primary. John Neel, chairman of the State Tax Commission and a member since it had been organized in 1913, announced his retirement in March, 1918. He commented bitterly about the opposition of special interests: "We have been criticised [sic], 'cussed' and abused—and our salaries held up for six months—because we were trying to do our duty." He had not supported the governor and had intended to resign until the executive committee removed the position from the governor's grip. Although urged by friends to run, he had discovered the field of contenders already crowded and had resigned rather than face the series of hurdles before him. In order to win, a candidate had to suffer through the Bryan primary confusion and then risk the chance that the governor would refuse to appoint him even if he captured the nomination, that the senate might not confirm him, or

10. Jacksonville *Florida Times-Union*, December 21, 1917.

that the legislature might abolish his job. His lengthy resignation did include praise for Catts's 1917 veto of the bill abolishing the commission.[11]

Neel's resignation came amidst a series of statewide meetings begun by Catts to stir up support for tax reform and conducted by J. V. Burke of the State Tax Board, who was also one of the governor's key aides. The ten meetings in different sections of Florida brought together the state commissioners, county assessors, and boards of county commissions and had been designed to equalize assessments. Burke argued that Florida's tax system dated from three-quarters of a century earlier, that it was hopelessly chaotic, and that each county was "a law unto itself." Offering specifics, Burke provided a carefully documented analysis of inequities: Gadsden and Jackson counties in rural northwest Florida assessed land at an average rate of $3.44 and $3.13 per acre; Hillsborough and Pinellas, both urban counties in west central Florida, appraised land at $7.21 and $17.03 per acre. Burke explained that this inequity meant that the affluent did not pay their rightful share and that the poor had to shoulder disproportionate burdens: "The poor man cannot conceal his meager possessions... the man of means can conceal from the assessor his cash, mortgages, notes, stocks, and bonds." In the past the public had been unaware of such injustices, but now that he had revealed the true conditions, he begged the public to support the commission and endorse its survival. According to Burke, the February and March conferences resulted in agreement, with "one or two minor exceptions," to implement the recommendations for equalized assessment which had been adopted by the state tax assessors at their Jacksonville meeting during December, 1917.[12]

Burke's confident prediction of tax reform proved naïve. He had not reckoned with the powerful influence of corporations over local tax policy, and it was precisely at this level that Catts's push

11. For text of resignation, see *ibid.*, March 24, 1918.
12. J. V. Burke to editor, *ibid.*, March 17, 1918.

for uniform assessment floundered. Leon County, containing the capital city of Tallahassee, was among the worst offenders. When Catts determined to enforce the agreements that had been reached during the wintertime conferences, he discovered that one "minor exception" to Burke's consensus was Leon County tax assessor E. B. Eppes. Despite the understanding reached between tax assessors, the board of county commissioners, and the tax commission, Eppes refused to assess railroad property at the same rate imposed by other counties. The governor, infuriated at the tax assessor's recalcitrance, requested an opinion from Attorney General Swearingen as to whether the state could require equalization. Swearingen issued an atypically independent ruling that a county commissioner was not bound by the agreements between tax assessors and the state commission. There was no convincing evidence that Eppes had abused his privileges as county assessor.[13]

The state's conservative press, led by the Tampa *Tribune*, also attacked the tax commission. In some respects the newspaper assault aided Catts, providing additional fuel for a full fledged tax revolt among Florida voters. Joe Earman's Palm Beach *Post* enunciated the administration's defense of the commission, and even the anti-Catts Jasper *News* said a good word on behalf of the agency: "Big business may succeed in doing away with the tax commission, but the people have learned of its value and if the legislature should abolish it the next one will re-establish it with more power. The tax commission is the people's commission."[14] This editor, however, like Burke and Catts, underestimated the influence of special interests over Florida government, for barely a year later the board was abolished.

Attitudes toward tax reform on the state Democratic executive committee heightened the continuing factionalism within the party. The fiasco over the Sturkie resolution had left the committee embarrassed but still dominated by party regulars. Shortly after Catts's installation as chief executive, he had inaugurated a strategy

13. For text of ruling, see *ibid.*, July 1, 1918.
14. *Ibid.*, August 29, 1918, quoting the Palm Beach *Post* and Jasper *News*.

to usurp control of the policy-making committee. John R. Rogers of
Lynne sought J. B. Hodges' backing in his campaign for chairman
of the committee, and offered Hodges the post of secretary-
treasurer should he win. Hodges declined the offer, though he did
recommend an associate for the post.[15]

This first abortive assault on the old guard was only a prelude to
a second engagement which occurred after the 1917 legislative session. When the committee met on February 25, 1918, at Jacksonville's Seminole Hotel, the skirmish lines had already been staked
out on either side of basic policy positions. Attendance included
not only members of the committee, but also most of the party and
administration hierarchy: Senator Duncan Fletcher, speaker of the
house Cary A. Hardee, state treasurer J. C. Luning, state auditor
J. Will Yon, labor inspector J. C. Privett, J. V. Burke of the tax
commission, and J. S. Blitch, Catts's secretary. The first resolution
provided that members of the tax commission run at large, confirming rumors that the committee intended to strip the governor of his
appointive powers. J. B. Hodges led the governor's forces who attempted to strike the key paragraph. The Lake City attorney argued that the commission was part of the governor's office and its
members should include whomever he chose. The resolution was a
subterfuge; its real intent was to prevent the chief executive from
equalizing taxes, argued Hodges. The regulars, led by Chairman
George P. Raney and W. W. Davis of Orange County, acknowledged the accuracy of Hodges' charge. Davis questioned rhetorically when it had become the duty of the governor to equalize
taxes. The administration faction lost the roll call to the regulars by
a vote of 19 to 10.

In a change of strategy by the Catts forces, Judge Hal W.
Adams introduced a resolution endorsing efforts of the governor to
enforce the laws of Florida. Duval County "boss" Pleasant Holt
countered that if the committee started commending people, he
intended to add names of the sheriffs, state attorneys, and county

15. J. R. Rogers to J. B. Hodges, January 10, 1917, Hodges to Rogers, January 11,
1917, in Box 13, Hodges Papers.

solicitors who had been removed by the governor. Chairman
Rainey became so overwrought that he left the chair to speak
against the resolution, which was finally withdrawn.

The committee members, their energies drained by the vitriolic debate over the governor and his politics, dealt with two
additional matters of considerable consequence, but without division along party regular-administration lines. Judge H. S. Glazier
of Manatee County shocked the assembled Democrats with an
amendment to voter qualification rules for the June, 1918, party
primary. He proposed to strike the paragraph which read that the
election would be open to whites only. Though claiming to be a
native southerner who was not particularly pro-Negro, he argued
that prohibiting Negro males from voting was undemocratic.
Glazier apparently was the only member cognizant of any injustice,
for he cast the lone vote for his own resolution.

William Crawford of Osceola County admitted that inequality
of the franchise existed, but he believed that the real victims were
Florida's females rather than the blacks. He offered a resolution
endorsing a woman suffrage amendment, but Pleasant Holt and
most regulars joined ranks to defeat the measure twenty-two to six.
Obviously, Governor Catts and his policies would win no popularity contest among angry regulars who would neither forgive nor
forget the heresies of 1916.[16]

If they expected the governor to truckle beneath their offensive
or blandly resign himself to their control, they inaccurately mea-
sured their adversary. Catts had already launched a movement to
wrest control of the state legislature from them, which, if successful, would allow him to enact the remainder of his legislative program. In a typical rally in the Duval County armory on June 30,
1917, only weeks after the end of the legislative session, he had
appealed to his overflow audience to elect a senate that would uphold him. Four months later the Miami *Herald* had reported activity in Dade County to elect a pro-Catts delegation and predicted

16. For proceedings of the executive committee, see Jacksonville *Florida Times-Union*,
February 26, 1917.

that loyalty or opposition to him would be the real issue in the 1918 primary.[17]

The governor also encouraged his aides to challenge regulars for cabinet and congressional offices. Their response constituted a powerful threat to traditionalist party spokesmen. J. Will Yon ran for the post of state auditor; Van C. Swearingen sought election to a full term as attorney general; Ion Farris opposed incumbent Congressman W. J. Sears. Farris, though not officially linked to the administration, had voted consistently for its reforms in the 1917 state senate. His decision to oppose Sears confirmed his connection with Catts in the opinion of many regulars; the Fellsmere *Tribune* editorialized that Farris had no chance unless he called "lustily for help from his Catt-ocratic party and send Billie Parker abarkin' in the wilderness."[18]

The conservative urban press became so deeply distressed at the uprising that the Tampa *Tribune* proposed that Democratic clubs be formed in each precinct. Membership in the clubs would be restricted to those who would pledge to abide by the platform and rulings of the party. Clubs would name delegates to county meetings which would in turn select representatives to the state convention; this statewide assembly would choose two names for each state office to be entered on the primary ballot. Most newspapers endorsed the plan, at least in principle.[19] The proposal could not be implemented in time for the 1918 summer primary, however, so party regulars rallied behind administration opponents.

The clearest midterm election test of public sentiment toward the administration came in the attorney general's contest between Cromwell Gibbons and Swearingen. This race was a microcosm of the 1916 gubernatorial campaign between establishment regular and maverick. Conservative Gibbons had ascended a familiar path

17. *Ibid.*, July 1, 1917, and November 2, 1917, quoting the Miami *Herald*.

18. Jacksonville *Florida Times-Union*, September 21, 1917, and March 21, 1918, quoting the DeLand *Record* and Fellsmere *Tribune*.

19. Kenneth R. Johnson, "The Woman Suffrage Movement in Florida." 175.

from Jacksonville lawyer to municipal court judge, state legislator, and speaker of the house. Swearingen was a farmer's son, born in Nassau County in 1873 and orphaned while still a youngster. He went to work as an office boy at twelve and at fifteen became apprenticed to a blacksmith in whose shop he labored for ten years. After taking a law degree at Mercer College in Georgia, he returned to Jacksonville and opened a law office, then was elected municipal judge and mayor. Lacking both prominent Jacksonville family and influential party connections, his career might well have peaked with his upset mayorality triumph of 1913 had it not been for his support of Catts. During the 1918 campaign Swearingen, perhaps sensing a decline in Catts's popularity or just fearful of riding anyone's coattails, did not emphasize his alliance with the governor and omitted any mention of the chief executive in advertisements.[20] Swearingen's opponents, however, did not allow him to disassociate himself from the governor, making his political affiliation their major issue. Although Gibbons disagreed with Swearingen on substantive issues, he centered his attack on what he called "cronism," warning voters against "Old Catts and all the kittens."

Catts's clique was not without certain assets, one of which was the belligerent Jacksonville *Free Press*. Created during the gubernatorial campaign, it had continued operation under editor A. B. Cargile, who also published the Lake City *Florida Index*, and J. B. Hodges, who ran the business end of the paper. It incited one particularly lively controversy by charging that officials of the Jacksonville *Florida Times-Union* had approached Governor Catts with a proposal that the large conservative daily become the official organ of the administration. Catts recounted the incident in private correspondence and urged Hodges to use the story in the *Free Press*.[21]

20. Gibbons' newspaper support included the Punta Gorda *Herald*, Ocala *Star*, Titusville *Advocate*, Lakeland *Telegram*, Carrabelle *Citizen*, Tampa *Tribune*, and Bartow *Record*. See Swearingen's advertisement in Jacksonville *Florida Times-Union*, June 2, 1918.

21. J. B. Hodges to Hal W. Adams, April 13, 1917, Sidney J. Catts to Hodges, April 17, 1917, in Box 13, Hodges Papers.

Although the new legislature would demonstrate that the 1918 election had not altered the anti-Catts bias of the senate, the referendum did expose considerable support for men who were clearly identified with the administration. J. Will Yon captured the state auditor's post, and Van Swearingen won easily over Cromwell Gibbons, 25,413 votes to 18,453 votes.

Gibbons amplified dissension within the state in postelection telegrams to newspapers in which he charged that a Catts appointee on the state payroll had sabotaged his campaign. The official had "worked over the state and circulated at the eleventh hour the false information that it would be a menace to the state to vote for Gibbons, as he is a representative of the Pope of Rome in Florida. This was like setting a house on fire in many strong Guardian of Liberty centers and accomplished its purpose." He accused Swearingen of complicity for saying that a vote for Gibbons meant "Pope rule in Florida." These religious charges had failed in the cities but had cost him the election in rural areas. He did agree with the governor on one point: the 1918 referendum constituted "an endorsement of Gov. Catts' administration, Mr. Swearingen being his appointee and first lieutenant in the cause." Furthermore, he believed that "the Cattites, having reorganized," would "offer again for office two years hence, Gov. Catts for senator and Mr. Swearingen for governor." He deplored the activities of these traveling state officials, proposing that "vigorous, timely, firm and unrelenting measures should be immediately taken" to stop them, and that the Democratic party in Florida should conduct an educational campaign to "thoroughly advise the people on . . . relieving us of a religious issue in the Democratic primaries."[22] His prognosis, while slanted by personal involvement, forecast the strategy of both Catts and regular Democrats in the ensuing two years.

Actually, the election returns suggest a more complicated analysis than Gibbons was willing to admit. Many smaller and rural north Florida counties—including LaFayette, Liberty, Manatee,

---

22. Text of telegram and interviews in Jacksonville *Florida Times-Union*, June 7, 1918.

Marion, Suwannee, Taylor, and Walton—voted for Gibbons. Neither do the facts support his charge that less prejudiced urban voters rejected Swearingen. Profiting from the support of organized labor, Swearingen carried Duval County (Jacksonville) 3,346 to 2,270, Hillsborough County (Tampa), and Dade County (Miami). In counties with smaller towns, the attorney general split the vote, carrying Leon (Tallahassee) by a two-to-one margin, while losing Escambia (Pensacola). Analysis of the returns suggests that Swearingen's convincing victory represented an endorsement of the administration, and that the erosion that resulted in humiliating defeats for both Catts and Swearingen in 1920 had not yet begun. Florida's regular Democrats still could not perceive that the Catts phenomenon was more than just a temporary aberration sustained by evangelical Protestant emotionalism.

Election results in various regions of Florida provide less decisive conclusions than the statewide races. The senate, which had been the stronghold for anti-Catts regulars, showed a remarkable fluidity. Senators ran in staggered years with sixteen members or half the total standing for election in 1918. Of these sixteen, thirteen either did not offer for reelection, or were defeated. Superficially, this tends to confirm the success of Catts's purge, and he did fare slightly better in the 1919 senate than he had in 1917; but many of his most loyal stalwarts were among the casualties, including his senate leader, James E. Alexander. Also, the majority of those elected in 1918 opposed Catts in the 1919 legislature. Even so, few legislative candidates ran with exclusively antiadministration platforms, and local issues oftentimes decided such contests.

One case study reveals how internal state politics affected local races. A bank failure in Live Oak in 1917 had created such emotional tension that Catts had summoned eighty county guards from Jacksonville to preserve order. This affair catapulted the issue of a bank guarantee law to the forefront of the 1918 election. Joe Earman and Hodges particularly emphasized this issue, and Hodges boasted that in Columbia County all the legislative candidates advocating the bank guarantee bill had won by margins of over two hundred votes. Senator Plymton, usually an administrative stalwart and a Hodges protégé, won easily over R. T. Boozer to become one of only three incumbents who won reelection. Hodges also commented that all defeated candidates in Columbia County had attacked Catts's Board of Control for squandering funds. He considered the election results to be a vote of confidence, writing Joe Earman boastfully that "We're some Board." The same day he informed Catts that "our legislative ticket won out easily, Plympton returning to the Senate and Roebuck and Bill Phillips to the House."[23] He assured the governor that the newly elected Phillips had been an original supporter in 1916, "one of the old Catts kittens."

The contradictory Hodges was still playing both sides of the political fence, however. While managing Catts's forces in the county elections, he also advised his railroad friends as to whom he considered "safe" candidates insofar as corporate interests were concerned.[24]

Governor Catts hardly paused to rest between the 1918 Democratic primary and the November general election. Two issues motivated his energetic participation in the fall ballot: the statewide prohibition referendum and a ten-mill tax increase for public education. Despite Catts's private enthusiasm for Christmas eggnog and stronger stuff on occasion, he crusaded vigorously for statewide prohibition. Realizing, perhaps, that his evangelical constituents were more committed to the cause than himself, he made the elimination of liquor a major division between his administration forces and party regulars.

Events in Jacksonville demonstrated how shrewdly Catts understood the growth of vocal public support for prohibition. Party stalwart Pleasant Holt opposed prohibition, and in 1917 had won reelection to the city council by the largest majority of any candidate. A year later conditions had changed so dramatically that the city scheduled a referendum to decide the liquor question. Drys,

23. J. B. Hodges to Joe L. Earman, June 7, 1918, Hodges to S. J. Catts, June 7, 1918, in Box 28, Hodges Papers.
24. J. B. Hodges to John L. Doggett, December 26, 1917, in Box 25, *ibid.*

supported by the War Department, argued that eliminating the whiskey traffic would provide a more healthful atmosphere for the soldiers stationed at Camp Joseph E. Johnston. The camp commander even threatened to declare the city off limits because of excessive drinking by his troops. The drys, perhaps exaggerating a bit, argued that a ballot for their cause was a vote for: "Uncle Sam. For home and country. For happy wives and children. For a better manhood. For a cleaner Jacksonville. For more prosperity. For better business for the legitimate merchant. For better wages for honest labor." Conversely, they observed that of the 120 Germans in Jacksonville, 20 owned saloons. Thus, a wet ballot was a vote for: "the Kaiser. For Moerlier. For 'old Heidelburg.' For Weidemann. And for all the German breweries in the United States. AND EVERY BREWERY IN THIS COUNTRY IS OWNED BY GERMANS." The drys received the endorsement of the Chamber of Commerce which was more concerned about the future of Camp Johnston than morality on either side of the drinking issue. Even the obstreperous Pleasant Holt deserted the wets to cast his lot with moral reform and against Germany. Aided by an eleventh-hour telegram from William G. McAdoo applauding efforts to end the liquor trade, the drys won by a seven-hundred-vote majority. The result even forced Ion Farris, long an opponent of prohibition, to reverse himself. Farris explained that he had voted for legalized sale in the state legislature only because Duval County was wet, but that he personally was a dry.[25] As a prelude to the November statewide referendum, the Jacksonville results presaged the drift of public sentiment.

The 1918 election also presented a perfect opportunity to harness anti-Catholicism in the service of social reform. The best single example of this confluence of bigotry and reform is found in Catts's address to a Jacksonville Labor Day rally on September 2, 1918. Speaking on the program with Mayor John W. Martin, a prolabor politician and sometimes ally, and Attorney General

25. Advertisement in Jacksonville *Florida Times-Union*, May 11, 1918; *ibid.*, June 2, 1918.

Swearingen, Catts began by lauding the workers. He urged them to pay their poll taxes so they could vote for prohibition in the general election and for compulsory education in the county referendum. According to the chief executive, the school referendum would be a vote against the Catholics who desired a parochial school system. In a rambling diatribe, Catts predicted that there would be war between labor and capital unless they could learn to cooperate. Borrowing from the anti-intellectual rhetoric of evangelist Billy Sunday, he warned workers not to count on anyone who had a "D.D., LL.D., A.M., Ph.D. or Ass after his name," because such "men belonged to the plutocrats" and were "owned by the rich."

The conflict between labor and capital, however, was only preliminary to the ultimate confrontation between Protestants and Catholics. The governor related an incident involving a Floridian who had called him to inquire if it were true that he opposed allowing Catholic teachers to be employed in parochial schools; when Catts admitted the charge, the caller informed him that to fight Catholics was to be pro-German. The governor assured the laborers that such a premise was an "infernal lie," that he had been elected on an anti-Catholic platform, and that he would remain faithful to it. In retaliation, Catholics, led by James Cardinal Gibbons, archbishop of Baltimore, had hounded his son out of military service.[26]

Bishop Michael J. Curley of St. Augustine replied to Catts's Labor Day speech, emphasizing that there was nothing new in the "anti-American" address: "just the same old spirit of stupid hate and bigotry which has actuated the governor and his ilk during the past four years." The prelate denied that Catholics had anything to do with young Sidney's army experiences and dismissed the governor by a reference to his "mission in life" which was "to keep the pope from building a new Vatican in Palm Beach or Moore Haven, and by so doing to feather his own political nest." In his most force-

26. Jacksonville *Florida Times-Union*, September 3, 1918.

ful rejoinder, Bishop Curley charged that Catts could be quite kind
to Catholics when it suited his political pleasure, thus reducing the
entire issue to a cynical expediency employed for the governor's
self-interest. The quarrel received national attention, and Louis
Silverstein, a prominent New York lawyer, wrote Catts inquiring
about allegations of anti-Semitism. The governor replied that, contrary to rumors circulating in Florida, he was fond of Jews.[27]

Catts spent the last week before the general election in
Jacksonville conferring with state prohibition leaders and working
for the school tax proposal. The state press swallowed its resentment for the governor and generally supported both measures. The
powerful Jacksonville Central Trades and Labor Council (AFL) endorsed the school tax, as did Senator Duncan Fletcher. The governor's efforts paid off handsomely; even his opponents among party
regulars had been forced into the prohibition camp, and both measures passed easily. Statewide, the ten-mill school tax amendment
carried 21,936 to 10,723. In Duval County, prohibition won by a
350-vote margin, while the school tax passed by a ratio of 4 to 1.

The summer primary and fall election buoyed the administration and convinced Catts of his support among rank and file voters.
The immediate consequence was a determination to storm the remaining redoubts of the establishment party faction. Bryan Mack
announced in July, 1918, that he was considering a race for state
treasurer in 1920. The same month, rumors intensified that Catts
intended to oppose Duncan Fletcher for the Senate in 1920, while
Swearingen planned a race to succeed his mentor in the statehouse. Party regulars countered by intensifying their opposition on the state committee and in the upper house. Senator
Fletcher also effectively utilized patronage against the Catts administration, and especially sought to destroy the formidable Columbia
County organization that had been constructed by J. B. Hodges.[28]

27. Bishop M. J. Curley to editor, *ibid.*, September 5, 1918, and *ibid.*, September 18,
1918.
28. Jacksonville *Florida Times-Union*, July 11, August 3, 1918, quoting DeFuniak
Herald and Jasper *News*. For the patronage struggle, see J. B. Hodges to Joe L. Earman,
August 29, 1919, in Box 32, Hodges Papers.

Noting both the election returns and ensuing struggle for party control, the editor of the conservative Jacksonville *Florida Times-Union* penned a blistering editorial on Democratic factionalism. There was no party, he wrote, but only a mad "scramble for office." Many of Florida's best men had withdrawn from politics because of the gutter level of campaigning: "The last gubernatorial campaign in Florida . . . was a farce, a disgrace to a civilized commonwealth, and its echoes are still such as to make the intelligent and right thinking people stop their ears." The editorial ignored, however, the real nature of the factionalism which was not so much a contest between respectability and demagoguery as it was a struggle for control of state government. A better explanation of the factionalism is found in the alternative to Catts proposed by the editor. The "right kind of government" proposed by the journalist meant returning the governor's office to party regulars; the newspaperman championed a government "conducted fairly and honestly, with the fewest possible laws and the least possible enfringement [*sic*] upon the business and pleasure of the governed."[29] His was the inevitable cry of every corporate power threatened by change: leave business alone and enact as few laws as possible.

Election returns were barely complete from the November referendum when Catts summoned the legislature into special session. The governor explained that the session was to implement the newly enacted prohibition amendment to Florida's constitution. He also appended to the call proposals for an automobile tax for road maintenance, for additional funds to operate the state's public institutions, for action to provide land for returning servicemen, and to attract more farm laborers. Many legislators opposed the special session, with the most vociferous criticism located in areas such as Tampa and Key West which had voted negatively on prohibition. They cited costs of the session as their primary objection, but Catts countered with reports showing deficits in road department funds that jeopardized the state's highway construction and

29. Jacksonville *Florida Times-Union*, February 22, 1919.

maintenance programs. The governor expected a hostile legislature to assemble and asked A. B. Small, Fred Cone, and Hodges to provide legal help to speed legislation should it become necessary.[30]

The special session convened on November 25 and remained in Tallahassee until December 7, 1918. In his address to the legislature, Catts restated the reasons for the special call. The upper house selected Senator James E. Calkins of Nassau County to preside, while the lower body elected George H. Wilder of Hillsborough as speaker. To cut costs of the special session, the legislature appointed four joint committees each with ten members divided equally between both houses. Senator W. A. MacWilliams of St. Augustine conceived the plan to allow both houses to work on the governor's proposals at the same time. Each committee assumed responsibility for one project: enforcing prohibition: stabilizing the labor force and levying an auto tax: settling soldiers; and providing money for public institutions, particularly the boys' industrial school.

Before any of these major items could be disposed of, numerous bills were dropped into the hopper dealing with a variety of issues. The new senate almost immediately declared war on the chief executive by repassing a bill vetoed by Catts in the previous session which paid officials whose suspensions by the governor had not been upheld by the legislature. The senate also refused to sustain a number of Catts's dismissals, most notably the suspensions of hotel inspector A. L. Messer, whose job had been given to Jerry Carter. Approximately one-third of Catts's suspensions were overruled, although the senate upheld the removals of tax collectors in Washington and Liberty counties, the sheriff of Citrus County, the Duval County constable, the clerk of the Manatee County circuit court, and the Polk County superintendent of public instruction. Despite one legislator's attack on the governor for his politically motivated suspensions, an embarrassed senate found charges serious enough to uphold two-thirds of his removals. In another slap at

---

30. *Journal of the State Senate of Florida of the Extraordinary Session of 1918*, p. 1; Sidney J. Catts to J. B. Hodges, November 21, 1918, in Box 30, Hodges Papers.

Catts disguised as an economy measure, the lower house voted to abolish the hotel commission and to cut the salary of the adjutant general. The governor demonstrated remarkable candor despite this legislative sniping, asking the lawmakers to reinstate two pure food and drug inspectors and to pay them back salaries. With characteristic frankness, he explained that he had made a mistake in dismissing them.[31]

The most explosive issue of the special session had nothing to do with the formal agenda outlined in the governor's call. The legislature was barely organized when Catts dropped a bombshell: he urged passage of bills abolishing the tax and railroad commissions. Previously, he had considered opposition to these two regulatory agencies to stem from the devil and the big corporations, which he could hardly separate. Only his veto had saved the tax commission in 1917. The most cynical explanation for his dramatic reversal was that the railroads, perhaps working through Hodges, either persuaded or bought him; but this is inconsistent with his increasing flirtation with radical unionism, and there is no evidence to support such a conclusion.

His own explanation, while strained, is still the most likely reason for the reversal: altered circumstances and a critical need for additional funds necessitated the action. Prohibition would deny the state a considerable amount of tax revenue which had to be compensated for by reduced expenditures. Abolition of the tax commission would save fifteen thousand dollars annually, while ending the railroad commission would reduce expenditures an additional seventy thousand dollars per year. Catts reaffirmed his original goals by attacking counties which assessed property too low, but fixed blame partially on the tax commission itself; the best way to obtain tax equalization was to abolish the commission. As for railroad regulation, wartime government control had left the commission powerless anyway.[32]

31. Jacksonville *Florida Times-Union*, December 3, 1918. For list of suspensions and senate action, see *ibid.*, December 6, 1918.
32. *Ibid.*, November 30, 1918; Deal "Sidney Johnston Catts," 143–44.

The legislature took only one day to accomplish the governor's recommendation. Bewildered defenders of the agency sought vainly to save it in the house, but were swamped by a forty-eight to seventeen vote. The senate confirmed the action twenty to four, and Catts signed the bill throwing tax commissioners J. V. Burke, R. J. Patterson, and John Neel out of work. Ironically Patterson and Burke were both Catts's aides whose appointment to the commission had provoked a storm of controversy. To add to the confusion of the situation, the state senate, addled by the transformation of its antagonist, refused to concur in the abolition of the railroad commission, thus temporarily saving it from extinction.

On matters central to the session, Catts won most of what he requested. The senate created the mechanism for enforcing prohibition in a bill that passed by an eighteen to four vote. At 9:45 A.M. on December 4 the governor signed an emergency prohibition law drying up the state from December 9 when it went into effect until January 9 when the newly passed constitutional amendment became operative. On December 3, 1918, the Florida legislature ratified the Eighteenth Amendment to the Constitution which made prohibition a national law.[33]

The governor was also successful on a number of other matters. As a result of his exposé of wretched conditions at the state reform school for boys, the legislature appointed an investigatory committee. The legislative report confirmed Catts's estimate of the situation and led to fundamental reforms. Florida's lawmakers also levied an automobile tax to provide critically needed funds for the state's highways. On December 7 the governor signed the "soldiers and sailors" bill, which authorized the Internal Improvement Fund trustees to cooperate with the federal government in securing homes for returning servicemen. This action completed a clean sweep for Catts, a remarkable success for his major proposals considering the antipathy of the legislators. The triumph resulted from a combination of obvious necessity (the need for additional reve-

33. Florida, *General Acts and Resolutions Adopted by the Legislature of Florida*, Extraordinary Session, November 25–December 7, 1918, p. 109.

nue), changes in Catts's own policies (abolishing the two commissions), and the weight of popular opinion (prohibition).

On one issue the governor received a setback. After initial hesitation, Catts had become an enthusiastic spokesman for woman suffrage. In a January, 1918, speech at the University of Florida, he had strongly endorsed female voting as a measure required by wartime circumstances. He proposed a resolution to the special session endorsing woman suffrage, but the house narrowly defeated the resolution, thirty-seven against to thirty-one for passage. The historian of the franchise movement in Florida suggests that Catts believed his support of this reform might aid in his race against Senator Fletcher; newly enfranchised women would perhaps prove less tightly bound to the regular wing of the Democratic party. Loyalist Democrats in the legislature, more concerned with party fidelity than with enfranchising women, may have voted against the resolution for the same reason that Catts favored it.[34] This strategy made good political sense, especially considering Fletcher's vigorous opposition to federal enactment of woman suffrage.

The thirteen-day session ended on December 7, 1918, setting the stage for some dramatic confrontations over enforcement of prohibition. Catts demanded that county sheriffs begin immediately to enforce the statute, a move that caused considerable resentment in communities which had voted against such restrictions. Hillsborough County, which contained a high ratio of Latin immigrants, precipitated the first crisis. When the liquor traffic in Tampa and Clearwater did not end, Catts considered invoking martial law. J. B. Hodges once again exercised a moderating influence over the impulsive chief executive. He advised that the situation did not warrant such drastic action, since small quantities of liquor could still be sold under Florida law until the prohibition amendment became operative in January, 1919. Martial law could not be invoked until there was some general disorder that the civil authorities were unable to control. Fortunately for Tampa and

34. Johnson, "The Woman Suffrage Movement in Florida," 178–79.

Florida, the advent of national prohibition and the end of the Catts era in 1920 eliminated the impasse. During the following decade the state of Florida became a major source of illegal liquor importation, and Tampa police and city officials were the most unreliable and unsympathetic of any in the state. Furthermore, the entire climate of public opinion changed with the advent of the Florida land boom, and the state became by some accounts one of the wettest in America.[35] One can only imagine the colossal chaos had Sidney Catts been elected governor in 1920 instead of 1916.

International events propelled Florida in new directions during the war years, and beginning with United States entry in 1917, the First World War confronted Catts with difficult problems. After some initial hesitancy, the state press endorsed an interventionist foreign policy which closely paralleled the Wilsonian approach. Catts's temperament seldom allowed cautious consideration, and he never shared the early reservations about American policy which characterized some Florida newspapers. He even felt compelled to advise the entire nation, and did so in a jingoistic letter to the New York *Times*. The newspaper had asked various governors for their reactions to renewed German depredations on American shipping, and Catts responded characteristically with the most belligerent opinion of any chief executive. Other governors praised the cool response of President Wilson; but Catts would have sent a twenty-four hour ultimatum "telling them that if they killed a single American citizen they would have me and the whole United States to whip, and I would direct the Admirals of the Navy and the Generals of the United States Army to prepare for battle, and in twenty-four hours we would meet them." The governor concluded the entire matter in two arrogant paragraphs: "I do not know whether this is proper or not, nor do I care, but these are my sentiments, and they would be the ones that I would live up to in regard to the loss and destruction of American lives. My idea about

35. J. B. Hodges to Sidney J. Catts, December 19, 1918, in Box 30, Hodges Papers; for a fuller discussion, see James A. Carter, "Florida and Rumrunning During National Prohibition," *Florida Historical Quarterly*, XLVIII (July, 1969), 54–56.

the whole business is that the American flag should protect American lives anywhere on land, sea, sky, earth or ocean, and when it fails to do so, we cheapen ourselves and cheapen the nation. If this answer does not suit you, don't publish it."[36]

As American involvement in the war began, he sought to harness Florida's public opinion and that state's resources to support the military effort. He scheduled a series of patriotic speeches in January and February, 1918, speaking in Gainesville, Ocala, Tampa, Tarpon Springs, and elsewhere. A typical speech, delivered in a crowded chapel at the University of Florida, surveyed the rise of democracy around the world, including the new "liberal movement" in Russia. Imperialism must be eliminated, and America should claim the leadership of the anticolonialists. He spoke strongly in favor of woman suffrage, moral courage, and the need for high standards of personal conduct.[37]

Provision for state military forces also required action. The Florida press agitated for the creation of paramilitary groups to defend communities during the absence of the federalized National Guard. Home guard units already had begun to appear in towns throughout the state by March and April, 1917. In December, 1917, Catts called for the establishment of a home guard in every Florida county to handle potential domestic emergencies. Implementation of his request caused some problems, and he issued another proclamation requesting that the home guard units not drill on Sunday. The commander of the Miami unit considered the German menace to Dade County so imminent that he refused to obey Catts's order and continued Sunday practice. At Gainesville vast crowds gathered on July 4, 1918, to watch the guards drill, and prizes were awarded to the best units.[38]

36. Sidney J. Catts to editor, New York *Times*, February 2, 1917. For a general survey of Florida newspaper sentiment, see C. Peter Ripley, "Intervention and Reaction: Florida Newspapers and United States Entry into World War I," *Florida Historical Quarterly*, XLIX (January, 1971), 255–67.

37. Jacksonville *Florida Times-Union*, January 15, 1918.

38. Ripley, "Intervention and Reaction," 256–66; also see Jacksonville *Florida Times-Union*, December 14, 1917, June 24, July 6, 1918.

In order to mobilize Florida's economy, Catts created several administrative agencies. Early in the war he established a Food Conservation Committee, and in July, 1918, he appointed four men from each of four congressional districts to coordinate all wartime activities in the state. The black community in Jacksonville asked to be included in the war effort and invited the governor to speak at the Ebenezar Methodist Episcopal Church. More than four thousand black citizens attended the June 29, 1917, rally, less than half of them able to crowd inside while the rest listened in the streets. Catts spoke mainly of the patriotic duty of every citizen to conserve food, but added that he performed his duty as chief executive for the good of all the people of the state, regardless of color.[39]

His agitation awakened Florida to the problem of food production. The *Bradford County Telegraph* described the objective in the folksy language of rural Florida: the war demanded food production, and "the best patriot, therefore, is he who raises the most grub. Let us, then, be valiant soldiers of the hoe."[40] To dramatize his concern for food production, the governor persuaded the city of Tallahassee to set aside a local ordinance in order to allow him to keep a pigpen behind the governor's mansion. Jerry Carter's sons, who lived nearby, visited the governor's home to help with the butchering back of the mansion. In return the governor could be seen occasionally passing through the neighborhood, a pork shoulder resting heavily on his shoulder, cutting off chunks for neighbors as he headed for the Carters' house.[41]

All segments of Florida's economy experienced a wartime boom. Military facilities were located here because of good climate and extensive natural resources, especially in timber. Of the thirty-five flying schools in the United States, five were located in

39. Jacksonville *Florida Times-Union*, June 30, 1917.

40. Ripley, "Intervention and Reaction," 264, quoting Starke *Bradford County Telegraph*, April 29, 1917.

41. Tebeau, *A History of Florida*, 373. Pages 368–75 of this study contain an excellent brief account of war conditions in Florida. Interview, Mike Carter, May 15, 1973, Birmingham, Alabama.

Florida. Naval bases and army installations also sprang up across the state. Maritime construction, heavily subsidized by the United States Shipping Board, became a major industry in Jacksonville, Tampa, and Pensacola. Thanks largely to the energetic lobbying of Senator Duncan Fletcher, shipyards in the three cities obtained contracts for thirty-five ships valued at $46,500,000 and increased their work forces to over eleven thousand employees. Supportive industries thrived on the construction boom. The Shipping Board, under prodding by Fletcher, agreed to ship lumber and other products from Georgia through the port facilities at Jacksonville. The result was a $1,500,000 expansion of the municipally owned terminals which allowed 80 percent of lumber purchased by the board in the Jacksonville vicinity to move through the city.[42]

Even with the closing of some facilities and the rapid dismantling of the federal presence in Florida, the state's economy did not decline to prewar levels. The number of manufacturing industries increased from 2,518 in 1914 to 2,582 in 1919. The number of employees working at these establishments increased from 63,204 to 82,986 in the same period. Wages and salaries more than doubled, and the use of power increased by 40 percent. Census experts emphasized in 1920 that the increase in wages, cost of materials, and values of products from 1914 to 1919 resulted mainly from advances attributable to the war; but the increases in the number of wage earners and in the use of electric power indicated a "decided growth in the manufacturing activities of the state." Analysis of industrial growth reveals the solid advance about which these experts commented. Ranked by value of products in 1920 the leading four revenue producers were: lumber and timber products, employing 21,058; the tobacco industry, with 12,393 average wage earners; steel shipbuilding, with 7,832 employees; and naval stores, employing 11,748 persons.[43]

42. Jacksonville *Florida Times-Union*, July 28, 1918; Duncan U. Fletcher to Edward N. Hurley, March 5, 1918, Hurley to Fletcher, March 15, 1918, in United States Shipping Board Papers, Record Group 32, National Archives, Washington, D.C.

43. *Fourteenth Census of the United States, 1920*, IX, *Manufactures* (Washington: Government Printing Office, 1923), 241, 243.

Urbanization kept pace with industrialization. Of the fifty-four counties in the state, Duval (Jacksonville) which was dominated by wooden shipbuilding, and Hillsborough (Tampa) which relied primarily on the cigar industry, reported 45 percent of the wage earners. The combined population of the six cities with over ten thousand inhabitants amounted to nearly one quarter of the state's total population. Although the countryside lost residents, farmers participated in the unprecedented prosperity. The value of farm property increased 130 percent between 1910 and 1920, while the average value per farm more than doubled.[44]

A major problem posed by this economic expansion was an inadequate supply of labor. Severe shortages in Jacksonville prompted advertisements for skilled workers in papers as far north as Tennessee. The government established an industrial school in the port city to train unskilled laborers and lauded the great opportunities available for women workers. Wages ranged from a low of thirty cents per hour for unskilled labor to eighty cents an hour for skilled.[45]

One reason for the critical manpower shortage was the exodus of blacks who moved north to assume higher paying jobs. Labor recruiters tapped the vast reservoir of underemployed and underpaid blacks, especially in the cities. Catts devoted much effort to reversing this drain, first by persuasion and then by force. He spoke to members of the Negro Protective League in Jacksonville on September 14, 1917. This newly formed group had undertaken to improve wages and conditions in Florida so blacks would not desire to leave the state. Catts's speech, pretentiously entitled "What God Had Done for the Colored Race and the Attitudes of the Administration," began with paternalistic references to Florida's racial peace which had resulted from whites Christianizing blacks during slavery. He advised policies of thrift which would enable blacks to purchase land. The chief executive urged them to

44. *Ibid.*, 241; *Fourteenth Census of the United States 1920*, VI, Pt. 2, *Agriculture*, 355.
45. Lewis M. Stoddard to Jesse F. Salyers, October 11, 1918, in U.S. Shipping Board Papers, RG 32, NA.

plant gardens and practice temperance while assuring them of protection against racial outrages. Closing with a plea for unity among all Floridians, he reminded his audience that northerners did not like Negroes because they threatened to take jobs away from whites, and he advised blacks to stay in a warm climate where "the Creator had put them."[46]

Many blacks apparently concluded that God would care for them as well in the northern cold as in the sunny South, for the labor crisis intensified in 1918. In July the governor summoned the State Council of Defense to a Jacksonville conference on the problems of black workers to which he invited Negro leaders and labor agents from across the state. Catts also experimented with a more direct method, dispatching a letter to each county sheriff telling him to enforce vagrancy laws against vagabonds, idlers, and other able-bodied men who refused to work. A month later he enlarged this authority to provide for the arrest of any labor recruiter entering Florida in order to recruit sawmill workers, who were usually doing work under government contract. When these drastic actions did not substantially improve labor supply, he urged the State Council of Defense and local officials to mobilize labor reserves in any way they could. As a result, some towns issued "work or fight" orders to all able-bodied males, a policy advised also by the United States provost marshal. Any male between the ages of eighteen and forty-five must seek employment in the war effort or face immediate conscription.[47]

The drain north was not the only labor problem. Farm workers left for better paying jobs in the cities, and laborers had to be imported from the Bahamas. Although the total number of tenant farmers without land increased slightly during the war years, the percentage of tenants compared to the total farm force declined slightly from 26.7 percent of the total in 1910 to 25.3 in 1920. A vast inequity existed in the racial composition of tenancy, however; only 17.4 percent of white farmers were tenants, while 50.4 per-

46. Jacksonville *Florida Times-Union*, September 15, 1917.
47. *Ibid.*, July 11, April 1, 28, August 23, 30, 1918.

cent of black agrarians labored under the system. Black tenancy actually increased nearly a percentage point during the prosperous decade.[48]

Although tenancy concerned him very little, inflation and profiteering infuriated Catts, and he instructed state agencies to take direct action. Attorney General Swearingen issued orders to the state attorneys to investigate ice and grocery companies for possible antitrust violations. The following day the governor warned that he was aware of profiteering in house rentals where owners were taking advantage of people forced to rent because of housing shortages. Some corporations and trusts also charged exorbitant prices. As chairman of the Council of Defense, he instructed Swearingen to use his power to see that such combinations be prosecuted under state antitrust laws. No one doubted the governor's determination to do exactly what he threatened, and by the end of the week ice companies in Jacksonville agreed to provide better service, though the St. Augustine city council began regulating the price of ice in that city.[49]

Stabilizing prices proved an illusory goal when confronted with the vast inflationary pressure of wartime spending. The cost of clothing doubled, and the price of most goods and services advanced correspondingly. Those persons on fixed income suffered most, but all Floridians were affected. As a dramatic gesture to reverse the pattern and also to aid his senatorial campaign against Duncan Fletcher, the governor called for a state convention to meet in Jacksonville on August 14 and 15, 1919. He specified that delegates chosen by him would include prominent state officials, Baptist and Methodist laymen, representatives from the Presbyterian and Catholic churches, organized labor, and all newspaper editors and mayors. The grandiose scheme failed because of poor planning, lack of publicity, and growing disaffection with the governor. When aides neglected to rent the Morocco Temple, a favorite city meeting place, the convention had to be moved to the Duval County Armory. Only two hundred delegates and curious town

48. *Fourteenth Census of the United States, 1920*, VI, Pt. 2, *Agriculture*, 356.
49. Jacksonville *Florida Times-Union*, August 23, 25, 29, 1918.

folk attended, electing J. B. Hodges chairman and Bryan Mack secretary. Judge Isaac A. Stewart of DeLand spoke on war profits, while a Catts legislator, W. W. Phillips of Lake City, discussed the economy. Hodges wrote Joe Earman concerning the meeting, providing perceptive insights into its origins and failure: "THE HIGH COST OF LIVING MEETING that Catts held in Jacksonville last week was not a success, such failure was due to his political opposition. Catts is going to have a hard fight, and his hope lies in the country."[50]

Although his attempts to control inflation faltered, Catts did offer some financial reflief to his hard pressed citizenry. On June 28, 1918, the governor announced that Florida's economic growth had made it possible to lower the general revenue tax. He also addressed a letter to every board of county commissioners in the state urging them to lower the millage for county taxes, thus providing more money to purchase government bonds.

Other wartime problems caused less trouble than economic difficulties. Rumors of espionage and sabotage appeared in Florida, but the governor maintained an atypical equilibrium. There was some antiwar sentiment—state senator J. L. Sheppard of Gadsden vowed that he would not permit his son to register for the draft and was himself indicted by a federal grand jury—but the governor's appointees on state agencies followed the calm lead of the chief executive. The Board of Control dealt sanely with rumors concerning professors at state institutions, including charges of disloyalty made against a Professor Bucholtz at the University of Florida. The board investigated, but J. B. Hodges dismissed the allegations as "only Tampa politics and a fight against masonry." One German-American piano instructor was dismissed for refusing to remove a picture of the Kaiser and a German flag from her studio, but such incidents were rare.[51]

The war years were significant ones for Catts. He still believed

50. *Ibid.*, August 8, 15, 1919, J. B. Hodges to Joe L. Earman, August 20, 1919, in Box 33, Hodges Papers.

51. J. B. Hodges to J. S. Blitch, November 12, 1918, in Box 30, Hodges Papers; and Ripley, "Intervention and Reaction," 265.

that legislative opposition could be overcome, and that the people supported him. Wartime measures provided a rallying place above partisanship, and he skillfully presided over the state's economic growth with its attendant dislocation. At the fundamental level of government, his appointees were changing state institutions to make them more democratic and efficient.

EIGHT

Failures of the Mind, Successes of the Heart

THE POLITICAL MAXIM that war preempts social reform was not demonstrable in Florida in the years during and immediately after World War I. Governor Catts had filled state agencies with enthusiastic neophytes who were determined to change existing conditions, and the result was a remarkable era of social progress.

Florida's commitment to education had not been on a par with her resources, and the result was an irregular patchwork of counties with excellent facilities beside counties with obviously inferior ones. Florida ranked above other southern states in most educational categories but exceeded the national average in few. By 1920 her schools enrolled 79 percent of the total school age population (the national average was 75.3). The average school term in the nation was 160.7 days compared to 133 in the Sunshine State. Florida expended an average of 7.24 dollars per capita for schools, compared with a national average of 7.26.[1] Teachers complained of inadequate salaries and lack of books. The Ocala *Star*, a perpetual foe of the Catts administration, complained in 1919 that "the school affairs of the state of Florida in the year three of the reign of Catts are in the blamedest muddle ever known." Blaming Catts, however, was an expedient diversion to explain a lack of fundamental educational commitment; indeed, the Ocala *Star* itself had ad-

1. Florida, *Bi-ennial Report of the Superintendent of Public Instruction*, for the Two Years Ending June 30, 1920 (Gainesville: Pepper Printing Co., 1920), 24–25, 27–28.

vised its readers in 1918 to vote against a ten-mill tax for state schools, saying that taxpayers could not shoulder additional burdens.[2]

Whatever progress Florida made in public education can be attributed at least partly to Catts. State Superintendent of Public Instruction William N. Sheats praised the service of the politically appointed rural school inspectors who had come under much criticism from hostile legislators. These experts had traveled the state in the interest of rural schools, conferring with county superintendents and school boards. The superintendent noted that the General Education Board contributed $5,000 a year to supervise Florida's high schools, and concluded that the state could surely afford a pittance for rural school inspection.[3]

Statistical evidence confirms the progress about which Sheats boasted. Illiteracy among those ten years and older had declined from 13.8 percent in 1910 to 9.6 in 1920. Total school enrollment for whites was up from 92,834 in 1910 to 157,666 in 1920; Negro enrollment had increased from 55,255 to 67,494. Thanks to the new 1918 assessment, tax revenue for schools had increased from $165,649,406 in 1910 to $356,880,187 in 1920.[4]

Disappointing the predictions of Catts's enemies, his appointees to the Board of Control seldom interfered with the institutions of higher learning. They did introduce some creative concepts into higher education. Following a precedent established in making general appropriations for public schools, the legislature used the pretext of opposition to Catts to threaten appropriations for higher education.[5] Catts's majority on the board countered with a vigorous building program and an innovative extension service. Beginning with the August, 1917, meeting of the board, Hodges and Earman pushed for both the physical and intellectual expansion of the

2. Jacksonville *Florida Times-Union,* October 6, 1919, quoting the Ocala *Star.*

3. *Ibid.,* September 10, 1918, quoting the Ocala *Star;* Florida, *Bi-ennial Report of the Superintendent of Public Instruction,* 37.

4. *Fourteenth Census of the United States, 1920,* III, *Population,* 186; Florida, *Biennial Report of the Superintendent of Public Instruction,* 12, 16.

5. Joe L. Earman to J. B. Hodges, April 26, 1919, in Box 32, Hodges Papers.

colleges. They appropriated $90,000 for additional buildings at Florida State College for Women in Tallahassee, and drafted plans for three new student residencies at the University of Florida.[6]

Extending the influence of the university into surrounding communities was a relatively new idea and one enthusiastically endorsed by Catts. The man most responsible for the idea of university extension in Florida was Claude L'Engle. It was he who primarily drafted the bill that instituted the program in 1919. Although a spokesman for organized labor, L'Engle never liked Catts. Despite their personal antipathy, the governor championed the extension philosophy, and Joe Earman lobbied it successfully through the 1919 legislature.[7]

The extension service coincided with the governor's concept of applied education, particularly in the field of agriculture. In addition to his philosophical affinity for the plan, two other factors influenced him: Professor P. H. Rolfs, director of extension work at the University of Florida, was a political ally who even accompanied Catts on tours; and the people of the state viewed university extension favorably.[8]

Catts's philosophical preference for applied training overshadowed academic programs. In a speech to the Florida Press Association on June 30, 1917, Catts had appealed for industrial education as a prime consideration: "This is no time for the study of Latin roots and translations to be made from the classics or solutions to be sought from problematic Euclid; this is the time to 'saw wood,' which means work practical and necessary alike for man and woman." From the outset of his term of office, he sought to create industrial schools to fulfill this need, and he won important converts. Ion Farris, the Jacksonville progressive who had

6. Jacksonville *Florida Times-Union*, August 14, 1917; J. B. Hodges to Sidney J. Catts, November 14, 1917, Hodges to Bryan Mack, November 22, 1920, in Box 25, Hodges Papers.

7. Jacksonville *Florida Times-Union*, November 7, 1919; for insights into both his muckraking labor reform and his opposition to Catts, see Claude L'Engle Papers, P. K. Yonge Library of Florida History, University of Florida, Gainesville.

8. Jacksonville *Florida Times-Union*, July 1, 1917; Sidney J. Catts to *Palm Beach Post*, April 10, 1918; J. B. Hodges to Joe L. Earman, January 30, 1919, in Box 32, Hodges Papers.

opposed him in the gubernatorial primary, had written superintendent Sheats only weeks after the 1916 general election praising
Catts's advocacy of industrial education and urging the superintendent to coordinate his education plans with the administration's.[9]

The most notable application of his concept came in black education. Booker T. Washington had already pioneered a curriculum
devoted to practical industrial arts and agriculture at Tuskegee.
Catts may have borrowed from Washington's theories, since the
governor was well informed about the school because of his service
as pastor of the Tuskegee Baptist Church during the 1880s. Although the causal effect is only inferential, Washington had been
advocating for blacks at Tuskegee what Catts proposed for Florida's
entire population.

Joe Earman enthusiastically seconded the governor's proposal.
Together they pushed through the legislature a sizable appropriation for a new mechanical arts building at Florida Agricultural and
Mechanical College for Negroes in Tallahassee. After investigation,
Earman was so impressed with the industrial orientation of the
black institution that he asked the 1919 legislature for a large
budget increase for the school. The momentum of improvements
prior to 1917 coupled with the activities of the black community
and Earman's enthusiasm greatly improved the quality of black
education. The historian of black higher education in Florida questions the validity of degrees granted prior to 1919 but maintains
that by that year the standards had been raised to acceptable quality for bachelor degrees.[10]

The improved standards at A. & M. created ambivalent feelings
in at least one Catts appointee. Although J. B. Hodges had endorsed the practical curriculum of the school, the new academic
emphasis disturbed him. He protested in 1920 that students at the
Tallahassee institution spent only 2 percent of their time in agri-

9. Jacksonville *Florida Times-Union*, July 1, 1917.
10. *Ibid.*, August 14 and 15, 1917; Leedell W. Neyland, "State-Supported Higher
Education Among Negroes in the State of Florida," *Florida Historical Quarterly*, XLIII
(October, 1964), 111.

cultural and mechanical subjects as opposed to 67 percent on academic courses. He protested to Earman that "You have no idea about the things the Negroes have in their minds." In a letter to Board of Control secretary Bryan Mack, he complained about "too much Greek and Latin" and "not enough work," and urged that some sort of action be taken to reverse this trend.[11] Before Hodges could convert his fellow board members and the governor, the Catts administration had ended.

Another potentially explosive issue died without reaching crisis proportions. Bryan Mack argued that the board should abolish fraternities and sororities at the Gainesville and Tallahassee schools. He believed such organizations to be "undemocratic societies in college life," and won the support of Dr. Edward Conradi, president of the State College for Women. Although Mack claimed that sentiment against social clubs was growing at the University of Florida, President A. A. Murphree resisted attempts to abolish them.[12] With so many other controversies swirling around his administration, Catts wisely decided to forego combat over the Greek system.

Besides, the governor was already embroiled in a bitter controversy with President Murphree over an incident that had occurred on April 17, 1917. The affair began when Anthony Goins, a ten-year-old black child, went to the room of two college students at the University of Florida to collect laundry. J. K. Fuller, son of a prominent Orlando family, was asleep, so his roommate told the boy to return later. The boy knocked again, and Fuller, trying to frighten the child away, fired a pistol shot through the door, killing young Goins.

The representative from Orange County (Orlando) asked the governor to appoint a joint legislative committee to examine conditions at the University of Florida, and the senior Fuller also contacted Catts, grief-stricken because his son was accused of murder.

11. J. B. Hodges to Joe Earman, November 19, 1920, Hodges to Bryan Mack, November 22, 1920, in Box 25, Hodges Papers.
12. Jacksonville *Florida Times-Union*, October 8, 1917.

He blamed the university for allowing its students to bring pistols on campus. Catts, only recently installed in office and fearing "a great deal of newspaper notoriety" that might jeopardize his appointments to the Board of Control, refused to take any action until he had investigated, personally, reports that many students at the university possessed firearms. Murphree replied to Catts's proposed investigation with a telegram mentioning legal action, which the governor interpreted as a hostile gesture aimed at him.[13]

Catts, his notoriously short patience now fully extended, replied with a blistering rebuke. Calling the telegram "a little heated for a man of your standing," he warned that if Murphee instituted legal proceedings or caused the Fuller family "any trouble you will have me to deal with on his side and possibly the Board of Control will also have something to say about what you do in the matter. . . . The less you agitate . . . and the more careful you are in regard to discipline in your University it seems to me the better it will be for you." This response was a thinly disguised threat to use the Board of Control to retaliate against him, and to Murphree it seemed to confirm election rumors that Catts was determined to remove him. The president wrote despondently to his friend P. K. Yonge, who was still a member of the board but soon to be replaced, threatening to resign: "It is needless for me to say that I feel very much discouraged and undone. It was a great trial to me to respond as I did to the impertinent letter. . . . For the good of the cause, however, I put my pride in my pocket and wrote the most conciliatory letter I could."[14]

The president's reply to Catts's angry letter of June 4 assured the governor that he had misinterpreted the telegram. Murphee had not threatened to sue the governor, but only proposed legal action against young Fuller. Realizing perhaps that no Florida court was likely to be harsh to a prominent young white accused of killing a black, Catts allowed the controversy to end with a terse note

13. Sidney J. Catts to A. A. Murphree, June 9, 1917, in Box 4, P. K. Yonge Papers.
14. Sidney J. Catts to A. A. Murphree, June 4, 1917, Murphree to P. K. Yonge, June 9, 1917, in Box 4, Yonge Papers.

regretting "the little misunderstanding," adding that "all is well that ends well." Mollified by what he interpreted as an apology, the governor contented himself with packing the Board of Control with Earman, Hodges, and Mack, and young J. K. Fuller went unpunished.[15]

With this introduction to the Catts administration, it is no wonder that Murphree feared that the board would make decisions based on political considerations. Credit for restoring strained relations between Murphree and the board belongs primarily to Hodges and Earman, who labored prodigiously to convince the college president that they would not meddle with university administration. Hodges assured Murphree and the governor that the new board would be able to "maintain harmony" and provide for university growth. Earman developed genuine respect for Murphree and wrote him in May, 1918: "There ain't going to be any politics in any way, shape or form connected with the Higher Institutions of Learning in Florida if the writer can help it. This statement not only applies to the faculties, but [to] all other influences." John B. Sutton, appointed to the board by Catts in 1919, also wrote Murphree assuring him that he had nothing to fear from the board, which would protect the university from political meddling.[16]

Although available correspondence of the Board of Control reveals little actual interference by the governor in university affairs, there is strong evidence that he recognized no restrictions on his right to intervene in educational and administrative policy. Earman wrote Murphree in 1919, suggesting that the impetuous chief executive sometimes exerted pressure on financial proceedings: "the governor SUGGESTS, which from a practical standpoint means that he BOSSES and Comptroller Amos Vises, [sic] audits and passes upon all bills. These two officials can make members of the Board of Control... jump sideways." That Catts seldom meddled is evi-

15. Sidney J. Catts to A. A. Murphree, June 9, 1917, Catts to Murphree, June 16, 1917, in Box 13, A. A. Murphree Papers.
16. J. B. Hodges to Sidney J. Catts, November 14, 1917, in Box 25, Hodges Papers; Joe L. Earman to A. A. Murphree, May 1, 1918, John B. Sutton to Murphree, June 7, 1919, in Box 4, Murphree Papers.

dence of his growing confidence in Murphree and the judicious restraint exercised over the governor by Earman and Hodges. Relations between Catts and the university president improved to such an extent that Catts appointed Murphree to numerous boards and commissions, and Murphree invited the chief executive to speak on campus. The faculty at the university did not aid the rapprochement, however, rejecting a proposal to award an honorary degree to one of the governor's friends whom he had recommended for such recognition.[17]

In time, Murphree reciprocated the confidence of Earman. The president wrote the board chairman in the fall of 1919 concerning a former teacher, Leroy D. Householder, who had written Catts demanding Murphree's removal because of "perjury, moral unfitness, ET CETERA [sic]." Householder wrote the governor that his salary had not been paid. Catts took no action except to forward Householder's complaints to Hodges for advice. Earman wrote Hodges interceding for Murphree: "nothing must happen to 'KID MURPH.' Please let me know if this matter is serious enough for me to hotfoot it to Tallahassee."[18] Once again the crisis passed without incident when the board solidly backed Murphree.

In some respects Earman espoused an even broader definition of freedom than President Murphree. The university official, accustomed to playing politics in order to win appropriations, was extremely sensitive regarding any embarrassing statements emanating from his institution. When student editors of the Florida *Alligator*, campus newspaper, criticized proposals for two additional "normal schools," Murphree moved to curb their hostile columns. Earman urged Murphree not to interfere, defending the students and reminding the college executive that the Constitution guaranteed the right of free speech.[19]

By the end of the Catts administration, substantial changes had

17. Joe L. Earman to A. A. Murphree, July 9, 1919, in Box 4, Murphree to Sidney J. Catts, June 8, 1918, in Box 16, Murphree Papers.

18. Joe L. Earman to J. B. Hodges, October 15, 1919, Hodges to S. J. Catts, October 20, 1919, in Box 9, *ibid.*

19. Joe L. Earman to A. A. Murphree, May 3, 1919, in Box 4, *ibid.*

occurred in the original personnel on the education board. The governor requested that Earman take over the chaotic Board of Health in the summer of 1919, and Hodges was chosen to replace him as chairman of the Board of Control. Bryan Mack resigned as secretary in September, 1920, to move to Atlanta, Georgia, where he became secretary-treasurer of a china import firm. J. T. Diamond—a Catts protégé, former superintendent of public schools for Santa Rosa County, and officer of the state school superintendent—replaced him.

Despite all the politically inspired changes, the initial predictions that Catts would tamper with internal policies and personnel of the colleges never materialized. He contented himself with political control of the board. As a matter of fact, the establishment-oriented governor, Cary A. Hardee, who followed Catts to Tallahassee, manipulated the board as much as his maverick predecessor. Hodges learned in November, 1920, only weeks after Hardee's election, that the new governor would not reappoint him or W. W. Flournoy, another Catts appointee, to new terms. Governor Hardee also refused to reappoint John B. Sutton despite endorsement by the University of Florida alumni association and many others. Hardee, in short, played politics with the Board of Control as fully as Catts had before him.[20] The difference between the two governors seems not to have been their policies toward the board, but their affiliations with regular and maverick wings of the Democratic party.

Joe Earman's dubious reward for his service as chairman of the education agency was transfer to the factionalized Board of Health. His service to education and his chairmanship of the State Plant Board, whose membership was identical to that of the Board of Control, elicited praise from the press. Journalists applauded his progressive ideas, especially the establishment of the university extension system, and his employment of skilled scientists to protect the state from tree and plant pests. His administration of the

---

20. J. B. Hodges to Bryan Mack, November 22, 1920, in Box 25, Hodges Papers; John B. Sutton to G. P. Garrett, June 9, 1923, in Box 4, Murphree Papers.

dual agencies had been "business like, economical and efficient."[21]

Earman's new task would utilize every ounce of this administrative skill. Governor Catts had removed the state's two highest health officers at the first of his administration, and had replaced them with two of his political cronies, Dr. W. H. Cox and Charles T. Frecker. In contrast to his selections to the Board of Control, the governor's nominees for the health agency did not prove so competent or dedicated. The 1918 session of the legislature appointed two special committees to investigate the department, and they blasted the board for inefficiency and internal dissension.[22] Catts, now embarrassed and angered by the malfeasance of his subordinates, tried to remove his own appointees but was blocked by court action. Finally, on June 19, 1919, Catts and Earman forced state health officer Cox out of office and replaced him with Dr. Ralph N. Greene.

Greene's credentials were impressive. He had served for seven years as chief of the medical staff at the Florida Hospital for the Insane. He had then entered the army medical service where he had performed with such distinction that he had been selected as clinical director for nervous and mental diseases for the Southern Department of the Army, stationed at Fort Sam Houston, Texas.

Greene provided vigorous, intelligent leadership, although he proved to be as controversial as the unfortunate Cox. His interest in public health conditions in Jacksonville led to the first of two controversies. For several years, Governor Catts had been disturbed over reports of drunkenness and prostitution in the port city, which was swelled to overflowing by expansion of the shipbuilding industry and the construction of Camp Joseph E. Johnston. In January, 1918, the governor had visited the military facility unexpectedly in the company of Joe Earman. He delivered an impromptu speech to the camp's enlisted troops, begging them not to "besmirch the womanhood of the city and state, but to marry . . . and leave an honorable name behind them." Should any

21. Jacksonville *Florida Times-Union*, July 7, 1919.
22. *Ibid.*, June 4, June 26, 1919.

soldier lack funds for a marriage license, he could write the governor who promised to arrange nuptials. There is no record of any such requests, but when the Camp Johnston bar association invited the governor for an encore two months later, he again urged the five thousand soldiers who attended his speech to live moral lives and not to stain the "fair name of Southern womanhood."[23]

Although the city, responding to military pressure, abolished liquor sales, prostitution presented a more complicated problem. Dr. Greene confronted the issue in an address to the Jacksonville Kiwanis Club in December, 1919; he charged that timidity of city officials contributed to a spiraling epidemic of venereal disease. Mayor John W. Martin, temporarily out of favor with the chief executive, precipitated a collision in his rebuttal before the same club. Martin questioned Greene's veracity and reminded the Kiwanians that the doctor was an appointee of Sidney Catts, presumably clinching the issue of credibility. Greene relished a battle, and replied that the issue was not a question of his veracity but of the "irrefutable fact" that U.S. health department statistics showed that five thousand cases of venereal disease had been reported in the city during 1919. Marshaling additional evidence, he reported that when Jacksonville inductees underwent medical examination during the first draft of World War I, nineteen out of every one hundred was suffering from venereal disease. These statistics more than any abstract argument provided "concrete and undeniable evidence and proof that the mayor of Jacksonville is not doing his duty in suppressing vice." Joe Earman also refuted Martin's claim and announced that Greene had asked the help of Jacksonville's police force in abolishing the city's "restricted district."[24]

Greene broadened his audience in a speech to the Florida State Conference of Social Work convened in Jacksonville in March, 1920. Florida led the United States with both the highest percentage of syphilis and the largest ratio of feeblemindedness. Dr. D. C. Campbell, director of the State Board of Hygiene, reinforced

23. *Ibid.*, January 16, March 6, 1918.
24. *Ibid.*, December 19, 20, 1919.

Greene's findings and proposed to help young people by instituting sex education in the public school curriculum from grammar school through college. He reported that 60 percent of Florida's convicts had syphilis, while the ratio of infection in large cities and lumber mill communities ranged from an estimated 36 to 40 percent of the male population. Only strict law enforcement could end the epidemic spread of syphilis and other "social diseases." Joe Earman, perhaps despairing of medical or political remedies, sought a spiritual solution. He invited the Reverend Billy Sunday to conduct a crusade in Jacksonville, confiding to the preacher that Florida's six thousand cases of syphilis per year had won her the dubious distinction of the highest rate of venereal disease in any state in the nation.[25]

When not crusading against vice, Greene proposed numerous reforms of Florida health practices. Noting that the state was a dumping ground for inefficient physicians because they could secure licenses to practice so easily, he criticized the legislature for blocking all remedial laws to correct this condition. During the disastrous influenza epidemic of 1919–1920, he also issued detailed instructions to state newspapers on proper health practices. The Board of Health, in a desperate measure to prevent spread of the epidemic, authorized railroad employees to arrest any travelers who persisted in spitting in railroad cars or waiting rooms. Greene urged urbanites to avoid crowded or poorly ventilated places, and authorized health officials in small towns to quarantine flu patients.[26]

His expert and dedicated service won the respect of his associates and the people of Florida. When Governor Catts was asked to recommend someone for the position of superintendent of St. Elizabeth Hospital, a government facility for the insane at Washington, D.C., he recommended Greene for the lucrative post.

25. *Ibid.*, March 14, 1920; and Joe Earman to Billy Sunday, November 9, 1920, in Box 25, Hodges Papers.
26. Jacksonville *Florida Times-Union*, March 14, January 26, 1920.

Greene turned down the job preferring to remain in Florida, a decision which brought praise from the state press.[27]

Controversy developed on the Board of Health, however, when Earman split with Greene over a construction proposal. Earman had functioned in the Catts administration as a conciliator, a role he performed with considerable skill. Even opposition newsmen liked their fellow editor. The antiadministration St. Petersburg *Times* proposed that he be sent to Russia to pacify the country's contending political parties: "Joe's ability to bring together the warring elements of Gov. Catts' followers leads his friends to believe that he might even compose the differences of the various elements in Russia." Earman admitted, however, that Catts exercised as tight a reign over his new board as over the educational agency.[28]

His powers of compromise faded in a dispute with Greene and Catts over the location of an orthopedic hospital. Word reached Catts from two political henchmen in the fall of 1920 that his chairman was causing trouble on the Board of Health by insisting that the hospital be built in Earman's hometown of West Palm Beach. Dr. Greene proposed a different priority, advocating a comprehensive health program funded by the state, and threatened to resign. Catts believed that Greene's resignation would "be one of the greatest losses the State of Florida has obtained since my coming to office," and asked Hodges to use his influence to reconcile the dispute. Catts's letter to J. B. Hodges revealed the friction that would soon cost him the friendship of his once valued ally:

Joe Earman is so touchless with me, I hate to write him about it, but if you could get it to him someway that he is going to injure himself, his Board, State Health Department, and the state by putting this building in this rich tourists town, where prices are higher than any other city in the state except Miami . . . you can do a great favor to the state as well as to me. I don't see what Joe Earman can be thinking about for it certainly looks like either he is trying to appease the enemies he made in Palm

27. *Ibid.*, January 17, 24, 1920.
28. *Ibid.*, quoting St. Petersburg *Times*, January 1, 1918; Joe L. Earman to A. A. Murphree, July 9, 1919, in Box 4, Murphree Papers.

Beach during the late campaign or pull off some other stunt for which there can be no sensible reason.[29]

Hodges revealed the correspondence to Earman and promised to defend his friend's position to the governor. Earman dissuaded him, expressing regret that the matter had reached Tallahassee and assuring Hodges that he and Greene were reconciling their differences. Hodges, summoned to Tallahassee by the governor, found him poring over files submitted by Greene for a comprehensive state medical program, together with Earman's hospital files. He persuaded Catts that since Greene's project was well underway, state tax funds could support it, and the two of them worked out a compromise.[30]

Days later, at the insistence of Hodges and Catts, Earman and Greene met at Delray and achieved a reconciliation. They agreed on overall health proposals for the state. Greene outlined a pilot project in four counties where health care was substandard. He would launch a massive effort against trachoma, hookworm, and various other diseases, and provide two or three dentists who would check the teeth of all children. Greene proposed Taylor, LaFayette, Suwannee and Madison counties; Earman suggested that Columbia County be substituted for Madison as a political maneuver to win the legislative support of influential Lake City Representative W. W. Phillips for the Board of Health appropriation. When the conference ended, Earman reported to Catts that amicable relations had been restored.[31]

No single area of social reform attracted more of Catts's energy than attempts to rehabilitate wayward young people, the mentally ill, and state prisoners. Close associate Jerry Carter remembered his concern as almost a passion.[32] The governor expressed this

29. Sidney J. Catts to J. B. Hodges, September 17, 1920, in Box 25, Hodges Papers.

30. J. B. Hodges to Joe Earman, September 22, 1920, Earman to Hodges, September 23, 1920, Hodges to Earman, September 28, 1920, Sidney J. Catts to Earman, September 27, 1920, Catts to Ralph N. Greene, September 27, 1920, all in Box 25, Hodges Papers.

31. Joe Earman to J. B. Hodges, October 4, 1920, Earman to Sidney J. Catts, October 4, 1920, in Box 25, Hodges Papers.

32. Interview, Jerry W. Carter, July 29, 1970, Tallahassee.

interest in many ways including regular private inspections of all state institutions for whites.

This busy schedule was more than a mere political gesture, a fact demonstrated by his prompt action to correct inadequacies which he discovered on such trips. He was quick to praise when he discovered good conditions and efficient management, but his wrath knew no bounds when he found suffering due to misman-agement or brutality. The school for boys at Marianna provided an early test of the governor's resolve on juvenile correction.

Attorney General Swearingen had been interested in delin-quent children since his days as a municipal judge in Jacksonville. As a member of the board of state institutions which ran the Marianna facility, he launched an investigation which he described in a bitter interview in the *Florida Times-Union*. The school was more a prison than an industrial or reform school, he reported. He refused to criticize school officials, blaming the plight on over-crowding and on a philosophy that treated the boys like hardened criminals, which they might become if they remained in the facil-ity. Problems were multiple: too much idleness; lack of eating utensils, which forced the boys to eat with their fingers; and too few blankets, which required the boys to sleep in their clothes dur-ing winter months.[33] He instituted two policies to correct condi-tions: he paroled one hundred boys whom he felt could be better handled by county probation officers, thus reducing expenses and making available more money for education; and he proposed that the legislature increase the superintendent's annual salary of fif-teen hundred dollars in order to attract a more capable man.

All such ameliorative measures failed to correct the personnel problems, but only Swearingen on the Board of Commissioners of State Institutions was willing to dismiss the superintendent. The board membership consisted of the governor's cabinet which was elective and allied to the regular wing of the party. They were ignorant of conditions, having demonstrated little interest in actu-ally inspecting the facilities they governed; without personal im-

33. Jacksonville *Florida Times-Union*, September 29, 1917.

pressions of their own, they interpreted Catts's demand for dismissal as just another personal vendetta. A year after Swearingen's first disclosure, a scandal finally forced the cabinet to concede that Superintendent Boone should be fired. An influenza epidemic swept the school, and the physician summoned to care for the boys discovered wretched conditions: lack of clothing, body lice, inadequate hygiene practices, and malnutrition resulting from lack of meat, especially among Negro boys. There were 264 cases of influenza with only three boys escaping the disease, and six patients had already died. Catts blasted the cabinet for its delay, and the conservative *Florida Times-Union* finally included establishment Democrats in its criticism of patronage abuse: politics had always determined appointments of staff at the industrial school and reform was critically needed, including employment of a warden of "exceptional abilities." Even Democratic regulars in the legislature belatedly recognized the problem. The 1918 special session appointed a committee to investigate conditions at Marianna, and its report confirmed Catts's judgment by condemning management of the school.[34]

During the month in which Catts took office he had launched an investigation of the state prisons. He found conditions at Raiford Prison Farm particularly appalling, but all attempts at reform were blocked by recalcitrant prison officials. He soon discovered allies among humanitarians of many persuasions, including prison reformer Mrs. Maude Ballington Booth who investigated Raiford and then delivered a series of addresses in Florida churches. In speeches at Jacksonville's First Presbyterian Church and the Memorial Presbyterian Church in St. Augustine, she argued that a prisoner was entitled to good food, air, clothing, plenty of work, and some money when he completed his term. Prisons should reform men and prepare them for good citizenship, a task that Raiford was not performing.[35]

As in the boys' school episode, Catts finally won his battle; in

34. *Ibid.*, November 9, December 1, 1918.
35. *Ibid.*, March 26, April 1, 1917.

July, 1918, his secretary J. S. Blitch resigned to assume the superintendency of the state prison farm at Raiford, elected to the office by the Board of Commissioners. Blitch was no novice to prison work, his father having served many years as physician for the state prison system. Even the antiadministration Tampa *Tribune* praised the new superintendent as a practical man who would make "Raiford farm blossom like a striped lily."[36] No prophesy was more completely fulfilled.

When the special legislative committee appointed to investigate state institutions turned its attention to Raiford, it once again had to concur with Catts—this time in glowing tribute to the governor's appointee. Although Blitch had been at the farm for only nine months, he already had increased receipts over 100 percent, reduced costs by half that much, and made the prison self-sufficient. He had terminated the practice of hiring forty local men as gun-carrying guards. After dismissing all salaried watchmen, he allowed the prisoners to select foremen who assumed this function with the result that there had been no escapes during 1919. Blitch also recommended that a number of responsible prisoners be paroled to the institution to serve as foremen, crew leaders, and office staff in place of free labor, thereby economizing while at the same time affording convicts a more humane life. The farm provided more recreational activity, including an auditorium for lectures and plays, a moving picture each Saturday night, and baseball and football fields. A historian of Florida's penal system claims that the convicts' health had never been so good nor the prisoners better cared for than under Blitch; and W. T. Cash wrote that Blitch was considered "one of the outstanding prison superintendents in the United States."[37]

Blitch energetically lobbied to win support for his concepts of penology. He frequently spoke to church groups where he cham-

36. *Ibid.*, July 22, 1918, quoting the Tampa *Tribune*.
37. Kathleen Falconer Pratt, "The Development of the Florida Prison System" (M.S. thesis, Florida State University, 1949), 101–102; W. T. Cash, *History of the Democratic Party in Florida*, 132.

pioned the application of the Golden Rule to prisoners. Another project that he instituted brought prominent guests to visit the Raiford Prison Farm in order for them to procure a better understanding of its operation. Many visitors subsequently became effective lobbyists for prison reform. Two visiting Jacksonville women carried away a view which obviously coincided with the superintendent's; they reported: "The visitor to the state farm comes away with the belief that a prison is not primarily solely a place for retalative [sic] punishment, but a training school in which a man is prepared for spending what years of freedom may come to him a decent, self-respecting citizen."[38]

The humanization of conditions in state institutions during the Catts adminstration ranks as his major accomplishment as governor. During the war, Catts had seen a report prepared by two representatives of the Russell Sage Foundation at the request of West Virginia's governor. He was so impressed by their recommendations on social welfare that he telegraphed the two investigators —Hastings H. Hart, who was director of a division of the foundation, and Clarence L. Stenaker, secretary of the New Jersey State Charities and Prison Reform Association—asking them to survey Florida. The two arrived in April, 1918, and undertook a comprehensive study of the state. Their lavish praise of Raiford Prison Farm raised Blitch to the status of a national expert in penology. They suggested even more effort at rehabilitation but noted that farm productivity surpassed comparable programs in other states, and called Blitch one of the abler prison superintendents in America. Although critical of the state's inadequate support for teachers, the report noted that Florida appropriated more money for public health services in proportion to her size than any state other than Pennsylvania.[39]

Perhaps influenced by the Russell Sage report, Catts took greater pride in his contributions to social welfare than in any other

38. Jacksonville *Florida Times-Union*, September 12, 1920.
39. For a summary of the report, see Deal, "Sidney Johnston Catts, Stormy Petrel of Florida Politics," 164.

facet of his service as governor. He boasted upon leaving office that state institutions were more efficiently and humanely conducted than at any time in Florida history, enumerating reforms at the boys' school at Marianna, the facility for the deaf and blind, and establishment of the girls' industrial school at Ocala. His crowning pride, however, was the state prison farm. Formerly it had bristled with guns, but under the honor system, cooperative prisoners were allowed considerable freedom. The reforms introduced by Blitch had reduced escapes and focused national attention on the prison.[40] The governor had a right to boast; despite the bitter partisanship of these years, even his opponents had grudgingly acknowledged his contribution to protecting and rehabilitating defenseless Floridians.

---

40. Jacksonville *Florida Times-Union*, January 5, 1921.

NINE

The Politics
of Disquietude

TWO SIGNIFICANT EVENTS struck Florida politics with resounding force in 1919: an increasingly militant labor movement and the 1919 session of the legislature. The resultant clamor set the stage for a political confrontation over "Cattsism" in the 1920 statewide elections. Labor unrest was not unique to Florida in the tumultuous year of 1919 but paralyzed much of the nation; however, the state situation contained some unusual elements.

Unionism in other parts of the South had encountered great difficulty because of prevailing social customs and mores. Otherworldly religion, ethnic homogeneity, individualism, ruralism, the paternalism of management, and many other distinctive cultural elements made the task of organizing southern workers more demanding than in the Northeast or Rocky Mountain states. There were really two labor movements in Florida, each of which had developed along its own lines. Craft unions were composed of shipyard and railroad employees, phosphate workers, transit operators, and building trades artisans. Such unions drew craftsmen mainly from rural Anglo-Saxon southern origins, with Negro laborers gradually forced out of skilled trades in the first decades of the twentieth century. As a consequence, this segment of Florida labor was somewhat traditionalist, corresponding to the pattern found in other southern states.[1]

---

1. The use of the term *traditionalist* does not, of course, preclude the use of strikes and even of occasional violence. Both had occurred in Florida labor history, though not to the

An unusual element within the state's labor movement was the extensive presence of Latin immigrants, concentrated mainly in the cigar industry of Key West and Tampa. By the beginning of the twentieth century, Tampa was producing more clear Havana cigars than any other American city, and the high-grade luxury smokes were as famed for their quality as Tampa was for its quantity of production. The Knights of Labor had first begun organizing the cigar workers, but not until 1899 did the most important phase of the organizing effort begin. The cigar workers had experienced the frustrations of many workers in the same era: ineffectual strikes, management retaliation, worsening labor conditions, child labor, seasonal layoffs, and unsanitary, dangerous plants. As a consequence of ethnic diversity and management opposition, the immigrants experimented with new approaches to labor problems. Some workers adopted the doctrines of anarchism, while others pioneered projects such as socialized medicine which operated through a health care cooperative.[2]

Although these two segments of labor had developed independently of each other, both figured prominently in the clash of economic interests which convulsed Florida in 1919. Conflict stemmed from three interrelated developments: wartime industrialism, inflationary pressure on worker pocketbooks, and the insecurity caused by wartime business retrenchment.[3] Labor upheaval occurred throughout the state but was most intense in six pockets where urbanization, inflation, and economic readjustment created labor unrest.

Key West, located at the tip of the peninsula and long a center

---

extent or with the intensity of other states. See, for instance, Wayne Flynt, "Pensacola Labor Problems and Political Radicalism, 1908," *Florida Historical Quarterly*, XLIII (April, 1965), 315–32.

2. Professor Durward Long has written a number of perceptive articles on immigrant unionism in Florida; the most representative and helpful are: "An Immigrant Cooperative Social Medicine Program in the South, 1887–1963," *Journal of Southern History*, XXXI (November, 1965), 417–34; "La Resistencia: Tampa's Immigrant Labor Union," *Labor History*, VI (Fall, 1965), 193–213; "The Open-Closed Shop Battle in Tampa's Cigar Industry, 1919–1921," *Florida Historical Quarterly*, XLVII (October, 1968), 101–21; "Labor Relations in the Tampa Cigar Industry, 1885–1911," *Labor History*, XII (Fall, 1971), 551–59.

3. For a more thorough overview, see Wayne Flynt, "Florida Labor and Political 'Radicalism,' 1919–1920," *Labor History*, IX (Winter, 1968), 73–90.

for the cigar industry, experienced an active organizing campaign in 1919. Creation of the Federation of Federal Employees and the Key West Police Local, which included the city's patrolmen and even the chief of police, provided greater respectability for unionism. Strikes occurred in August and September among electricians, construction workers, and five thousand laborers in the tobacco factories.

The bustling tourist resort of Miami had grown from a swamp to a city of 35,000 inhabitants in only twenty years and had been well organized by the AFL. In early September, 1919, construction workers struck in order to force a local lumberyard to discharge nonunion Negro deliverers. The strike paralyzed nearly $2 million in new construction and threatened to disrupt the lucrative tourist season. Angry businessmen founded the Greater Miami Association, declared for the open shop, and began to import strikebreakers. Under prodding from the city council and stymied by the strike, the association finally capitulated to worker demands on September 10. A general strike was renewed in October, however, when one of the companies refused to recognize the closed shop agreement.

Labor unrest in St. Petersburg contained elements of racial conflict. The city was experiencing a building boom similar to Miami's, with a consequent shortage of labor. Unskilled workers, most of them black, formed an AFL local and declared in favor of a minimum salary of four dollars a day. Rumors of a general strike by all Negro laborers circulated through the west coast resort community amidst newspaper reports of outside agitators and a local "radical labor element."[4]

Nor did the Florida panhandle escape ferment. Pensacola, long-time base of unionist activity, experienced labor strife throughout the spring and fall. In April, shipyard workers unsuccessfully struck the Pensacola Shipbuilding Company. All coastwise steamers and tugs were tied up by a strike of port engineers in October, and in November the city's construction workers walked out demanding a closed shop.

4. Tampa *Tribune*, June 7, August 31, September 10, 11, November 27, 1919.

Despite such dispersed activity, the cities of Jacksonville and Tampa remained the most potentially explosive centers of labor unrest. Jacksonville's history of unionism dated back well into the nineteenth century and involved a multiplicity of skilled workers.[5] Some thirty-eight AFL locals thrived in the city by 1919, with twenty-four of them united in the politically potent Central Trades and Labor Council. A labor newspaper, the *Artisan,* helped mobilize laborers and had played a key role in the election of John W. Martin as mayor. In addition to national strikes which affected the city's railroad and telephone employees, there were local walkouts by tractionworkers and city firemen. Violence became a frequent occurrence, and the Central Trades Council averted a citywide sympathy strike only by allowing its constituent unions to individually call workers off their jobs in support of the firemen.[6]

Tampa was the other great citadel of unionism in Florida, with major strength among shipyard and cigarworkers. A violent seven-month strike had occurred in 1910 among cigarworkers, and trouble broke out again in 1919. Sporadic walkouts began in April and intensified by the end of the year. Although numerous minor issues were involved, the primary demands were a 25 percent increase in wages and institution of the closed shop. Industrialists countered with a well-organized trade association which effectively blocked corporate members from dealing separately with the unions. Union membership increased steadily from 3,000 members in 1919 to over 7,000 members in 1920, a year during which some 6,400 cigarworkers left their jobs. The ensuing ten-month strike was the longest in the history of Tampa's cigar industry and ended in the defeat of labor demands for a closed shop.[7]

Another prominent Tampa industry, ship construction, experienced statewide labor difficulties, although the local situation was relatively tranquil. At the large Oscar Daniels yard, 96 percent of

5. For an interesting vignette, see Jerrell H. Shofner, "The Labor League of Jacksonville: A Negro Union and White Strikebreakers," *Florida Historical Quarterly,* L (January, 1972), 278–82.

6. *Artisan,* March 1, 1919; in Records of the United States Shipping Board, RG 32, NA.

7. Long, "The Open-Closed Shop Battle in Tampa's Cigar Industry, 1919–1920," 105, 120.

the employees were American born, a notable contrast to the work force of the city's cigar industry. Most of the workers were Florida natives, some 40 percent were black, and 25 percent of the laborers belonged to unions. This figure would have been much greater had Negroes been included in the union, but most blacks refused to join a Jim Crow affiliate. A secret service investigation among shipyard workers in March, 1919, revealed no radical activity among Daniels' ship-builders.[8] By December, however, the national reduction in shipping created insecurity among these same employees. Complaining of lower wages than were being paid in other yards, they struck Oscar Daniels to enforce their demands. Union spokesmen claimed that 1,300 workers walked off their jobs, although the company reported that of its total 2,150 employees (which included 600 blacks), only 570 white and 16 black workers participated in the strike. The hostile Tampa *Tribune* blamed the trouble on union demands for a closed shop and on "outside agitators" who had caused division among the workers; strikers denied both charges.[9] Daniels pledged to replace each striker and by December 9 announced that the number of workers had reached 1,627 employees.

The Tampa Bay Dry Dock Company suffered less labor trouble but still experienced serious economic dislocation. The government had approached Tampa financial tycoon Peter O. Knight during the war and had persuaded him to utilize land he owned to construct a facility for building wooden vessels. Knight agreed and spent a substantial sum of money recruiting skilled labor from across the country. The yard was 75 percent unionized but cuts in government contracts caused many of the skilled unionists to seek employment in the Oscar Daniels facility. Despite Knight's vigorous protest of government injustice, two ships that were 40 percent complete lay rotting in the ways, no longer needed after the armistice in Europe.[10]

8. Morton Watkins to Charles Piez, March 10, 1919, United States Shipping Board, RG 32, NA.

9. For an account of the trouble, see Tampa *Tribune*, December 4–8, 1919.

10. Morton Watkins to Charles Piez, March 10, 1919, United States Shipping Board, RG 32, NA.

Shipbuilders in Florida feared most for the situations in Jacksonville and Pensacola. Oscar Daniels reported privately to one
government official that labor was making a determined effort to
unionize the Jacksonville yards, and that the Jacksonville Ship
Outfitting Company was prepared to sign a closed shop contract.
Union leaders, considering this an opening wedge, would then
conduct a determined campaign statewide. President Temple of
the Jacksonville Outfitting Company reportedly had told A. D.
Grout of the city's Industrial Relations Board that he favored a
union agreement and would have operated a closed shop but for
the government's edict against such policy.[11]

Morton Watkins, who reported on Florida labor relations for
the Emergency Fleet Corporation of the United States Shipping
Board, interviewed W. A. Wallace, president of the Jacksonville
Metal Trades Council, in order to obtain labor's viewpoint. Wallace revealed that his council had organized 75 percent of the
workers at the antiunion Merrill-Stevens Yard and that membership was increasing daily. He admitted charges of labor inefficiency
at the facility but blamed the trouble on management which spent
more time fighting unionism than building ships. Also, the company allowed no union officials or supervision in the yards, a
marked contrast with Temple's company which was in almost daily
contact with union headquarters.[12] As a result of such disagree-
ments, labor problems plagued Merrill-Stevens. In April, 1919,
Governor Catts visited Jacksonville to confer with William B.
Wilson, a representative of the secretary of labor, who was in the
city to examine labor-management problems at the Merrill-Stevens
facility. In December, 1,500 workers walked out for a week over a
minor dispute.

Across the state in Pensacola, rumors of political radicalism
complicated unrest in the shipyards. According to one report,
members of the radical Industrial Workers of the World had left
Mobile, Alabama, and had obtained jobs in a Pensacola yard. Subsequently, local residents blamed a "run" on a Pensacola bank on

11. *Ibid.*
12. *Ibid.*

"two ship yard [sic] workers who could not identify themselves . . . and . . . started stories of the bank's insolvency."[13] In April, 1919, the Pensacola Shipbuilding Company was struck by 652 members of the Boilermakers and Iron Shipbuilders' Union, who demanded that Negroes be removed from certain skilled jobs and be employed only as helpers. They also called for removal of the company superintendent.

Florida's labor unrest involved inevitable political consequences. For some years the state's labor leaders had shied away from politics. Influenced, however, by the increasing political involvements of the national office, the Florida affiliate became more active in government during the Catts administration. Claude L'Engle, publisher of the Jacksonville *Sun*, applauded the decision of AFL president Samuel Gompers to thrust labor into the political arena. L'Engle argued that most great reforms had been born in labor organizations, and argued that if laborers and their sympathizers voted, they could abolish trusts and end corruption.[14] Elected as a prolabor candidate, L'Engle had served one term in Congress (1913–1915). In 1919 he praised profit sharing, advocated the equality of workers with management, and tried to arrange a statewide ticket for the 1920 elections that would be sympathetic to labor.[15]

The efforts of L'Engle and others bore fruit in 1919 when workers, prodded by economic unrest, participated in a wide range of political activities. Key West unionists endorsed a candidate for mayor, while Negro workers in St. Petersburg sponsored a drive to persuade blacks to pay their poll taxes, prompting a police investigation and charges of "bolshevism" from the mayor. The eighteenth session of the Florida Federation of Labor convened in Tallahassee in April, 1919, with its over one hundred delegates constituting the largest attendance in history; and the laborers endorsed a variety of

13. *Ibid.*
14. Joel Webb Eastman, "Claude L'Engle, Florida Muckraker, " *Florida Historical Quarterly*, XLV (January, 1967), 249.
15. MS of article, 1919, in Claude L'Engle Papers.

legislative measures. When the Tampa *Morning Tribune* complained about the formation of a new party in Florida, a reader named E. L. Clarke responded by outlining the objectives of this new coalition: it would unite the "A. F. of L., non-partisans, single-taxers, socialists, various farmers' unions, unorganized labor and legitimate business and professional men." Its platform called for confiscation of some land and property which the government would rent for revenue to replace taxes. The *Tribune* raged that such a platform constituted "the most complete bolshevikism, [sic] socialism and redism we ever have seen."[16]

The actual expression of labor's political activity was considerably less radical than Clarke's proposal and usually emerged in response to local economic conditions. Jacksonville provides a good example of the interaction between localized working-class problems and state politics. The Jacksonville Chamber of Commerce and Senator Duncan Fletcher tried to minimize labor trouble by persuading the federal government to reduce expenditures in the city by gradual closings of facilities rather than by sudden, wholesale cutbacks.[17] The strategem did not work, and violence exploded during summertime strikes among the city's firemen and communication workers. Mayor John W. Martin, who owed his election to labor backing, assured strikers of his sympathy and fired three policemen for taking money from company officials while on duty. Governor Catts conferred with Martin several times about the strike situation, and on July 16, 1919, held a conference with striking firemen. He later addressed a large audience at the Jacksonville Labor Temple. The governor pledged himself to the cause of unionism and against the "absolute monarchy and autocracy" of the city commission; he assured workers that he had few friends among bankers, capitalists, and other "plutocratic" classes. After reviewing his unsuccessful efforts to place city commissions under control of the governor, he said: "If Catts had the power and

16. Tampa *Tribune*, November 16, June 19, July 19, 1919.
17. Duncan U. Fletcher to Charles Piez, March 5, 1919, United States Shipping Board, RG 32, NA.

right you'd see how long these firemen would be out of work and how long the city commission would be in power." Catts urged strikers to obey the law and assured assembled firemen that three-fourths of all Floridians supported their attempt to form a union. The chief executive praised Mayor Martin and advised workers to register to vote in order to put men into office who would "look at this labor proposition in your way, and before placing them into office, impress upon them that the will of the workingmen is unionism and to override this will mean their expulsion from office."[18]

The governor also became embroiled in a violent strike in Florida's phosphate belt. The War Labor Board had investigated charges of company exploitation of labor in the Polk and Hillsborough county mines, and unanimously had recommended a shorter workday and the right of collective bargaining. Peter O. Knight, conservative Tampa industrialist and counsel for the phosphate companies, rejected the recommendations.

Some 3,500 miners walked off their jobs in April, demanding implementation of the government recommendations and paralyzing the mining district. In May the operators began importing strikebreakers, many of them blacks, and by June the mines had reopened. Incidents of violence increased steadily throughout the summer, and on July 23 a Negro strikebreaker was murdered. On the night of August 7 a convoy of forty-six automobiles, each carrying two armed men, drove to Haines City to escort one hundred blacks from Georgia to the mines. While returning, the convoy was ambushed near the mining town of Mulberry, and a Negro strikebreaker and deputy sheriff were killed. The same night two other incidents occurred: guards at the Pierce mine mistook storekeeper J. H. Hudson for a striker and shot him; and Rodney Wilson, an employee of the Nichols Mine died from knife wounds received while trying to separate a striker and "scab" who were fighting.[19]

18. Jacksonville *Florida Times-Union*, June 25, July 17, 1919.
19. *Ibid.*, August 8, 1919; the Tampa *Tribune*, August 17, 1919, quoting Haines City *Herald*.

The phosphate workers won support from other Florida laborers. The Brotherhood of Locomotive Engineers and Firemen refused to transport materials to the affected mines, and the Tampa Labor Temple opened its doors to strikers. One angry miner related wretched conditions in the mining towns, then conjectured that the Boston Tea Party, which had been a strike, "would doubtless have been called the work of the I. W. W. or bolsheviki" had it occurred in 1919.[20] The executive council of the state federation of labor considered a general strike in support of the miners, although adequate support for the project failed to materialize. Sympathy also came from the population of the mining towns. The pastor of the First Baptist Church in Plant City offered his church facilities for a strike rally should rain drive the workers inside; he also attended the meeting and led in prayer. The Reverend Thomas McDowell of Fort Meade was a prominent figure at labor rallies in the district, and L. W. Bloom, editor of the Lakeland *Star,* also took the side of the strikers.

By springtime the strike was enmeshed in Florida politics. Representative Samuel Williams of Polk County introduced a resolution in the state legislature calling on the governor to investigate conditions in the mining district. Catts subsequently toured the area, expressing sympathy for the miners. On July 14 the governor addressed a mass meeting of two thousand laborers in Tampa. Declaring that eighty-six of the phosphate operators were from outside the state, he threatened that inasmuch as "the owners have defied the legislature and executive branches of the government of Florida, I can declare their charters forfeited." He proposed to refer this to Attorney General Swearingen for possible legal action. Warming to his subject, the governor directed his attention at management counsel Peter Knight who was also an officer in the giant government shipbuilding complex at Hog Island, Pennsylvania. When Catts vilified "Hog Island Pete," the crowd roared its approval: "'You tell 'em, Guv'nor!' 'Ye-e-e-o-u!!' 'That's the stuff!'"

20. Tampa *Tribune,* June 9, 1919.

Months before, the governor announced, he had written both mine owners and unionists offering to name mediators from each branch of the legislature, but attorneys for the operators had rejected arbitration. Next, Catts paid his respects to the Florida press: "I'm tired of hearing these daily papers talk about Catts and Van Swearingen being bolshevists and anarchists. They're damned liars, and if they don't like it they can lump it."[21]

Reaction to his outburst ranged from the predictable hostility of the Florida press to the perplexed disbelief of the attorney general. The Jacksonville *Metropolis* accused the governor of insincerity, pointing to a March, 1919, speech to the conference of governors and mayors where he had criticized exorbitant labor salaries. The Tampa *Tribune* blamed the entire dispute on the "infamous intermeddling of politicians and scalawag agitators." And the editor asked rhetorically if violence by strikers had not resulted from Catts's inability to annul corporation charters: "Have they, because he could not do the wild bolsheviki thing he promised... determined to institute such a reign of terror in the area as will accomplish their purposes?"[22] Two weeks after his speech, the governor still had not referred the matter to Swearingen, who allegedly questioned the chief executive's knowledge of corporation law and declared that Catts had no authority to annul charters. A perceptive historian of the Florida phosphate industry has concluded that Catts's speech was an insincere political gesture to win labor support for his senate race.[23] Although the tactical suggestion to revoke charters may have been a characteristically impulsive gesture of defiance, Catts's alliance with labor was both genuine and consistent and cannot be dismissed by reference to political expediency. Throughout his gubernatorial career Catts counted heavily on labor to counter the opposition he received from business.

21. *Ibid.*, July 15, 1919.
22. *Ibid.*, July 29, 1919, quoting Jacksonville *Metropolis; ibid.*, August 20, 9, 1919.
23. A. Fred Blakey, "A History of the Florida Phosphate Industry, 1888–1966" (Ph.D. dissertation, Florida State University, 1967), 147–49; see also shortened published form, *The Florida Phosphate Industry: A History of the Development and Use of a Vital Mineral* (Cambridge: Harvard University Press, 1973).

During August the governor's involvement in the strike deepened. He dispatched Florida's new adjutant general, James McCants, to New York to talk with phosphate operators and also to request the aid of the Department of Labor in reconciling the dispute. Striking miners told the governor that they would drop their demand for union recognition and would settle for an eight-hour day and a minimum salary of thirty-seven cents an hour. The operators refused to make any concessions, however, and the violence continued. Company guards fired a fusillade into the town of Mulberry on August 10, killing a two-year-old Negro child and seriously wounding a black man and woman. When the town's mayor asked the governor to declare martial law, Catts and Assistant Attorney General Worth W. Trammell visited Lakeland for a personal investigation; on August 22 he mobilized the Gainesville National Guard Company for service in the phosphate district. Major John L. Crary, a regular army officer, was placed on active duty for two months as the governor's representative in Mulberry, which was located in the center of the strife-ridden mining belt.[24]

The next day, August 23, the chief executive removed Polk County sheriff John N. Logan from duty, a move that triggered immediate reaction from nonmining elements of the county population. Striking miners had complained that Logan could not maintain order and that he was partial to the operators. Working through the unofficial Polk County Law and Order League, Logan had attempted to break the strike. In late June, A. H. Wilder, his chief deputy for the previous seven years, had resigned after complaining that Logan refused to investigate claims of peonage in the phosphate mines at Fort Meade. The day following Logan's dismissal, twenty-five hundred angry citizens attended a mass meeting sponsored by the Law and Order League, the mayor of Bartow, and the county's state senator. Logan refused to vacate his office, and Adjutant General James McCants, who had served as state mediator in the strike, resigned protesting that he opposed the removal of the sheriff and had advised Catts to stay out of Polk

24. George G. Bittle, "In the Defense of Florida: The Organized Florida Militia from 1821 to 1920" (Ph.D. dissertation, Florida State University, 1965), 430.

County. Major Crary, fearing further violence, mobilized the Daytona National Guard unit, creating rumors that Catts planned to use force to remove Logan; the governor reduced tensions by demobilizing the unit, explaining that Crary had acted on his own initiative without instructions from the governor's office. The sheriff finally resigned in early September.[25]

J. M. Langford, the man Catts chose to replace Logan as sheriff, was both more cooperative and sympathetic to the strikers. The new law officer confided that if the companies would cooperate with him as much as the strikers, he could maintain order and peace. When incidents of violence continued through mid-September, Lakeland state senator Oscar M. Eaton telegraphed Polk County representative W. O. Williams in Tallahassee, asking him to talk with Catts about the almost daily gunfire and lawlessness. Some local citizens were demanding that soldiers be sent to the county to preserve peace. Major Crary, who investigated Eaton's charges, concluded that since no one had been hit, the situation in the violence-prone region was not serious; furthermore, he telegraphed the governor, "suspicion points to guards doing shooting themselves to prolong jobs or on orders." Catts agreed with Crary's estimate and wrote Senator Eaton that the request for troops was a "red herring" contrived by Peter O. Knight to prolong the strike. Apparently pressure from local citizens, particularly the Law and Order League, did influence the governor, for during the first week of November he returned Logan to office. The reinstatement elicited praise from local citizenry as well as from the Lakeland *Advertiser*.[26]

The governor's abusive feud with Peter O. Knight did not end so amicably. The Tampa industrialist was not only a financial tycoon, but also a power in the conservative wing of the Democratic party and a confidant of Senator Fletcher. His dispute with Catts operated at both personal and philosophical levels, and the chasm

25. Tampa *Tribune*, June 30, August 5, 25, 30, September 3, 4, 1919.

26. *Ibid.*, September 28, 1919; Jacksonville *Florida Times-Union*, November 4, 1919, quoting the Lakeland *Advertiser*.

between them was unbridgeable. During 1918 the Tampa *Tribune* had interviewed Knight on Florida politics. The industrialist had praised the state's concern for property rights and, even though a resident of underrepresented Hillsborough County, opposed Catts's scheme to reapportion Florida: "We have had this state remain conservative because of the sober, common sense of the representatives and senators from the small middle East and West Florida counties, who have been willing to administer the affairs of this state in an old-fashioned, common-sense way." Knight proposed a legislative program by which lawmakers would limit state expenses, abolish the tax commission, freeze the tax levy, and impose no further burdens of any kind on property or individuals. After enacting this agenda, the legislators should have the United States Constitution read at each morning session after which they should adjourn; on alternating weeks the same schedule would be followed substituting the Florida Constitution and Bible passages until the session ended.[27]

Knight's attitude toward organized labor was equally hostile. He deplored the AFL decision to enter politics, arguing that the central issue in American life was whether the nation was to "live under the constitution of the United States or . . . the constitution of the American Federation of Labor. Both cannot exist." Speaking to the Southern Hardware Jobbers Association in 1921, he praised President Warren G. Harding as "that magnificent gentleman who sits in the White House" and whose election notified Samuel Gompers that Americans were "not going to live under the red flag of Socialism." In the 1920 presidential election "liberty-loving and constitution-loving men, real Americans, said they were through with phrase-making, half-baked theories, damn-foolism, mental joy-riding and intellectual sky-climbing and were going to get back to the Constitution and common sense."[28]

27. Interview with Peter O. Knight, Tampa *Tribune*, June 17, 1918.
28. P. O. Knight to editor, *Manufacturers' Record*, April 8, 1920. Copy in Peter O. Knight Papers, P. K. Yonge Library of Florida History, University of Florida. MS of speech in Knight Papers.

When the War Labor Board submitted its recommendations on phosphate workers to Knight, he peremptorily rejected it, denying the authority of the government agency to enter the dispute. Throughout the strike, Knight remained the spokesman for operators and a key advisor on company strategy. So far as Knight was concerned, the industrialists should negotiate nothing with workers, but instead fire them all and employ a new labor force: "To hear some of the flannel-mouthed, pin-headed, brainless anarchistic, bolsheviki labor agitators talk about questions of this kind, you would think we were living in Russia."[29]

Such tirades incited the worse side of Catts, who could not contain his rage. Beginning with the July reference to Knight as "Hog Island Pete," the governor escalated his personal attacks. In a Labor Day speech to Pensacola workers, he said that Knight was so despised in Tampa that he could not walk the streets for fear of being killed. Tampa's mayor and city council demanded a retraction, which inspired another of Catts's bellicose public statements. His September 16 reply, addressed to the city council and Tampa mayor D. B. McKay, read: "Your contemptible resolution concerning what I said about Peter O. Knight has been received. If you think you can make me take back what I said suppose you come up to Tallahassee and try it, or the next time I am in Tampa, suppose you try it there. Respectfully, S. J. Catts, Governor." The city council ordered the letter framed to be displayed on the walls of the council chamber as "a fine example of the retort discourteous."[30] The affair was celebrated nationally: the New York *Times* published Catts's telegram and the resolution of the city council to frame the reply; *Manufacturers' Record* commented that the incident was typical of the humiliation Florida had endured under the administration "of the man who has been such a phenomenal misfit in the gubernatorial chair. Well may every friend of Florida hope for better things for that splendid state, whose people are thus

29. Tampa *Tribune,* June 29, 1919.
30. For text, see Jacksonville *Florida Times-Union,* September 17, 1919.

made to suffer by a mistake which they made when Catts was elected governor."[31]

The furious confrontation between labor and management provided the backdrop for the regular session of the Florida legislature which met in the spring and summer of 1919. Catts, interviewed in early March, 1919, while attending a governors' conference in Washington, said that he expected great accomplishments from the Florida legislature when it convened in April; but this public optimism belied his real feelings. In private correspondence he expressed concern over rumors that the senate intended to institute impeachment proceedings against him. The governor expected much trouble from the legislature, particularly from Amos E. Lewis of Marianna who represented Jackson County in the lower house, and from three lobbyists he identified only as Mayfield, Burke, and Hayes. He asked J. B. Hodges, whom he called "my chief lawyer and advisor," to visit Tallahassee in order to discuss the situation in the legislature.[32]

Catts and Joe Earman prepared a directory of individual legislators who were favorable to the administration. A majority of the state senate opposed him, as they had in 1917. J. B. Hodges listed Columbia County's W. W. Phillips on the administration list, calling him a staunch loyalist who had campaigned for Catts in 1916. The Lake City attorney also volunteered to use his influence with several other legislators, especially Senator John Bradshaw of Jasper who had opposed Catts but whom Hodges thought could be persuaded to a more sympathetic stance.[33]

Phillips fulfilled Hodges' prediction of loyalty, traveling to Tallahassee a week before the session began to lobby for Catts's legislative program. He was a favorite with his house colleagues, and

31. New York *Times*, September 18, 1919; Jacksonville *Florida Times-Union*, October 4, 1919, quoting *Manufacturers' Record*.

32. Jacksonville *Florida Times-Union*, March 5, 1919; Sidney J. Catts to J. B. Hodges, March 18, 1919, Hodges to Catts, April 8, 1919, in Box 32, J. B. Hodges Papers.

33. J. B. Hodges to Sidney J. Catts, March 14, March 22, 1919, in Box 32, Hodges Papers.

this personal popularity helped broaden the administration faction. Phillips announced before the session that he intended to introduce bills to guarantee bank deposits, to abolish the convict lease system, and to establish a workman's compensation act, all of which were key administration measures.

Catts's address to the legislature, delivered April 4, 1919, contained bold proposals for reforming Florida although much of the impact of the speech was lost because Joe Earman summarized the program in minute detail a week before the governor delivered it. Many of the themes were continued from the unfulfilled agenda of 1917 and 1918. On the controversial issue of taxation, he condemned unequal and unjust assessments, recommended a franchise tax on all corporations, a state income tax, and a levy on inheritances. He asked that the legislature pass a bank deposit guarantee bill patterned on Oklahoma's statute, and urged a fair hearing for woman suffrage, which he endorsed. Catts also renewed his request for a sixth judge to relieve congestion of cases on the supreme court. New recommendations included: creation of a second Board of Control called the Efficiency Commission which would investigate the manner and method of transacting business in the state's institutions; establishment of a university extension program to eliminate adult illiteracy and which would reach not just farmers, but fishermen, laborers, clerks, and merchants; strengthening child labor laws to prevent exploitation of children; advocacy of a workman's compensation law which would allow the employee at least two-thirds of his salary in event of personal injury; creation of a Bureau of Labor Statistics; institution of universal compulsory education from age seven through the eighth grade for at least eight months a year; and legislation to protect the citizenry of Florida from loan sharks who were charging as much as 33 percent interest a month. Under a section on espionage, the governor also deplored laws which restricted the exercise of free speech. National espionage legislation had alienated millions of democratic Americans whose "mouths were shut to hundreds of cases of injustice wrought through military, judicial and legislative channels, which was not right to be borne by a free people and which they now deeply resent." The Florida legislature should demand that Congress repeal the espionage act.[34]

The address elicited a surprisingly mild reaction, perhaps because the Florida press was secure in the knowledge that his more liberal proposals stood little chance among conservative legislators. A *Florida Times-Union* editorial on April 10 agreed with repeal of the espionage laws, Catts's attack on profiteers, and his recommendation on budgetary revision which provided for specific appropriations; the editor even endorsed the philosophy of a tax on landholders, though he warned that such a levy might slow Florida's economic development.

In addition to obtaining a fair hearing for his legislative program, the governor also won his first skirmish in the lower house. His bitter antagonist Amos Lewis contested the speakership of the house with George H. Wilder from Plant City. Lewis planned to introduce a bill prohibiting the chief executive from appointing a member of the legislature to public office during the official's term of office. Otherwise, he argued, a governor could barter public office for legislative support. When organization of the house came to a vote, Wilder defeated Lewis, misleading J. B. Hodges to conclude "that the House is very strong for you and your friends."[35] Senator James E. Calkins of Fernandina, who was elected presiding officer in the upper house, represented the senate opposition which would block so much of Catts's program.

Despite a recalcitrant senate, Catts was not without powerful allies in the state of Florida. Foremost among these was organized labor. Brought into politics by the strife which tore the state in 1919, the federation of labor looked to Tallahassee for relief. The eighteenth session of the federation convened in the capital on April 8, the first full legislative day, with a record attendance of more than one hundred delegates. Not all laborites were allied to Catts; T. J. Appleyard, representing the Tallahassee Typographical

---

34. *Journal of the House of Representatives, 1919*, pp. 9–38.
35. Jacksonville *Florida Times-Union*, April 8, 9, 1919; J. B. Hodges to Sidney J. Catts, April 8, 1919, in Box 32, Hodges Papers.

Union, was an old foe, and rumor had it that the governor did not get along well with state federation president J. H. Mackey. The rank and file still admired the chief executive, however, and Catts welcomed the delegates and entertained them at the governor's mansion. The unionists quickly settled down to the serious business of drafting an agenda of labor proposals to submit to the legislature. They called for tax reduction by transferring revenue levies to the intangible property of the wealthy. The delegates also endorsed workman's compensation, woman suffrage, statewide compulsory education, free schoolbooks, a mother's pension, a laborer's lien law, vocational education, and a two-shift system for city firemen in cities of over twenty-five thousand residents.[36]

After the convention adjourned, some labor leaders remained in Tallahassee to lobby among legislators. The state federation kept at least one representative in the capital throughout the session. Their success, however, depended less on their efforts than on the philosophical bent of the lawmakers with whom they dealt. Many representatives and senators shared Catts's vision that the political decisions of the future would be molded by aroused laborers. In the senate, Lincoln Hulley, an ambitious educator from DeLand, introduced an entire package of labor measures. Senator John B. Stokes from labor-oriented Pensacola managed the critical workman's compensation bill in the upper house, and was also a key backer of the laborer's lien bill, compulsory school attendance, vocational education, and child labor reform. Doyle E. Carlton, who represented the powerful labor center of Tampa in the upper house, led forces trying to pass a child labor bill. In the lower house as in the senate, leading advocates of labor's program usually came from cities experiencing worker unrest: Edgar W. Waybright of Jacksonville had campaigned for Catts in 1916 and sponsored the workman's compensation bill, the two-platoon firemen bill, a steam boiler inspection law, and legislation creating the Bureau of Labor Statistics; E. R. B. Kite of Alachua County led the fight for a strong

36. Jacksonville *Florida Times-Union*, April 9, 17, 1919; Tampa *Tribune*, April 10, 11, 1919.

child labor law, and John W. Watson of Miami led backers of the laborer's lien law.

The most hotly contested part of the package was the proposal for workman's compensation. Senator Hulley's bill prescribed the liability of an employer for injuries received by his employees, established a schedule of compensation, and provided methods for paying compensation; Representative Waybright's measure incorporated most of the same features. The proposals made progress in both houses; the House Committee on Organized Labor amended the bill, but then reported it favorably by a narrow five-to-four margin. Hulley's proposal passed the senate by a surprisingly wide margin of seventeen to eleven, with Doyle Carlton, W. T. Cash of Perry, Oscar Eaton from Lakeland's phosphate district, M. L. Plympton of Lake City, and John Stokes of Pensacola leading the labor forces. Corporations and the press, propelled to a sense of urgency by the rapid progress of the bill, launched a counteroffensive on May 20. The Tampa *Tribune* carried a negative editorial, and the Georgia-Florida Sawmill Assocation adopted a scathing denunciation. Complaining that even the mildest version of workman's compensation would double the costs of their liability insurance, the association concluded that passage of the measure would "place such a hardship upon the industries of this state as to make it practically impossible to operate."[37] Jacksonville unions rallied labor strength by a resolution supporting the measure, but proved no match for organized business. Four separate bills were introduced in the legislature incorporating different concepts of compensation, making it impossible to solidly unite labor forces behind any one. As a result, W. W. Phillips, fearing the defeat of all of them, offered a resolution appointing a joint committee of two representatives and one senator to draft a consensus workman's compensation bill which would be presented to the 1921 legislature. This unsatisfactory compromise ended chances for passage of any effective reform in the 1919 session.

37. *Journal of the House of Representatives, 1919*, pp. 1651–52, 2063; *Journal of the Florida Senate, 1919*, p. 1257. For text of resolution, see Tampa *Tribune*, May 20, 1919.

The phosphate strike presented another provocative labor issue. Representative W. O. Williams of Polk County introduced a
resolution directing the governor to investigate conditions in Polk
and Hillsborough counties. If both parties to the dispute agreed,
the governor should offer to appoint a mediator to represent the
public interests and resolve the differences between the contending parties. Subsequent criticism of Catts's involvement in the
strike ignored the fact that the legislature had requested that he
intervene, apparently not anticipating his prounion sympathies or
his proposals for ending the conflict. After his initial forays into the
mining towns, he forwarded a number of affidavits alleging peonage by the companies to Attorney General Swearingen for possible
legal action. Swearingen responded in an advisory opinion saying
that if the conditions described in the affidavits were accurate,
"these laborers are held in a virtual state of peonage, for which the
parties responsible are amenable to the Federal Laws governing
that offense." He urged the miners to seek redress in the federal
courts.[38] Senator John E. King of Inverness introduced a bill to tax
the output of phosphate mines as personal property, but Peter O.
Knight registered violent opposition, and the bill failed to pass the
senate by a vote of fourteen to sixteen.

The crisis posed by black workers demanded a different kind of
response. There were two segments to the problem: a labor shortage caused by the migration of blacks to better paying jobs outside
Florida, and the attempt of Negro laborers to organize collectively
in order to take advantage of the manpower shortage. Catts appointed W. W. Phillips, his Lake City aide, to represent Florida at
an April meeting in Washington, D.C., to discuss labor conditions
in the state. The conference centered on the activities of E. W.
Armwood, a Negro agent of the Bureau of Home Economics for
Negroes which was headquartered in Jacksonville. Armwood allegedly had sent his agents across the state "preaching social
equality to the colored people, telling them not to work for less

38. *Biennial Report of Attorney General, Florida, from January 1, 1919 to December
31, 1920*, p. 90.

than forty cents an hour, etc." His agency was often implicated in the attempt to organize unskilled St. Petersburg blacks. Governor Catts lodged a protest, and dispatched Phillips to demand that the secretary of labor take action. Phillips accomplished his mission in three days of conferences, securing the recall of Armwood and persuading the Department of Labor to allow each state to name a director for the government labor bureau.[39]

Measures to improve working conditions in the state suffered a fate similar to workman's compensation. Doyle Carlton proposed a child labor bill which provided for an assistant state labor inspector, but it died in the house labor committee, together with most reforms touching working people.[40]

The failure of the labor package contrasts with the success of many measures of broader application which labor endorsed, such as compulsory school attendance, vocational and extension education, and child welfare. The Jacksonville Central Trades and Labor Council also adopted a resolution opposing a bill to reduce appropriations to the Board of Health, emphasizing that contagious diseases spread more rapidly among poor workers. When unionists made common cause with education forces, they succeeded in 1919; when they focused on narrower "class legislation," the labor coalition proved feeble.

Aided by labor support and women's groups, educators managed to pass an impressive package. As with so many reforms of the era, the drive for compulsory education had originated at the local level. In Duval County where two thousand school age children did not attend public schools, a campaign had been launched in 1918 to require all children under fourteen years of age to enroll in school for at least four months of the year. Organized labor backed the reform but had to share credit statewide with Florida women. Mrs. May Yancey Lesley, granddaughter of Alabama's William L. Yancey and a long-time teacher in Hillsborough County, drafted Florida's attendance law using an Indiana statute as her guide. She

39. Tampa *Tribune*, April 29, 1919.
40. *Journal of the House of Representatives, 1919*, p. 388.

took it to Hillsborough's Senator Doyle Carlton, who agreed to introduce it.[41] The Florida Federation of Women's Clubs lobbied for the bill through Mrs. J. D. Coughlin, who chaired the federation's committee on legislation. The final version of the bill provided that beginning in July, 1919, every child between the ages of seven and sixteen must attend either a private or public school. Aided by labor backing, the bill passed the senate by a vote of twenty-six to four, was quickly approved by the house on June 11, and signed into law by Governor Catts.[42] According to Dixie M. Hollins, superintendent of Pinellas County schools, it was the first statewide compulsory attendance law with adequate enforcement provisions to be passed by a southern legislature, and was the most "progressive educational step ever taken by Florida." Although Mrs. Lesley conceded that Catts was always a friend of education during his four years in Tallahassee, she also contended that Catts's signature on the bill was his only contribution to compulsory education.[43] This is a misstatement, however, for his initial message to the 1919 legislature listed this reform as a major priority, and Catts labored industriously for its passage.

The governor's role in creating a university extension system and saving the 1919 educational appropriations bill was far more significant. University of Florida president A. A. Murphree joined Catts and Board of Control chairman Earman in proposing creation of a state system of extension education. The proposal became enmeshed in a bitter struggle over the record wartime appropriations bill recommended by the Board of Control and provoked negative reaction from economy-minded legislators. Joe Earman wrote Murphree complaining about the niggardliness of the lawmakers. Murphree suggested that members of the board ought to go to

41. Theodore Leslie to author, November 17, 1970.
42. For lobbying efforts, see Mrs. J. D. Coughlin to A. A. Murphree, March 18, 1919, in Box 17, Murphree Papers. For provisions of the bill, see *General Acts and Resolutions Adopted by the Legislature of Florida*, 17th Regular Sess., April 8–June 6, 1919, Vol. I, 59–65.
43. Quoted in Jacksonville *Florida Times-Union*, June 4, 1919; Theodore Leslie to author, November 17, 1970.

Tallahassee to actively lobby, a course that Earman considered more proper for the university president than for the board members. Earman changed his mind when parsimonious legislators emasculated the $1,800,000 appropriations bill for higher education, cutting it by nearly 20 percent. Students at the University of Florida, which suffered most from the cut, circulated petitions condemning the legislature, while Eli Futch and W. W. Phillips fought to restore the funds, and Earman summoned the Board of Control to Tallahassee for an emergency meeting.[44] Earman said on May 12 that the board members planned to remain in the capital until the education bill was passed; they were not there to lobby, he explained, but only to "answer questions." He recommended passage of the original appropriations bill, establishment of two normal schools, and endorsed the compulsory attendance bill, free textbooks, the child welfare proposal, and an increase in the maximum tax levy for schools. As for the legislative mood of economy, he commented pointedly: "I have been dealing with the extreme all my life. Extremes of any kind spill the beans. Extreme economy will also spill the beans. . . . The institutions are greater than any 104 men of the state. The institutions of higher education should not be made to suffer because of the fear that inheritance or franchise tax will be necessary to take care of them."[45]

Reaction to Earman's statement was mixed. The proposal for creation of normal schools in north and south Florida was crippled by amendments, and finally killed; however, a joint legislative committee conducted new hearings and restored the original appropriations bill. On May 24 the house also approved by a two-to-one margin creation of the university extension system. The bill, sponsored in the house by W. W. Phillips and in the senate by Theodore T. Turnbull, incorporated a long-time notion of both Governor Catts and Earman that it was the job of the state "to seek out, among all the schools of Florida, every student who may by

44. Joe L. Earman to A. A. Murphree, May 5, 1919; Eli Futch to Murphree, May 12, 1919, in Box 17, Murphree Papers.
45. See statement in Jacksonville *Florida Times-Union*, May 13, 1919.

nature have a special aptitude and genius for some one branch of learning, and to encourage him in the prosecution of the study."[46] After a bitter debate in the senate, the bill passed by a vote of twenty-one to eight.

The new law established salaried instructors at the University of Florida, the College for Women, and Florida Agricultural and Mechanical College, who would provide correspondence courses to anyone who could not attend college. President Murphree would recommend a director and field agent for the Florida Extension Division, who would be appointed by the Board of Control. Earman, who deserves primary credit for the extension system, declared that he had rather see this act pass than become governor. He attributed to Turnbull and Phillips responsibility for guiding the measure through the legislature and jubilantly wrote Murphree that the legislature had passed every major item that the Board of Control had requested. As for the extension act, it would "bring great honor in time to come to the present Board of Control. We have wrought well for the poor boys and girls in Florida who for any reason are unable to attend college."[47]

Governor Catts added another victory in the termination of the convict lease system. Although he had succeeded in modifying the leasing of prisoners in 1917, he determined to abolish the system altogether in 1919. Abolitionist sentiment had increased in Florida, and the Carlton-Igou bill introduced in the senate established a state convict road force consisting of all male prisoners except for a contingent who would work the prison farm at Raiford. A companion measure levied a three-eights-of-a-mill tax to fund the program. The bill profited from newspaper support and passed easily. Although the leasing of convict labor continued on a county level and turpentine operators maintained a system of virtual peonage into the 1920s, state convicts were treated more humanely than ever

46. Florida, *General Acts and Resolutions Adopted by the Legislature of Florida*, 17th Regular Sess., Vol. I, 284–85.
47. Telegram from Joe Earman to W. W. Phillips, May 24, 1919, Earman to A. A. Murphree, May 24, 1919, in Box 4, Murphree Papers.

before in Florida history.[48] This dream of the governor, stemming from his early contact with the brutality of the west Florida turpentine industry, constituted one of his proudest achievements.

The issue of reapportionment surfaced again in 1919 to balance the governor's success on prison reform. Although Catts was determined to reapportion the state, political observers predicted less chance of reform in 1919 than in 1917. Despite such pessimistic estimates, Catts called for reapportionment in his address to the legislature and in a special message sent to the house on May 28. Representative Francis W. Perry of Fort Myers introduced a reapportionment measure which lost twenty-two to forty. Although most of the support came from south Florida, many urban legislators from underrepresented counties did not even bother to vote (including both Duval County representatives), while legislators from many overrepresented north Florida counties (Baker, Alachua, Hamilton, Holmes, Jackson, Walton, and Washington) supported the compromise.[49]

While reapportionment involved the governor in some controversy, the seemingly bland issue of good roads provided the most rancorous debate of the session. In a special message during late April, Catts recommended a statewide highway system to replace county roads controlled by boards of county commissioners. He reasoned that local boards were only interested in county needs because they were susceptible to political influence. The governor felt that a state road department would not be so politically vulnerable. Newspaper response was favorable, and the senate, with only two negative votes, quickly passed a two-mill tax to match three million dollars in federal road funds. The bill created a highway network to be administered by a state road department. The house, feeling that the senate bill included too few safeguards, narrowly passed the Wilder-Scruggs amendment which surrounded

48. Carper, "The Convict-Lease System in Florida, 1866–1923," pp. 301–10; *General Acts and Resolutions Adopted by the Legislature of Florida*, 17th Regular Sess., Vol. I, 66.
49. For a vote tally, see Jacksonville *Florida Times-Union*, June 5, 1919.

the state road department with protective devices, including a competitive bid provision and limitations of employee salaries. The two houses had reached an impasse when Catts threw legislators into a dither with yet another special message on May 31. The governor threatened to veto any bill which did not place the road department under the board of state institutions, or which did not provide for periodic audits and competitive bids. In a complaint characteristic of his insistence on careful supervision to prevent governmental corruption, he explained that he would not allow $6 million to be expended by any department without some sort of countercheck. His proposal resembled the Wilder-Scruggs house version except for his insistence on control by the board of institutions. Many legislators condemned Catts for waiting so near the end of the session to issue a virtual ultimatum to the legislature. On June 2 Catts denied that he had told a special legislative delegation that he would veto the bill unless it placed the department under the board of institutions, but he affirmed that his entire philosophy throughout his administration had been to put the duties of one department under the supervision of another in order to insure honesty. He warned that the legislators had only four more days to pass the measure because he would not summon a special session. The house receded from its restrictions in order to save the bill, then reacted emotionally to Catts's message. Representative E. O. Miller, "the usually imperturbable gentleman from Duval" who had conferred with the governor, lost "his equilibrium" and, in "a voice high pitched with excitement and shaken with emotion," vowed that the governor had threatened a veto: "So help me God he said it. What kind of a governor do we have." Other legislators joined in the attack, and the house symbolically repudiated the governor by tabling his message of June 2 without printing it in the house journal.[50] The event was celebrated by the press as one of the most dramatic incidents ever to occur in the legislature. Catts reluctantly signed the final bill although it did not provide supervi-

---

50. For this affray, see *ibid.*, June 1–3, 1919.

sion as he had requested; it did include provisions for competitive bids and regular audits.

The issue of who should vote in Florida also attracted much attention. As the legislative session approached its close, Congress passed the woman suffrage amendment. A coalition immediately tried to persuade the legislature to make Florida the first state to ratify the amendment. Among the activists were Mrs. William S. Jennings, wife of a former governor and active in the Florida Federation of Woman's Clubs, a group of Jacksonville suffragists, and Catts. The governor had already appointed a female to his staff, Marion Horwitz O'Brien, who was mayor of Morehaven; she was reportedly the only female member of a southern governor's executive staff. Although he had received no official notification from Washington, he sent a message to the Florida legislature on June 4 based on an Associated Press announcement of congressional passage of the Nineteenth Amendment, asking the legislators to ratify the measure before adjourning. Mrs. Jennings, lobbying in Tallahassee at the time, pressured the Duval delegation into polling the house and senate; while a majority in the house favored extending the franchise to women, proponents could not muster the two-thirds majority necessary to waive house rules in order to consider the measure.[51] Not even a majority of senators favored taking up the issue. The state of Florida, which could have become the first state to ratify female suffrage, did not finally approve the Nineteenth Amendment until 1969.

Determining how men should cast their ballots concerned the legislators more than whether women should vote. Senator W. T. Cash proposed replacing the controversial Bryan primary with a runoff election. Arguing that the confused first- and second-choice votes had been responsible for the 1916 gubernatorial fiasco, he won senate passage by a sixteen-to-thirteen vote. The house passed

51. *Ibid.*, March 3, 1918; *Journal of the Florida Senate, 1919*, p. 2264; Kenneth R. Johnson, "Florida Women Get the Vote," *Florida Historical Quarterly*, XLVIII (January, 1970), 303–305.

an emasculated version of the Cash bill the day before adjournment. Though much amended, the bill did abolish second-choice
voting. A senate filibuster in the closing hours of the session killed
the reform, saving Catts from vetoing the ineffective compromise.

One of the most explosive issues to plague Florida during the
war years was the issue of cattle dipping. The State Livestock Sanitary Board had recommended that the legislature compel all cattle
to be dipped into a solution of chemicals in order to eradicate cattle
tick which threatened the state's developing livestock industry.
The proposal required a two-mill tax to construct dipping vats in
each county. A substantial lobby gathered in Tallahassee to oppose
the legislation; lawmakers split, with some opposed to any action,
some fighting only the compulsory aspect of the bill, and others
supporting the board's recommendation. South Florida legislators
provided the bill's major support, while west Florida representatives preferred the status quo which left the dipping issue as a
county option. The *Florida Times-Union* endorsed the compulsory
measure, pointing out that counties could not eradicate ticks by
local-option dipping while adjacent counties refused to require
similar action. The bill providing for compulsory dipping was heavily amended until it became useless and unworkable, and finally
died in the senate. The lack of uniformity plagued the state for
many years, and local option dipping did not always solve the problem even locally. In 1920 three dipping vats in Duval County were
dynamited by irate citizens.

Throughout the session, legislators sniped at the governor on a
variety of issues. Many regular Democrats were particularly anxious to embarrass Catts, who was already campaigning for the
United States Senate seat of Duncan Fletcher. A committee appointed by the 1919 legislature to investigate the adjutant general's
office submitted a negative evaluation. Adjutant General J. B.
Christian had been one of Catts's first appointees and was closely
identified with the administration. Christian and Catts had parted
paths during the war when Catts had requested a federal official to
handle Florida's selective service program. Christian refused to
pay the salary from his funds, arguing that the federal government

should provide the money. Catts threatened to dismiss Christian unless he paid the disputed salary, a decision bitterly contested by the legislative committee. Christian also lacked records, inaccurately recorded the composition of National Guard units, and employed associates for whom no work existed. The historian of Florida's militia concludes that although Christian may not have been dishonest, he was certainly a slipshod administrator.[52]

On May 28 Catts replaced Christian with Major James E. McCants of Tampa, a Spanish American War veteran and major in the coastal artillery guard. The governor also sent a special message to the legislature calling for reorganization of the National Guard and urging the transfer of its headquarters from Catholic-dominated St. Augustine to Tallahassee. The end of the war had heightened both racial unrest and "Bolshevism," and the state required a strong militia to counteract potential strife.[53] The legislature did not see fit to enact any of these proposals.

Legislators also found a new method of countering Catts's spoils system. They abolished the office of assistant health officer and the entire hotel commission. Senator W. J. Singletary explained that the hotel board had been created to give "people jobs to run around over the state," and had done little good. Similar criticisms helped defeat Senator Doyle Carlton's bill to establish a volunteer board of charities to oversee all the state's correctional institutions. Opponents of the measure protested that inspectors would have to be employed; as Catts's long-time enemy Senator J. B. Johnson of Live Oak quaintly expressed it: "the whole state is over run with traveling inspectors and it seems that soon we will have somebody to look after every boy baby in Florida."[54]

Catts, never cowed by prospects of a battle, tried to whip the legislature back into line by aggressive exercise of the veto. In April he sent a message to the legislature warning that many bills being introduced affected the financial conditions of local com-

52. Bittle, "In the Defense of Florida: The Organized Florida Militia From 1821 to 1920," pp. 428–30.
53. *Journal of the House of Representatives, 1919,* p. 1959.
54. Jacksonville *Florida Times-Union,* April 30, May 25, 1919.

munities or abolished offices; he threatened that any such local legislation which did not include a provision for a referendum of the people affected would be vetoed. To the consternation of many legislators, he did precisely what he promised, even vetoing one innocuous bill prohibiting the seining of fish because it did not submit the issue to a countywide vote. The senate became so infuriated that it voted to expunge his message relating to vetoes from the official journal.[55]

The state senate also provided impetus for changing the procedure for choosing Democratic nominees for public office. Several papers, fearful both of a repetition of 1916 and the spector of bolshevism and labor unrest, suggested in 1919 that the Democratic party drop the primary in favor of a state nominating convention. The senate added its voice to the cause, requesting Executive Committee Chairman George P. Raney to call a party convention to adopt a restrictive platform. Raney, fearful of repeating the disastrous strategy of the Sturkie resolve, denied that he possessed authority to call a meeting and opposed substituting a state convention for the open primary. He admitted that the most pressing issue facing the party was the need to "suppress the demagogue with the ballot," but when the executive committee met in January, 1920, he led the party hierarchy in quashing a resolution summoning a state convention.[56]

Catts's program in the hostile 1919 legislature suffered many defeats: the Committee on Banks and Loans killed his bank guarantee plan; his entire package of labor bills failed, as did his request for two new state auditors to allow more careful monitoring of financial transactions in the state; the legislature rejected woman suffrage, election reform, revision of the state constitution, reapportionment, and reorganization of the National Guard. It defeated his proposals for franchise, corporation and inheritance taxes, and re-

---

55. *Ibid.*, May 23, 1919; *Journal of the House of Representatives, 1919*, p. 326; *Journal of the Florida Senate, 1919*, p. 2013.

56. Jacksonville *Florida Times-Union*, March 5, 12, 1919, quoting Eustis Lake *Region* and Palatka *News*; Jacksonville *Florida Times-Union*, September 11, 1919; Johnson, "The Woman Suffrage Movement in Florida," 176.

fused to equalize tax assessments. Since this constituted a significant portion of his legislative agenda, the governor can be tagged a
failure in his dealings with the 1919 legislature. Personal animosity
and a conservative senate once again doomed most of his reforms.

There is a more constructive evaluation of the session, however. Three of his major projects were adopted: university extension education, compulsory schooling, and some tax reform. Although the legislators did not add a sixth judge to the supreme
court, they did establish two new judicial circuits to reduce
crowded court dockets. The legislature submitted a constitutional
amendment providing for taxation of intangible property such as
bank deposits and providing for property assessment based upon
its revenue production. The legislature also adopted several measures not in his message but which he had advocated earlier and
endorsed again in 1919: creation of a farm for the "feeble-minded";
the abolition of the convict lease system; state assistance to women
with dependent children; establishment of a state road department
supported by a tax levy and a convict work force which replaced the
leasing of prisoners; an appropriation for vocational education to
qualify for federal matching grants; and a new revenue bill.

The passage of so many reforms cannot be attributed wholly to
Catts's initiative. He faced conservative, alienated legislators,
many of whom despised him as a party irregular and religious demagogue. Where the reform propensity of hostile lawmakers coincided with the beliefs of Catts's faction, as on abolition of the convict
lease system or education, the two forces combined to enact significant changes; but such reform resulted from the confluence of
two separate streams of reformism rather than from the effective
leadership of the chief executive. The governor's successes came
on issues which had accrued a substantial amount of public support
over the years. He was a personal leader, not the leader of a progressive coalition. As the focus of an antiestablishment mentality,
he proved the chief impetus for change; at least he could advocate
reform, and when passed he would not veto it as Governor Albert
Gilchrist had in a previous administration. Furthermore, Catts's
advocacy of class legislation and the cause of organized labor repre-

sented one of the few times in Florida history when workers felt the chief executive sought actively to help them. The legislative rejection of such measures diminished only slightly the luster of his frank espousal of labor's demand for a greater share of Florida's prosperity.

Nor could the extent of his reforms be determined when the legislature adjourned on June 6, 1919. Only subsequent years demonstrated the vision of Catts's legislative programs. The agricultural extension system enrolled 1,305 persons from fifty-four counties in its first ten months of operation. During the first year of compulsory schooling, average attendance in public schools increased 27 percent, while enrollment went up 12 percent.[57] However, in subsequent years Catts boasted most loudly of ending the convict lease system and instigating prison reform. When leaving office he reminded Floridians: "The time was a few years ago, when a man was incarcerated and imprisoned and sent to the turpentine farms of the state, he had as brutal a time as if he had been in darkest Africa. That has been changed by taking those men from the turpentine farms and putting them on the state highways." By any objective standard, the governor had reason to be proud of his 1919 accomplishments for the people of Florida.

57. Florida, *Report of Board of Control, 1920*, "First Annual Report General Extension Division, University of Florida," 170–72; *Bi-ennial Report of the Superintendent of Public Instruction*, 32.

TEN

The Eulogies of
a Tomcat

THE LABOR PROBLEMS and legislative wranglings of 1919 were only two acts of a much longer drama, for Catts had decided to unseat incumbent United States Senator Duncan Fletcher. Despite a long tradition of defeat for chief executives who tried to move from Tallahassee to Washington, the governor had relished combat with Fletcher almost from the inception of his administration. The senator was the very embodiment of the Democratic establishment: a product of genteel Jacksonville reform who had ascended the political ladder in traditional fashion and who was backed by the state's bankers, businessmen, and prosperous farmers. Although capable of advocating moderate reform when the political climate demanded it, he was tightly bound to the Florida Democratic hierarchy.

As early as June, 1917, Florida newspapers published rumors that Catts would oppose Fletcher in 1920. Given the factional nature of politics in the state and Governor Park Trammell's successful challenge of incumbent Senator Nathan Bryan in 1916, this prediction may have been a logical conjecture rather than informed opinion. At any rate the rumor persisted, and by August, 1918, the name of Jacksonville real estate man Telfair Stockton had been added to Catts's as a prospective senatorial aspirant. As late as March, 1919, Catts still refused to comment on such speculation, although it is clear that by the middle of the year he had definitely decided to enter the race.[1]

The state's Democratic leadership never doubted Catts's intentions and tried desperately to block his candidacy. Such opposition motivated Florida's senate to request that the executive committee hold a state nominating convention rather than a primary. Alexander St. Clair-Abrams, an oldline party functionary, dropped the policy subterfuge in November, 1919, and frankly tied the proposal to a "stop Catts" movement. He urged that a state convention nominate Democratic candidates for governor and senator; otherwise the well-organized faction headed by Catts and Van Swearingen which had "perverted the principles of the Democratic party, usurped its name, and brought the people of this state to the brink of bolshevikism and socialism" would win a plurality against a splintered field of regular party candidates. The alliance of Catts and Swearingen for the Senate and governorship represented the "steady drift into socialism, [and] labor servitude, through the so-called labor unions and religious intolerance."[2]

George Raney resisted such pressure, not because he disliked Catts any less, but from fear that any executive committee action against the governor might incense Floridians and propel him into the senate. J. B. Hodges anticipated that the Fletcher contingent on the committee would try to "put something over" at the January, 1920, meeting, but promised to prevent such action.[3] Raney and many regulars joined Hodges and other pro-Catts members in rejecting a proposed state convention. The committee did pass an innocuous motion requiring each applicant for registration to swear that he would support all nominees chosen in the Democratic primaries. Editorials in the *Florida Times-Union* on February 1 and 16 opposed such action as unwise and useless; a Catts follower who believed the governor had been unjustly denied

1. Jacksonville *Florida Times-Union*, June 25, 1917, August 3, 1918, March 5, 1919.
2. Alexander St. Clair-Abrams to editor, Tampa *Tribune*, November 26, 1919.
3. J. B. Hodges to Sidney J. Catts, January 9, 1920, in Box 33, J. B. Hodges Papers.

the Democratic nomination would feel no compunction in taking the oath and then voting for Catts as an independent.

The senatorial field began to emerge in mid-1919. When W. W. Flournoy of DeFuniak Springs announced his candidacy in June, he temporarily confused political observers because he had handled the legal appeals for Catts in 1916 and was considered an intimate friend of the governor. One Jacksonville newspaper speculated that Catts had pledged to support Flournoy against Fletcher, an allegation which the chief executive promptly and emphatically denied. Catts stated that he had no prior knowledge of Flournoy's entry and had reached no final conclusion about the race himself. Actually, Flournoy had never been as close to the governor as the superficial evidence indicated, supporting Catts when it suited him and opposing the governor when it did not. The two had not been on cordial terms since 1918, and Flournoy's decision to enter the race was unrelated to his former alliance with Catts. In fact, a more logical explanation may be that he entered the primary to split the west Florida vote and defeat Catts.[4] Whatever his motivation, Catts soon adopted a strategy that bypassed his erstwhile ally; on January 15, 1920, he appointed Flournoy to the Board of Control, thus eliminating him from contention.

Telfair Stockton entered the race in mid-August, 1919, creating a stir with his initial announcement that Fletcher was an "autocrat" and Catts a "pole cat," and prompting the St. Petersburg *Times* to conclude that Stockton must be a "regular hell-cat." Trying to gain the middle ground, he said that Florida's Democratic party was divided into two factions, one socialistic and the other reactionary; he offered the option of progressive change without radicalism. One paper, fearful that Stockton would only divide the anti-Catts vote, reported that Joe Earman and other friends of the governor

---

4. Jacksonville *Florida Times-Union*, June 12, 1919. For press reaction to Flournoy's anouncement, see *ibid.*, June 12, 17, 18. Jerry Carter considered Flournoy an opportunist who supported Catts when it was in his self-interest to do so, then dropped him. Interview, Jerry W. Carter, July 29, 1970, Tallahassee.

had raised four thousand dollars in order to get the Jacksonville resident into the primary.[5]

Friends such as Earman were in shorter supply than in 1916. Many close associates from the earlier race had become casualties of Catts's tantrums, from which he quickly recovered but which others seldom forgot. Adjutant Generals Christian and McCants, W. W. Flournoy, Dr. W. H. Cox, and Charles T. Frecker had all fallen from grace; only J. V. Burke, Bryan Mack, Jerry Carter, Joe Earman, J. S. Blitch, and J. B. Hodges remained from those prominent in the maverick gubernatorial coalition. Jerry Carter, who had replaced J. V. Burke as chief strategist for the 1920 race, arranged Catts's campaign itinerary, introduced him at rallies, and stumped north Florida on his behalf. Second only to Catts as a magnetic orator before cracker audiences, Carter kept the governor's cortege in good spirits with his rollicking stories and mimicry. While crossing a river en route to a rally in west Florida, he entertained a ferryboat operator with stories and alcohol; then he persuaded the happy fellow to join him at the rally, leaving Fletcher's aide stranded on the far bank of the river. Carter told his rural audience that the incumbent senator cared so little for the plain folk of the panhandle that he did not even send a representative to address them. As an amateur cartoonist he had few peers in Florida, and, despite occasional protests from Catts's lieutenants about his atrocious spelling, Carter wrote the 1920 campaign pamphlets. His pictorial satires delighted crackers and so infuriated Duncan Fletcher that he threatened to have Carter confined to a penitentiary.[6]

J. B. Hodges and Joe Earman provided important support, as did Jacksonville mayor John W. Martin who offered energetic assistance among Jacksonville workers. Hodges continued to play all sides of the political fence, maintaining close ties with his conserva-

5. Jacksonville *Florida Times-Union*, August 14, 1919, quoting St. Petersburg *Times; ibid.*, October 8, 30, 1919.

6. J. B. Hodges to Jerry W. Carter, April 28, 1920, in Box 34, Hodges Papers; interview, Jerry W. Carter, May 15, 1964, Tallahassee.

tive railroad friends while at the same time helping Catts appeal for the support of organized labor. He did break completely with his old friend Duncan Fletcher, even writing the senator curt letters. He drifted into the Ku Klux Klan and, when informed that Fletcher was being considered for an ambassadorship to Italy, predicted that Catts would smash the senator if the incumbent did not move to Italy to "take up his residence with the Dagos and Catholics."[7]

The labor unrest which figured so prominently in the 1919 legislative session also emerged as a critical issue in the senate race. Throughout the year businessmen had responded to most labor demands with charges of "bolshevism" and "socialism." By 1920 an element of "radicalism" actually *did* emerge amidst the class conflict and violence, and this development seemed to lend credence to their persistent charges.

Socialist labor protest was not a new phenomenon in Florida. Economic radicalism had increased steadily from 1900 to 1912, and the Socialist party had become more a method of protest than a well-organized party structure. With the single exception of 1916, Floridians cast the highest percentage of left-wing votes of any southern citizenry in presidential elections from 1904 until 1932. Only nine states in the nation recorded a higher Socialist presidential vote in 1912 when Eugene V. Debs finished second in Florida with 9.3 percent of the vote, putting him ahead of both Republican William Howard Taft and Progressive Theodore Roosevelt. Most of this vote came from poorer farmers and industrial workers.[8]

The labor unrest of 1919–1920 intensified this traditional radicalism, particularly in Jacksonville and Tampa. The *Artisan,* a

7. Ralph Greene to Joe Earman, February 26, 1924, in Box 52, J. B. Hodges to Sidney J. Catts, November 27, 1919, Hodges to John L. Doggett, October 24, 1919, Hodges to F. P. Fleming, October 25, 1919, Hodges to Kligrapp of Great Wizard, October 28, 1919, all in Box 33, and Hodges to Duncan U. Fletcher, December 4, 1919, in Box 34, Hodges Papers.

8. Three studies treat this aspect of Florida "radicalism": George N. Green, "Florida Politics and Socialism at the Crossroads of the Progressive Era, 1912" (M.A. thesis, Florida State University, 1962); Ray F. Robbins II, "The Socialist Party in Florida: 1900–1916" (M.A. thesis, Samford University, 1971); Flynt, "Florida Labor and Political 'Radicalism,' 1919–1920."

labor paper published in Jacksonville, carried announcements of weekly Wednesday night Socialist meetings and defended strikers from charges that they were "Bolsheviki, rapists, free lovers, anarchists and I. W. W.'s."[9]

Across the state in Tampa the foreign-born population provoked even more suspicion. The first incident occurred in April, 1919, when Juan Garcia Guiterrez was arrested for writing a letter to relatives in Spain containing "radical and Bolshevist" expressions. The second incident involved two Socialists, Frank Lehti, a shoemaker, and John Sprunk, a tailor. Lehti had a local reputation as a troublemaker; during the war he had been accused of German sympathies and brought before a local judge who required him to kiss the American flag, presumably assuring his patriotism. Lehti and Sprunk requested the directors of the Tampa Labor Temple to allow a rally protesting the jailing of American Socialist leader Debs. Local labor leaders rejected the request and attacked the Socialists. When Lehti finally obtained a hall for a May 1 protest rally, Tampa's mayor and chief of police announced that they would tolerate no anarchistic or un-American speech in their city, and arrested the Finnish shoemaker for nailing up posters advertising the rally. Some activists allegedly agitated among cigarworkers to stage a sympathy strike for Debs, but while labor leaders expressed their sympathy, they protested that a strike of Tampa cigarmakers could not help Debs.[10]

Labor's rejection of socialist "radicalism" did nothing to dissuade conservatives from the notion that socialism was synonymous with organized labor. The conservative Tampa *Morning Tribune* launched a campaign of verbal violence which more than equaled the rhetoric of the socialists. On April 21 the editor blamed unrest among the city's cigarmakers on "about a dozen bolshevists or IWW's" who were "agitating overtime among the unsophisticated." Three days later the editor reported the distribution of much radi-

9. *Artisan*, March 1, 1919, in United States Shipping Board, RG 32, NA.
10. Tampa *Tribune*, April 20, 26, July 1, 1919.

cal propaganda including a copy of the constitution of the "communists in Russia" together with a proclamation from the Workers' Council of Butte, Montana, calling for a general strike in support of Debs. The editor praised the arrest of Lehti and warned those of similar persuasion in two defiant editorials:

The crowd of reds operating in this city under the guise of anarchists, bolshevists, socialists, or anything else thay may call themselves, are put on notice that the first aggregation of them caught attempting to hold a Debs imprisonment protest meeting May 1—or any other day—is going to be awfully sorry.

Tampa has had enough of war and Hun hellishness for the past ten years, and of Russian treachery and damn foolishness generally to do it for some time. In fact, we are "fed up" on that stuff. We want to get back to business. . . . The *Tribune* believes that these I.W.W. leaders when caught should be promptly hung before the masses of the people and celebration held over the occasion. This would serve as a warning to those others of the bolshevist tribe that none of their action was wanted in this country.[11]

Nor was the *Tribune's* response unusual. Labor spokesman Claude L'Engle proposed the cessation of all immigration and the deportation of all foreign radicals: "Those who talk about righting wrongs, real or fancied, by violence are not the stuff from which real Americans are made and whether they are classed as Bolsheviki, Anarchists, I.W.W. or any other thing, they have no business in a country where an intelligent use of the ballot will correct all evils that come into a system built on a sound foundation of justice and equity."[12]

The climax of this unrest came in January, 1920, in the massive arrests conducted nationwide by the Department of Justice. Jacksonville was one of only two southern cities involved. Eight aliens were arrested in a raid on what was reputed to be Communist party headquarters for the city. Justice Department officials discovered membership cards of the Communist party, minute

11. *Ibid.,* April 27, July 14, 1919.
12. MS in Claude L'Engle Papers.

books and a charter for a Communist organization, and speeches by
Eugene V. Debs. The only American citizen arrested was J. A.
Adams, a machinist at the Merrill-Stevens shipyard.[13]

Shortly after the first arrests, the "red round up" struck the
University of Florida where Professor Newell L. Sims, instructor
in sociology and political science, was asked to resign by the Board
of Control. A native of Indiana and former Congregationalist minister, Sims had taught at the Gainesville institution for five years and
defined himself as a "liberal." The British government had inter-
cepted a letter from him to a college friend who served as a missionary in the Belgian Congo. The letter included a reference to
the "hellish American government and its espionage act," and
cheered the Communist revolution in Russia: "I glory in the soviet
republic of Russia and pray for the day when it shall be established
in all of the world. Jesus of Nazareth was the moral Messiah to the
oppressed of the earth. Lenine [sic] is the economic deliverer of
Humanity, both are of God and all hell fights against them and will
destroy them, if possible."[14]

Sims protested that he had written the letter only to spark debate with his friend from undergraduate days at the University of
Kentucky. Faculty members at the University of Florida disliked
him, he explained, because he had refused to buy Liberty Bonds
and had ordered a radical newspaper for the university library.
Some alumni rallied to Sims's defense, calling him "one of the
strongest men of the Florida faculty" and challenging the dismissal
as a violation of freedom of thought; but most Floridians applauded
the expulsion of a dangerous "radical."[15]

Such evidence of radicalism aided Duncan Fletcher's bid for
reelection. He had supported the espionage act and had proposed
even more stringent legislation in the aftermath of the violent Cen-
tralia, Washington, strike in 1919. He had drafted a bill that would

13. For the "Red Scare" in Jacksonville, see Jacksonville *Florida Times-Union*, January
3–22, 1920.

14. See complete text, *ibid.*, January 17, 1920.

15. For a defense of Sims, see H. L. Dewolf to A. A. Murphree, January 28, 1920, in
Box 18, Murphree Papers.

have imprisoned or deported to the island of Guam anyone who advocated the overthrow of the American government.[16]

To many Floridians the displays of radicalism both nationally and locally provided convincing evidence that most labor agitation was subversive or at least suspect. Political candidates pandering to the labor vote incited unrest, strikes, and violence. The 1920 campaigns for senate and governor centered on attempts to link Van Swearingen and Catts to radical labor; and since both candidates desperately needed solid labor backing to win, the charges assumed added credence.

In September, 1919, the Jasper *News* demanded that each candidate for a major office state his position on labor because the people wanted to know "whether they justify organized labor in its Bolshevist attempts to overthrow the government and how they will handle the strikes, outbreaks and disturbances of labor if elected to office." There was a time, added the editor of the Brooksville *Argus*, when the "labor candidate" was a popular figure; but recently "union labor has threatened the country with strikes, with unreasonable demand for wage increase," and the "labor candidates" had been replaced by conservatives who would save the country from financial bankruptcy.[17]

Such dire predictions ignored the essentially conservative nature of American unionism, including the fact that many laborers supported Fletcher. The Palmetto *News* predicted that although a majority of workers would vote for Catts, the "best element" of union labor was working for Fletcher's reelection. The *Journal of the Knights of Labor* endorsed the incumbent as a proven friend of working people and farmers.[18]

By whatever standard the Palmetto *News* determined the "best element" of unionism, the fact remains that most rank and file unionists backed Catts. Fletcher had alienated labor by voting for

16. *Congressional Record*, Vol. LIX, 66th Congress, 2nd Sess., 1919, p. 69.
17. Jacksonville *Florida Times-Union*, September 25, October 1, 1919, quoting the Jasper *News* and the Brooksville *Argus*.
18. Jacksonville *Florida Times-Union*, November 17, 1919, quoting the Palmetto *News*; *Journal of the Knights of Labor*, May, 1920, pp. 7–8.

the Esch-Cummins bill to return railroads to private control after
the war. The AFL bitterly opposed the bill as did Catts, and the
governor used the issue frequently against Fletcher.[19] The prolabor editor of the Lakeland *Star*, which was one of the few papers
sympathetic to the phosphate strikers, was almost alone in its endorsement of Catts.

If union support helped the chief executive, the reaction to
labor "radicalism" and violence more than countered it. One paper
after another linked Catts and Swearingen together as a team
which appealed to the narrow class interests of organized labor.
They alleged that since most striking phosphate workers were
black, Catts sided with Negroes against his own race.[20]

Cary A. Hardee, who challenged Swearingen in the gubernatorial race, sent a letter to Florida voters opposing nationalization of
railroads and claiming that a great crisis threatened the collapse of
law and order and might plunge the state "into a vortex of anarchy
and Bolshevism." Catts replied angrily that the blast seemed to be
aimed at him and "this... seeming insult will throw me on my
mettle against you if you mean to involve me in this fight between
you and Van Swearingen." Hardee replied that he assumed since
Swearingen was a close political associate of Catts that the governor
had already entered the race on his behalf. The Tampa *Morning
Tribune* analyzed Catts's speech before city laborers and summarized: "His platform was 'down with the employer—every time,'
'Up with organized labor, right or wrong.' He waved the red flag
of socialism high over his head." The Jacksonville *Metropolis* contended that Catts was cynically using labor strife in 1920 just as
he had exploited religious conflict in 1916. A "Liberty Council"
was formed at Bradenton by professional men, bankers, and businessmen to oppose Catts's attempt to array one class against

19. See Warren A. Jennings, "Sidney J. Catts and the Democratic Primary of 1920,"
Florida Historical Quarterly, XXXIX (January, 1961), 203–20.
20. Tampa *Tribune*, May 21, 1920, and Jacksonville *Florida Times-Union*, May 7, 1920,
quoting St. Andrews Bay *News*.

another.[21] Sidney Catts suddenly found himself lumped together with Communists, anarchists, and the IWW in the minds of many Floridians.

The main focus of antilabor rhetoric was the alleged cabal between Swearingen and Catts. The two officials were personal friends, and Catts had appointed Swearingen to the post of attorney general, so there was no way to escape the inevitable conclusion that Swearingen represented a continuation of the Catts style and philosophy. In addition Catts's political associates such as J. B. Hodges and Joe Earman backed Swearingen, who often drew contributions from the same backers as the governor. The former Jacksonville blacksmith adopted a platform that promised to complete the unfulfilled goals of the Catts administration: opposition to the special corporate interests which had dominated Florida for so long; a full eight-month school term with free textbooks and reapportionment of the state legislature.[22]

The two men also focused their campaigns on the same laboring precincts. Swearingen established district headquarters in four geographical regions of Florida, and each was located in an area of labor unrest: Jacksonville, Pensacola, Tampa, and Miami. His speaking forays into urban Florida almost always centered on laborers. At Arcadia he visited the railroad shops to talk with workers; at Bartow he addressed several hundred laborers; his main speech in Tampa was delivered at the Labor Temple.

This labor strategy exposed him to the same charges of radicalism that plagued Catts's campaign. Lincoln Hulley, state senator and president of Baptist-affiliated Stetson University in Deland, Florida, entered the gubernatorial race with a blast at Swearingen's motto, "with the masses, against the classes." Hulley

21. See Sidney J. Catts to Cary A. Hardee, October 2, 1919, in Jacksonville *Florida Times-Union*, October 6, 1919; St. Petersburg *Times*, June 6, 1920, quoting the Jacksonville *Metropolis*; Tampa *Tribune*, July 16, 27, 1919.
22. Hodges worked for Swearingen but expected him to have a hard race against Cary Hardee; J. B. Hodges to Van C. Swearingen, March 16, 1920, Swearingen Campaign Pamphlet, in Box 34, Hodges Papers; Tampa *Tribune*, May 27, 1920.

termed it "a dangerous doctrine," "wholly unAmerican," "rank
Russian bolshevism," "unworthy of an American citizen," and appealed to organized labor to repudiate this divisive platform. The
Hastings *Herald* endorsed Hardee because he promised "a business like administration, thorough Americanism," fearless enforcement of the law, and would use every means available to "oppose and stamp out Bolshevism, Syndicalism, the I. W. W. and
every similar organization opposed to America."[23]

Even some labor leaders reacted negatively to Swearingen and
searched desperately to find an alternative to the gubernatorial
field. Claude L'Engle tried to persuade Major Charles B. Parkhill,
who was on the advocate general's staff in Washington, to offer
laborers a choice between the "deadening conservatism of Hardee
and the uninformed radicalism of Swearingen." L'Engle criticized
Hardee, who had been "trained in the way of business" and regarded the "maintenance of the established order" as the noblest
function of government; he represented the "old forces of selfish-
ness and greed" composed of bankers, businessmen, and corporations. Swearingen, on the other hand, favored the people but
lacked the mental equipment and training to be governor. He represented the "new forces of ignorance, self interest, passion and
prejudice gotten together by Catts." Some considered Swearingen
the favorite because he had support from Catts's courthouse officials
and appointees, the Guardians of Liberty, and labor. But L'Engle
accurately summarized Swearingen's liabilities: the Guardians were
not nearly so united or powerful as in 1916; many officeholders
were angry at Catts and planned to "double cross Swearengen
[*sic*] to get even"; and labor could never win in Florida because the
rank and file voted from "blind prejudice" instead of "fundamental
principles." Thousands of Floridians who had followed progressive
Governor Napoleon B. Broward between 1904 and 1908, men with
"progressive, liberal ideas" who should naturally vote for Swearingen, could not abide his rhetoric and affiliation with Catts and

23. Lincoln Hulley to editor, Tampa *Tribune*, October 7, 1919; Jacksonville *Florida
Times-Union*, February 26, 1920, quoting the Hastings *Herald*.

were going to vote for Hardee.[24] L'Engle's perception of the mood of Florida voters was prophetic.

All the gubernatorial candidates joined L'Engle in tying Swearingen and Catts together. Hardee constantly referred to the "present Catts-Swearingen regime in Tallahassee." The Tampa *Tribune* editorialized on June 6, 1920, that there was only one issue facing voters in 1920: "Cattsism, or anti-Cattsism." Swearingen was "the creature of Catts" as proven by the papers supporting him which included the Palm Beach *Post* owned by Earman, the Arcadia *Enterprise*, owned by Andrew Carter, whom Catts had appointed to a three-thousand-dollar job as "fire warden of the Everglades," and Bill Maypoles' Okaloosa County paper whose owner had been appointed state gasoline inspector. The Tampa *Tribune* even extended the factionalism to local contests where "Cattsism" meant appeals to one class against another.

Swearingen perceived the effect such attacks had on his race and sought to dissociate himself from the governor. He denied that he intended to forfeit the charter of phosphate companies operating in Florida and repudiated charges that his campaign drew from the same contributors and appealed to the same groups as Catts. He even ran an advertisement in the *Florida Times-Union* on June 2, 1920, which attempted to link Hardee and Catts by charging that Hardee had approved the governor's legislative program and had voted to sustain his vetoes.

Such attacks greatly aided Duncan Fletcher, who conducted a low-key campaign against Catts. He disliked Catts intensely and privately predicted a contest with "the delivery of blows below the belt."[25] The incumbent senator did not begin his bid for reelection until March 21, 1920. Three days later a number of his supporters met at the Law Exchange Building in Jacksonville to determine

24. Claude L'Engle to Major Charles B. Parkhill, September 19, 1919, Parkhill to L'Engle, September 27, 1919, L'Engle to Parkhill, October 2, 1919, all in L'Engle Papers.
25. Duncan U. Fletcher to Joe L. Earman, October 6, 1919, in Box 33, Hodges Papers. For a more thorough treatment of Senator Fletcher and his campaign, see Wayne Flynt, *Duncan Upshaw Fletcher: Dixie's Reluctant Progressive* (Tallahassee: Florida State University Press, 1971), especially 128–34.

strategy. Campaign manager A. T. Williams named an executive committee, warned against overconfidence, and organized Fletcher clubs down to the precinct level. In his speeches Fletcher emphasized his service to Florida farmers through creation of the Federal Farm Loan Bank Act, his advocacy of a strong American merchant fleet under federal control, and his support of the League of Nations. He emphasized his role in bringing defense industry to Florida, and especially sought out labor audiences to try to win the more conservative elements of unionism.

Catts launched his campaign in 1920 in the same old Ford that had carried him to the governor's mansion. He delivered three or four speeches a day, oftentimes ending his busy schedule with an address to a Sunday evening worship or Wednesday night prayer meeting at the nearest Baptist church. His bombastic speeches invariably closed with prayer. Although he lacked the support that Fletcher had, his friends did organize a number of Bear Catt Clubs, headed by state president Albert W. Boatwright. The clubs operated from headquarters in Tallahassee, and members contributed one dollar each. Most of the literature distributed through the clubs contained Jerry Carter cartoons to delight cracker readers; a typical one depicted a cat astride a dog whose face resembled Fletcher's, while the phosphate operators, railroad owners, Peter O. Knight, and other prominent Florida industrialists cheered the incumbent senator. The masses cheered the cat: "Hurrah! for the Tom Catt and to H—l with your corporation pup." W. H. McIntosh of Graceville contributed his own unique cracker lyric:

> It matters not what papers say,
>   Nor corporation firms,
> It's the wool hat boys that wins the day,
>   That scatters catching germs.

> It matters not who runs the race,
>   Nor who plays at the bats,
> He'll appreciate a seat in D.C.'s Hall
>   Who beats old Sidney Catts.[26]

---

26. Catts Campaign Sheet, 1920, P. #93, in Jerry W. Carter Papers, Florida State University, Tallahassee.

In most of his literature and speeches, the governor began by defending his stewardship of the four years in Tallahassee. He boasted of his vetoes during the 1919 legislative session by which he had safeguarded the road fund, saved the appropriation for the Board of Health, and defended the rights of poor Floridians. On the affirmative side, he had improved the quality of government by replacing corrupt officials with honest ones, enacted and enforced prohibition, saved the boys at Camp Wheeler by exposing unhealthful conditions, and provided the most efficient draft system in the United States. In his administration he had always stood "for the common people, he himself being an ordinary, everyday Florida Cracker," and he had opposed corporations and "the Plutocratic power which others in this race stand for."[27]

Three of these issues—prison reform, the Camp Wheeler episode, and prohibition—dominated his speeches. He frequently contrasted prison conditions before his term to the model farm at Raiford, and at almost every rally he proudly displayed a ring which had been presented to him as a present from convicts grateful for his introduction of the honor system. Regarding Camp Wheeler, he claimed that the incumbent senator had done little to improve conditions and that only the governor's persistence had prevented disaster. According to one account, the governor said in a St. Petersburg speech that three German spies had inoculated the food at the military facility with poisonous germs. Fletcher released letters which he had received from the War Department and Secretary of War Newton Baker alleging that Catts was not even present in Washington when he claimed to have been and charging that the governor greatly exaggerated mortality at the camp. Fletcher suggested that Catts suffered from a disease of his own: an "overfed imagination." The governor made another sensational charge that three unnamed men from Tampa had offered him fifty thousand dollars not to call the 1918 session of the legislature to enact the prohibition amendment, and then had threatened to murder him if he summoned it anyway. One incredulous editor

27. Catts Campaign Sheet, 1920, in the Diamond Papers.

offered five hundred dollars each for prosecution of the three mysterious gentlemen.[28]

The governor also offered some positive proposals. He promised to support measures that would curtail immigration, provide Protestant ministers equality with Catholic priests in military camps, develop Florida's economy by constructing canals and encouraging commerce, and enact labor reform.[29] His blasts at corporations, railroads, and phosphate companies appealed to the labor vote, although conservative unionism responded unenthusiastically. The craft unions opposed Fletcher because of his vote to return railroads to private ownership and endorsed Catts, albeit without any real enthusiasm for him. Cigar, phosphate, and shipyard workers responded more affirmatively to the governor's appeals. Catts also proposed that the government give every soldier who had served in France forty acres of land and one hundred dollars in cash.

None of Catts's issues struck with more impact than his opposition to the League of Nations. Fletcher had been one of the Senate's most persuasive spokesmen for the league, and had fearlessly championed internationalism in every Florida speech. J. B. Hodges considered the league charter to be a "Godless document," and sent a copy to the governor together with a prediction that if Fletcher did not reverse himself on the league, Catts would "sweep him off his feet." Jerry Carter proposed an even bolder strategy, visiting Washington in February of 1920 to arrange for the isolationist senator James A. Reed of Missouri to make four or five antileague speeches in Florida. Carter conferred with Hodges in Jacksonville on the most effective utilization of Reed in behalf of Catts.[30] Progressive politician John S. Beard wrote a scathing denunciation of the league and gloomily prophesied that its adoption would mean the end of the union.

28. Jacksonville *Florida Times-Union,* March 28, April 1, 1920, July 1, 3, 1919.
29. Catts Campaign Sheet, 1920, in the Diamond Papers.
30. J. B. Hodges to Joe Earman, November 19, 1920, in Box 25, Hodges to Sidney J. Catts, June 21, 1919, Jerry W. Carter to Hodges, February 3, 1920, Hodges to Carter, February 12, 1920, all in Box 33, Hodges Papers.

Catts wasted no time emphasizing his own opposition to the league. In one of his earliest campaign documents, he said that United States participation in the league would link America to "the landgrabbing schemes" that England, Japan, and other nations had "engaged in during the late war." Fletcher's vote for the league was a vote to underwrite the "worthless European bonds and securities now owned and held by the money hogs of Wall Street." He argued that the league could not prevent war and that the United States should mind its own business.[31] Charles P. Sweeney, who was working on an article, "Bigotry in the South," for the *Nation*, became fascinated with Catts and recorded a speech that the governor used to entertain a Fort Myers audience. According to Sweeney's account, the governor stated that if America joined the league, nine men, "one of them a thick-lipped gazabo [*sic*] from Liberia, would run everything over here." He described the consequences of such a calamity in vivid language:

Why feller [*sic*] citizens, if we had a League of Nations, those foreigners would take Jedge [*sic*] Whitehurst off this bench here and what would they do? I'll tell you what they'd do. They'd go to your homes here in Fort Myers, and look at your washing hung on the line in the back yard; they'd glance into your garbage pails; they'd pry into your kitchens, and they'd peer into your bureau drawers. And they wouldn't stop there. What else would they do? These foreigners would peer into your wife's closets and examine her clothes—her intimate wearing apparel. And you know what would happen, don't you? I'll tell you. There'd be black eyes and broken bones next morning. That's what those foreigners would get.[32]

Both the issue and the rhetoric touched a responsive nerve among some Florida voters. The Lakeland *Star* admitted that Catts had made many mistakes as governor but added: "He meant all right, and if Fletcher don't change his attitude on this league of nations business, Catts will be the next United States Senator."[33]

31. Catts Campaign Sheet, 1920, P. #93, in Carter Papers; Jacksonville *Florida Times-Union*, May 15, 1920.
32. Charles P. Sweeney, "Bigotry in the South," *Nation*, CXI (November 24, 1920), 586.
33. Jacksonville *Florida Times-Union*, January 17, 1920, quoting the Lakeland *Star*.

Another emotional issue for Catts was opposition to location of a leprosarium in Florida. The United States Public Health Service had made a topographical survey of an island eight miles off the Florida Coast at Cedar Key, and proposed to construct there a two-hundred-thousand-dollar colony for lepers. State officials fought locating the colony there with a fear born of ignorance: the facility would jeopardize the industrial and commercial interests of the area around Cedar Key; it might poison the excellent oyster waters surrounding the island; and finally, families of the lepers would move to Cedar Key enhancing the danger of escapees from the island who might spread the disease. State health officer Dr. Ralph N. Greene complained that Florida already led the nation in venereal disease and did not need any additional health problems. Joe Earman, president of the Board of Health, wired Fletcher, who was lobbying for the bill, to pressure Washington officials to locate it elsewhere. Governor Catts launched a petition drive with the warning that California, Florida's rival for tourism, would change the nickname of the Sunshine State to the Leper State. On October 23, 1919, Catts and Greene visited Washington to lodge their complaints in person. Despite such pressure, Senator Fletcher defended the project, refuting the wild rumors with expert medical opinion. He did acknowledge, however, that if the furor in his home state continued, it would jeopardize plans to locate the facility in Florida.[34]

On October 12 Catts and Greene took their cause to Cedar Key where virtually the entire population turned out for a rally. Greene presented rationally the medical opposition to the colony, but "when Gov. Catts mounted the platform the fur began to fly." He asked his auditors how many opposed location of the colony in their area, and virtually every hand was lifted. The board of county commissioners had endorsed the colony, and Catts threatened that unless every commissioner removed his name from the petition by the following Wednesday, the governor would remove each one of them. Thunderous applause greeted this statement. Despite en-

34. *Ibid.*, October 7, 10, November 2, 1919.

dorsement of the colony by the Duval County Medical Association, Fletcher backed away from the controversy, writing public health officials that in light of the opposition in Florida, the colony should be located elsewhere. National health officials agreed, but Catts had a new issue: Fletcher had tried to make Florida "a dumping ground for lepers."[35]

One of the strangest issues to emerge in the campaign was the subject of free speech. Catts had long opposed the national espionage act as a violation of the right to criticize the government, but during the senatorial race he extended his criticism. He condemned the New York state assembly for expelling duly elected Socialist members. No state assembly or even Congress had the right to expel a member because of his political beliefs. Directing his fire at Fletcher, Catts frequently referred to his senatorial opponent as "a first cousin to the Czar of Russia."[36]

In a curious mingling of religious prejudice and defense of free speech, he blasted Fletcher's "Guam bill" as part of a Catholic conspiracy. Catts noted that the legislation had been proposed by Fletcher in the midst of the national "red scare" and would allow permanent deportation of dissidents to the island of Guam at the discretion of a federal judge; but he discovered a more sinister motivation. The Catholic Knights of Columbus, exuberant because of their victory in putting priests into all the cantonments and army camps, had duped Senator Fletcher into proposing a bill that would deny the American people freedom of speech, press, and worship. With this accomplished, the Knights, aided by Fletcher, would "hold up the Roman Catholic dogma and creed and say to despised Protestants, 'You worship as the Holy Mother Church says, or you go to prison or the fires of persecution. . . .' Do you think for a moment he can fool the people of Florida into voting for him when he wants to put all of us on the Island of Guam."[37] Catts gleefully concluded the point by telling cracker audiences that so

35. *Ibid.*, October 13, November 6, 30, 1919; Catts Campaign Sheet, 1920, in Park Trammell Papers, Lakeland Public Library, Lakeland, Fla.

36. Catts Campaign Sheet, 1920, in Trammell Papers.

37. Catts Campaign Sheet, 1920, P. #93, in Carter Papers.

long as his trigger finger remained limber, no one would deport
him.

Running like a thread throughout Catts's campaign was a consistent populist theme of little, inarticulate people battling the special interests. Catts oftentimes referred to himself as "the Ben
Tillman of Florida," evoking memories of the Negro-baiting South
Carolina reformer. Fletcher's vote for the Esch-Cummins bill had
denied railroad workers the right to strike and demonstrated that
the incumbent senator served "the big railroads, the big corporations and the big interests." Three major Florida railroads—the
East Coast, Atlantic Coast Line and Seaboard Air Line—opposed
Catts because they could not "boss him" as they did Fletcher. The
Senator had also helped the "Big Five Corporations" control the
meat supply in Florida by means of a secret buyer in every big
town who had run independent meat-packers out of business. Such
corporate connections explained Fletcher's vote against a federal
child labor bill and his opposition to the poor man who was forced
by necessity to work from dawn and who "comes home at night to
his wife and children smelling like a Billy Goat with the honest
perspiration of a hard day's toil." By contrast Catts had always sided
with the workers as demonstrated by his support of the phosphate
strikers. He also related an incident about one of his son's service
with a National Guard unit during a Jacksonville streetcar strike.
According to the governor, he told the boy that if he fired on the
strikers, "he need never put his feet under Catts' table again."[38]

Such substantive issues constituted the major thrust of Catts's
offensive but were overshadowed in the public mind by his religious and personal attacks on Fletcher. Even legitimate questions
such as free speech or the League of Nations often became so enmeshed in religious emotionalism that the public lost sight of the
real point. As in 1916, there is much evidence that Catts detected a
strong anti-Catholicism and harnessed it to his campaign. It is true
that he genuinely feared Catholic political involvement, and that
he felt the church had undue access to military audiences during

38. *Ibid.*

the war. He bordered on paranoia in his fear of a Catholic conspiracy aimed at himself and his family; but when he personally encountered Catholics, he was not the raving bigot described by his enemies. In an ironic twist of fate, his son, Rozier, married a Catholic girl from Key West where he had been stationed during the war. The governor offered no criticism of the decision in family councils and welcomed her into the family. During the 1920 campaign the marriage was mentioned occasionally to refute Catts's charge of a Catholic menace. Most reflective of his personal relationship was an incident aboard a train when he approached a group of strangers to solicit their votes. One man took the campaign material, commenting that he appreciated the way that Catts had welcomed the Catholic girl into his family. The governor reached out to take his material back with the statement that this was an insufficient reason for casting a ballot; any father should welcome his son's wife into the family regardless of her religion.[39]

As an organized religious body, however, Catholics seriously threatened religious freedom, and if Floridians reelected Fletcher, "they can just say that they have bowed their knee to the corporations and Catholics of the state."[40] In his speeches Catts predicted that he would carry every panhandle county west of the Apalachicola River except Escambia, which was controlled by Pensacola's Catholic population. One of his early circulars explained the nature of the opposition: "These Catholic toe-kissers of the pope know very well that if Catts goes to the senate they will hear his strong, fierce vote urging that the United States shall not be sold to the pope of Rome."[41]

As campaigning moved into the spring of 1920, the rhetoric became more vituperative. Even at the beginning of the race, Catts had made oblique references to the fact that he was "not ashamed to confess that he believes that Christ is the Son of God"; but as emotions heated, he made less subtle references to Fletcher's

39. Interview, Mrs. Ruth Cawthon, May 8, 1972, DeFuniak Springs, Mrs. Elizabeth C. Paderick, and Mrs. Alice May Stiegel, May 12, 1972, Jacksonville.

40. Catts Campaign Sheet, 1920, in Trammell Papers.

41. Jacksonville Florida Times-Union, February 2, 1920, quoting the Ocala Star.

Unitarian faith: "Catts is informed that Fletcher's church, the Unitarian, does not even believe in the divinity of Christ, but makes him a bastard."[42] Fletcher had to spend much of his time explaining Unitarianism and his own beliefs, and grew increasingly irritated at Catts. The climax came in a joint debate at Titusville on May 6. Fletcher, usually unperturbable on the stump, became infuriated and accused Catts of blasphemy for attacking someone's religion while at the same time linking Jesus Christ to his own name and that of Sears and Roebuck. Observers agreed that it was "the warmest debate of the campaign."[43]

Such a response only aroused the governor to greater personal abuse. Two weeks later in Tampa he added a cranial argument, telling a riotous crowd that Fletcher's frequently cited mental capacity did not impress him since the incumbent wore a 6½ inch hat compared to his 7¼. Examining the senator's physique more closely, he observed that "further down in his anatomy where he carried his beer and champagne," he was "much better developed." A heckler took offense and asked why Catts had been run out of Alabama. "The man who says I was run out of Alabama is a liar," shouted the chief executive. "You'll go back after June 8," came the reply. "I'll go back when I pardon your daddy from the pen," retorted the governor. When the angry Catts rested his hand on a heavy object in his coat pocket which reporters said resembled an automatic pistol, one heckler jeered: "What is that you have in your pocket?" Catts responded: "What I've got in my pocket can settle you quick enough!"[44]

Fletcher became enraged by such attacks and sank to the lowest level of his long career. For the only time in his fifty years in Florida public life he resorted to the Negro issue against a political opponent. In the same May 6 debate at Titusville, Fletcher created a sensation by charging that Catts had appointed a Negro Republi-

42. Catts Campaign Sheets, 1920, in Diamond Papers, and P. #93, in Carter Papers.
43. Jacksonville *Florida Times-Union*, May 7, 1920.
44. *Ibid.*, May 23, 1920.

can, R. R. Robinson, as assistant probation officer for Duval
County. The senator then produced the February 28, 1920, issue
of the Chicago *Plain Dealer*, "a negro paper which advocated social
equality, repeal of Jim Crow laws, etc." The newspaper contained a
picture of Catts and Robinson above an article about the appointment. The Florida press publicized the charge in many editorials,
sometimes embellishing the facts with rumors that Catts clubs
were being formed among Florida Negroes.[45] Even Catts's proposal to reward servicemen with land grants became suspect according to the Jasper *News:* "Give to the nigger who saw service in
France one hundred dollars and forty acres of land . . . and the
white man will have to hew all the wood, and draw all the water."[46]
Catts admitted appointing Robinson but vehemently denied that
this implied any belief in social equality for blacks. In one campaign circular, he offered Fletcher one thousand dollars if he would
try to put a "negro" in the governor's parlor on terms of social
equality, pledging "that he will not settle with the Negro until he
finishes with [Fletcher]."[47]

Fletcher also utilized substantive rebuttal. His opposition to
woman suffrage and child labor was based on technique rather than
principle. Suffrage should be submitted to the people of Florida for
a referendum, not dictated by the federal Congress; and the child
labor bill as drafted by Congress had violated the Constitution, a
view subsequently upheld by the Supreme Court which ruled the
measure unconstitutional. On labor matters, he argued that he had
not supported the Esch-Cummins bill until an antistrike clause had
been eliminated. He also blasted Catts's record as governor, noting
that he had entered the statehouse with a pledge to lower taxes and
instead had nearly doubled them during his four years. Even more
telling was his assault on nepotism. Research revealed that members of the Catts family on the state payroll received total salaries of

45. *Ibid.*, May 7, June 7, 1920.
46. Jasper *News*, March 27, 1920.
47. Catts Campaign Sheet, 1920, P. #93, in Carter Papers.

thirty-two thousand dollars a year. If the governor remained in office another year, Fletcher predicted that "he will have an inspector of icebergs on the St. Johns river."[48]

The Florida press formed in solid ranks against the governor. Many papers which had supported him in 1916—including the Williston *Progress,* Fort Lauderdale *Sentinel,* Palmetto *News,* Lake Wales *Highlander,* and Miami *Metropolis*—joined the opposition in 1920. The *Metropolis* regretted its support of a man who had made himself a laughingstock by his "buffonery [*sic*] and his ignorance;" the Palmetto *News* rejoiced that Catts had entered the senate race so it could correct its mistaken 1916 support and "relegate him to the scrap heap of political oblivion." "If such a thing is possible," wrote the editor, "we hope he will be buried so deep he will leave the state, never to return."[49] The Avon Park *Pilot* said that the only thing Catts had said that it believed was his promise if elected to raise more hell in six months than Fletcher had done in eleven years.

Even the Baltimore *Sun* entered the affray, though more perceptively than the Florida press. The *Sun* believed that the only explanation for a demagogue such as Catts was that the old factions had abused the poor cracker of Florida. Had the masses not been aggrieved by corporations and the wealthy who had been favored by government at their expense, Catts could not have set Florida afire. Nevertheless, opined the editor, if a man with Catts's platform and emotional appeals could be elected to the United States Senate, "the current belief in the saving grace of democracy will receive an extremely severe shock": "A lower, more blatant or more blasphemous campaign of demagogy was never staged in this country. 'Sockless Simpson' never came anywhere near it; Blease's methods were refined in comparison; Vardaman was a knightly figure contrasted to the new political hero of Florida."[50]

48. Jacksonville *Florida Times-Union,* June 4, 1920.
49. *Ibid.,* July 8, 1918, quoting the Palmetto *News;* Tampa *Tribune,* May 22, 1920, quoting Miami *Metropolis.*
50. Jasper *News,* March 5, 1920, quoting the Baltimore *Sun.*

Newspapers refused to announce Catts's speeches, and this, coupled with the general abuse by the press, infuriated the governor. He did not consider the newspapers "any more than he did grasshoppers and crickets," he wrote. The editor of the Branford *Progress* should be confined to an insane asylum, and he assured a Moore Haven audience that the newspapermen of Florida would "be cast into hell, every one of them." The belligerent editor of the Lakeland *Telegram* hoped he was mistaken: "Don't want to be bothered with him in the next world, as we certainly will be if we have to reside in the hot place." The Sebring *White Way* dismissed the speech as an "hour long harangue," the "Eulogies of a Tom Cat."[51]

Returns in the June 8 primary demonstrated that voters as well as newspapers had defected from the administration camp. Catts received only 28.6 percent of the senatorial vote in losing to Fletcher 25,007 to 62,304. He carried only three counties, all in the northwest panhandle section. Even in this traditional stronghold, however, Fletcher carried eleven of the fourteen counties from Leon west to Escambia, winning 12,302 votes to 7,553 for Catts, who even lost his home county of Walton. Catts also carried his compatriot, Van C. Swearingen, down to defeat; the attorney general lost to Cary Hardee, 30,240 (34.1%) to 52,591 (59.5%). Although Catts and Swearingen appealed to essentially the same voters, the attorney general ran ahead of the governor in forty-one counties and trailed him in thirteen, most of them in the panhandle. Swearingen carried only one county but received more than 40 percent in nine additional counties.[52]

The much heralded and quietly feared "labor coalition" materialized only in impotent form. Of the five counties most affected by the labor disorders of 1919–1920—Polk, Duval, Dade, Escambia, and Hillsborough—Catts and Swearingen lost all five. The

51. Catts Campaign Sheet, 1920, P. #93, in Carter Papers; Jacksonville *Florida Times-Union*, May 5, 6, 1920, quoting Lakeland *Telegram* and Sebring *White Way*.
52. *Report of the Secretary of State, 1919–1920*, insert; Annie Mary Hartsfield and Elston E. Roady, *Florida Votes: 1920–1962* (Tallahassee: Institute of Governmental Research, Florida State University, 1963), 56, 77. See map, page 272 herein.

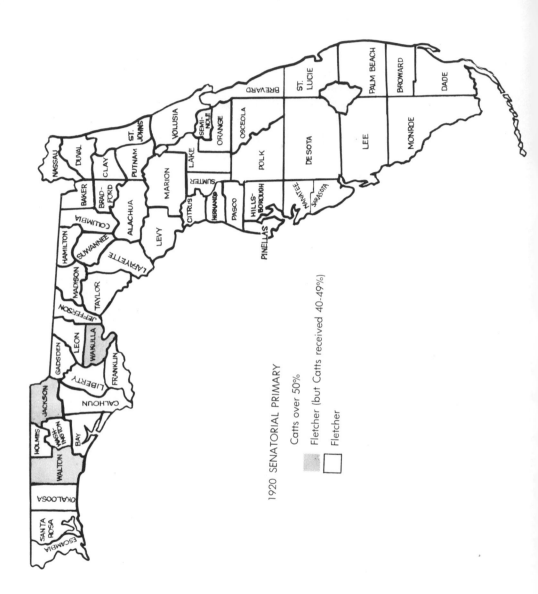

1920 SENATORIAL PRIMARY

Catts over 50%

Fletcher (but Catts received 40-49%)

Fletcher

governor ran below his statewide average in two of the counties, almost exactly the same in one, and slightly stronger in two (Hillsborough and Polk, where the most violent labor disorders had occurred). Swearingen led him in each of the five counties by margins ranging from 3 to 15 percent. In Hillsborough, for example, Swearingen carried 14 of 55 precincts; Catts won 7 of the same 14, plus three additional voting places. Despite the presence of a third candidate in the gubernatorial field, Swearingen still led Catts in 32 of the 55 precincts. Yet the vote for the two men was about the same, and available evidence in Tampa and statewide suggests that labor voted for both, though in slightly smaller numbers for Catts.[53]

Several factors influenced the 1920 results. Catts's intimate flirtation with unionism in a time of constant labor tension and violence created a reaction that associated his candidacy with radicalism. Also, Duncan Fletcher was a powerful figure in state affairs whose federal farm loan bank system had provided long-term agricultural credit and endeared him to precisely the north Florida small farmer constituency which had elected Catts in 1916. Despite such ameliorative factors, W. T. Cash accurately termed Catts's defeat one of the worst political eclipses in the history of the state.[54] Fletcher's winning margin over Catts was by far the widest of his four senatorial contests.

Reaction from the Florida press was unrestrained; editors unashamedly rejoiced. The Gainesville *Daily Sun* concluded that the primary had ended "Catts and Cattism . . . in Florida" and factionalism within the Democratic party. The Tampa *Morning Tribune* agreed, adding that June 8 was a victory for the "principle of the open shop" which had terminated "four years of Cattism with its appealing prejudices, its personal aggrandizement and its selfishly hoping to withstand attack by pledging its loyalty to organized labor." In a jibing editorial entitled "The Passing of Sidney," the Miami *Herald* rejoiced that Catts's ignorance would no longer send

53. Hartsfield and Roady, *Florida Votes*; Tampa *Tribune*, June 10, 1920.
54. Cash, *History of the Democratic Party in Florida*, 134.

the nation into "veritable guffaws of amusement and laughter": "And, hence, passes Sidney J. Catts.... He came to us like a cyclone, he goes out with the mildness of a June Zephyr. He has disturbed our political peace and has kept the state embroiled in controversy. He now goes his way, with few to lament him, and thousands to rejoice that his political day is over." The tiny Baldwin *Sun* shared the vitriolic delight of its larger sisters: "Catts was Blease, Vardaman and half a dozen other demagogues in one, and he could descend lower and roll deeper in the political mire than all of them put together.... But Florida has waked up from her Midsummer Night's Dream and has divorced herself from this repulsive political beast."[55] All such obituaries were premature.

55. Gainesville *Daily Sun*, June 10, 1920; Tampa *Tribune*, June 10, 1920; Miami *Herald*, June 10, 1920; Jacksonville *Florida Times-Union*, June 24, 1920, quoting the Baldwin *Sun*.

ELEVEN

Let Old Acquaintance Be Forgot

THE PUBLIC REJECTION documented by the June primary matched the nadir of Catts's personal relations with his political associates. His strange behavior in the last months of his "lame duck" administration reveals the effect of the years of criticism and vilification that culminated in the press assault during the 1920 campaign. This, and his subsequent annihilation by Fletcher, left him angry and cynical. He had broken the old Democratic establishment by forging a coalition of personal friends, opportunists anxious to win a place for themselves in public life, and idealists who shared his objectives but became increasingly disenchanted with his crude techniques of government. Opportunists such as J. B. Hodges drifted away because of his explosive temper, his unwillingness to compromise more completely with the old politics and its practitioners, his oftentimes ineffectual dealings with the legislature, and his loss of popularity. Idealists such as Joe Earman became disgusted with Catts's cynicism and his ever more frequent compromises of conviction. The governor was too inept and rigid to please his expedient allies and too flexible and inconsistent to placate his idealists.

Opponents who accused Catts of attempting to build a political machine were correct, but he never succeeded. His failure was more the consequence of his own limitations than of their actions. He lacked the broad vision of some demagogues. In his younger years he had only a vague interest in politics, not the single-minded purpose of a Huey Long. Once in office, he could be vindictive, but he lacked the quality of sustained ruthlessness that was necessary to crush his enemies. Even had he possessed sufficient will to construct a machine capable of eliminating opposition, his violent temper and unreasoning animosities would have doomed any long-range plans. The governor treated close associates as valued confidants on one day, only to banish them as hated traitors the next.

Angry and disillusioned by public rejection in 1920, Catts wrote J. B. Hodges days after the June election: "There are just a few men who stood square all the time, but most of them ditched me every chance they got. However, my shoulders are broad enough to stand it and I think I will never deal in politics again." Chief among the defectors that Catts listed was Joe Earman, who was either a "traitor or a fool." It was Earman who had obtained from the governor the appointment of a Catholic friend as sheriff of Brevard County and the removal of a very popular local official. Catts decided that this unfortunate advice had cost him the entire lower east coast in the election. The disgruntled chief executive even charged that Earman had favored Fletcher from the beginning and had purposely sabotaged his campaign; a stiff denial from Hodges failed to convince him otherwise.[1]

The rift between Earman and the governor widened in July when Catts wrote the West Palm Beach publisher an abusive letter for refusing to sanction the removal of J. Ed Graves from the State Board of Health. The only reason for such pressure, concluded Earman, was that Graves had refused to support the governor for the United States Senate.[2]

In December the clash finally broke into public over control of local patronage. Judge E. B. Donnell of Palm Beach, a political ally of Catts, wanted to resign as presiding magistrate of the Fifteenth

1. Sidney J. Catts to J. B. Hodges, June 16, 1920, Hodges to Catts, June 17, 1920, in Box 34, Hodges Papers.
2. Joe L. Earman to J. B. Hodges, August 1, 1922, Box 197, *ibid.* This letter, filled with venom, may overstate Catts's "crimes" and certainly was written in a moment of high passion against the governor.

Judicial Circuit. A local official wanted the job, and Earman charged that Catts demanded money for the appointment. He angrily announced on the pages of the Palm Beach *Post* that "Joe and Sid have Dissolved." Catts had also reinstated Edgar C. Thompson as state's attorney for the Fifteenth Judicial Circuit. Thompson had been removed from office by the governor, then reelected by his constituency, and reappointed by Catts over Earman's objections. Privately, Earman charged that Thompson had paid Catts to reinstate him;[3] publicly, he vented his frustration over losing influence with Florida's chief executive:

Sid Catts has sold his PRICELESS HERITAGE OF CONSISTENCY and FIDELITY for a mess of POLITICAL POTTAGE, said POTTAGE being Thompson's promise of political support to Sid Catts in 1922.
I HAVE GONE ALL THE WAY THROUGH FOR A FRIEND.
I have no apologies to make for sticking with Catts down to his and my defeat.
I have been a CONSISTENT friend.
His INCONSISTENCY has torn the blanket and we have parted politically FOREVERMORE.
During 1918, he wrote me a vicious letter.
I WROTE HIM ONE BACK.
. . . .
I hooked in with Old Catts in 1916.
I believed in him.
At the finish, he has disappointed me.
POLITICS IS HELL.
. . . .
Reverend S. Johnson [*sic*] Catts had the golden opportunity of being the GREATEST MAN IN ALL FLORIDA.
He has PETERED out.
The LAST MAN WHO TALKS TO HIM IS THE INFLUENCE.[4]

Jerry Carter, one of Catts's few friends who remained loyal throughout the 1920s, denied that the governor ever took bribes or payoffs for jobs. Perhaps in his frustration and bitterness, Earman overstated Catts's offense, or it may have been that the "pay" which

3. *Ibid.*
4. Palm Beach *Post*, December 12, 1920; copy in Box 39, *ibid.*

Thompson gave the governor was only a promise of future political support as Earman suggested in his editorial. Carter did substantiate the charge of infidelity; Catts did not consider consistency a critical virtue, and his unpredictability soured the governor's relationship with all of his associates. He would work with them loyally on one issue, then reverse himself and attack them mercilessly if they disagreed with him on another matter. A second factor which contributed to the fissure with Earman was local patronage. Catts allowed no one, not even Carter, to dictate appointments, and often rejected the advice of his better-informed friends on local appointments. Carter considered him essentially a fair man, but those who unsuccessfully sought favors did not consider him equitable.[5]

Hodges, who remained a confidant of both Earman and the governor throughout the crisis, regretted that Earman had published the article. He wrote his publisher friend that Catts had given assurances that Earman would not be removed from the Board of Health despite their differences. This assurance had been given before the governor read Earman's polemic, however, and Hodges expressed concern over Catts's reaction.[6]

The governor's response was both public and emotional. He assured Floridians that he was not mad at Earman and did not intend to remove him from office; but neither would he allow Earman to "boss" the governor:

> The truth of the business is that your tyranny, arrogance and big stick bossing has run all your friends away from you.... Now, I have got to speak plainly with you. I am willing to let you and yours alone, you to do the same with me and mine, but if you publish one more page in your paper like the last one, or bother me or my children anymore, I will go to West Palm Beach, Fla., with my double-barrel shotgun loaded with buck-shot and I will have a final settlement with you.
>
> . . . .
>
> You say your printer's ink is worth 1-cents [sic] a drop, but I say fourteen buckshots in each gun barrel with a man who will pull the trigger, weighs one thousand pounds each.[7]

5. Interview, Jerry W. Carter, July 29, 1970, Tallahassee.
6. J. B. Hodges to Joe L. Earman, December 15, 1920, in Box 39, Hodges Papers.
7. S. J. Catts to Joe Earman, in Palm Beach *Post*, December 18, 1920; also in Jacksonville *Florida Times-Union*, December 17, 1920.

The state's regular Democrats gleefully watched this spectacle, while the New York *Times* delighted its readers with detailed descriptions of the bizarre public correspondence by two of Florida's most prominent citizens. Catts warned Hodges privately to use his influence to moderate Earman: "I guess you see all the fool stuff Joe Earman wrote and I wrote him . . . and I meant every word I told him, so if you have any influence over him and don't want a tragedy in Florida you had better ask him to stop his foolishness, for I am tired of it." Hodges apparently took the governor's threat quite seriously and begged Earman to make no reply to Catts's letter.[8]

The south Florida publisher, unwilling to let the affair end, told a New York *Times* reporter that he would remain in Palm Beach to "welcome" the governor, and that his controversy with Catts was a struggle between "good government and demagogy." To local citizens, he announced that "THREATENED MEN LIVE A LONG TIME. OR UNTIL THEY DRY UP."[9]

Hodges apparently considered Earman's vendetta unjustified and sided with Catts, at least in correspondence with the governor. He deplored the entire episode and explained that he had written "Joe several times to lay off." He even predicted that such "unfair tactics" had swept Catts into office in 1916 and might "sweep you out of the Governor's chair to a great service to the people." Catts replied that he had learned on December 20 that Earman had collapsed physically as a result of "our differences, so I 'called the dogs of war off.'"[10] The combination of physical collapse and political disenchantment caused Earman to sell his newspaper, and the furor finally subsided.

Catts had disputes with other friends during the same months, and his vitriolic scorn for his Democratic antagonists intensified. Although he gained some measure of control over his tongue, his pen recorded a torrent of abuse. Since his early days as a minister

8. New York *Times*, December 18, 1920; Sidney J. Catts to J. B. Hodges, December 17, 1920, Hodges to Joe Earman, December 18, 1920, in Box 39, Hodges Papers.

9. New York *Times*, December 18, 19, 1920, unidentified newspaper clipping in Box 39, Hodges Papers.

10. J. B. Hodges to Sidney J. Catts, December 20, 1920, Catts to Hodges, December 21, 1920, in Box 39, *ibid.*

in Alabama, he had filled the margins of his sermons and books with notations. Now, these scribblings dealt with the betrayal of his friends and the corruption of his enemies. He always had been a man of strong language, and profanity toward friends and enemies alike pushed aside thoughts of history, mythology, and theology, spilling onto the margins of his books.[11]

Psychologist Jerry Carter, Jr., provides insight into this chaotic period of the governor's life. Catts had entered the governorship as a genuine idealist determined to use his victory over the party bosses to enact fundamental reform. Frustrated by four years of confronting entrenched interests and hostile legislators, and poorly served by his own uncontrolled emotions, his idealism had turned sour. By the end of his term he was a cynical, "professional" politician. Although the images may be overdrawn, they help explain the near paranoid last months of his incumbency. The senior Carter reached the same judgment, expressing it in simpler terms by emphasizing Catts's duality: when in good spirits, he was a consistent and compassionate man, but when angry, he lost every vestige of the Christian spirit.[12]

On policy matters, an air of tranquility pervaded the last days of the adminstration. Hodges arranged a meeting with officials of the *Florida Times-Union* who agreed that they would publish no further "adverse statements in the columns of the *Times-Union.*" One of the paper's officials even volunteered the opinion that Catts "had made a much better governor than some people desired to give you credit for, and that you had performed great service to the people of Florida."[13]

Hodges' relay of such flattering opinion masked his defection from Catts. The first hint came from Hodges' old friend, Joe Earman. When a hostile Lake City newspaper editor castigated

---

11. Interviews, Mrs. W. O. Willham, May 8, 1972, DeFuniak Springs, Mrs. Elizabeth Paderick and Mrs. Alice May Stiegel, May 12, 1972, Jacksonville. Also, see Joe L. Earman to J. B. Hodges, August 1, 1922, in Box 197, Hodges Papers.

12. Interviews, Jerry Carter, Jr., May 8, 1972, Tallahassee, Jerry Carter, July 29, 1970, Tallahassee.

13. J. B. Hodges to Sidney J. Catts, September 8, 1920, in Box 39, Hodges Papers.

Hodges as "an UNDERSTUDY of Sid Catts," the editorial drew an immediate rejoinder from Earman who suggested that "if Sid Catts would always heed his advice, there would be no trouble." Hodges had already begun "mending fences" with party regulars. Less than two months after Duncan Fletcher's resounding triumph, the Lake City attorney wrote the senior senator admitting his support of Catts: "He has been my friend, and I have not found him to be the unwise Governor that some of the newspapers are charging him with." On the other hand, he assured Fletcher that he had been "your personal friend for a long number of years, and I propose to remain such personal friend to you."[14] This cautious detente was the harbinger of a complete split with the unpopular governor.

As his four years of service came to an end, evaluations of Catts's administration ranged across the entire continuum of opinion. By his own estimate, the successes outweighed the failures. When introducing governor-elect Cary A. Hardee at the January 4, 1921, inaugural ceremonies, Catts discussed the complicated structure of government that had frustrated so many of his reforms. Despite such complexities, he boasted that as he left office state institutions were in the soundest condition in history. He pointed proudly to the Marianna boys' school and the honor system on the state prison farm at Raiford as examples of his enlightened attitude toward penology. Institutionalized Floridians never had received so much attention from a governor: permanent brick buildings had replaced wooden shacks to serve the mentally ill at Gainesville; the school for the deaf and blind had been restored to good condition; a girls' school had been opened at Ocala; the Board of Health had operated at a level of efficiency seldom equaled before. In a moment of candor, Catts admitted many mistakes, but insisted that they were "of the head and not of the heart."[15]

His enemies found no more charity for him at the conclusion of his term than during the fierce controversies that had swirled around his office. The Miami *Herald* spoke bitterly for those who

14. Joe Earman to Herbert L. Dodd, December 16, 1920, in Box 39, J. B. Hodges to Duncan U. Fletcher, August 4, 1920, in Box 34, Hodges Papers.
15. Jacksonville *Florida Times-Union*, January 5, 1921.

could not forgive Catts's apostacy. The lesson of his administration
was that people had deserted the principles of the Democratic
party and had "wandered after radical leaders." These years had
provided a "solemn warning to the people for all time to come, that
extremists, theorists, radicals are not safe political guides for this or
any other people." The editor concluded: "His term of office has
been characterized by incompetence, by a course of action that has
made every intelligent Floridian hang his head with shame. He
became a disrupter and a disturber and ends his term without a
political friend. The state rejoices that he goes out of office within
a few days and hopes that never again will the state of Florida be
afflicted with the brand of politics adopted and pursued by the
present governor."[16]

A kinder view prevailed among some of his critics. William T.
Cash attributed to him honest motives and some success. Whether
they mourned the fact or not, most Floridians thought that they
had heard the last of Sidney Catts, and many welcomed the advent
of a post-Catts era; but "old Sid" had expended only one of his
political lives and soon reneged from his vow to forsake public life.

The return to DeFuniak Springs brought a traumatic confrontation with severe economic problems. Eschewing the ministerial
career which had frustrated him earlier, the governor dabbled in
agriculture and real estate. He had acquired a patch of land where
he planted orchards, one product of which was peach brandy,
whose personal use he considered consistent with his prohibitionist
sentiments. He opened a small real estate office, occasionally sold
insurance, and spoke frequently on the lecture circuit. None of the
ventures was financially successful, and the family recalls these
years as hard ones. Catts wrote J. B. Hodges of financial woes,
asking him to use his influence on the Board of Control to get Sidney, Jr., a job in order to allow him to complete law school at the
University of Florida.[17]

16. The Miami *Herald,* December 31, 1920.
17. Interviews, Mrs. Elizabeth Paderick, May 12, 1972, Jacksonville, Mrs. Ruth
Cawthon, May 8, 1972, DeFuniak Springs; Sidney J. Catts to J. B. Hodges, no month or
day, 1921, in Box 42, Hodges Papers.

In February, 1921, Catts moved his family to Atlanta, Georgia, where he investigated the possibilities of opening an insurance business. This venture failed so the former governor, now low on funds, established the American Purchasing Company, which served as agent for Consumer Owned Stores. He also established the Catts Pep Company with home office in Atlanta. Switching from political to health panaceas, the company advertised medicinals good for man and beast: Pep Man's Restorative, Catts' Hog Tonic, Catts' Cow Tonic, Catts' Chicken Tonic, and Catts' Horse and Mule Tonic.[18] These enterprises were no more successful than the earlier ones, and the governor lost what little capital he had accumulated. In the spring of 1921 he traveled to the northwestern states and to British Columbia investigating business opportunities.

Economic problems were not the only ones bedeviling the harried former governor. In mid-April he received a call from a representative of the Jacksonville *Metropolis* informing him that state senator Harry Wells planned to introduce a resolution to investigate his administration. The legislator charged that Catts had received large sums of money for pardoning prisoners and appointing officeholders. Catts asked J. B. Hodges of Lake City and W. C. Hodges, a friend from Tallahassee, to represent him should the charges result in legal action, although J. B. Hodges advised that nothing was likely to come of the investigations.[19] Wells's resolution was adopted on April 15 by an almost unanimous state senate.

No sooner had the legislature launched its inquiry than the Bradford County grand jury meeting at Starke indicted Catts for allegedly accepting bribes to pardon prisoners. A life termer, J. J. Mendenhall, testified before the jury on May 4 that he had acted as procuror for J. J. Coleman, a convicted murderer, who paid Catts seven hundred dollars for executive clemency. The grand jury returned its indictment on May 5, and Mendenhall traveled to Tal-

18. John R. Deal, Jr., "Sidney Johnston Catts, Stormy Petrel of Florida Politics," (M.A. thesis, University of Florida. 1949), 185.
19. Sidney J. Catts to J. B. Hodges, April 15, 1921, Hodges to Catts, April 20, 1921, in Box 42, Hodges Papers.

lahassee to make his charges before the legislative committee.
Catts shrugged off the allegations as typical abuse from his party
enemies. He explained to his family that such accusations were an
integral part of politics, assuring the children that their friends
would understand and would dismiss them.[20]

Rozier Catts traveled to Jacksonville to console his distressed
mother. She told him that Catts had retained W. C. Hodges and
Senator Atkins of Starke and also hoped to persuade J. B. Hodges
to help. The boy confided to Joe Earman that his father had made a
mistake by not immediately going to Starke after the indictment.
Rozier feared that his father's hesitation had created the impression
that he was a fugitive, and might even result in his arrest by the
Bradford County sheriff.[21]

J. B. Hodges displayed his usual sagacity during the legal
wrangling. Catts, still convinced of Hodges' friendship, considered
him one of only two completely trustworthy friends.[22] He soon
discovered that his confidence was misplaced. On April 23 he
asked the Lake City attorney for assistance in handling the legislative investigation but received a negative response from Hodges,
who had spent several days in conference with legislators and personal friends in Tallahassee. Hodges did not believe the charges,
considering them to be politically motivated, and feared that the
attendant publicity would harm the state; but in a confidential note
to Joe Earman, he sketched his strategy to avoid further identification with the governor:

I am staying out of this thing.

I charged him more than he would pay, so I did not refuse to represent him.

Of course, if he was to pay my fee I would try him, but he says it was to
[sic] much.

20. New York *Times*, May 6, 1921; interviews, Mrs. Ruth Cawthon, May 8, 1972,
DeFuniak Springs, Mrs. Elizabeth Paderick and Mrs. Alice May Stiegel, May 12, 1972,
Jacksonville.

21. Joe Earman to J. B. Hodges, February 10, 1921, Hodges to Catts, May 14, 1921, in
Box 42, Hodges Papers.

22. Sidney J. Catts to J. B. Hodges, February 10, 1921, Hodges to Catts, February 12,
1921, *ibid.*

Catts says that there are some Georgians that are after him.

Neither you nor I are responsible for the acts of Catts, and I do not believe that any right thinking man will hold our connection with his administration to be a reflection on us.

I regret it very much.[23]

Catts's troubles deepened on May 18 when a federal grand jury in Pensacola indicted him on charges of peonage. Three days later, on May 21, he was arrested at the railway station in Albany, Georgia. A clothing store clerk from whom Catts purchased a collar noticed the initials "S.J.C." in the discarded garment and notified police. The governor made no effort to conceal his identity, protesting that he had been to British Columbia and had not learned of the indictments until he had received a telegram from his wife while on his way home. When arrested he did have a railroad ticket from Cincinnati to Jacksonville. A search of his possessions also revealed "a short leather billy [club], loaded with lead," which he explained as a highly prized gift from a friend.[24] A subsequent trial would exonerate him of the peonage charge, but this accusation was not the worst of his legal problems.

The negative publicity which J. B. Hodges feared extended beyond the borders of Florida. The New York *Times* ran complete stories about the indictments and arrest, and carried a feature article on Catts's remarkable career in its May 29 issue.

The state legislature provided sensational evidence for such stories in its final report submitted on June 1, 1921. One significant issue was the quantity of pardons granted during the Catts administration. The pardons board, consisting of the cabinet and governor, had granted pardons to 451 convicts, including 156 convicted of murder, of whom 140 were serving life sentences. Such a rate of pardons was not extraordinarily high, however, for in the two years before Catts took office, the board had granted 187 pardons, commuted 18 sentences, and granted 9 paroles.[25]

23. J. B. Hodges to Joe L. Earman, May 11, 1921, *ibid.*
24. New York *Times*, May 22, 1921.
25. *Ibid.*, April 16, 1921; *Journal of the House of Representatives, 1917*, p. 1679.

The investigating commitee probed a wide range of accusations against the former governor. Florida's new attorney general grilled D. W. Stevenson concerning rumors that a group of phosphate operators in Polk County and Sheriff Logan had collected a purse of $7,500 to pay Catts to reinstate the law officer. Stevenson allegedly had paid the money to the governor, for which services he subsequently was appointed by Catts to the Board of Managers of the Florida Farm Colony for the Feeble-Minded and Epileptic, then to the State Road Department. Stevenson said he had heard rumors of a bribe attempt but knew of no such transaction, and he offered an entirely different version of the Logan affair. Convinced that the sheriff had done nothing wrong, he had persuaded Catts that the dismissal was ill-advised. Catts had agreed but said he could not restore the officer without losing face; Stevenson then had suggested that he submit the entire matter to Attorney General Swearingen and secure an opinion favoring reinstatement. This strategy had been followed, Logan had regained his job, but not a dollar had changed hands.[26]

Several prisoners testified, including J. J. Coleman who was serving a life sentence for the murder of a Bay County deputy sheriff. He swore that another convict, J. J. Mendenhall, had told him that a pardon could be secured for $700. Coleman had given the money to his fellow prisoner and soon afterward had received notice of his clemency. He also testified that he knew of five other pardons purchased for sums ranging from $1,000 to $2,000. A Negro prisoner, John Henry Rogers, alleged that he had paid Catts's attorney W. C. Hodges $50 for a pardon and had agreed to work for the governor on his farm to pay the "bribe" plus 8 percent interest. Another prisoner testified that he had paid state hotel inspector Jerry Carter $300 and a double-barreled shotgun to obtain a pardon.[27]

26. State of Florida, "Report of Joint Committee to Investigate the Official Acts of Sidney J. Catts, while Governor of Florida, under Senate Concurrent Resolution No. 4," p. 12, copy in Box 197, Hodges Papers.

27. "Report of Joint Committee to Investigate Catts," 14–18, 21, 23; New York Times, June 2, 1921.

The key figure in the investigation and subsequent trials was J. J. Mendenhall. A convicted murderer who had won Catts's friendship, he presented contradictory testimony in his two appearances before the committee. During his first session he disputed Coleman's testimony. He discussed the phenomenal improvement in conditions at Raiford under Blitch and explained that Catts had befriended him and had plead his case unsuccessfully before the pardons board. Mendenhall then had persuaded the governor to urge Coleman's parole. The convict admitted that he had kept Coleman's $700, explaining to his fellow convict that the money would be used to hire an attorney. He also acknowledged receiving funds from other prisoners to recommend their pardons to Catts, but denied that he had given any of this money to the chief executive. He had offered the governor sixteen hundred dollars after a certain pardon had already been granted, but Catts had rejected the money.

Later in his testimony Mendenhall elaborated, adding that Catts had asked prisoners to pay what they could in order to determine if they were willing to obtain an attorney to handle their cases properly; but he had taken none of the money himself. According to the convict, Catts had told him to keep the money because he represented his fellow prisoners better than an attorney would have. The governor had urged Mendenhall to recommend pardons only for deserving convicts. Subsequent evidence confirmed that many prisoners had paid money to Mendenhall, but there was no evidence that any of it had found its way to the governor.

Mendenhall was recalled on May 5 following his testimony before the Bradford County grand jury which had led to the bribery indictment against Catts. He completely contradicted his earlier statements, saying that he had given Catts a $2,200 bribe.[28]

Additional witnesses included Duval County sheriff W. H. Dowling, a political enemy of the governor in 1916 and 1920, who had been suspended and then reinstated by Catts. Dowling denied

28. "Report of Joint Committee to Investigate Catts," 29–42, 65, 69–70.

rumors that he had bought back his office and substantiated his rebuttal with a witness who had accompanied him to the governor's office to receive his commission.

Other testimony linked Catts to David Sholtz of Daytona, allegedly a "wire tapper" who had given the governor a payoff. Sholtz, who was later elected governor in 1932, had supported Catts while serving in the legislature. Henry T. Titus testified that Sholtz was influential with the governor, but denied knowledge of any bribery.[29] Additional accusations of corruption elicited similar denials, and no real evidence was presented to substantiate the charges. Most of the testimony was based on political rumors which had circulated almost from the beginning of Catts's administration.

The probe besmirched not only Catts's reputation, but also that of most of his political associates. W. C. Hodges and Jerry Carter were accused of accepting bribes, and by implication everyone close to the administration seemed involved in some sort of complicity. As a consequence, the fragmented Catts coalition rallied one last time to the defense of the governor. Many of his alienated friends offered unenthusiastic assistance, perhaps more to protect their own reputations than to acquit him.

Dr. Ralph Greene, state health officer and a man highly regarded by Catts despite their differences, conferred with Joe Earman and suggested that the legal defense should be based on mental instability. Greene's extensive military experience with mental cases had convinced him that the former governor suffered from delusions of persecution. He believed that Catts was insane and "a danger to one for whom he has formed a dislike real or otherwise." J. B. Hodges replied that such a legal defense would be of no use; besides this practical point, Hodges detected the political motivation for the charges and noted that Catts "has now realized his delusions. They are real and not imagined."[30] Greene's analysis may offer a better insight into Catts's twisted mind, however, than Hodges cared to admit.

29. *Ibid.*, 72–75.
30. Joe L. Earman to J. B. Hodges, August 1, 1922, in Box 197, Hodges to Earman, May 17, 1921, in Box 42, Hodges Papers.

Even the embittered idealist Joe Earman found some compassion still remaining for the Catts family. During the governor's last year in office, he had appointed Rozier harbor master for the port of Key West. The boy lost this position when Catts left office and moved to West Palm Beach, which was Earman's hometown. Rozier worked there as an electrician but did not prosper. In the spring of 1921 he moved his wife and infant to Hastings where he found employment picking potatoes. He had left a debt of two hundred dollars in West Palm Beach, and when he returned broke to seek employment in mid-May, he visited Earman and "broke down." The boy's wife and child were stranded in Hastings and could not leave until he returned to pay two weeks' board of twenty dollars. He had sought money from his mother, but there was none to spare. Rozier begged Earman for the money, a request the kindhearted businessman could not ignore: the boy looked "like a tramp, his shirt and pants are dirty, he smells and needs a bath. He got the twenty bones."[31]

Young Rozier also informed Earman that his family desired the legal services of J. B. Hodges, though they had been unable to retain him. Earman was touched by the family's predicament and persuaded Hodges to take the case and provided the fee. Catts furnished Hodges with as much information as possible, thanking him profusely for remaining a friend through his troubles and asking the attorney to thank "Mr. E." for paying the legal fees. Catts desired a personal reconciliation with Earman, but Hodges advised that any public notoriety would harm his case. Despite the former governor's overtures, Earman refused direct communication with his old friend and did not attend the trial. Earman also helped persuade former Catts henchman Judge E. B. Donnell of Palm Beach to enter the case.[32]

In November, 1921, Catts's family enjoyed a cordial visit in the Hodges' home at Lake City while the two politicians discussed

31. Joe Earman to J. B. Hodges, May 14, 1921, in Box 42, Hodges Papers.
32. Sidney J. Catts to J. B. Hodges, August 1, 1921, Hodges to Catts, August 3, 1921, Catts to Hodges, September 29, 1921, Hodges to E. B. Donnell, August 2, 4, 1921, in Box 197, Hodges Papers.

legal strategy. Hodges, ever the consummate politician, delighted Catts by announcing that he was considering joining the Baptist church. Catts exuded the old time enthusiasm in a note of appreciation: "Nothing *could make me happier* than to receive a letter saying you both have been baptized" in "my beloved Baptist Church."[33]

The first of the trials began at Starke in November, 1921. E. B. Donnell was convinced that the indictment would not be substantiated because it did not charge that Catts had made promises to prisoners nor that he had been paid anything for the specific purpose of influencing his vote on the pardoning board. The only allegation in the indictment was that the governor had accepted a gratuity after certain pardons had been granted.

The major barrier to winning the case, Donnell believed, was Catts himself. The former governor wanted to participate in his own defense, and his quick temper might undermine their arguments. Donnell warned Hodges that "the old Governor is pretty brilliant in some things, I suppose, but he does not know how to try a law suit and particularly a suit against himself"; therefore "we will simply have to handle him discreetly but firmly." The judge was unconcerned about the political implications of the case, either to "make political capital necessarily for somebody in the future, neither to dig a political grave for someone who has died in the past."[34]

In both this trial and the succeeding ones, the star prosecution witness was J. J. Mendenhall. Fortunately for Catts, the governor had heard rumors only days before leaving Tallahassee that Mendenhall had made slanderous charges against him. To protect himself, Catts had taken all correspondence concerning Mendenhall to DeFuniak Springs. This correspondence was turned over to J. B. Hodges for use in the case and became the crux of defense rebuttal. Hodges argued that the file was complete and established that the association between Catts and Mendenhall was completely proper.

---

33. Sidney J. Catts to J. B. Hodges, November 27, 1921, *ibid.*
34. E. B. Donnell to J. B. Hodges, August 6, 1921, *ibid.*

Mendenhall simply had tried to use the governor's friendship to gain a pardon.[35]

The relationship which emerges from this correspondence provides the most likely explanation for the entire episode. Mendenhall had been sentenced to life for the murder of two Clearwater women in 1914. He killed them and overturned their car and burned it because the mother of one of the women was demanding five thousand dollars not to prosecute him on charges of "white slavery." The girl allegedly was pregnant with Mendenhall's child. Mendenhall gained Catts's attention in 1919 when the convict had taken a leading part in collecting funds from Raiford convicts to purchase a ring to be given in appreciation for the governor's prison reforms. This gesture so pleased Catts that he proudly displayed the ring in his subsequent campaigns. In thanking Mendenhall for the 1919 ceremony at Raiford, he wrote the convict that "this has touched my heart as nothing else has done since I have been Governor of this State." He discussed his reforms at Raiford, his success in removing convicts from the west Florida turpentine camps, and improvements in the State Road Department prison facilities. Such activity had "been done through love and devotion to those unfortunates, whose life is shut off from the freedom of the world, and not because I desired any compensation for what little I could do." The governor enclosed copies of his messages to the 1917 and 1919 legislatures which included his concepts of prison reform.[36]

During subsequent conversations, it seems likely that they discussed further the governor's abortive 1917 proposal for appointment of a "friend of the convicts" who would live with the prisoners and become their advocate. Although the legislature had rejected his idea, Catts may have thought that Mendenhall represented a perfect substitute. He could observe fellow prisoners, then relay recommendations to the governor to be used before the board of

35. J. B. Hodges to E. B. Donnell, August 6, 1921, *ibid.*
36. Sidney J. Catts to J. B. Hodges, October 18, 1921, Catts to J. J. Mendenhall, December 17, 1919, *ibid.*

pardons. If prisoners sought legal representation, why shouldn't they pay Mendenhall, whose advice to the governor was more reliable than a paid attorney's? Mendenhall thus became a surrogate "friend of prisoners," performing the role he first discovered in the pages of Catts's 1917 message.

Mendenhall gained considerable freedom on the Raiford farm thanks to Blitch's relaxed trustee system and perhaps also due to his friendship with the state's chief executive. He received a female visitor from Jacksonville, Miss Helen M. Carline, and drove her to the Raiford railroad station in a state owned buggy; there, witnesses said, they would sit "until the late train for Jacksonville with the buggy top up and side curtains up." [37]

Despite their friendship, Mendenhall seems to have exercised no undue influence on Catts. If, as the prisoner later claimed, he could purchase pardons for other prisoners through Catts, he was amazingly inept at winning concessions for himself. The convict hinted at a bribe in a letter to the chief executive in September, 1920: "I fully realize that I have a difficult case *but* I am *sure* I can make an *easy* one of it, if you will give me the respite I ask for [a sixty-day leave to visit Jacksonville], you do not answer me on this subject, *please* do." [38]

Mendenhall elaborated in a letter two days later, explaining that such a furlough would allow him to obtain a statement vindicating him of the murder conviction and also to "see parties that I am quite sure I can get $1500.00 worth of pardon business for my friend, that cannot be gotten unless I do see him [*sic*]. This friend is handling my case and unless I can get home for a day, one half of what I agreed to pay him will be . . . recalled, and that means insufficient funds to get him to go in with the case." [39]

Catts agreed to propose the pardon only because he was convinced that the convict was innocent of any crime. As Mendenhall discovered, however, the governor did not dominate the pardons

---

37. Sidney J. Catts to J. B. Hodges, October 18, 1921, *ibid.*
38. J. J. Mendenhall to Sidney J. Catts, September 13, 1920, *ibid.*
39. September 15, 1920, *ibid.*

board. Cabinet members Amos, Crawford, and even Catts's ally
Swearingen rejected a pardon, and the governor could persuade
only Commissioner of Agriculture McRae to favor Mendenhall's
release. Although Catts agreed "to stick by you through the whole
thing . . . and you have a right to bring the case up when you want
to," he advised Mendenhall to delay his appeal for four years when
he might have a better chance. The convict pressed the issue,
reapplying for a pardon in December, 1920.[40]

Mendenhall also applied for a thirty-day furlough in December,
but Catts explained that he could not grant it since he would leave
office in a matter of days. The governor's last correspondence expressed hope "that you will be a free man some good day," and also
"that we can do a nice business in the future with regard to the
Pardon Board, which I spoke to you about." This last phrase is the
only hint of bribes or of special favoritism in the lengthy correspondence.[41]

Preparations for the trials in Starke (November, 1921) and Lake
Butler (May, 1922) were handled by a team consisting of A. Z.
Atkins, Judge Donnell, and J. B. Hodges. Jerry Carter feared that
the Lake Butler region was so prejudiced that the former governor
could not receive a fair trial, but Catts disagreed and sought
Hodges' advice; the Lake City attorney approved the site. Catts
furnished a list of witnesses who could refute details of Mendenhall's testimony. These included A. B. Carter of Lakeland,
Florida, who would testify that he had talked with the convict
while visiting Raiford in the summer of 1920 to investigate several
pardons appeals: "He asked *M* about taking his case and *M* said
'No, that I have my arrangements made and that if Gov. Catts did
not pardon him before his term was out that he *M* would get Catts
[*sic*] *goat good* and *hard.*'"[42]

The Starke trial in November featured a series of witnesses who

40. Sidney J. Catts to J. J. Mendenhall, December 14, 1920, Catts to Miss Florence
Mendenhall, December 14, 1920, Mendenhall to Catts, December 21, 1920, *ibid.*
    41. Sidney J. Catts to J. J. Mendenhall, January 3, 1921, *ibid.*
    42. Sidney J. Catts to J. B. Hodges, October 18, 1921, *ibid.*

both refuted Mendenhall's testimony and questioned his integrity. Hodges skillfully utilized the hostile legislative report to demonstrate how the state's star witness had contradicted himself before the joint committee. The defense witnesses, together with Hodges' adroit legal maneuvers, won acquittal for Catts.[43]

After victory in the Starke trial, J. B. Hodges sought to avoid further involvement in the legal proceedings. When Catts requested that Hodges be present on May 15, 1922, at the opening of the Lake Butler peonage trial, the attorney consented, but in a cold letter which reminded the former governor that the relationship of attorney and client "in this matter was not established by your procurement, but you agreed . . . to the establishment of the relation and my fees was [sic] paid by a friend of mine, so I am of the opinion that it would be unprofessional on my part to sever this relation . . . except upon your assent thereto."[44]

On May 15 Judge Donnell submitted a motion to quash the indictment because it was faulty in not specifically including Coleman's and Mendenhall's roles in the alleged affair. The presiding judge upheld the motion and dismissed the case. The state's attorney privately assured the defense that he would not resubmit it to that session of the grand jury, and Hodges correctly concluded that the charges would be dropped. Hodges was relieved to see the matter finished and wrote Joe Earman: "I am very glad that this case has terminated. It has not been altogether pleasant. Since this case is out of the way, the old man will have no excuse for any further operations. I did not talk to him about his future plans, nor about any other matter. However, he had the nerve to ask me to take his son in my office after he graduates at the university this year. I told him I could not do it. Some people have nerve, and others have more nerve."[45]

The last scene of the protracted legal drama occurred in

43. For Hodges' strategy in the trials see "Official List of Witnesses," "Instructions Requested by the Defendant," and J. B. Hodges to A. Z. Atkins, October 20, 1921, all *ibid*.
44. Sidney J. Catts to J. B. Hodges, May 5, 1922, Hodges to Catts, May 8, 1922, *ibid*.
45. J. B. Hodges to Joe L. Earman, May 16, 1922, Box 44, *ibid*. For the "Brief to Quash," see Box 197, *ibid*.

Pensacola in November, 1922, when Catts was tried on federal peonage charges. He asked Hodges, as a personal favor, to present a summons to a witness, but this appears to be the only involvement that the Lake City lawyer had in the case. Catts's youngest daughter, Alice May, accompanied her father to Pensacola to drive him about. She recalls that he was calm and confident that the trial would finally exonerate him. At night in the hotel room, they would read the Bible together, with Catts explaining the text. He was hurt by the proceedings but not "as badly as someone who had a weaker faith would have been." He had known that his political enemies were determined to destroy him, and the accusations had not come as a complete surprise.[46] In the Pensacola trial, Catts contended that he had paid a fair wage to the Negro convicts who had worked his farm under terms of the Raiford honor system, and the jury deliberated only nine minutes before acquitting him on November 20, 1922.

The charges stemmed initially from his antagonists in the state senate and may have been politically inspired, as Catts claimed. Based largely on the unreliable and contradictory testimony of Mendenhall, prosecution evidence was circumstantial. The governor could not control hostile cabinet officials on the pardons board and hence the logic of bribing him seems unreasonable. Mendenhall could not even convert his friendship with Catts into a furlough, much less a pardon. J. B. Hodges and Judge Donnell both rejected the allegations as politically inspired, though neither was any longer friendly to the former governor. Jerry Carter in the last year of his life denied that Catts had taken bribes for pardons or jobs; he admitted that some men contributed to campaigns, then later asked for favors, but no one paid the governor for a job, a favor, or to grant a pardon.[47]

A more likely explanation is to be found in Catts's inability to

46. Sidney J. Catts to J. B. Hodges, November 10, 1922, Hodges to Catts, November 10, 1922, in Box 197, Hodges Papers; interviews, Mrs. Alice May Stiegel, Mrs. Elizabeth Paderick, May 12, 1972, Jacksonville.
47. Interview, Jerry Carter, July 29, 1970, Tallahassee.

judge character and his gullibility concerning his legislative proposals. Prison reform had always been a major concern of his, both
for philosophical and personal reasons. Catts's brother-in-law,
Blake Campbell, was serving a prison term during the gubernatorial years. Urged on by the governor, Joe Earman had accumulated
fifteen hundred dollars in expenses attempting to gain Campbell's
release from the Atlanta Federal Penitentiary.[48] The central pillar
of Catts's penology, which included the Raiford honor system and
abolition of convict leasing, was the "friend of the convict" concept.
Thwarted by the legislature, he bestowed his confidence on Mendenhall and perhaps even allowed the convict to filch money off
fellow prisoners to represent them before the governor. The only
evidence to substantiate the charges of bribery and peonage which
grew out of his connection with Mendenhall was Catts's reference
to doing "a nice business in the future with regard to the Pardon
Board." The former governor's inconsistencies on other issues such
as drinking make it clear, however, that he was capable of
rationalizing almost any moral lapse, and the bribery and peonage
charges cannot be entirely dismissed.

His public ordeal ended, Catts returned to DeFuniak Springs
where he had purchased the comfortable home of Peter H. Miller.
Considering the drain on his financial resources by nearly a year of
legal maneuvering and trials, such an outlay of funds raises perplex-
ing questions. Joe Earman may have resolved this mystery as well
as the ultimate source of J. B. Hodges' legal fees in an angry letter
written to Hodges in August, 1922. The former publisher alluded
to a letter from Catts written on August 28, 1921. The governor
seemed to "have a mania, or is obsessed with the thought to regain
my friendship," a move which Earman considered only a ruse to
obtain more funds. At the bottom of the August letter "was an appeal that under an obligation most sacred I could not disregard
even to an enemy." In subsequent correspondence Earman alludes

48. Catts blamed opposition to Campbell's release on Catholics who were retaliating
for his 1916 campaign. See Sidney J. Catts to J. B. Hodges, April 23, 1917, in Box 13, also,
Joe L. Earman to Hodges, August 1, 1922, in Box 197, Hodges Papers.

to Catts's violating the "sacred obligations of Masonry to further his own financial ends and then further attempt to use it to Blackmail": "Men of Masons go into the Gutter and sometimes they go to jail but I have never heard of one violating the sacred obligations they solemnly take upon themselves until Old Catts violated and violated most grievously in a letter to me and the demand was for money in connection with violating the sacred and in fact most sacred of obligations."[49] Apparently Earman referred to a Masonic pledge not to reveal any private matters related to him by a fellow Mason. The only exception to this "most sacred of obligations" is when the private information involves treason or murder. It appears that Earman had shared some compromising secret with his Masonic brother, Sidney Catts, and the former governor was now threatening to reveal it to obtain funds from Earman's contacts with local gamblers.

Under the threat of blackmail, Earman complied with the "request" to forward the letter to a notorious gambler, perhaps a man named Bradley, with instructions to send Catts's attorney, A. Z. Atkins, $500. The letter further directed that Pensacola attorney John B. Stokes be sent two checks, one for $500 and another for $750. Earman knew the alleged gambler, though he claimed never to have dealt with him: "This party took the position that while he did not owe Catts anything, that . . . Catts did not trouble him during his four years incumbency of the Governorship, and sent him the seventeen hundred and fifty dollars, which was forwarded from Ithaca, New York, on September 24, 1921." Earman regretted his actions despite the profuse gratitude of the former governor.[50]

Nor did this end Earman's dealings with Catts. On March 17, 1922, Catts wrote Earman once more demanding money and cursing his attorneys, A. Z. Atkins and John B. Stokes. The letter contained a proposal quite out of character: Catts asked that Earman request his Palm Beach gambler acquaintance, who was a Catholic, "to intercede with Archbishop Curley of Baltimore to get him to

49. Joe L. Earman to J. B. Hodges, August 1, 6, 1922, Box 197, Hodges Papers.
50. August 1, 1922, *ibid.*

put the Catholics in Pensacola to work for Catts on the peonage cases and also to pull other wires in the Lake Butler case." Apparently the governor genuinely believed that the "Catholic hierarchy" possessed vast political power and might be persuaded to use it in his behalf. Catts also sent his former Palm Beach ally a "blackmail" letter claiming that Earman owed him money for lands they had owned.[51] Earman's angry letter to Hodges is a most severe challenge both to Catts's private integrity and public morality. Whatever idealism and honor Catts had carried into office seems to have expired.

Joe Earman had sold his newspaper in 1920, and though he remained active as a writer, he was elected West Palm Beach municipal judge. He retained political interests despite his unfortunate experiences with Catts, forcefully advocating reapportionment and more equitable taxation. In 1922 he wrote an April Fools' satire on Catts which elicited a concerned letter from his friend J. B. Hodges warning him to leave Catts alone before the fiery former governor really did use his shotgun on Earman.[52]

Catts and his former aide continued to argue over land they had owned jointly, with Hodges playing the role of mediator. In the summer of 1922 Earman learned that Catts planned to initiate bankruptcy proceedings and implored Hodges to represent his financial claims. In an eleven-page indictment, he claimed that his relationship with Catts had cost him some fifteen thousand dollars. He still held seven notes from Catts totaling seven hundred dollars dating from 1916. This did not include expenses incurred working for the parole of Blake Campbell or the sum spent to purchase Catts's embarrassing letter to Carter R. Bibb in 1916, or loans to Rozier Catts. He also alleged that the former governor had been "paid" to reinstate several local officials in West Palm Beach. A bitter concluding paragraph pleaded with Hodges "to help eliminate Old Catts from my existence whereby I will never hear his detestable name again or receive a letter from or be further annoyed by him."[53]

51. *Ibid.*
52. Clipping in Box 44, J. B. Hodges to Joe L. Earman, April 5, 1922, in Box 44, *ibid.*
53. Joe L. Earman to J. B. Hodges, August 1, 1922, in Box 197. Also, see Sidney J.

Hodges restrained Earman, advising that he had no basis for legal action except on one land transaction and warning that such an examination "would put both of us in the ridiculous position of the Florida State Senate... and will have the tendancy [sic] for Catts to play the myrtar [sic]."[54]

Earman reluctantly accepted his friend's counsel, though he protested bitterly that his political experience had been "rotten and expensive," and blamed Catts for his unhappiness: "But Jim old man it does seem dam hard that that old skunk can get away with the cussedness he has put over and is still attempting to put over me." Hodges did submit to the court Earman's petition concerning land transactions, thereby earning the former governor's wrath. Catts replied angrily that he had sold his equities in the disputed land and referred to Hodges as the "Little Lacky [sic] boy for Little Joe Earman."[55]

The Lake City attorney informed Earman that he had "run this old man in a hole, and I presume he has now made a bogus deed, dated it back for more than two years, and... had it recorded." He predicted that this would be Catts's "last squel [sic]" and recommended that his friend forget about him. Earman promised to do so but seemed obsessed. In October, 1922, he visited a man named Bradley, alleged to be a gambler and power broker in south Florida, to ask if he was supplying money to Catts. Bradley denied that he was furnishing any funds, and volunteered the opinion "that he [Catts] is an insane man and expressed sympathy for him." Bradley also suggested that Mrs. Catts was "the balance wheel to keep him out of jail."[56]

Earman never completely escaped the presence of Sidney Catts. Ironically young Sidney, Jr., opened a law office in West Palm Beach upon finishing law school in 1922, and maintained

Catts to Hodges, February 10, 1921, Hodges to Catts, February 12, 1921, in Box 42, *ibid.*

54. J. B. Hodges to Joe L. Earman, August 4, 1922, in Box 197, *ibid.*

55. Joe Earman to J. B. Hodges, August 6, 1922, Sidney J. Catts to Hodges, August 30, 1922, in Box 197, Hodges Papers. For the legal aspects of the bankruptcy trial see Hodges to Catts, August 8, 1922, Hodges to Clerk, U.S. District Court, August 4, 1922, and S. J. Catts Bankruptcy File, all *ibid.*

56. J. B. Hodges to Joe Earman, September 1, 1922, *ibid;* Earman to Hodges, undated, though written in October, 1922, Box 44, *ibid.*

practice there until his death in June, 1969. Earman lived in constant dread that Catts would stop for a visit while in Palm Beach to see his son. He would have found contentment in the knowledge that Catts had more important considerations on his mind than Joe Earman, for the former governor was determined to seek his vindication from the voters of Florida.

TWELVE

From Messiah
to Pariah

THE YEARS OF CATTS'S POLITICAL EXILE brought rapid growth to Florida. American affluence and the state's mild climate combined to attract tourists, retirees, and new citizens to serve the increased population. Jerry Carter began promoting tourism which also was encouraged by the road building program of the Catts and Hardee administrations. A road network financed partially by federal grants made possible a vast expansion of leisure time activities when automobiles began to replace railroads as the nation's primary source of transportation. The effect of the good roads movement, which began before Catts entered the governorship but was accelerated by his endorsement, has received inadequate attention. Its impact was obvious, however, in a state where tourism became the largest single source of revenue. By 1925 Florida had 9,200 miles of roadways, and her 6,000 miles of railroad track were almost twice as much mileage per one thousand population as any other southern state.

The nature of Florida's population growth seemed to substantiate the political obituaries that had been written for Catts in 1920. The 30.4 percent gain in population between 1920 and 1925 occurred mainly in urban, lower peninsula counties such as Dade and Broward which recorded phenomenal increases of 160.6 percent and 177.6 percent. Some 45 percent of Florida's people lived in towns of over 2,500 inhabitants by 1925; conversely, the rural population in twenty of her sixty-seven counties declined during the same half decade, and it was among these people that Catts had run best in 1916 and 1920. Agriculture, on which the rural areas depended for livelihood, declined, trailing far behind tourism and manufacturing in economic significance to Florida.[1]

Urbanization and rural malaise affected Catts ambivalently. Agricultural depression in rural Florida, particularly in the panhandle, seems to have strengthened him in that traditional bastion which had deserted the governor in the 1920 senatorial primary. Yet, the relative importance of these regions in general elections declined as the balance of power shifted toward the burgeoning towns of central and south Florida. Although the rural sections maintained their stranglehold on the malapportioned legislature, the three governors following Cary Hardee all came from more urbanized counties—John W. Martin from Duval (Jacksonville), Doyle E. Carlton from Hillsborough (Tampa), and David Sholtz of Volusia (Daytona Beach). In addition, the Republican party, aided by prosperity and the migration of nonsoutherners into Florida, offered a more significant challenge to one-party democratic rule.

The diversity which characterized the 1920s in America also posed a serious challenge to traditionalist values in Florida. Social change combined with economic difficulties to trigger an inevitable reaction. The Ku Klux Klan constituted one element of the traditionalist response to upheaval in the 1920s. It aimed more at enforcing community moral standards than at attacking Negroes or Catholics, although its members did perpetrate isolated acts of violence. It flourished in rapidly expanding cities where the clash of values became most intense. In attempting to understand the Klan, too much blame may fall on individuals such as Georgia's Tom Watson or Florida's Sidney Catts. Although both men symbolized the nativism and anti-Catholicism of the era, this personality orientation loses sight of the basic nature of the Klan. It was a folk movement, tremendously popular among masses of deeply re-

---

1. In 1925, for instance, tourism contributed $250 million income to the state compared to $150 million manufacturing revenue and $85 million income from agriculture. For statistical analysis of economic and population growth, see *Fifth Census of the State of Florida, 1925*, 9–10, 15–17, 21, 61.

ligious and patriotic people who saw their values eroded by strange new forces they could not understand. Unable to reverse the avalanche of change, they formed rank in opposition to it. Catts might have articulated their fears, but the nativism predated him.

Jacksonville became a Klan stronghold in the 1920s. The organization dominated local politics, using many of the same appeals that Catts had popularized in 1916. No doubt the Klan numbered among its members many battle-hardened veterans of the Guardians of Liberty and the True Americans. Outside the port city, the Klan spread rapidly; it attacked dog and horse racing and other forms of gambling in south Florida, endorsed prohibition and opposed Catholicism. Unlike some other states where the Klan collapsed after 1925, it continued to thrive until the end of the decade in Florida and played a prominent role in the campaign against Catholic presidential candidate Alfred E. Smith in 1928.[2]

Many pragmatic Florida politicians joined the Klan for the same expedient reasons that they had followed Catts in 1916. J. B. Hodges represents a microcosmic case study of the reactionary politics of the 1920s. Despite private reservations about the religious and racial prejudices of men such as Catts and Tom Watson, he endorsed the goals of the Ku Klux Klan. His anti-Semitism and opposition to organized labor drove Hodges toward the secret order. When writing of the American Federation of Labor, he expressed his contempt for "any organization that will follow the leadership of a Jew." After listening to a Labor Day speaker at High Springs, in 1921, he called the speech revolutionary because it denounced Wall Street for being "tenented [sic] by scoundrels, and rascals, who were robbing off the poor people." Hodges even blamed unemployment on the excessive demands of labor unions.[3] A similar climate of unrest and disgust with the times had pro-

2. For the Klan in Florida, see David M. Chalmers, *Hooded Americanism: The First Century of the Ku Klux Klan, 1865–1965* (New York: Doubleday and Co., 1965), 225–28; David M. Chalmers, "The Ku Klux Klan in the Sunshine State: The 1920's," *Florida Historical Quarterly*, XLII (January, 1964), 209–15.

3. J. B. Hodges to Joe L. Earman, August 12, 1924, in Box 53, Hodges to Earman, March 30, 1921, Hodges to F. L. Scofield, September 6, 1921, in Box 42, J. B. Hodges Papers.

pelled Catts into the statehouse in 1916 and would nearly accomplish that feat twice more in the twenties.

With the enervating trials ended in November, 1922, Catts had more time for personal interests. He sold insurance and lectured to raise money and maintain political contacts. Both he and Mrs. Catts assumed an active role in the DeFuniak Springs Baptist Church, contributing heavily of their time and of their limited resources to its activities. With the children gone, Catts directed more of his attention toward his wife. Their family had always been close, and he expressed a warmth toward his wife and children that only his closest political friends perceived. When Catts traveled, no matter how short the distance, he invariably wrote Alice May. Always addressed to "my dearest gerlie [sic]," the letters were so affectionate that the children considered them "mushy." When the daughters returned home on visits, they noted the devotion which their parents demonstrated and the increased frequency with which their father talked about his "gerlie." The reserved, shy woman did not approve of his drinking peach brandy, his temper, or his continued political ambitions, but she remained as genuinely devoted to him as he was to her.[4]

The general prosperity that prevailed in Florida during the first half decade of the 1920s influenced the 1924 gubernatorial contest. Affluence ended the older corporation/anticorporation clashes which had characterized twentieth-century elections before the Catts era.[5]

Potential candidates began to cultivate support early in the 1920s. Three-term mayor John W. Martin of Jacksonville had supported Catts in 1916 and 1920 and had compiled a prolabor record as chief official of Florida's largest city. Worth Trammell, another

4. Interview, Mrs. Elizabeth Paderick, Mrs. Alice May Stiegel, May 12, 1972, Jacksonville.

5. This opinion of William T. Cash seems to be confirmed by both the 1924 and 1928 campaigns, although economic reform remained an issue in both races. See Cash, *History of the Democratic Party in Florida*, 134. For a fuller discussion of the 1924 race, see Victoria H. McDonnell, "Rise of the 'Businessman's Politician': The 1924 Florida Gubernatorial Race," *Florida Historical Quarterly*, LII (July, 1973), 39–50.

candidate for the state's highest office, was a brother of former governor and incumbent United States Senator Park Trammell, and
also had maintained close ties with Catts, even testifying on his
behalf during the 1922 trials. Charles H. Spencer, a successful
Hillsborough County farmer and chairman of the county Democratic committee, represented the state's most populous county in
the contest. Frank E. Jennings, former speaker of the Florida
house of representatives and long-time power in state politics, also
jumped into the race. A state senator contemplated entering the
contest, but Frank Jennings frightened him out by threatening to
reveal that the man had leased convicts prior to his political
career.[6] All the candidates, including Catts, fashioned similar platforms. They agreed on the need for some sort of reapportionment,
lower taxes, better schools and teacher salaries, and especially better roads.

Catts had decided in 1923 to seek vindication for the abuse he
had suffered, and by spring of the following year, he had recon-
structed an effective campaign organization. Friends established
the Tallahassee *Dispatch* to champion his candidacy for governor,
and J. J. McCasskill, a wealthy DeFuniak Springs admirer, once
again provided financial backing.[7] Ira Sanborn, former state
senator from Carrabelle, directed the organization of Catts clubs in
every part of the state. The effort was particularly successful in
north Florida counties such as Liberty, Calhoun, and Putnam.[8]
Catts also published a pamphlet which recorded the reforms
wrought by his administration. His platform enumerated the same
issues as his opponents with added emphasis on enforcement of
prohibition. He also opposed compulsory cattle dipping, which was
still a heated subject in agricultural counties.

In a typical rally before approximately eight hundred persons in
Tallahassee, Catts spent equal time on his past record and propos-

6. J. B. Hodges to Joe L. Earman, November 14, 1923, in Box 52, Hodges Papers.
7. Interview, Mrs. Elizabeth Paderick, Mrs. Alice May Stiegel, May 12, 1972,
Jacksonville.
8. Tallahassee *Dispatch*, April 11, 1924, copy in Florida, "VF Governors, Catts, Sidney
J."

als for the future. He emphasized the reforms enacted during his previous term and the need for a strong executive who would dismiss any official who refused to enforce state and federal prohibition laws. Under Hardee's leadership, he reminded, taxes had increased from $4.11 to $28 per capita. There were familiar oratorical outbursts against the daily newspapers and the state's corporations which he would not allow to "put a yoke around my neck."[9]

Religion played a role in the gubernatorial campaign, though it did not become so significant as in 1916. Klan opposition to immigration and Catholicism no doubt aided him, though there is no evidence that the hooded order specifically endorsed him. Joe Earman dismissed the support of one Catts partisan by explaining that he was "agin' the Catholics *tooth* and *toe nail.*" The *Florida Christian Advocate,* serving Methodist parishes, publicized anti-Catholic statements by some of its ministers, and the Baptists continued their suspicious distrust.[10]

Catts also profited from the federal woman suffrage amendment. Mrs. W. S. Jennings, state director of the General Federation of Women's Clubs, spread rumors that he had made improper "advances" to a matron of the Girls' Reformatory at Ocala; however, the story does not seem to have lessened his appeal to female activists who appreciated his early endorsement of equal suffrage. J. B. Hodges complained that a women's club leader in Lake City favored Catts for governor: "I feel considerably disappointed in what the women are going to do about political matters. I do not know what Catts has promised these women, but she tells me that there will be more women that vote for Catts than any other candidate."[11]

J. B. Hodges also attributed to Catts one of the shrewdest stratagems of the contest. Campaign cards appeared in May, printed at Capitola near Tallahassee, which read on one side: "Vote for John W. Martin First Choice and Frank E. Jennings Second

9. *Ibid.*
10. Joe Earman to J. B. Hodges, no date, 1924, Hodges to Earman, April 24, 1924, in Box 53, Hodges Papers.
11. Joe Earman to J. B. Hodges, November 27, 1923, Hodges to Earman, December 7, 1923, in Box 52, *ibid.*

Choice AND SAVE THE STATE." On the other side, the same statement appeared except that the names of the candidates were reversed. Catts's newspaper, the Tallahassee *Dispatch*, first revealed
the cards, and Hodges concluded that Catts had them printed in
order to charge his opponents with forming a conspiracy to block
his election.[12]

Such strategy had to compensate for the lack of newspaper
coverage. Florida's press switched from its earlier vilification to a
self-imposed moratorium on any mention of Catts. The *Florida
Times-Union* featured almost daily coverage of Jennings and Martin, but had not a single word concerning the former governor. The
Miami *Herald*, Gainesville *Daily Sun,* and Tampa *Morning Tribune* carried neither Catts's advertisements nor summaries of his
appearances. One reads daily papers in vain to discover where the
former governor spoke or what he said. Probably no prominent
Floridian ever conducted a serious race for high office with such a
total absence of media coverage.

Faced with what can only be called a conspiracy of silence,
Catts created his own publicity. Using the Tallahassee *Dispatch* as
a forum, he attacked former friends such as Joe Earman and J. B.
Hodges, who refused to support him in 1924. He claimed that his
henchmen had misappropriated campaign funds in 1916, a charge
that elicited a private denial from Earman as well as a promise to
"publish the actual facts" if "Catts and his crowd keep on."[13]

Most of Catts's former allies endorsed Frank Jennings, a Kan-
sas native who had served as speaker of the Florida house in 1921.
He won backing from many conservative Democrats, including
Senator Duncan Fletcher, and from small-town newspapers. He
emphasized his philosophical agreement with prohibition, while
claiming that Mayor Martin proclaimed himself prohibitionist but
winked at violations in Jacksonville. Jennings also advocated re-
forestation of Florida's woodlands and creation of a state marketing
bureau. J. B. Hodges became Jennings' "inside man" in northeast

12. J. B. Hodges to Joe Earman, May 27, 1924, and campaign card in Box 53, *ibid.*
13. Joe Earman to J. B. Hodges, May 27, 1924, Hodges to Earman, May 24, 1924, *ibid.*

Florida, playing the same role that he had so astutely filled for Catts in earlier days. The Lake City attorney persuaded many of his former associates to back Jennings, including Joe Earman, Dr. Ralph Greene, and Representative Bill Phillips of Columbia County. Not all such efforts were successful, for Jerry Carter supported Catts while Bryan Mack remained aloof, fearing that Jennings was too closely alligned to the old establishment.[14]

Hodges figured in two strategic decisions in the 1924 governor's race. First, he attended the February meeting of the state Democratic committee determined to block a return to the convention system of nominating Democratic officeholders. Any "fool resolutions" might be used against the committee by Catts, and when George Bassett of St. Augustine insisted on submitting such a proposal, Hodges led the battle to kill it.[15]

The second decision involved recommendations by Joe Earman and Ralph Greene that Jennings conduct a more vigorous campaign, especially against Catts: "put on the political brass knucks at once and fight everything in sight, otherwise the anti-Catts sentiment will shift to Martin as the only available man." Jennings urgently requested Hodges' advice, and the attorney contradicted his friends. He argued that it was precisely Martin's frontal assault on the former governor that had fueled the Catts resurgence. Such attacks had caused many Catts partisans to decide in favor of Jennings as their second choice on the June ballot; any aggressive campaign by Jennings against the former governor could only help Martin in second-choice votes.[16]

Jennings' decision to follow Hodges' advice and confine his attention to Martin unquestionably hurt him. Many Floridians, especially urban editors and the Democratic leadership, consid-

14. For Hodges' participation in Jenning's campaign, see Hodges to Joe Earman, February 18, 1924, January 4, 8, 15, 1924, *ibid.*; Jennings to Hodges, January 2, 1924, Hodges to Jennings, January 5, 26, 1924, in Box 52, *ibid.*; interview, Jerry Carter, July 29, 1970, Tallahassee.

15. J. B. Hodges to Joe Earman, February 23, 1924, in Box 53, Hodges Papers.

16. Frank E. Jennings to J. B. Hodges, November 15, 1923, Hodges to Jennings, November 16, 1923, in Box 52, Hodges to Joe Earman, April 24, 1924, in Box 53, *ibid.*

ered the crucial issue to be the defeat of Catts; whether Martin or Jennings won was a secondary consideration. John Martin, pro-labor Jacksonville mayor who had backed Catts in 1916 and 1920, suddenly found himself the leader of a "stop Catts" coalition which included even conservative industrialist Peter O. Knight. Ralph Greene noted that Democratic cabinet officials John Luning and W. V. Knott also backed Martin from fear of a possible Catts triumph. The Jacksonville offical turned the surging Catts strength in the panhandle to his advantage by warning that the real contest was between himself and the former governor and that Jennings ought to drop out of the race in order not to fragment the anti-Catts vote. By election day, Martin's major issue had become the "Catts' Menace."[17]

Martin was no match for Catts on the stump, but he did offer a colorful alternative to the drab Jennings. At one rally, a fanatical Catts partisan threatened to disrupt the meeting. Each time Martin reached a dramatic moment in his address, the man would shout "Hurray for Catts!" Finally, Martin paused and quieted his antagonist with a paragraph worthy of Catts: "My friends, you gave your support once to Catts on his promise to run the Pope out of business. Did he keep his promise? NO! While he was Governor, mind you, and supposed to be looking after his promise he made you, one Pope died and he let them appoint another without raising a finger to stop it!"[18]

Ralph Greene sensed the potency of anti-Catts sentiment and urged Jennings to emphasize Martin's prior connection with the governor. Jennings should ask the people "if they would not rather have the Cat than the kitten."[19] Hodges disagreed, however, and Jennings' ambivalence gave a critical advantage to Martin.

The urban newspapers climbed aboard the Martin bandwagon, viewing it as the most feasible alternative to Catts. The Miami

17. Ralph Greene to Joe Earman, February 26, 1924, Box 52, *ibid.*; Miami *Herald*, May 24, 1924.
18. Quoted in Fuller Warren, *How to Win in Politics*, 173.
19. Ralph Greene to Joe Earman, February 26, 1924, in Box 52, Hodges Papers.

Herald presented the clearest rationale for supporting him in an editorial comparing the campaigns of 1916 and 1924. In both, wrote the editor, there had been five candidates with one man the acknowledged leader (Knott in 1916, Martin in 1924). Attempts had been made each time to persuade several minor candidates to withdraw, but to no avail. Both times the leading candidates had fought one another while ignoring Catts, who had developed surprising strength in north and west Florida. The *Herald* feared that history might repeat itself in 1924 with voters splitting to give Catts victory in a disputed election. The only way to prevent "a state calamity" was for voters to unite behind Martin. The Gainesville *Daily Sun* and Tampa *Tribune* backed Martin and obviously considered Catts the primary challenger because they urged Martin voters to cast second choice ballots for anyone but Catts. They also advised supporters of Trammell, Jennings, or Spencer to vote Martin for second choice.[20]

The best account of the phenomenal impact of Catts on the gubernatorial election is a series of unofficial surveys taken by J. B. Hodges on behalf of Jennings. Hodges first expressed concern after talking with a phosphate operator from central Florida who informed him that Catts was very strong from Live Oak to Brooksville down the west coast. A traveling salesman confirmed Catts's strength in central Florida, and added to it the east coast up to St. Augustine. A Hillsborough County contact noted a drift away from Martin and toward Catts by rank and file Democrats in Tampa. A political friend from Milton told Hodges that the former chief executive would carry everything in north Florida from Lake City to Pensacola. Catts had also made a deal with two prominent Jacksonville citizens—J. E. T. Bowden, a former mayor and archenemy of Martin, and John Alsop—which had strengthened him in Duval County. These impressions were confirmed by Hodges' own business trips across north Florida, and by Bill Phillips' speaking tours on behalf of Jennings. Phillips reported that Catts

20. Miami *Herald*, May 24, 1924; Gainesville *Daily Sun*, June 2, 1924; Tampa *Tribune*, May 28, 1924.

was drawing much larger crowds in south and central Florida than either Jennings or Martin. Hodges noted that Jennings was slipping even in Lake City and might well lose the county despite the support of both himself and Phillips. The attorney complained that Jennings' publicity was too sophisticated and was "slipping over the heads of the people."[21]

Hodges' mood of despondency deepened as election day arrived. After voting, he wrote Earman a bitter letter which anticipated Jennings' defeat: "You and I have made a bad guess. We have played bone head politics." Earman consoled him by reminding that they lived in an age of ignorance which had produced prejudice, suspicion and jealousy. These, in turn, had caused "all the damn trouble in the world. The votes that Catts was given were inspired by prejudice. Every man that can think who lives in Florida knows this."[22]

Election returns confirmed Hodges' predictions. Jennings received 37,962 votes (25.9 percent) but won a plurality in only six counties—five of them the contiguous central Florida counties of Lake, Polk, Pasco, Hillsborough, and Manatee. Apart from this cluster, he won only Leon containing the capital city of Tallahassee. John Martin, shrewdly comprehending the population shifts that were transforming state politics, conceded north Florida and the Gulf coast, concentrating his time on the Atlantic side of the peninsula and in the south. This strategy worked perfectly; he carried every county in south Florida and lost only one on the east coast. His 55,715 first-choice votes (38 percent) included victories in urban counties containing seven of the ten largest cities. Martin's strategy of emphasizing the "Catts menace" paid handsome dividends best demonstrated in second-choice votes: Catts received only 6,067 such ballots, whereas the second-preference Jennings votes went heavily to Martin, who received 17,339.

21. J. B. Hodges to Joe Earman, December 7, 1923, in Box 52, Hodges to Earman, April 16, May 15, 27, 29, 30, 1924, in Box 53, Hodges Papers.
22. J. B. Hodges to Joe Earman, June 3, 1924, Earman to Hodges, June 5, 1924, in Box 53, ibid.

Considering his disadvantages, Catts ran a remarkable race. Running this time against four other candidates instead of one, he increased his total vote from 25,007 (28.6 percent) in the 1920 senatorial primary to 43,230 (29.5 percent). He won a plurality in twenty-nine counties compared to only three, four years earlier. In Leon County, for example, he doubled his 1920 primary vote. He barely lost Escambia County, but carried the rest of the panhandle; he dropped Leon (Tallahassee), and Columbia (Lake City), Alachua (Gainesville), Duval (Jacksonville), and St. Johns (St. Augustine), but carried every other county in north Florida. South of this, however, he won only three adjoining west coast counties (Levy, Citrus, Hernando) which traditionally had voted for him, and one isolated county in central Florida (Hardee); he lost heavily in south Florida and on the east coast. Urban areas and rapidly expanding southeast Florida voted against Catts as heavily as the rural counties supported him. He did not win a single county containing one of the state's ten largest cities; in Dade County he won only 3.7 percent of the vote, in Monroe (Key West) 9.9 percent, in Broward, 12.9 percent. He carried the same number of counties as Martin, and had no population shifts occurred in the preceding eight years, Catts's percentages won in the same counties would have given him the election; but changes had tipped the balance slightly in favor of central and southern counties with the critical addition of Duval in the north.[23]

The election results were sufficiently close to create some doubts in Catts's mind. He launched a "trial balloon" days after the election, printing a circular that threatened once again to challenge the returns in court. The circular claimed that the "ballot box stuffers and nighthawks of Florida politics" had discovered a new way to cheat him; instead of changing second-choice ballots as they had in 1916, they had "a slick artist call the votes and in place of Catts or Jennings call Martin and then have an accomplice change the tickets at once, leaving no trace behind." Catts notified Floridians

23. For demographic data, see Hartsfield and Roady, *Florida Votes, 1920–1962*, 75–76. See map, page 313 herein.

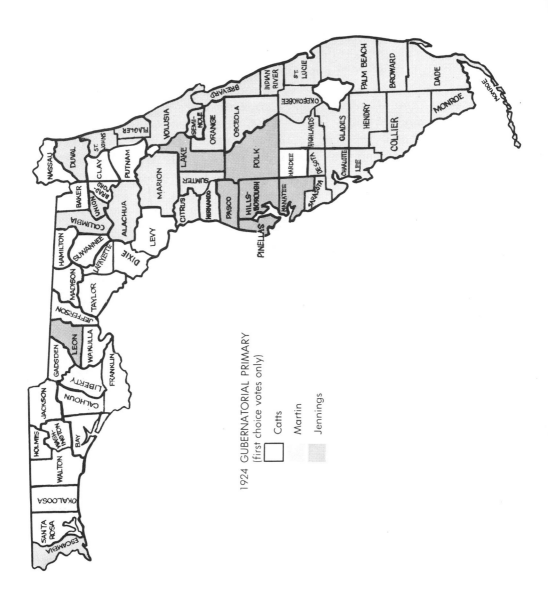

1924 GUBERNATORIAL PRIMARY
(first choice votes only)

Catts

Martin

Jennings

that "unless I am beaten fairly, I will not stand for it," and predicted that his real battle had only just begun.[24] Although many urban newspapers fully expected Catts to run as an independent in the fall, the former governor finally conceded defeat.

Joe Earman discovered a different kind of chicanery in the election, and his witness is revealing since he obviously retained no affection for Catts. The Palm Beach resident received information that Martin had made enormous campaign expenditures: "It seems that the corporation crowd were [sic] scared to death that old Catts would win, and a barrel of money was expended and many men hired to make accurate surveys and report daily for four or five weeks preceding the primary." He also mentioned the mysterious use of printed facsimiles of express receipts which he had learned about: "it seems that the matter was hatched and cooked up at Tallahassee: that the present statehouse officials were solidly against old Catts." Although Earman could obtain no further information, he concluded that "vast influences that permeated all over the State" did not want their "cussedness interfered with" and exerted pressure and influence in the election.[25]

The 1924 combat only whetted Catts's appetite for more, and he campaigned almost continually for the next four years. For Catts, the 1928 gubernatorial race was just an extension of the previous campaign, though with different issues and opponents; and he had saved the best effort of his career for last.

The early frontrunner in 1928 was Martin's heir apparent, Fons A. Hathaway, who represented the powerful Jacksonville dynasty. Hathaway, a native of Holmes County, had served as school superintendent in Orlando and Jacksonville before leaving education to become chairman of the State Road Department in the Martin administration. He received the blessing of Martin and much of the state press corps, and ran on an uninspiring platform which promised to continue policies of the prior administration, especially state construction of roadways.

24. Quoted in Tallahassee *Florida Democrat and Weekly Record,* June 13, 1924.
25. Joe Earman to J. B. Hodges, June 26, 1924, in Box 53, Hodges Papers.

Other candidates soon joined Hathaway. James M. Carson, a
Jacksonville attorney, entered the race, dividing the port city vote,
and state senator John S. Taylor of Pinellas County gave south
Florida a representative; but none of these altered Catts's strategy
to regain the state's highest office.

The former governor formally launched his campaign on May
27, 1927, at the traditional location for such announcements, the
Wakulla Springs barbecue. He appeared as before, wearing white
coat and pants, a vest, white tie, wide collar and white shoes, all of
which accented his round, red face. Predictable planks appeared in
his platform: better schools financed by an additional two cents per
gallon gasoline tax, and if necessary, a levy on tobacco; since the
real estate collapse of 1926 had impaired state finances, he advocated stringent economies such as reduction of all state salaries,
including the governor's, whose pay would drop from ten thousand
to six thousand dollars annually; he attacked his successors in the
statehouse for squandering a surplus of two million dollars which
he had left in the treasury; he championed revenue-sharing by ap-
plying half of the state gasoline tax to retire state and county municipal bonds; he also attacked Fons Hathaway for discrepancies in the
road department and promised to have each county audited at
three-month intervals.

Although Catts largely ignored religion in 1928, he did emphasize moral issues. He promised to enforce rigidly the state's
prohibition laws, opposed capital punishment for anyone under
twenty-one years of age, and advocated abolishing the death penalty for some crimes. A morals scandal which he alleged at the
woman's college in Tallahassee also received much attention. Although these were typical of his past campaigns, one proposal
shocked friend and foe alike: he advocated the legalization of bet-
ting on horse and dog racing on a county option basis.

Declining agriculture and the Florida real estate collapse in
1926 complicated the social problems facing rural people. Added to
their financial woes was the plethora of social changes which
seemed to threaten traditional morality: automobiles (those "hotels
on wheels"), rising hem lines, sensuous dances to the accompani-

ment of jazz, "liberated" women who smoked and drank, and the teaching of evolution and Freudian psychology in public schools and colleges. Catts perceived this new threat as keenly as he had the people's fear of Catholicism in an earlier era. Fortunately for him, a *cause celebrè* appeared at precisely the right moment.

A group of Tallahassee deacons, disturbed about iniquitous teachings and books circulating on the campus of the Florida State College for Women, organized an Impurity League. Subsequent investigation confirmed their worst fears and led to publication of a pamphlet documenting the circulation of "obscene books" and immoral teachings at the college. Dean Nathaniel M. Salley replied to the charges, arguing that the pamphlet was filled with lies.[26]

With a few of his own embellishments added for dramatic flair, Catts made conditions at the girls' school a major campaign issue. In the Wakulla speech announcing his candidacy, he described how a professor at the college, "wearing a coat with tail so long that he had to carry it in order to walk," took a younger girl for a walk. After vividly depicting the improper advances, Catts asked that voters send him to Tallahassee to clean up the mess. It would take him "only a minute to put my foot half as far as the length of that coat into the area that it should have covered."[27]

In subsequent speeches the former governor suggested less violent palliatives: at a Tallahassee rally, he promised to remove obscene books from the state colleges, even if he had to appoint a new Board of Control every week to accomplish it; he told a Leesburg audience that his basic beliefs were in God, the Savior, and the Holy Ghost, and that his platform consisted of reading the Bible in public schools, abolishing the teaching of psychoanalysis in the colleges, and firmly establishing belief in God. In Wauchula he discussed immorality at the state woman's college, and when two

26. Tallahassee *Florida Morning State*, May 26, 1928.

27. Jerry Carter, Jr., attended the barbecue at Wakulla Springs and vividly recalls the speech. It became the basic address used in 1928, although Catts sometimes altered it to fit local situations. Carter, a brilliant mimic, recites the speech in the same raspy, strained voice which made Catts a hypnotic orator. Interview, Jerry Carter, Jr., May 8, 1972, Tallahassee.

coeds in the audience asked for a chance to reply, the former governor stormed that they "probably didn't have sense enough to graduate." The editor of the Miami *Herald*, incensed over the incident, wrote that from any audience other than "a densely ignorant type such as would be recruited from the outposts of Hardee County, the girls might have had some help, but education among the Catts supporters there is regarded as a curse and a blight."[28]

Educators tried unsuccessfully to quell the emotional issue. Dean Nathaniel Salley replied to Catts's Tallahassee speech, but Catts continued to blast away at the climate of immorality that flourished at F.S.C.W. President A. A. Murphree of the University of Florida discussed the matter with his Administrative Council in October, 1927. He believed the situation would aid that gubernatorial candidate who sought "to gain office by sensationalism": "I fully believe that the whole force of mementum [*sic*] in this thing has been generated by Ex-Governor Catts. I understand he is going all over the county districts telling these things."[29] The editor of the Panama City *Pilot* wrote a more cynical explanation in August of 1927:

One aspect of the Tallahassee deacons' findings that has come in for only casual comment is its political possibilities. What a wonderful opportunity for the perenial [*sic*] Mr. Catts! How much more tangible and concrete an issue than the impending conquest of Florida by the Pope and his armed minions, of which we heard so much a few years ago! If this business can just be kept alive and kicking until the next gubernatorial campaign, it is quite possible that we will learn of a great deal of evil teachings that the Capital city churchmen overlooked.[30]

The other issue that enlivened politics in 1928 contrasted dramatically to Catts's enraged indignation over declining morality: he advocated legalized gambling for Florida. His explanation was as carefully reasoned as it was sensational. Catts explained that he did

28. Tallahassee *Florida Morning State*, May 26, 1928; Leesburg *Commerical*, quoted in the Suwannee *Democrat*, April 6, 1928; the Miami *Herald*, April 28, 1928.
29. "Discussion by the Administrative Council," October 8, 1927, in Box 22, Murphree Papers.
30. Panama City *Pilot*, August 18, 1927, copy in Box 22, Murphree Papers.

not advocate gambling or any other vice, but he did believe that each county should practice "home rule," with the people of the area deciding the racing issue for themselves through a referendum. This was consistent with states' rights and was opposed to the dangerous centralization of power. Furthermore, moralistic "blue laws" hindered Florida's economic growth as "the World's Greatest Winter Playground," and caused racing enthusiasts to spend their vacations in Cuba. Where local people opposed racing it should not be imposed on them, but "it is high time that some voice should be lifted, in FLORIDA and elsewhere, against the tide of fanaticism which seeks to engulf the United States—the desperate effort which is being made by a certain class of people to bring all citizens under the sway of their own particular beliefs through legal compulsion."[31]

In many speeches he further developed the basic theme of home rule. It was the only way to prevent the separation of the state because the interests of north and south Florida had diverged so widely. The tourist sections in the south must construct facilities to attract winter visitors. If the north and west vetoed racing, the south might withdraw and form a separate state. He told a cheering throng in the Gulf coast resort town of Sarasota that he favored a "wide open state, with horse racing, dog racing, and cat racing if you want it." Burton Lee Mank, a Miami lawyer and racing enthusiast, accompanied Catts around the state introducing him and explaining the plight of south Florida. Illegal racing had operated despite the law, and during the previous year alone Miami had lost $44 million in revenue to Cuba.[32]

Catts's advocacy of pari-mutuel, local option gambling was certainly the most contradictory act in a career characterized by inconsistency. It violated not only his moral sensibility, but his own pejorative attitude toward prohibition which demanded statewide enforcement of rural Protestant standards of private morality. The Catts family remembered his "home rule" concept as a method of

31. Advertisement in the Tallahassee *Florida Morning State,* May 20, 1928.
32. *Ibid.,* May 15, 26, 1928.

guaranteeing fairness to south Florida, a notion which corresponds to his earlier advocacy of reapportionment.[33] The disastrous hurricane and the real estate collapse had nearly paralyzed southeast Florida, perhaps another reason for his drastic change of heart.

There are at least two additional explanations. The 1924 election had demonstrated beyond debate the shifting realities of political power in Florida. Catts had won the same number of counties as Martin, but had lost by a sizable margin because he had received less than 20 percent of the vote in many southern counties. Catts did not need the demographic studies made during the interim between elections to tell him the hard facts of Florida politics. The total vote in 1924 of 137,000 would likely increase to 160,000 in 1928. Virtually the entire increase would occur in central and south Florida where Pinellas County alone had 12,000 registered Democrats in 1928 compared to only 2,859 voters four years earlier. Catts's territory in west Florida was becoming relatively weaker compared to the rest of the state. So, he had to find new issues that would appeal to the more tolerant and broad-minded south Floridian who might not have been a resident of the state when Catts first had begun haranguing against Catholics in 1916.[34]

A more sensational explanation was advanced by Jacksonville lawyer and gubernatorial candidate James M. Carson, who entered the race specifically to discredit Catts. He claimed that Catts was the candidate of the criminal element who would use him as a "front man" for their operations. He claimed to have documentary evidence that a south Florida gambler named Bradley was financing Catts's campaign to the extent of twenty thousand dollars. The opposition even released a photograph of an American Express receipt that Catts allegedly had signed to receive his money. Catts dismissed the indictment as just another politically inspired attempt to wreck his career; in a Tallahassee speech, he jokingly announced: "All I've got to say is any man who don't like a good dog, a

33. Interview, Mrs. Ruth Cawthon, May 8, 1972, DeFuniak Springs.
34. See Aloysius Coll, "A Pre Election Analysis of the June Primary," in Tallahassee *Florida Morning State*, May 19, 1928.

fast horse, and a good looking woman just ain't in my class."[35] The
tremendous applause that greeted his "explanation" did not sub-
merge the issue.

Joe Earman's revelation of Catts's contact with gamblers in
1921 seems to add credibility to this charge, as does the former
governor's connection with several unsavory Tampa characters,
which was revealed later in his 1929 counterfeiting trial. At any
rate, the charges clouded the last years of his life and emphasize
the political cynicism that became increasingly apparent in the
1920s. Two Florida historians state categorically that "a lawless
gambling element in Florida's east coast resort area was in charge
of Catts's campaign."[36]

This strange development caused as much contemporary consternation as Catholicism had in 1916. The Tampa *Tribune* referred
to Catts as the "God and gambling candidate" and predicted that he
would renege on his promise even if elected: "O, what a 'double-
crossing' they [racing element] will get if the old hypocrite is elected!" Catts discovered that his stand had not only alienated many of
his Baptist brethren, but had so infuriated some ministers that they
came out in open opposition to his candidacy. The Reverend A. C.
Shuler of Jacksonville's Calvary Baptist Church told his congregation that Catts "has gone over lock, stock and barrel, bag and baggage, to the other crowd. I have been a personal friend and supporter of Catts for many years. I regret that he, a Baptist minister,
should be willing to sell his birthright for a mess of pottage in order
to obtain a few votes." Shuler apologized for entering the political
sphere but argued that the moral principles involved were too fundamental for Florida Baptists to support Catts.[37]

The Reverend Len G. Broughton, pastor of the influential First
Baptist Church of Jacksonville, was widely respected for his religious tolerance. The 1928 campaign brought him into politics. He

35. Interview, Jerry Carter, Jr., May 8, 1972, Tallahassee.
36. See Charlton W. Tebeau and Ruby Leach Carson, *Florida: From Indian Trail to
Space Age*, II (Delray Beach, Fla: Southern Publishing Co., 1965), 67. Tebeau does not
repeat the charge, however, in his *A History of Florida*, 389.
37. Tampa *Tribune*, May 27, 28, 1928; Panama City *Pilot*, May 10, 1928.

could "conceive of nothing that would be a greater calamity to the state of Florida," he told his congregation on May 2, 1928, "than to put a man of Catts' low grade moral conception into the governor's chair." He endorsed Dr. Fons A. Hathaway, but told his packed congregation that his main concern was defeating Catts. The sermon, which was widely reprinted in state newspapers, drew round after round of applause from his congregation.[38] The press ridiculed Catts for trading his church support for the backing of east coast gambling interests, and considered it a fatal political blunder.

Such journalists misjudged the uncanny capacity of Catts to stir Florida crackers and failed to understand the heterogeneity of the "Baptist vote." Urban Baptists and socially conscious pastors of the "first churches" might oppose him, but even religion contained its quota of "woolly hats." In Miami he ridiculed his antagonists, claiming that he would still win even if only the bootleggers and gamblers in Florida voted for him. After a speech in Tampa, he was verbally attacked by Dr. A. M. Bennett, pastor of Palm Avenue Baptist Church. Catts replied that a gubernatorial candidate had paid Bennett "$600 or $700 to pray Uncle Catts out of heaven," that personally he had never bet a nickle on a race, that many church people supported legalized gambling, and that his religious heritage was "just a two-by-four preacher and two-by-four farmer," an "exponent of the great common masses" against the rich and the corporations.[39]

In rural areas he regularly was asked to fill the pulpit of the local Baptist church, but on occasion temper overwhelmed reason when the issue of religion arose. While addressing a wildly cheering, overflow crowd in Tallahassee, he criticized preachers for attacking him from their pulpits, arguing they probably were for hire, had desecrated the holy places, "and if they would come down from their pinnacles and make the same base charges, I will beat hell out of them." Manipulating a favorite theme, he described himself as

---

38. Panama City *Pilot*, May 10, 1928; Tallahassee *Florida Morning State*, May 2, 1928.
39. Tampa *Tribune*, May 15, 1928.

just a plain man from the people who had asked his wife to bury him with a wool hat.[40]

Catts's campaign organization boasted many new faces in 1928. Technically, J. V. Burke, who had guided his 1916 race, again served as director; but the mysterious and ever present Burton Lee Mank of Miami really managed the campaign. Governor John W. Martin, himself a candidate for the United States Senate seat held by Park Trammell, charged that Mank was a former convict, race horse gambler, and rum runner, all of which Mank denied. Sidney Catts, Jr., provided transportation for his father, who usually spoke three or four times a day. The entourage included a calliope which attracted crowds to impromptu street corner rallies. The Miami *Herald* charged that on approaching the little hamlet of Wauchula, Catts had undressed, clothed himself in a pair of patched trousers, a ragged, frayed coat, worn-out shoes, and broad-brimmed felt hat. Then, "he shambled into town to meet the brothers and sisters, followed by his calliope." His audiences in such towns drew heavily from the surrounding rural districts where he seems to have maintained formidable strength despite his attitude on racing and the epithets hurled by his opponents.[41]

The most serious handicap in 1928 was his own temper. When speaking at Groveland in April, a disabled veteran disputed his remarks, provoking Catts to such a rage that he threatened "to beat hell out of" the unfortunate man. Members of the local American Legion post drafted a resolution critical of Catts's temper and calling him an unfit candidate; they sent copies of the resolution to every American Legion post in Florida.[42]

All such episodes failed to dampen the Catts movement which seemed to gather strength from each new confrontation. The Lakeland *Journal* believed that Catts was in first place.[43] The unalterably hostile editor of the Miami *Herald* could not understand Catts's

40. Tallahassee *Florida Morning State*, May 26, 1928.
41. Miami *Herald*, April 28, 1928; Suwannee *Democrat*, March 2, 1928.
42. Miami *Herald*, April 29, 1928.
43. Clipping from the Lakeland *Journal*, April 13, 1928, in William J. Howey Scrapbook, Florida State University Library, Tallahassee.

continuing popularity. The former governor held the church people of west Florida spellbound relating his role in bringing prohibition to Florida; then he told audiences in little towns like Caryville that he was their friend because prohibition forced prices higher for their corn and grain. In one locality he would promise prohibitionists that he intended to remove every sheriff in Florida if necessary to enforce the Volstead Act, but elsewhere he assured farmers that he would never molest men who "used up their skimmins." The editor, mirroring H. L. Mencken's contempt for the masses, disgustedly concluded that "every county in the state where there are neither good roads, newspapers, telephones nor telegraph, apparently is for Catts, now and forever, one and inseparable, *E. Pluribus Unum.*"[44]

Distraught Democrats searched for some means to block Catts. One group of Tampa party leaders decided that the crisis demanded a man not closely associated with the corporations, an orator "who could scatter as many firebrands from the stump" as Catts. They approached State Senator Doyle Carlton of Hillsborough County and persuaded him to enter the contest. Carlton's announcement temporarily muddled the political situation. Mayor W. A. MacKenzie of Leesburg had entered the race briefly, but withdrew and endorsed Fons Hathaway when Carlton announced, fearful that the new candidate would split south Florida's votes and elect Catts. The St. Petersburg *Times* had endorsed Senator John S. Taylor of Largo, arguing that south Florida could unite behind him and defeat Hathaway and Catts. The furious editor dismissed the Catts menace as a spurious issue designed to conceal the attempt by a Tampa political clique to elect its own representative, Doyle Carlton, as governor. Carlton seemed to confirm this charge by maintaining a judicious silence about Catts while blasting Hathaway's record of ineptitude and waste in the State Road Department.[45]

44. Miami *Herald*, April 30, 1928.
45. Gainesville *Daily Sun*, May 6, 1928; St. Petersburg *Times*, May 30, 1928. Carlton was also an active Baptist layman who was later to serve as president of the state Baptist convention.

With Hathaway, Taylor, and Carlton bidding for the urban and south Florida vote, the election became hopelessly confused. Tallahassee's *Florida Morning State* joined the St. Petersburg paper by endorsing John Taylor. The Tampa *Tribune* assured its readers that only unity behind Doyle Carlton could prevent Catts's reelection. The Kissimee *Valley Gazette* and Gainesville *Daily Sun* were equally convinced that the only chance of defeating Catts was to support Hathaway; the almost frantic editor of the Miami *Herald* begged "in a pure spirit of patriotism and love for Florida, all other candidates should withdraw from the contest and get behind Hathaway."[46] Realizing the hopeless fragmentation among candidates, many papers urged voters to cast a first ballot for whomever they chose, but to vote their second choice "for anyone but Catts."

Fons Hathaway, suffering most from Catts's strength in west Florida, spent most of his campaign defending himself from Carlton's charges of malfeasance and desperately trying to cut into Catts's north Florida strength. Edgar W. Waybright, prolabor legislator from Jacksonville who had been a key supporter of Catts in the 1917 legislature, led Hathaway's assault. He accused the governor of switching from the "church crowd" to the "gambling crowd," attacked the Catts administration record on school appropriations and road building, and reminded his auditors of tax increases during the years from 1916 to 1920.[47]

Some Democrats fought Catts on his own terms and employed emotional prejudice that surpassed anything the governor had used. A circular issued in Hamilton County was entitled "The Unpardonable Crime Among Men and Part of the Record of Sidney J. Catts When He Was Governor." The pamphlet began with a query: "Suppose your mother, or wife, or sister, or daughter, had been the victim of a negro rapist—and the negro rapist had been sent to the chain gang—and then Governor Catts should give him a

---

46. Tallahassee *Florida Morning State*, May 2, 1928; Tampa *Tribune*, May 21, 1928; Gainesville *Daily Sun*, May 28, 1928, quoting Kissimee *Valley Gazette;* Miami *Herald*, April 28, 1928.

47. Suwannee *Democrat*, April 27, 1928; Jacksonville *Florida Times-Union*, May 10, 1928.

pardon for a Christmas present? What would you do?" The circular listed Catts's record of pardons which had included fifteen men who had been convicted of rape or attempted rape, then concluded: "For the love of your home, your loved ones and friends, for the love of righteousness and your native land—Don't vote for Sidney J. Catts."[48]

Editors gleefully reprinted the circular, adding embellishments as they wrote. The Tampa *Tribune* stretched newspaper ethics in its election eve editorial entitled "Rapists Should Vote for Catts." The editor argued that in addition to the support of "jail birds and rum runners," Catts should receive also "the solid vote of the rapists, would-be rapists and prospective rapists of the state, if these fellows look up the record and feel any sense of obligation to a friend and benefactor." The editor also reviewed Catts's record for pardoning rapists, although he added three more to the tally of the Hamilton County circular.[49]

The June primary demonstrated how well grounded had been the almost paranoic fear of Catts. Less than 4 percentage points separated Carlton, Catts, and Hathaway. Carlton won with 77,569 first-choice votes (30.4 percent) and a whopping 28,471 second ballots; Catts trailed narrowly with 68,984 (27.1 percent) to Hathaway's 67,849 (26.7 percent). The other candidates divided the remaining 40,595 votes (15.9 percent). Carlton won nine scattered counties through north and west Florida, but his major strength was across the central portion of the state from the Gulf to the Atlantic; anchored by powerful Hillsborough, he carried thirteen contiguous counties (for a total of 23 counties). Hathaway's support came from three clusters: four counties in the bend of the panhandle, the east coast where he won nine counties, and in southwest Florida between the Gulf and Lake Okeechobee where he carried five contiguous counties (a total of 20 counties). Catts could not translate his belated discovery of south Florida's political strength into victory. He won nineteen counties in north Florida, the

48. Quoted in Panama City *Pilot*, May 24, 1928.
49. Tampa *Tribune*, June 2, 1928.

panhandle, and down the west coast as far as Hernando, all traditional areas of Cattsism; but he won only boss-ruled Monroe County (Key West) in the south. In the duel for north and west Florida, Catts won sixteen counties, Hathaway nine, and Carlton eight.[50]

Despite Catts inability to carry south and central Florida, he did improve his showing considerably over 1924. In Dade where he had received only 3.7 percent of the vote in 1924, he won 22.7 percent in 1928; comparative figures in Hillsborough were 26.4 percent to 32.8 percent; in Pinellas 6.2 percent to 16.7 percent; Sarasota 6.2 percent to 29.4 percent. Not all counties fit this pattern, however, and in Brevard, Palm Beach, Broward, Orange, and Manatee counties his vote percentage either remained unchanged or declined between 1924 and 1928. Perhaps the most remarkable fluctuation in the state occurred in Monroe County where Catts had received only 9.9 percent in 1924. Four years later he won an absolute majority of 53 percent. This strongly suggests the enthusiasm of the county for legalized racing and also the machine control which delivered it to Catts. This incident offers persuasive evidence concerning the former governor's identification with gambling interests in 1928, although his family considered the charge just another political attempt to embarrass him. Undoubtedly Catts paid a price for this support among rural church people. William Cash has suggested that except for the defection of many religious folk in 1928, he might have won.[51]

Catts briefly threatened to contest the election, but decided against this option when a new political issue attracted his attention. The Democratic nomination of Alfred E. Smith for president aroused him to renewed fury. Religion and prohibition, which had played minor roles in the 1928 gubernatorial race, suddenly took on tremendous political impact in the national contest. In mid-

50. For statistical data, see Hartsfield and Roady, *Florida Votes, 1920–1962*, 74; State of Florida, *Report of the Secretary of State, 1927–1928* (Marianna: Printing Department, Boys' Industrial School, 1929), insert. Also, see map, page 328 herein.

51. Interview, Mrs. Alice May Stiegel, Mrs. Elizabeth Paderick, May 12, 1972, Jacksonville; Cash, *History of the Democratic Party in Florida*, 133.

September, Catts announced that he intended to conduct a state-wide campaign against Smith. The issue was a genuine one for the aging former governor, who did not believe that a Catholic should be elected president of the United States. He visualized basic conflicts between a Catholic president and his own deeply rooted Baptist heritage of church-state separation, and he took this issue to the voters of Florida.[52]

The state Democratic leadership, galvanized into action by Senator Duncan Fletcher, tried to counter the "Hoovercrats" with a vigorous campaign which included a visit from vice-presidential nominee Joseph T. Robinson of Arkansas. Counter efforts by the still powerful Ku Klux Klan and Catts cut deeply into Democratic support and frightened many party leaders into silence. Senator Park Trammell only reluctantly endorsed Smith after intense pressure from Fletcher. His belated support brought an avalanche of negative response from citizens who threatened to vote against him in the general election. Although both Democrats and Republicans denounced Catts, his activity helped make religion and prohibition major issues. Most historians of the election argue either that the two issues were inseparable in the minds of voters or that prohibition actually figured more prominently than religion; but certainly Catts's unequivocal emphasis on religion made it more significant in Florida than in most other southern states.[53]

Catts's influence in 1928, however, can be overremphasized. Hoover's greatest strength was in south and central Florida, while Smith ran best in precisely the same traditionally Democratic counties where Catts was strongest. Of the twenty counties which the former governor had carried in June, 1928, Hoover won only seven while Smith took thirteen. Perhaps one of Catts's earliest anti-Smith speeches at Tallahassee was an omen; the audience

52. Interview, Mrs. Ruth Cawthon, May 8, 1972, DeFuniak Springs.

53. For anti-Smith sentiment, see T. L. Gunter to Park Trammell, October 18, 1928, and telegram from Samuel F. Flood to Trammell, October 18, 1928; telegram from Gilchrist Stockton to Trammell, October 10, 1928, on Reel 3, Trammell Papers. For an excellent brief survey of the 1928 race in Florida, see J. Herbert Doherty, Jr., "Florida and the Presidential Election of 1928," *Florida Historical Quarterly*, XXVI (October, 1947), 174–86.

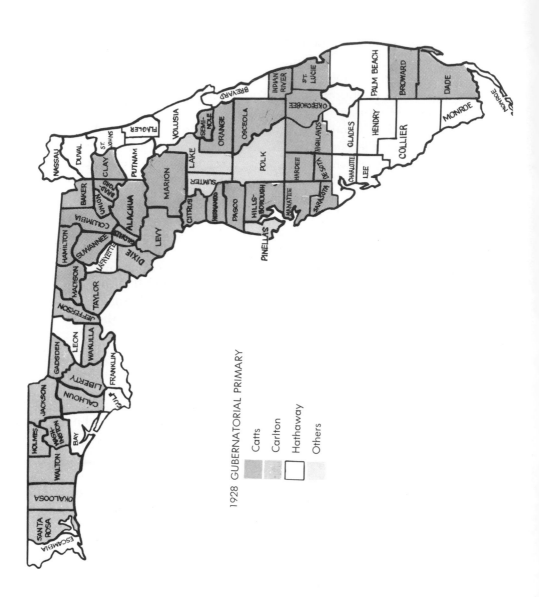

1928 GUBERNATORIAL PRIMARY

Catts

Carlton

Hathaway

Others

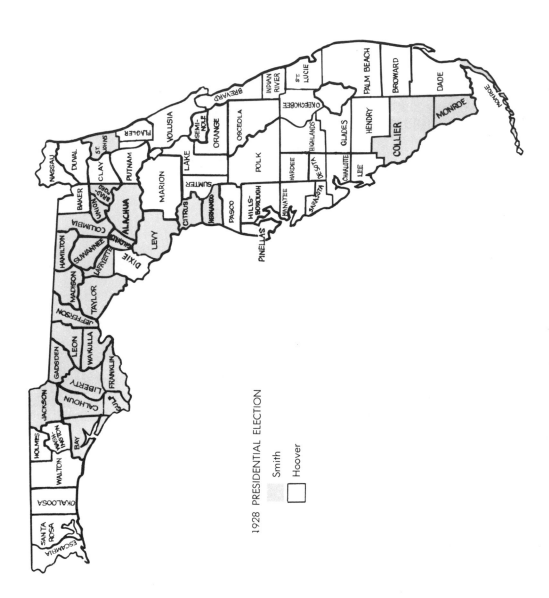

1928 PRESIDENTIAL ELECTION

Smith

Hoover

broke into near riot, forcing him to terminate his speech amid hooting and egg throwing.[54] Repudiated by many church people because of his gambling apostacy and by his rural constituency for his political treason in supporting the Republican party, Catts suddenly had become a pariah without a base of strength. Suffering from failing health and political disappointment, he sought the tranquility of DeFuniak Springs, but peace did not come so easily for "Old Sid" Catts.

54. Doherty, "Florida and the Presidential Election of 1928," 179. See map, page 329 herein.

THIRTEEN

The Failure and
the Hope

THE 1928 CAMPAIGN had barely ended when Catts found himself once again embroiled in legal controversy. On April 9, 1929, a federal grand jury in Jacksonville indicted the former governor on charges of counterfeiting. Catts allegedly had supplied $5,000 in the fall of 1928 to purchase plates which would manufacture fake $100 bills. The grand jury also indicted Tampa attorney Julian Diaz, his nephew Armando Dominguez, Diaz' lover, Madeline Leah Burwell, and his secretary, Mateo Mir, all of Tampa. In return for his investment, Catts allegedly took a fictitious mortgage on Diaz' office and law library, and would have received $25,000 in counterfeit money. When Catts paid his bond in Marianna on April 12, he was in a gay mood, laughing and joking with friends and predicting vindication: "The charges of counterfeiting $100 bills is especially ridiculous. Why, I'm still in the dollar bill class, but not in counterfeiting."[1]

Diaz, ringleader of the conspiracy, had been arrested some weeks earlier when government agents had discovered a bogus bill in his law office. Although the Tampa attorney had been a close associate of Governor Catts during the 1928 election, no suspicion had involved the DeFuniak Springs minister until Diaz specifically implicated him. Diaz pleaded guilty to the counterfeiting charges in May and began serving a five-year sentence.

1. Jacksonville *Florida Times-Union*, April 10, 13, 1929.

Catts's trial began on October 21, 1929, in Tampa. The sixty-seven-year-old former governor walked into the court chamber leaning heavily on the arm of Rozier, his youngest son. Already suffering from the early effects of the heart disease that would take his life, he also was losing sight in his remaining eye. Three attorneys represented him in the Tampa proceedings: his son Sidney, Jr., C. J. Hardee of Tampa, and J. Walter Kehoe.

The government case was carefully constructed, based almost entirely on the testimony of Leah Burwell, who had turned state's evidence, and Diaz. The government prosecutor quickly established the close relationship between the Tampa lawyer and Catts, even extending to the Baptist minister's christening one of Diaz' children in 1928. Miss Burwell's testimony, almost all of it based on conversations with Diaz, related that Catts had pledged $5,000 in November, 1928, to be used to gain the release of Mir who was being held for smuggling. Mir would then obtain the plates for reproducing counterfeit bills. Catts had gotten the money from his wife by showing her mortgages on land given by Diaz. Catts allegedly had carried five $1,000 dollar bills to a Tallahassee motel in the soles of his shoes. Diaz had used $1,000 to effect the release of Mir, and the remainder to establish the counterfeiting operation.

When two hundred $50 bills were completed, Diaz and Miss Burwell had met Catts at the Seminole Hotel in Jacksonville where the former governor had inspected the bills. Unhappy with the workmanship, Catts had gone with his accomplices to purchase a better quality of ink. Miss Burwell testified that after having a drink with Catts in their hotel room, they had returned to Tampa to run another batch of bills.

Diaz testified also, providing additional background. He had helped Catts organize the Guardians of Liberty in Tampa and had served actively in the 1928 gubernatorial campaign. During this association, the counterfeit scheme had been completed.[2] Catts had operated under the alias of Gato, Spanish for cat.

The defense case depended on strategies to discredit the two

2. Deal, "Sidney Johnston Catts, Stormy Petrel of Florida Politics," 202–207.

star prosecution witnesses and to provide a credible explanation for Catts's involvement with Diaz. The first task proved simpler than the second. Defense counsel C. J. Hardee left Leah Burwell weeping from a slashing cross-examination on October 23. Federal judge Alexander Akerman had already disallowed much of her testimony as inadmissable hearsay evidence. Under Hardee's prodding, she admitted sexual intimacies with Diaz during the previous eight years. She also admitted that in a letter to Diaz while in jail in Miami she had threatened to implicate Catts unless he posted bond to release her. Infuriated upon learning that her lover had accused her of masterminding the ring, Miss Burwell had sought to link the governor in hopes of forcing someone to help her. When Hardee reminded that in her initial statement she had not mentioned Catts, Miss Burwell replied that she had tried to protect Diaz and the former governor.[3]

Hardee also attempted to destroy Diaz' credibility as a witness. In cross-examination, he questioned the Tampa attorney about statements he allegedly made to a fellow prisoner in the Hillsborough County jail that although Catts was innocent of any complicity, he would involve the former governor unless Catts obtained his release. Diaz denied making the statement, but Hardee countered with a series of prominent Tampans who testified that they would not believe Diaz even under oath. Although the witnesses acknowledged Catts's political association with the Tampa attorney, they denied knowing of Catts's involvement with the counterfeiting ring.

After discrediting the key prosecution witnesses, Hardee based the defense case on 1928 political activities. Several witnesses testified that they had heard Diaz ask to borrow $5,000 from Catts in order to clear up personal debts and to finance the political appointments of two friends. Mallie Martin, secretary to newly elected Governor Doyle Carlton, took the stand to verify that Catts had worked with Diaz to get two men appointed as justices of the peace in Hillsborough County.

3. Jacksonville *Florida Times-Union*, October 24, 1929.

When Catts took the stand on October 26, he admitted that he had sought appointments for the two Tampans. In return for the favor, he had promised Carlton to deliver 1,500 votes in Ybor City, a Latin suburb of Tampa. Catts added that Diaz had planned to use the letter appointing his friends to demonstrate influence with Governor Carlton, thus obtaining legal business for himself and Catts. The attorney had estimated that income from handling pardons cases alone would bring in $3,000 a month.

Governor Doyle Carlton testified on the last day of the trial, denying that he had made any "trade" with Catts. He confirmed Catts's offer to deliver 1,500 Ybor City votes in return for the justice of the peace appointments. He refused the deal, however, and when Catts explained that he and Diaz could gain financially from legal business resulting from the appointments, Carlton promptly terminated the interview.[4]

Catts denied all the charges in his testimony on October 26. When questioned about carrying $5,000 for the alleged loan in his shoes, he belligerently acknowledged that this was his custom; he had carried as much as $30,000 in his shoes, "with two good guns on my hips and no body hadn't better bother me, either."[5]

After Judge Akerman had charged the jurors on October 31, they retired to decide the case. The first ballot was seven to five for acquittal, but each additional ballot deadlocked with six on each side. After twenty-four hours of deliberation, the jury remained hopelessly deadlocked, and Judge Akerman declared a mistrial. During the fall, 1930, session of the court, the former governor was acquitted.

Although Catts's explanation of the affair helped to win acquittal, it certainly did not reflect well on his integrity. The offer to swap votes for political appointments confirmed charges that long had been made by his antagonists. Furthermore, his admitted proposal to use his influence with Carlton to obtain pardons cases adds credibility to the allegations made against him in 1921. Although

4. *Ibid.*, October 22, 26, 30, 1929.
5. *Ibid.*, October 30, 1929.

none of this bargaining was illegal, it certainly was inconsistent with his earlier promises of reform and integrity in government. Despite such revelations, the counterfeiting charges seem to have been thoroughly squashed. Based solely on the testimony of Miss Burwell and Diaz, they were refuted by dozens of reputable defense witnesses. The explanation by Catts is a consistent if embarrassing account of what probably occurred.

After the trial ended, Catts retired to DeFuniak Springs to live out his remaining days in peace. Many political opponents, including W. V. Knott, felt sympathy for him during the 1929 episode, and W. T. Cash conceded in 1936 that Catts had "meant well" as governor. Since he was no longer a political factor in Florida, a fairer evaluation of his contributions began to emerge. When a resolution was introduced in the 1931 state legislature to have Catts's picture in the governor's office turned toward the wall, the proposal was defeated.[6]

To keep busy, Catts dabbled in real estate and farming. He also served as general manager of the West Florida Plant Food Company which manufactured fertilizers. Perhaps fearful of additional legal action against him, he placed most of the Catts property in the name of his wife, Alice May. He already owned several pieces of Walton County property before 1929, but acquired other lots in the 1930s. By 1936 Mrs. Catts held the title to seven pieces of property valued on the tax roles at nearly $4,000.[7] When Jerry Carter, Jr., became concerned about the former governor's finances and visited him in the 1930s, Catts reminded Carter of his maxim to save fifty cents out of each dollar and assured the young man that the family was financially secure.[8]

---

6. James R. Knott to author, August 6, 1970; W. T. Cash, *History of the Democratic Party in Florida*, 133; Deal, "Sidney Johnston Catts," 223. The Cash book, published in 1936, is the first serious attempt to deal with Catts in a balanced fashion which acknowledges his positive contributions.

7. Sidney J. Catts to Kempster Paderick, Jr., December 20, 1933; in possession of Mrs. Elizabeth Paderick, Jacksonville. For financial condition, see *Tax Assessment Roll, 1936, Walton County*, Walton County Courthouse, DeFuniak Springs; "Will of Alice May Catts," Case #2-138, in Probate Judge's Office, Walton County Courthouse.

8. Interview, Jerry W. Carter, Jr., May 8, 1972, Tallahassee.

Catts suffered from steadily declining health. For some eight years before his death, a cataract gradually reduced vision in his right eye. Upon seeing him denied his favorite pastime of reading, his family compensated by reading to him. Ruth Cawthon, his daughter, read at least three hours a day, and these sessions became the high point of his life. In the midthirties he had an operation at New Orleans Baptist Hospital to remove the cataract, and regained enough sight in his remaining eye to read with the aid of a magnifying glass.[9]

When he returned to DeFuniak Springs from his operation, newspapers from across the South called to ask if he planned to run for public office again. His wife and two of his daughters, Elizabeth Paderick and Ruth Cawthon, begged him to pledge never again to enter politics, but the old man left the question unresolved. Politician to the end, he recovered sufficiently to campaign actively in 1934 for his old friend Jerry Carter, who was running for the state railroad commission. He visited forty-five counties for Carter, assured him of a twenty-thousand-vote margin, and added: "If you are elected I have a scheme that I want to talk to you about in the next 6 months."[10] Carter won easily, though there is no further mention of Catts's "scheme." Perhaps his health prevented its implementation. He had suffered from heart trouble since the late 1920s, and on March 9, 1936, he died of heart failure at the age of seventy-three.

Within the next two months both of Florida's United States senators, Park Trammell and Duncan Fletcher, died, and the three deaths marked the passing of a political era in Florida's history. Catts's funeral was held at the Baptist church in DeFuniak Springs on March 10, and he was buried in a hillside cemetery east of town. Paradoxically, the Miami *Herald*, which seldom printed a kind word about him during his lifetime, tried diligently to be charitable at his death:

9. *Ibid.*, and Mrs. Ruth Cawthon, May 8, 1972, DeFuniak Springs.
10. Interview, Mrs. Elizabeth Paderick and Mrs. Alice May Stiegel, May 12, 1972, Jacksonville; Sidney J. Catts to Jerry W. Carter, June 25, 1934, copy in Florida VF, "Governor—Catts, Sidney J."

Sidney J. Catts has passed from the political scene of Florida, leaving behind a mixed heritage of love and hatred, of admiration and disgust. . . .

Perhaps it is better to remember the good and to bury the bad with his body. Whatever his most ardent enemies may have said about Governor Catts, even they admitted he was a strong man, a dominating individual, who protected his people and was afraid of nothing on earth. In these days such strength is a rare asset in public life. . . . He served his sort of people but the passing years decreed that his kind should dwindle to a minority.

Many will mourn his passing with earnest grief. Others who opposed him in all he did will at least grant that he was his own man, a character as picturesque as the Old South and as rugged as the great live oaks under whose shade Catts so often preached the gospel of the Lord.[11]

What the Miami *Herald* and many Floridians could neither forget nor forgive was his use of religion to seduce the gullible folk of rural Florida. The emotionalism which he generated could be switched on and off, as occasion demanded, a fact that Catts demonstrated many times. During one campaign, a popular high school principal died in Tallahassee and the whole town went into mourning. The next day Catts's entourage entered town, complete with blaring calliope. A huge, menacing crowd attended his rally that night, determined to shout down his grotesque stories and profane attacks. Instead, they listened in astonishment as Catts quoted in Latin from Virgil, then from a Greek funeral oration. In quiet voice with subdued emotion and perfect diction, he paid tribute to the town's fallen son. The eloquent oratorical masterpiece left his hostile audience stunned, and some angry townspeople reduced to tears.[12] Many were the dimensions of Sidney Catts.

To understand him one must take him altogether. Those who saw the governor as a bigot could find sound reasons, for lower middle-class bigotry often finds expression through religion.[13] Using this perspective, one can attribute Catts's religious intolerance to his Baptist fundamentalism, whereas his enlightened so-

---

11. Miami *Herald*, March 10, 1936.
12. Interview, Jerry Carter, Jr., May 8, 1972, Tallahassee.
13. For a defense of this thesis, see Gary M. Maranell, "An Examination of Some Religious and Political Attitude Correlates of Bigotry," *Social Forces*, XLV (March, 1967), 356–62.

cial views were an aberration from his provincial Christianity. Psychologist Robert Coles offers a sounder explanation, postulating that the religious beliefs of an individual correspond closely to a whole range of other beliefs and experiences within his life. Coles respects religion as an inseparable part of human meaning, which is neither escapist nor inconsistent.[14] Taking the first approach, one tries to decide which part of Catts does not belong—the social progressive deeply involved in politics or the fundamentalist evangelical demagogue. Application of Coles's viewpoint allows one to accept Catts on his own terms with his religion becoming an inseparable part of his reformism.

Despite the obvious moral inconsistencies of his later career when he used religion to fulfill his personal political ambitions, there is a profound level to the man. From his earliest pastorates, he took controversial stands for unpopular causes in which he believed. The conflict over moral standards in his Tuskegee church and his advocacy of missions at Fort Deposit presaged his later determination to ferret out corruption among local Florida officials even if such a course spelled political suicide. As governor his moralistic handling of governmental corruption constantly amazed pragmatists such as J. B. Hodges and destroyed any hope of detente with the old Democratic establishment.

There was an ironic ambivalence to Catts. He genuinely feared that Catholic political influence threatened American democracy, but he did not apply his anti-Catholicism in personal relationships. Individual Catholics found him anxious to help them, and he reacted with kindness when his son Rozier married a Catholic.

In Florida, he was more a product of the nativist movement than its originator. Anti-Catholicism preceded him to the Sunshine State by half a decade. His Baptist heritage shackled him with religious prejudice as it did most rural Protestants, and he verbalized his convictions as one tool to win political office; but neither the state's nativism nor the Ku Klux Klan of the 1920s owed much to

14. Of Robert Coles's many works, one of the most useful for application to Catts is "God and the Rural Poor," *Psychology Today*, V (January, 1972), 31–41.

him as opposed to the issues he expounded. Once in office he proposed little punitive legislation against Catholics. Some contemporary reformers perceived accurately the real impact of his administration. Legislators such as Arthur Gomez, Edgar Waybright, Ion Farris, and Doyle Carlton opposed his anti-Catholicism and sometimes even his prohibitionism, but enthusiastically supported his social and economic reforms. Entrenched conservatives, on the other hand, tried to brand him a baboon, a bigot, and a Puritan, in order to divert attention from his reforms and defeat them. They generally succeeded.

Catts, in the paranoid style of many American politicians, believed that a conspiracy of his antagonists sought to destroy him. Perhaps his paranoia was not entirely fanciful; the regular wing of the party did act in concert against him in the state senate and on the Democratic executive committee. Many of his problems, however, were of his own making. Long before his political career in Florida began, he could not reconcile his own temperament to what he interpreted as "God's call." He was never happy for long anywhere in his ministerial career, certainly not in Tuskegee, Fort Deposit, or DeFuniak Springs. The real problem that plagued him in Tuskegee was not the corrupt worldly faction that opposed his sermons against dancing, gambling, and juvenile vandalism; it was the faithful church women who resented his abrasive temper and his thoughtless, ill-conceived administrative bungling. The same misjudgment occurred later in his battle with Joe Earman. Catts magnified a simple controversy over control of local patronage into a test of personal loyalty, concluding in a fit of temper that one of his most trusted disciples had betrayed him.

The same fundamentalist theology that reinforced Catts's narrow viewpoint and anti-Catholicism also turned him toward politics. The same religion that narrowed his vision of Catholics and evolution enlarged his view of the rights of convicts, juvenile offenders, women, laborers, and children. If his Christianity made him regressive on some social issues, it made him progressive on many others. It also provided the empathy and jargon which allowed Catts to communicate effectively with the people of rural Florida.

When his religious convictions merged with his political ambition to challenge the whole structure of Florida government, his enemies sabotaged his legislative program and branded him a fanatic. They were willing to believe almost anything about him and to lodge the charges in court because they could not deal otherwise with the strange new forces that Catts unleashed. In a state which had relatively little Populist activity, a genteel kind of politics had replaced Bourbon conservatism. The new Democratic leadership had gravitated between respectable, urban reformers such as Napoleon Broward and Park Trammell to equally respectable conservative "courthouse gang" grandees such as W. V. Knott and Cary A. Hardee. In a sense, Catts became a surrogate for populism come to Florida two decades late. He provided a voice for the inarticulate "unwashed" against the carefully manicured and properly pedigreed, if sometimes progressive, Florida Democratic establishment. The "woolly hats" agreed with his anticorporation, prolabor reforms, they supported the termination of convict leasing, improved education, prison reform, and better care for the mentally ill; but it was his style they liked most. Utilizing their fundamentalist religious rhetoric, he articulated their frustration, and so they followed him from religious indignation and moral reform in 1916, to labor radicalism in 1920, to issueless rhetoric in 1924, and finally to local option gambling in 1928. He always provided a show and he abused the "courthouse gang."

The initial tragedy of this era was that it took such bigotry and cavorting for a reformer to win office in Florida. Having won power, "Cattsism" failed because of its inability to capitalize on its stunning initial triumph. The 1916 victory gave Catts a chance to make reform a respectable reality, but his antics and emotional immaturity embarrassed his cause, alienated possible middle-class allies, and played into the hands of conservative "old guard" Democrats. His demagoguery compromised his reform.

Despite the short-term legislative success of some reforms, Catts failed in his attempt to reorganize the party and government. This failure was partly the inevitable product of Catts's movement which focused on one charismatic, flamboyant man instead of a consistent reform credo or even a reform faction within the party. As such, it attracted men from too varied motives; it was a coalition of the "outs." Opportunists who would have stayed with the establishment had the regulars been shrewder and the party more inclusive, bolted to Catts. J. B. Hodges epitomized the type who gingerly climbed aboard the reform wagon in June, 1916, rode it as if it were his own, but kept all his options open. Hodges sought to moderate Catts, forcing the governor to reenter the old system or to create a viable new one; and when the "old man" either could not or would not play by Hodges' rules, he deserted Catts and returned to the regulars. On the opposite extreme was Joe Earman, the prototype of the urban idealist who believed in Catts and conceived of himself as the cosmopolitan balance to the eccentric, religious governor.

The best hope for "Cattsism" probably rested with the new leaders attracted to him, men who understood the need for factional loyalty and patronage but who were also genuine reformers. Devoid of the heavier emotionalism of rabid prohibition and anti-Catholicism, men such as Jerry Carter and J. S. Blitch learned to work with legislators who only occasionally cooperated with them. With Catts there was no partial loyalty: one either stood with him or against him. Catts's religion locked him into a mental frame of reference which saw only "good guys" and "bad guys," without the "proximate solutions" that make American politics work.

One final question remains. What of the people who followed him? Despite all the compromises and his growing cynicism, many Floridians continued to believe in "Old Sid." As the election returns demonstrate, there was a phenomenal cohesiveness to his constituency. Considering the variety of issues he espoused between 1916 and 1928, his appeal can be attributed mainly to his fundamentalist identification with rural Floridians. Both in style and philosophy, he came to personify an entire genre of "reform," and without understanding the enigmatic demagogue who voiced the frustrations of inarticulate white Protestants, one cannot fully comprehend southern politics.

Critical Essay
on Authorities

MANUSCRIPT COLLECTIONS

The richest single depository of materials on Florida politics is the P. K. Yonge Library of Florida History at the University of Florida in Gainesville. Among the collections located there and of value in understanding Catts are the Claude L'Engle Papers (which offer excellent insights into the conservative nature of labor leadership in Florida and its search for a political alternative to both conservative Democratic "regulars" and agrarian "demagogues" such as Catts); the Park Trammell Papers (on microfilm; the originals are located at the Lakeland Public Library, where they were first used for this study); the Peter O. Knight Papers; the P. K. Yonge Papers; and the William N. Sheats Papers. The latter two collections are useful for Catts's educational policy as are the A. A. Murphree Presidential Papers, located in another section of the library at Gainesville. By far the most valuable single collection used in this study was the James B. Hodges Collection, also located in the Yonge Library. This extensive collection of some two hundred boxes constitutes the richest single source of Florida political history between 1916 and 1930. Florida State University Library contains several collections of value to the study, including the Jerry W. Carter Papers (which are disappointingly incomplete for the years before 1920), the Ruby Diamond Papers, the William J. Howey Scrapbook, and a single file on Catts. Mrs. Elizabeth Catts Paderick of Jacksonville, now deceased, possessed numerous clippings concerning her father and also his sermon notebook (now on microfilm at the Samford University Library), which furnished invaluable psychological insights. The Thomas E. Watson Papers at the University of North

Carolina at Chapel Hill contain some material on anti-Catholicism in Florida, and the United States Shipping Board Papers, Record Group 32, National Archives, Washington, D.C., contain significant information on economic and labor conditions in Florida during the First World War.

INTERVIEWS AND ORAL HISTORIES

One of the most useful sources of information for a twentieth-century political figure is oral history. Of the many interviews conducted for this study, the most candid and useful were three interviews with Jerry W. Carter (deceased) (Tallahassee, 1962, 1964, 1970), and interviews with Jerry Carter, Jr. (Tallahassee, 1972), Mike Carter (Birmingham, 1973), Judge James R. Knott (Tallahassee, 1974), and Mrs. W. O. Willham (De-Funiak Springs, 1972). I also conducted lengthy interviews with Catts's three remaining children, Mrs. Ruth Cawthon (DeFuniak Springs, 1972), Mrs. Elizabeth Paderick (now deceased), and Mrs. Alice May Stiegel (Jacksonville, 1972). Mrs. Cawthon was reluctant and protective, Mrs. Stiegel extremely shy, and Mrs. Paderick, though loving of her father, quite candid and frank.

DOCUMENTS

State documents during the Catts administration were particularly helpful in establishing the quality and quantity of reform as well as the purging of public employees. Legal documents involved in the 1916 gubernatorial election also are listed: *Biennial Report of Attorney General, Florida, from January 1, 1919, to December 31, 1920* (Tallahassee, 1921); *Biennial Report of the Superintendent of Public Instruction* (Gainesville, 1920); *Cases Adjudicated in the Supreme Court of Florida*, LXXII (1916); *Democratic Primary, June 6, 1916, Office of the Secretary*, I (in the office of the Secretary of State, Tallahassee); *General Acts and Resolutions Adopted by the Legislature of Florida*, Extraordinary Session, November 25 to December 6, 1918, and Sixteenth and Seventeenth Regular Sessions (Tallahassee, 1917, 1918, 1919); *Journal of the House of Representatives* for 1917 and 1919 (Tallahassee, 1917, 1919); *Journal of the State Senate of Florida* for 1917, Extraordinary Session of 1918, and 1919 (Tallahassee, 1917, 1918, 1919); *Minutes of the Trustees of the Internal Improvement Fund*, XII and XIII (Tallahassee, 1919, 1920); *Report of the Board of Control, 1920;* "Report of Joint Committee to Investigate the Offical Acts of

Sidney J. Catts, While Governor of Florida, Under Senate Concurrent Resolution No. 4"; *Report, Secretary of State, 1915–1916, 1919–1920* (Tallahassee, 1916, 1920), and *1927–1928* (Marianna, 1929); *Report of the Attorney General of the State of Florida, From January 1, 1919 to December 31, 1920* (Tallahassee, 1921); *The Fifth Census of the State of Florida, 1925* (Tallahassee, 1925).

Federal documents of interest include the *1870* and *1880 Census Population Schedules, Alabama, Dallas County* (Microfilm, Samford University); *Fourteenth Census of the United States, 1920*, Vols. III, VI, IX (Washington, 1922–1923); *Religious Bodies, 1916* (Washington, 1917, 1919); *Congressional Record*, Vol. LIX.

Local and institutional documents of value include *Tax Assessment Roll, 1936, Walton County* (Walton County Courthouse, DeFuniak Springs); "Will of Alice May Catts," Case #2-138 (Probate Judge's Office, Walton County Courthouse, DeFuniak Springs); *Thirty-Eighth Annual Catalogue and Register of Howard College, 1880–1881* (Selma, Ala., James S. Jacob Publishers, 1881); *Catalogue, Cumberland University, Lebanon, Tennessee, 1881–1882* (N.d., n. p.); *Alabama Baptist State Convention, Report for 1904* (Archives, Alabama Baptist Historical Collection, Samford University, Birmingham).

NEWSPAPERS

Newspapers which helped reconstruct Catts's life in Alabama were the Montgomery *Advertiser*, the Haynesville *Citizen Examiner*, the Birmingham *Age-Herald*, and the *Alabama Baptist*. The New York *Times* found Catts fascinating even if somewhat bizarre. Most Florida papers opposed Catts, and those of most use were the Gainesville *Daily Sun*, Jasper *News*, Jacksonville *Florida Times-Union*, Panama City *Pilot*, St. Petersburg *Times*, *Florida Baptist Witness*, Tallahassee *Florida Morning State*, Tallahassee *Florida Democrat and Weekly Record*, Miami *Herald*, Live Oak *Suwannee Democrat*, and Tampa *Tribune*.

PERIODICALS

Thanks to editor Samuel Proctor's emphasis on twentieth-century Floridiana, the *Florida Historical Quarterly* contains a number of articles that provided background for this biography. Other journals contained useful perspectives, but I have listed only those articles of major importance:

James A. Carter "Florida and Rumrunning During National Prohibition," *Florida Historical Quarterly*, XLVIII (July, 1969); 47–56; David M. Chalmers, "The Ku Klux Klan in the Sunshine State," *Florida Historical Quarterly*, XLII (January, 1964), 209–15; Robert Coles, "God and the Rural Poor," *Psychology Today*, V (January, 1972), 31–41; Merlin G. Cox, "David Sholtz: New Deal Governor of Florida," *Florida Historical Quarterly*, XLIII (October, 1964), 142–52; J. Herbert Doherty, Jr., "Florida and the Presidential Election of 1928," *Florida Historical Quarterly*, XXVI (October, 1947), 174–86; Joel Webb Eastman, "Claude L'Engle, Florida Muckraker," *Florida Historical Quarterly*, XLV (January, 1967), 243–52; Editorial, *Independent*, LXXIII (July 11, 1912), 103–104; three articles by Wayne Flynt, "Florida Labor and Political 'Radicalism,' 1919–1920," *Labor History*, IX (Winter, 1968), 73–90; "Pensacola Labor Problems and Political Radicalism, 1908," *Florida Historical Quarterly*, XLIII (April, 1965), 315–32; "William V. Knott and the Gubernatorial Campaign of 1916," *Florida Historical Quarterly*, LI (April, 1973), 423–30; Warren A. Jennings, "Sidney J. Catts and the Democratic Primary of 1920," *Florida Historical Quarterly*, XXXIX (January, 1961), 203–20; Kenneth R. Johnson, "Florida Women Get the Vote," *Florida Historical Quarterly*, XLVIII (January, 1970), 299–312; four articles by Durward Long: "An Immigrant Cooperative Social Medicine Program in the South, 1887–1963," *Journal of Southern History*, XXXI (November, 1965), 417–34; "Labor Relations in the Tampa Cigar Industry, 1885–1911," *Labor History*, XII (Fall, 1971), 551–59; "La Resistencia: Tampa's Immigrant Labor Union," *Labor History*, VI (Fall, 1965), 193–213; "The Open-Closed Shop Battle in Tampa's Cigar Industry, 1919–1921," *Florida Historical Quarterly*, XLVII (October, 1968), 101–21.

Dorothy Lord, "Sidney J. Catts and the Gubernatorial Election of 1916," *Apalachee*, 1963–67, VI (1967), 45–64; Victoria H. McDonell, "Rise of the 'Businessman's Politician': The 1924 Gubernatorial Race," *Florida Historical Quarterly*, LII (July, 1973), 39–50. Gary M. Maranell, "An Examination of Some Religious and Political Attitude Correlates of Bigotry," *Social Forces*, XLV (March, 1967), 356–62; Leedell W. Neyland, "State Supported Higher Education Among Negroes in the State of Florida," *Florida Historical Quarterly*, XLIII (October, 1964), 105–22; George E. Pozzetta, "Foreigners in Florida: A Study of Immigration Promotion, 1865–1910," *Florida Historical Quarterly*, LIII (October, 1974), 164–80; David Page, "Bishop Michael J. Curley and Anti-Catholic

Nativism in Florida," *Florida Historical Quarterly*, XLV (October, 1966), 101–17; Robert B. Rackleff, "Anti-Catholicism and the Florida Legislature, 1901–1919," *Florida Historical Quarterly*, L (April, 1972), 352–65; C. Peter Ripley, "Intervention and Reaction: Florida Newspapers and United States Entry into World War I," *Florida Historical Quarterly*, XLIX (January, 1971), 255–67; Jerrell H. Shofner, "The Labor League of Jacksonville: A Negro Union and White Strikebreakers," *Florida Historical Quarterly*, L (January, 1972), 278–82; Charles P. Sweeney, "Bigotry in the South," *Nation*, CXI (November 24, 1920), 585–86; Charles P. Sweeney, "Bigotry Turns to Murder," *Nation*, CXIII (August 31, 1921), 232–33.

UNPUBLISHED MONOGRAPHS

A number of doctoral dissertations in history at Florida State University provided significant perspectives on Florida during the Catts years: George C. Bittle, "In the Defense of Florida: The Organized Florida Militia from 1821 to 1920" (1965); Fred A. Blakey, "A History of the Florida Phosphate Industry, 1888–1966" (1967; published by Harvard University Press in 1973); N. Gordon Carper, "The Convict Lease System in Florida, 1866–1923" (1964); Kenneth R. Johnson, "The Woman Suffrage Movement in Florida" (1966). Three M.A. theses in political science written at Florida State University provide important discussions: Richard E. Bain, "Legislative Representation in Florida: Historic and Contemporary" (1960); Alice S. Chambers, "The Governor as Chief Executive" (1953); Kathleen Falconer Pratt, "The Development of the Florida Prison System" (1949). Two M.A. theses in history, one at Florida State University and one at Samford University, treat "radicalism" in Florida: George N. Green, "Florida Politics and Socialism at the Crossroads of the Progressive Era, 1912" (1962); Ray F. Robbins II, "The Socialist Party in Florida: 1900–1916" (1971). Three M.A. theses at the University of Florida assisted my research. Two of them are in history: John R. Deal, Jr., "Sidney Johnston Catts, Stormy Petrel of Florida Politics" (1949); and Victoria Harden McDonnell, "The Businessman's Politician: A Study of the Administration of John Wellborn Martin, 1925–1929" (1968); Jean Carver Chance's, "Sidney J. Catts and the Press: A Study of the Editorial Coverage of the 1916 Governor's Race by Selected Florida Newspapers" (1969), was done in journalism and communications.

GENERAL STUDIES

The most useful published studies were: Ray Stannard Baker, *Woodrow Wilson, Life and Letters: War Leader, 1917–1918* (New York: Charles Scribner's Sons, 1939); Arch Frederic Blakey, *The Florida Phosphate Industry: A History of the Development and Use of a Vital Mineral* (Cambridge: Harvard University Press, 1973); Bessie Conner Brown, *A History of the First Baptist Church, Tuskegee, Alabama, 1839–1971* (Tuskegee: First Baptist Church, 1972); W. T. Cash, *History of the Democratic Party in Florida* (Live Oak: Democratic Historical Foundation, 1936); David M. Chalmers, *Hooded Americanism: The First Century of the Ku Klux Klan, 1865–1965* (New York: Doubleday & Co., 1965); O. T. Dozier, *Response of Doctor O. T. Dozier to Priest James E. Coyle* (privately published, 1917); Wayne Flynt, *Duncan U. Fletcher: Dixie's Reluctant Progressive* (Tallahassee: Florida State University Press, 1971); Joshua H. Foster, *Sixty-Four Years a Minister* (Wilmington, N.C.: First Baptist Church, 1948); Douglas S. Gatlin and Bruce B. Mason, *Reapportionment: Its History in Florida* (Gainesville: Public Information Clearing Service of the University of Florida, 1956); B. J. W. Graham, *Baptist Biography*, II (Atlanta: Index Printing Co., 1920); Annie Mary Hartsfield and Elston E. Roady, *Florida Votes: 1920–1962* (Tallahassee: Institute of Governmental Research, Florida State University, 1963); John Higham, *Strangers in the Land: Patterns of American Nativism, 1860–1925* (New York: Atheneum Press, 1963); Edward Earl Joiner, *A History of Florida Baptists* (Jacksonville: Convention Press, 1972); V. O. Key, Jr., *Southern Politics* (New York: Vintage Books, 1949); Samuel Proctor, *Napoleon Bonaparte Broward: Florida's Fighting Democrat* (Gainesville: University of Florida Press, 1950); Charlton W. Tebeau and Ruby Leach Carson, *Florida: from Indian Trail to Space Age*, II (Delray Beach: Southern Publishing Company, 1965); Charlton Tebeau, *A History of Florida* (Coral Gables: University of Miami Press, 1971); George B. Tindall, *The Emergence of the New South* (Baton Rouge: Louisana State University Press, 1967); Fuller Warren, *How to Win in Politics* (Tallahassee, Peninsular Publishing Co., 1949); T. Harry Williams, *Huey Long* (New York: Alfred Knopf, 1969).

Index